THE SUPREME COURT
AND THE PHILOSOPHER

THE SUPREME COURT AND THE PHILOSOPHER

HOW JOHN STUART MILL SHAPED US FREE SPEECH PROTECTIONS

ERIC T. KASPER AND
TROY A. KOZMA

NORTHERN ILLINOIS UNIVERSITY PRESS
AN IMPRINT OF
CORNELL UNIVERSITY PRESS
Ithaca and London

First published 2024 by Cornell University Press

Library of Congress Cataloging-in-Publication Data

Names: Kasper, Eric T., author. | Kozma, Troy A., 1969– author.
Title: The Supreme Court and the philosopher : how John Stuart Mill shaped US free speech protections / Eric T. Kasper and Troy A. Kozma.
Description: Ithaca : Northern Illinois University Press, an imprint of Cornell University Press, 2024. | Includes bibliographical references and index.
Identifiers: LCCN 2023029732 (print) | LCCN 2023029733 (ebook) | ISBN 9781501774515 (hardcover) | ISBN 9781501774522 (epub) | ISBN 9781501774539 (pdf)
Subjects: LCSH: Mill, John Stuart, 1806–1873—Influence. | Mill, John Stuart, 1806-1873. On liberty. | United States. Constitution. 1st Amendment. | United States. Supreme Court—History. | Freedom of speech—Philosophy. | Freedom of speech—United States—History.
Classification: LCC JC591 .K37 2024 (print) | LCC JC591 (ebook) | DDC 323.44/30973—dc23/eng/20230825
LC record available at https://lccn.loc.gov/2023029732
LC ebook record available at https://lccn.loc.gov/2023029733

To Maddie and Jackson
—E. T. K.

To Linus and Ned
—T. A. K.

Contents

ACKNOWLEDGMENTS

For two academics who enjoy discussing constitutional law, political philosophy, and the decisions of the US Supreme Court, this was an enjoyable book to research and write. We spent many hours rereading John Stuart Mill's *On Liberty*, relevant Supreme Court opinions, and countless germane books and articles on free expression, Millian theory, and the US Constitution. It was all quite worth it to build the tome that you have before you.

A bit of an explanation of how this book came about is in order. In the course of teaching classes on political philosophy and constitutional law, it became impossible for us to ignore the connections between John Stuart Mill's ideas in *On Liberty*, Oliver Wendell Holmes Jr.'s early twentieth-century First Amendment opinions, and contemporary Supreme Court free speech jurisprudence. These connections eventually led us to write a paper, "Absolute Freedom of Opinion and Sentiment on All Subjects? John Stuart Mill's Enduring (and Ever-Growing) Influence on the Supreme Court's First Amendment Free Speech Jurisprudence," which we presented at the 2016 Midwest Political Science Association's annual conference in Chicago, Illinois. We reworked this paper into a journal article that we published with the *University of Massachusetts Law Review* in 2020. Another conference paper on Mill's influence over the Supreme Court followed: "First Free Speech, Then 'Experiments in Living': John Stuart Mill's Influence over the U.S. Supreme Court on Constitutional Rights after the Freedom of Expression." That paper was revised into an article that was recently published by the *University of Kansas Journal of Law and Public Policy*. As proud as we are of these articles, we believed that a book-length treatment of these issues was needed to comprehensively show Mill's influence over the Supreme Court's free expression caselaw. Our continued work on the subject resulted in this book.

As was the case for past books we have authored together and separately, we are grateful to those who have helped us along the way to publish this book. Of course, we are indebted to everyone at Northern Illinois University Press and Cornell University Press who has labored to bring this project to fruition. We especially appreciate the efforts of our editor, Amy Farranto, who worked with us to ensure that our research met the highest standards and that our vision of a book became a reality. The same is true for Mary Kate Murphy and Michelle Scott, who managed the production side, and Anne Davidson, our copyeditor. Likewise, we are thankful to Jay Steinmetz and Jeff Kosseff, who reviewed earlier drafts of the manuscript and offered helpful feedback that made the finished product immeasurably better. Thank you particularly to the Menard Center for Constitutional Studies at the University of Wisconsin–Eau Claire. Support from the center enabled us to give multiple presentations on the subject matter of this book (including at conferences and at the UW–Eau Claire and UW–Eau Claire–Barron County campuses) and ultimately complete this work. Ideas for the book were also discussed with several personnel at the Menard Center for Constitutional Studies, most notably Phil Rechek and Adam Kunz.

Most importantly, we are grateful for the love and support given to us by our families: Eric's wife, Julie, his children, Maddie and Jackson, and his parents, Clint and Sharon, as well as Dick, Carol, Amy, Marshall, Cole, Andy, Jenny, and Eve; Troy's wife, Melissa, his sons, Linus and Ned, and his mom, Jacquie, as well as Trevor, Angela, Jen, Bob, Mike, Jody, and Mary.

Finally, if we have inadvertently neglected to thank anyone, we sincerely apologize. The oversight was purely accidental.

THE SUPREME COURT
AND THE PHILOSOPHER

Introduction
Mill's *On Liberty* and the US Supreme Court

Questions over the freedom to speak and the power to restrict its expression are at the core of our social, political, religious, economic, and personal lives. Modern struggles to find the proper emphasis between these interests would be familiar to humans throughout history. From our earliest historical records to now, this debate has roiled societies, faiths, countries, and empires. Nearly 2,500 years ago in Athens, Socrates was convicted and put to death for the ideas he expressed.[1] After the introduction of the printing press, England instituted a licensing law in 1538 that required government approval before any text could be published.[2] Galileo's book arguing that the earth revolves around the sun was banned in 1633 by Pope Urban VIII.[3] In 1735, John Peter Zenger was prosecuted for seditious libel in New York for publications critical of the colonial governor.[4] The Comstock Law of 1873 prohibited mailing obscene material through the US Postal Service.[5] Communists and socialists were prosecuted in the mid-twentieth century in the United States for expressing their political beliefs.[6] In the 1970s, the Federal Communications Commission restricted the use of "indecent" speech in broadcast media.[7] In more recent decades, questions over free inquiry and discussion on college campuses have taken on new meaning in the context of trigger warnings, lists of discouraged microaggressions, and bias reporting systems.[8] There has been much debate over free speech online, including the role of government in social media companies' content moderation relating to hate speech and "disinformation."[9] This includes decisions by social media companies to ban then-President Donald Trump from their platforms after the January 6, 2021 attack on the US Capitol, and billionaire Elon Musk's 2022 purchase of Twitter. By 2023, newly passed state laws like Florida's Stop WOKE Act, which restricts the teaching of race and gender in public educational institutions, have been challenged in the courts.[10]

Control of the freedom of expression is control over our shared lives. As long as there has been collective, organized power (social, political, institutional, and financial), there have been debates over the limits of speech. What are the boundaries of free expression? When are restrictions on expression unjustified censorship, and when are they necessary to prevent egregious harms, like imminent violence? Should lies or "disinformation" be protected speech? What power does the government have to dictate what subject matter may—or may not—be taught in schools and universities? In the United States, these questions cannot be answered fully until one understands the principles that have guided the US Supreme Court's First Amendment decision making. In the Constitution, the freedom of expression (including the freedoms of speech, press, and expressive association) is protected by the First Amendment: "Congress shall make no law . . . abridging the freedom of speech, or of the press."

Today, the US Supreme Court is an institution that tasks itself with the protection of minority rights from infringement by government institutions that are empowered by democratic majorities.[11] The Supreme Court held in a famous legal footnote in *United States v. Carolene Products* (1938) that it may apply a greater level of scrutiny "when legislation appears on its face to be within a specific prohibition of the Constitution, such as those of the first ten amendments."[12] The First Amendment has protected the freedom of expression against the federal government since 1791, and this right has been incorporated by the Fourteenth Amendment to protect the freedom of expression against infringement by state and local governments.[13] Further, the Supreme Court held in *Carolene Products* that it may give more scrutiny to government action involving "prejudice against discrete and insular minorities."[14]

Rulings like *Carolene Products* would have confounded justices serving during previous Supreme Court eras, as earlier Supreme Court rulings in free speech cases heavily relied on English common law and the writings of William Blackstone, a legal tradition that provided little of the protections we now associate with freedom of expression. In fact, as we will explain in succeeding chapters, the US Supreme Court did not overturn a single government restriction on expression on First Amendment grounds until 1931; hundreds of free speech constraints have been struck down since then. How did this extraordinary shift in jurisprudence occur, and what was the role of John

Stuart Mill's *On Liberty* (1859), a book penned by an English philosopher *seven decades* after the Bill of Rights was enshrined in the Constitution? The answer lies in the opinions of the justices themselves.

The Supreme Court issued relatively few decisions directly interpreting the First Amendment's protection of free speech before 1919, and virtually none were decided before *On Liberty* was published. Thus, Mill's theory was applied to what was, relatively speaking, a legal vacuum on free speech jurisprudence. As we will demonstrate through a close reading of Supreme Court opinions and other historical evidence, Mill's understanding of the freedom of expression was first adopted on the Supreme Court by Justice Oliver Wendell Holmes Jr. in 1919. Due to stare decisis and the growth of political liberalism on the Supreme Court, this approach to free speech has manifested itself in countless other opinions in more than a century since. Many justices' allusions to Mill's *On Liberty* have been subtle, involving the use of language and jurisprudence that clearly expresses a Millian attitude without directly citing Mill's name or the title of *On Liberty*. And as justices make use of stare decisis by citing past precedents that adopted Mill's philosophy, some justices may have been unintentionally embracing Mill. However, sometimes these references are more overt. The justices have cited or quoted Mill in their First Amendment opinions a number of times over the years. Sometimes this has been done approvingly, but sometimes it has been done to criticize other justices for adhering to Mill's approach.

The Supreme Court's contemporary interpretation of the freedom of expression—and its continued use of the marketplace of ideas analogy—traces directly back to John Stuart Mill and his book, *On Liberty*. *On Liberty* outlines the merits of limiting governmental and social power over the individual. Mill, an English politician and philosopher, advocated for a maximum protection of freedom.[15] Mill was particularly protective of the freedom of expression (and the concomitant freedom of thought). He understood it as foundational to promoting a society in which individuals flourished, pursuing lives that fit their own needs, even if this offended prevailing notions of a properly lived life. Without freedom of expression, a thriving society would not be possible, so Mill began his work with a detailed discussion of this liberty; approximately one-third of the text of *On Liberty* is devoted to this right.[16] Although Mill advocated for some limits on freedom, he argued that minorities should not be restrained by a tyrannical majority, whether acting from a good or ill will.[17] For Mill, the sole legitimate restraint exercised against one's will is to prevent harm to others; moral reasons or the good of the person in question are not satisfactory reasons to limit that person's freedom.[18] This is known as the harm principle, and it is a rule that Mill applied to the freedom of speech.[19]

This book will provide an examination of how Mill's views have displaced the previously prevailing Blackstonian common law tradition and have come to form a key philosophical foundation for US free speech jurisprudence, such that even its critics on the Supreme Court are forced to acknowledge its centrality. A Supreme Court case reviewing the federal conviction of Xavier Alvarez encapsulates this Millian understanding of free expression.

The Case of Xavier Alvarez and His Lies

Xavier Alvarez had a history of lying. He lied about playing in the National Hockey League. He lied about marrying a foreign actress. And in 2007, he lied about having been awarded the Congressional Medal of Honor.[20] Alvarez was an elected public official. He had just begun his term as a member of the Three Valley Water District Board in California. At his first meeting with the board, Alvarez introduced himself, stating, "I'm a retired marine of twenty-five years. I retired in the year 2001. Back in 1987, I was awarded the Congressional Medal of Honor. I got wounded many times by the same guy."[21]

For uttering those comments, federal prosecutors indicted Alvarez for violating the Stolen Valor Act, which made it a crime to make false claims about receiving military decorations or medals. Alvarez claimed that prosecuting him violated the First Amendment, but a trial judge rejected this claim. Alvarez eventually pleaded guilty, reserving the right to appeal his First Amendment claim. He was sentenced to pay a $5,000 fine and perform 416 hours of community service, and he received three years of probation.[22]

In 2012, the US Supreme Court overturned Alvarez's conviction. The justices held by a vote of 6–3 in *United States v. Alvarez* that the Stolen Valor Act as it was then written was unconstitutional. Justice Anthony Kennedy wrote for the Supreme Court that "falsity alone may not suffice to bring the speech outside the First Amendment."[23] Instead, Justice Kennedy proclaimed that the "remedy for speech that is false is speech that is true. This is the ordinary course in a free society. The response to the unreasoned is the rational; to the uninformed, the enlightened; to the straight-out lie, the simple truth."[24] As we will explain in detail, this understanding of the freedom of expression reflects the political philosophy espoused by Mill in *On Liberty*.

Other justices in *Alvarez* more directly demonstrated Mill's influence over the Supreme Court by quoting from *On Liberty*. In a concurring opinion, Justice Stephen Breyer argued that "false factual statements are less likely than are true factual statements to make a valuable contribution to the *marketplace of ideas*," but also that "false factual statements can serve useful human objectives."[25] According to Breyer, this includes "in social contexts, where they may prevent embarrassment, protect privacy, shield a person from prejudice, provide the sick with comfort, or preserve a child's innocence; in public contexts, where they may stop a panic or otherwise preserve calm in the face of danger; and even in technical, philosophical, and scientific contexts, where . . . examination of a false statement (even if made deliberately to mislead) can promote a form of thought that ultimately helps realize the truth."[26] To support this, Breyer quoted Mill's *On Liberty*: "Even a false statement may be deemed to make a valuable contribution to public debate, since it brings about 'the clearer perception and livelier impression of truth, produced by its collision with error' (quoting J. Mill, *On Liberty* 15 (Blackwell ed. 1947))."[27] For Breyer, *On Liberty* rightly reflects a utilitarian understanding of the freedom of speech and the importance of openness in debate on public issues, even if what is said is sometimes false.

Breyer's citation of Mill spurred a response from a colleague who also invoked Mill. Dissenting in *Alvarez*, Justice Samuel Alito made use of the same *On Liberty* passage quoted in Breyer's concurrence.[28] Alito agreed with Breyer that some false speech must be constitutionally protected to ensure that true speech is not improperly hindered, arguing that "it is perilous to permit the state to be the arbiter of truth."[29] Nevertheless, Alito dissented because he believed that "the Stolen Valor Act presents no risk at all that valuable speech will be suppressed. The speech punished by the Act is not only verifiably false and entirely lacking in intrinsic value, but it also fails to serve any instrumental purpose that the First Amendment might protect."[30] Thus, Alito cited Mill to explain what the First Amendment protects; Alito simply disagreed with Breyer about the application of Mill's philosophy to that case.

These opinions by Breyer and Alito in *Alvarez* that directly cite and quote Mill are the low-hanging fruit of Supreme Court opinions that make use of *On Liberty*'s theory for free expression. Much more prevalent than these outright citations are the hundreds of other opinions, such as the one by Kennedy, that implicitly draw on Mill by citing past precedents that clearly adhere to Mill or that use Mill's philosophical approach to free speech without stating his name.

The Argument for John Stuart Mill's Influence on the Supreme Court

We take a deep qualitative dive into the Supreme Court's First Amendment freedom of expression decisions to demonstrate conclusively how Mill's influence has increased over time to become the dominant understanding of this constitutional right today. We survey the entire catalog of Supreme Court cases on the freedom of expression, either in our main text or in our endnotes, to avoid the pitfalls of cherry-picking cases. Indeed, reviewing fewer than the entirety of the Supreme Court's free expression caselaw might allow one to select only the decisions that are most favorable to a particular outcome. Instead, we survey the vast number of free speech Supreme Court rulings to fully demonstrate how Mill has profoundly affected the Supreme Court's jurisprudence. This also permits us to show the reader how Mill was *not* always a dominant influence on the Supreme Court's free expression cases, as his influence was nonexistent before 1919, and it then was sporadic over the next few decades.

The modern Supreme Court has progressively adopted a view of the constitutional right of free expression that emulates Millian libertarianism. The justices have struck down numerous laws in recent decades for infringing on the freedom of expression; this has included cases involving a wide array of issues, such as campaign finance, offensive speech, symbolic speech, commercial speech, online expression, and false statements. The Supreme Court's approach to free expression now reflects a great deal of Mill's reasoning in *On Liberty*. This adoption of Mill's version of free speech began slowly with Justice Holmes more than one century ago, with other justices subsequently carrying this Millian torch, largely in dissent, for decades. However, support for Mill's free speech views has expanded over time, and this position now often prevails on the Supreme Court. Furthermore, in the cases where the Supreme Court has found expression not protected under the First Amendment in recent years, the majority in those cases arguably applies exceptions to Mill's harm principle; this includes cases involving student speech, public employee speech, and speech related to incitement. This embrace of Mill's rationale has led to a radical and unmistakable reorientation in the Supreme Court's understanding of free expression.

The outline of this book is as follows. Chapter 1 will explore the political philosophy that Mill expressed in *On Liberty*, starting with an analysis of the harm principle. While Mill built caveats into his theory (some reasonable, others racist and ethnocentric), Mill generally advocated for the protection of personal freedom.[31] Specifically, he applied his reasoning to the freedom of expression, proclaiming that we should have "absolute freedom of opinion and sentiment on all subjects."[32] As a utilitarian, Mill dismissed the notion of natural or inalienable rights. Mill maintained that protecting the freedom of speech was a means to an end. It facilitates a well-functioning democratic process, the search for truth, and the leading of autonomous, authentic, and flourishing lives.

In chapter 2 we explain that although the Supreme Court issued some early free expression decisions, before World War I, there were substantial limitations on the right to free expression. As the nineteenth century turned to the twentieth, Supreme Court rulings implied that this right, following English common law tradition, was largely limited to the prevention of prior restraints, which are suppressions of expression before it is even made public. In *Davis v. Massachusetts* (1897), the Supreme Court upheld the prosecution of a man who preached in a public park without a license. *Turner v. Williams* (1904) upheld a law that punished advocacy of anarchism. In *Patterson v. Colorado* (1907), the justices permitted punishing seditious libel. A series of decisions restricted the freedom of speech for unions and union organizers. The Supreme Court ruled in *Mutual Film Corp. v. Industrial Commission of Ohio* (1915) that states may require films to be approved by censorship boards. Not a hint of Mill's philosophy appeared in these cases. These decisions culminated in upholding the Espionage Act in *Schenck v. United States* (1919).

Things were about to change. Justice Holmes's decision in *Schenck* upheld the conviction of a man for distributing pamphlets urging resistance to the military draft. Nevertheless, Holmes introduced the more protective clear and present danger test into First Amendment jurisprudence. As chapter 3 details, Holmes was criticized for applying the test narrowly, including by the Harvard Law professor Zechariah Chafee Jr. Holmes was also lobbied by his friend, the Harvard Law School lecturer Harold Laski, to adopt Mill's approach to free speech. Holmes subsequently became a zealous advocate for Mill's understanding of free expression, making Holmes the vehicle to introduce *On Liberty*'s philosophy into US constitutional law. Holmes's adoption of Mill includes an understanding in *Abrams v. United States* (1919) that the First Amendment protects what would eventually be called a "marketplace of ideas."[33] This notion of letting ideas compete with each other (rather than the state deciding what speech was valuable) echoes Mill's *On Liberty*, especially in Holmes's defense of protecting even ideas we "loathe and believe to be fraught with death."[34] Holmes maintained a similar approach in his *Gitlow v. New York* (1925) dissent, and he was joined by Justice Louis Brandeis in his support for this view of free speech, particularly in Brandeis's concurrence in *Whitney v. California* (1927).

In chapter 4 we show how, as the first Red Scare ended, Holmes's and Brandeis's free expression jurisprudence gained traction on the Supreme Court. Joined by another admirer of Mill, Chief Justice Charles Evans Hughes, the Supreme Court would espouse a type of Millian approach to many First Amendment questions in the 1930s and 1940s. This began with *Stromberg v. California* (1931), which struck down a conviction for displaying a communist flag. Other cases during this era overturned prior restraints on the press, antisyndicalism laws, convictions for handbill distribution and picketing, and the expulsion of public school students for refusing to salute the US flag. *Thomas v. Collins* (1945) would emphasize "the preferred place given in our scheme to the great, the indispensable, democratic freedoms secured by the First Amendment."[35] With the exception of a few cases in the early days of World War II—including *Valentine v. Chrestensen* (1942), finding no constitutional protection for commercial speech, and *Chaplinsky v. New Hampshire* (1942), establishing categorical exceptions to the freedom of speech—the 1930s and 1940s were two decades of almost unimpeded expansion of free expression rights. In the early post–World War II period, it seemed as though a Millian understanding of this right was becoming accepted by the Supreme Court, but a close observation of the justices' divisions by 1949 showed that a move away from Mill was on the horizon.

In chapter 5 we investigate how the Supreme Court's growing adoption of Millian philosophy was halted, and regressed, in the early 1950s. *Dennis v. United States* (1951) succinctly exhibited the anti-Millian approach taken by the Supreme Court during the early years of the Cold War: "The societal value of speech must, on occasion, be subordinated to other values and considerations."[36] Another Red Scare gripped the nation, bringing with it a feeling that dangerous ideas needed suppression. Nevertheless, Justices Hugo Black and William Douglas dissented in *Dennis*, *Roth v. United States* (1957), *Barenblatt v. United States* (1959), and other key early Cold War cases. This pair of jurists harkened back to the free speech libertarianism of Holmes and Brandeis, with some of their opinions not only referring to the older dissents and concurrences but also reading like summaries of *On Liberty*, sometimes citing Mill. By referencing the opinions of Holmes and Brandeis, Black and Douglas—eventually joined by Chief Justice Earl Warren and Justice William Brennan—preserved Mill's thought in US constitutional law.

Chapter 6 illuminates how continuing advocacy of free speech principles moved the tribunal back to a more Millian approach to the freedom of expression in the mid-1960s. Personnel changes on the Supreme Court, as well as the plight of civil rights protestors and a thaw in Cold War relations, helped to bring a majority of justices closer to Black and Douglas on several First Amendment questions. Justice Brennan narrowed what constituted libel in *New York Times v. Sullivan* (1964). The justices tightened the definition of unprotected obscenity. The Supreme Court adopted the imminent lawless action standard for expression in *Brandenburg v. Ohio* (1969), embracing a view of expression that Holmes used in *Abrams* and that Mill supported in *On Liberty*. In *Tinker v. Des Moines* (1969), the Supreme Court recognized student expression as constitutionally protected. Although the Supreme Court deferred to the government on speech at county jails in *Adderley v. Florida* (1966) and on symbolic speech in *United States v. O'Brien* (1968), the period from 1963 to 1969 was one of the fastest shifts toward Mill in the Supreme Court's history.

In chapter 7 we show how the early Burger Court's free expression jurisprudence was very similar to that of the latter Warren Court. Prior restraints continued to be disfavored in *New York Times v. United States* (1971), offensive speech received protection in *Cohen v. California* (1971), and obscenity and libel remained narrowly defined. The Supreme Court found some protections for commercial speech over time, and public university students' expressive rights were established in *Healy v. James* (1972). However, personnel changes on the Supreme Court started to limit some of the most prominent Warren Court gains, with the definition of unprotected obscenity being expanded in *Miller v. California* (1973) and libel being expanded in *Gertz v. Robert Welch* (1974). The Supreme Court sustained the fighting words doctrine, restricted speech in broadcast media, and continued to permit significant restrictions on symbolic expression. Nevertheless, Brennan and Justice Thurgood Marshall became the new duo most forcefully expressing Millian themes, including in majority opinions. Furthermore, the Supreme Court consistently upheld the First Amendment rights of peaceful protestors, particularly in *NAACP v. Claiborne Hardware Co.* (1982). Unlike the retrenchment of the 1950s, the gains from the 1960s were largely maintained into the 1980s, with some advancements made.

As demonstrated in chapter 8, by the late 1980s, the Rehnquist Court began accelerating the pace of Mill-based reasoning in freedom of expression decisions. Especially after Justice Kennedy's appointment, Justice Brennan was able to initiate another Millian resurgence that endured long after the latter justice's retirement. For example, Brennan wrote in *Texas v. Johnson* (1989): "If there is a bedrock principle underlying the First Amendment, it is that the government may not prohibit the expression of an idea simply because society finds the idea itself offensive or disagreeable."[37] Cases like *R.A.V. v. St. Paul* (1992), *44 Liquormart v. Rhode Island* (1996), and *Virginia v. Black* (2003) continued this approach, allowing persons to express themselves without fear of excessive government restrictions, even if the expression was hate speech or commercial advertising. This was followed by more expressive libertarianism on the Internet, including *Reno v. ACLU* (1997) and *Ashcroft v. Free Speech Coalition* (2002).

In chapter 9 we demonstrate that the Roberts Court has made use of the Millian language regarding free expression more than any previous Supreme Court. This has been particularly true in opinions written by Chief Justice John Roberts and Justice Kennedy. A majority of justices now consistently uses Mill's harm principle to evaluate the constitutionality of restrictions on the freedom of expression. This is exemplified in the Supreme Court's defense of campaign finance related expression in *Citizens United v. FEC* (2010), depictions of animal cruelty in *Stevens v. United States* (2010), offensive speech in *Snyder v. Phelps* (2011) and *Matal v. Tam* (2017), false speech in *United States v. Alvarez* (2012), and expression on social media in *Packingham v. North Carolina* (2017). What is even more interesting is that the contemporary Supreme Court's views of expression outside of First Amendment protection arguably fit Mill's caveats with regard to the harm principle, including as they relate to performance of certain required public employee duties in *Garcetti v. Ceballos* (2006), to the young in *Morse v. Frederick* (2007), and to persons promoting incitement in *Holder v. Humanitarian Law Project* (2010). Some of these exceptions are what might be best characterized as misinterpretations of Mill, a point expressed in dissent by justices who embrace Mill's philosophy. Nevertheless, even in these cases upholding restrictions on expression, the majority on the Supreme Court is, knowingly or not, making use of a jurisprudence similar to Mill's harm principle from *On Liberty*, based on following Millian precedents.

US constitutional jurisprudence today has remarkably strong free speech protections when compared to other developed democracies.[38] Granted, the Supreme Court has not universally adopted Millian philosophy on free expression questions, including as it relates to the rights of broadcasters, prisoners, and foreigners. Furthermore, Mill is *not* the only influence on the Supreme Court's free speech jurisprudence. Traditionally, the Supreme Court accepted Blackstone's view that the freedom of expression prohibited the government merely from imposing prior restraints, and an originalist interpretation of the Constitution has been espoused by members of the current Supreme Court.[39] The Supreme Court has also been affected by Alexander Meiklejohn's self-governing theory of the First Amendment.[40] But the reach of Mill's influence over our free expression rights is stronger than any alternatives. This judicial adoption of Mill's doctrine to protect a greater amount of expression was not—and is not—without its share of critics. In the modern era there have been those who believe the law should punish those whose expression is disrespectful to the state, espouses immoral ideas, or promotes anti-egalitarianism.[41] Objections arose against the Supreme Court once it began to assert a right of individuals to express themselves in ways that were out of step with majority morality.[42] In the contemporary age, a new wave of disagreement over the Supreme Court's free expression jurisprudence has arisen, with some today arguing that the Supreme Court should uphold laws restricting protest activities, political campaigning, hate speech, commercial advertising, and religious expression.[43] The Supreme Court's march toward a Millian ideal of speech protection was not inevitable: it took years of dissents to germinate, almost died during the early years of the Cold War, and is under attack by new threats today. On the Supreme Court, new appointments could alter jurisprudence in the future, making it less protective of expression, just as the Supreme Court's jurisprudential trajectory has been altered in the past.

Finally, there are debates, even within the Supreme Court, as to how to best understand this Millian tradition; there is more than one case where opposing justices will cite Mill or a Millian principle to defend their disagreeing interpretations. These discussions and disagreements are examples of the free exchange of ideas that Mill himself found to be the sign of a healthy society and that he hoped to encourage with *On Liberty*. All told, John Stuart Mill has had a significant impact on the free speech jurisprudence of the US Supreme Court. Once his views were adopted by Justice Holmes, they became enshrined in Supreme Court opinions that took on their own precedential value, thus embedding them in US constitutional law. Although a statesperson of the United Kingdom like Mill probably did not set out to change the way the US Constitution is interpreted, Mill's indirect influence over this part of US law is as comprehensive as it is undeniable. This includes *Alvarez*, which might at first seem like a counterintuitive decision by the Supreme Court to protect lies as a part of the larger constitutional project of searching for truth in a marketplace of ideas. But as we will explain, restricting the government's ability to punish both truth and lies is precisely what Mill had in mind.

CHAPTER 1

Absolute Freedom

Mill's Free Speech Philosophy and the Harm Principle

To understand the extent to which the US Supreme Court has adopted John Stuart Mill's philosophy for the freedom of expression, it is necessary to recount Mill's arguments in *On Liberty*. Mill set out an expansive view of "civil" liberty, which he defined as "the nature and limits of the power which can be legitimately exercised by society over the individual," and Mill then had the goal of justifying these limits within a democratic society.[1] Mill expected that a just society would be governed by democratic principles, allowing for anything other than the consent of the governed under only a narrow set of circumstances, and he assumed his readers would think the same.[2] While Mill noted that a free society "is not likely to be contested in general terms," his project was in reconciling democratic rule and the restrictions that democratic governments might place on civil liberties in a free society.[3]

Although others have noted the tension between civil liberty and democratic rule, Mill argued the discussion had been too abstract; even in our mundane, ordinary lives, social expectations and seemingly trivial laws suppress civil liberty. *On Liberty* begins by tracing the evolution of the liberal democratic polity, from its initial incarnation as an absolutist state to the rebirth of democracies in France and the United States. These new democracies seemed to many nineteenth-century European liberals to represent the complete triumph of freedom: "The nation did not need to be protected against its own will. There was no fear of its tyrannizing over itself. Let the rulers be effectually responsible to it, promptly removable by it, and it could afford to trust them with power of which it could itself dictate the use to be made."[4] In theory, this appeared sound, but according to Mill, what remained was the "struggle between liberty and authority [which] is the most conspicuous feature" in history.[5] For Mill, the hypothesis that modern democracies were no longer a threat to liberty was disproven by some disappointing results of the American experiment, even against a variety of successes in promoting democracy and protecting various freedoms in the United States. Permitting "the people" to rule could create a paradox if a majority of the people decide to take away the rights of a minority. A student of Alexis de Tocqueville, Mill refined the concept of the tyranny of the majority.[6] Writing in 1859 as the United States teetered on the brink of a civil war over slavery, the most extreme example of tyranny, Mill noted that "such phrases as 'self-government,' and 'the power of the people over themselves,' do not state the true state of the case."[7] He further explained the problem as follows:

> The "people" who exercise the power are not always the same people with those over whom it is exercised; and the "self-government" spoken of is not the government of each by himself, but of each by all the rest. The will of the people . . . practically means the will of the most numerous or the most active *part* of the people—the majority, or those who succeed in making themselves accepted as the majority; the people, consequently, *may* desire to oppress a part of their number, and precautions are as much needed against this as against any other abuse of power.[8]

Mill further declared that "'the tyranny of the majority' is now generally included among the evils against which society requires to be on its guard."[9] Mill believed that democracy cannot ensure that individual rights will be protected without proper restraints on the majority to exercise unjust power over others.[10] According to Mill, "Like other tyrannies, the tyranny of the majority was at first, and is still vulgarly, held in dread, chiefly as operating through the acts of the public authorities."[11]

Although our analysis is of US legal jurisprudence limiting government power, Mill understood that private persons and organizations also engaged in tyranny over opinion and action.[12] Mill believed that social tyranny of the majority is often the catalyst for legal restrictions. We are inclined to want others to think and act like we do, because our customs *feel* right. Mill noted that people tend to believe "that their feelings . . . are better than reasons, and render reasons unnecessary. The practical principle which guides them to their opinions on the regulation of human conduct is the feeling in each person's mind that everybody should be required to act as he . . . would like them to act."[13] People typically cling to their prejudices, and they want others to think and act the same way, even if there is not a principled reason to justify it.[14] This can be very dangerous. It has been used to silence others and force their conformity to certain conduct. Irrational prejudice "gives rise to perfectly genuine sentiments of abhorrence; it made men burn magicians and heretics."[15] While Mill was particularly concerned about legally enshrined religious intolerance, his framework is broad enough to include freedom to promote all ideas.[16]

Mill's concerns about social and political tyranny continue in the United States of the twenty-first century, where public opinion polls show intolerance by many against atheists and certain minority religions, the growing influence of white Christian nationalism, the rise and activism of racist hate groups, and the alarming mainstreaming of the great replacement theory.[17] The Southern Poverty Law Center reports historic levels of hate group activity, especially on social media, with escalations to violence in recent years in the 2017 Unite the Right rally, portions of the 2020 George Floyd protests, and the January 6, 2021, Capitol insurrection.[18] Recent Pew research reveals religious and nativist attitudes remain strong, with a significant minority believing that to be "truly American," one needs to be Christian, be born in the country, or both.[19] Forty-nine percent of Americans believe the Bible should influence the legal system and 28 percent say that the Bible should take priority over the will of the people.[20] Public opinion data show a strong gap in attitudes between different religious groups, with atheists and certain minority religions viewed much less favorably.[21]

These points notwithstanding, Mill understood that every society must draw lines regarding what is legal speech and action. Mill acknowledged that "all that makes existence valuable to anyone depends on the enforcement of restraints upon the actions of other people. Some rules of conduct, therefore, must be imposed—by law."[22] Mill was no anarchist; he understood that government must make rules for human behavior.[23] Yet, he was concerned that such lines are often drawn arbitrarily, due to superstition, or out of prejudice: "There is, in fact, no recognized principle by which the propriety or impropriety of government interference is customarily tested. People decide according to their personal preferences."[24] Mill's project was to design a principled way to make these necessary decisions.

Mill's solution was the harm principle, which Mill defined as follows: "The sole end for which mankind are warranted, individually or collectively, in interfering with the liberty of action of any of their number is self-protection. . . . The only purpose for which power can be rightfully exercised over any member of a civilized community, against his will, is to prevent harm to others."[25] Mill thought this was necessary because "over himself, over his own body and mind, the individual is sovereign."[26] Therefore, Mill argued that a person's "own good, either physical or moral, is not a sufficient warrant" to limit one's freedom, and one "cannot rightfully be compelled to do or forbear because it will be better for him to do so, because it will make him happier, because, in the opinion of others, to do so would be wise or even right."[27] The harm principle, also known as the principle of liberty, does not just argue for a normative idea of freedom—Mill also presupposed empirically that we as humans desire this level of freedom.[28]

Following the harm principle does *not* mean we are forced to accept the speech or action of another person if we find it to be immoral or offensive. As Mill explained, these "are good reasons for remonstrating with him, or reasoning with, or persuading him, or entreating him, but not for compelling him."[29] We are free to express ourselves as we see fit and to do our best to convince someone else, but we cannot enlist the government to punish someone for nonconformity that poses no direct harm to others. Mill believed this, even if one is engaging in self-destructive activities and there is clearly a better option where that person will not cause self-harm.[30] The harm principle, as expounded by Mill, means that to justify the exertion of government power over someone, "the conduct from which it is desired to deter him must be calculated to produce evil in someone else" because "the only part of the conduct of anyone for which he is amenable to society is that which concerns others."[31]

For Mill, the harm principle solves the "struggle between liberty and authority."[32] In *Utilitarianism*, Mill argued that protection from harm is the foundation of justice: "Justice is a name for certain classes of moral rules which concern the essentials of human well-being more nearly, and are therefore of more absolute obligation, than any other rules for the guidance of life."[33] According to Mill, "human well-being" rests on this foundation: "All other earthly benefits are needed by one person, not needed by another; and many of them can, if necessary, be cheerfully foregone, or replaced by something else; but security no human being can possibly do without; on it we depend for all our immunity from evil and for the whole value of all and every good, beyond the passing moment, since nothing but the gratification of the instant could be of any worth to us, if we could be deprived of everything the next instant by whoever was momentarily stronger than ourselves."[34] People cannot even begin to live well without a sense of security, and security is a core function of the state. Yet, for Mill, security was not to be understood merely as physical safety: "The moral rules which forbid mankind to hurt one another (in which we must never forget to include wrongful interference with each other's freedom) are more vital to human well-being than any maxims, however important, which only point out the best mode of managing some department of human affairs."[35] For Mill, authority and freedom were two forms of the same concept of justice. Authorities must respect individual liberty and one's right to decide how to live one's own life.

Underlying this is an even more fundamental principle, that of utility. Mill summarized this doctrine as the greatest happiness principle: "Actions are right in proportion as they tend to promote happiness: wrong as they tend to promote the reverse of happiness."[36] Security is important, not because of some abstract concept of justice, but because of its practical consequences; it is an essential background condition for a life of flourishing. In *On Liberty*, this concept is foregrounded in the introductory chapter, where Mill declared, "I regard utility as the ultimate appeal on all ethical questions; but it must be utility in the largest sense, grounded on the permanent interests of man as a progressive being."[37] The remainder of the book argues why respecting individual autonomy is the best way to secure these utilitarian interests. This is utility broadly defined, designed to help individuals freely develop for their own benefit and to provide advantages that will accrue society-wide.[38]

Consistent with Mill's utilitarianism, the harm principle was not absolute and would not apply to certain portions of humanity. Mill believed that there were necessary personal and cultural antecedents, without which, liberty's exercise would be dangerous or ineffective. His first caveat was that the harm principle applies solely to persons of a certain age and intellectual capacity: "It is, perhaps, hardly necessary to say that this doctrine is meant to apply only to human beings in the maturity of their faculties. We are not speaking of children or of young persons below the age which the law may fix as that of manhood or womanhood. Those who are still in a state to require being taken care of by others must be protected against their own actions as well as against external injury."[39] Mill's freedom is meant for those who are capable of fully functioning intellectually, to be sure they grasp the results of their actions. Government may restrain one who is too young or whose mental state does not fully allow them to comprehend what they do.[40] They are not ready for all of the freedom protected by the harm principle, being unable to anticipate possible negative outcomes of their choices. They could be exploited. That children cannot legally vote or enter into certain agreements reflects Mill's admonition about when the harm principle cannot apply. This imposes a societal and generational duty to raise the young, to "make them capable of rational conduct in life. The existing generation is master both of the training and the entire circumstances of the generation to come."[41] The state must impose additional restrictions on children, who must still be educated.[42]

While there is broad agreement on this first restriction, Mill's second caveat is unabashedly racist. Mill proclaimed that "we may leave out of consideration those backward states of society in which the race itself may be considered as in its nonage."[43] Mill believed that like children, certain cultures lacked the requisite experience, education, or material wealth to be mature enough to exercise full freedom.[44] In these cases, "despotism is a legitimate mode of government in dealing with barbarians, provided the end be their improvement, and the means justified by actually effecting that end. Liberty . . . has no application to any state of things anterior to the time when mankind have become capable of being improved by free and equal discussion."[45] Mill suffered from the very ethnocentrism that he warned his readers about, as he espoused in this passage from *On Liberty* a fundamental misunderstanding of non-European cultures and the diverse concepts of the individual, society, freedom, and power that exist in various civilizations around the globe.[46]

Although horrifying, this caveat rejects racial and ethnic essentialism, the ascendent view among Westerners during the mid-nineteenth century.[47] As the first caveat can be resolved by one sufficiently maturing, Mill thought the same with a state of society. As Mill put it, "As soon as [a society has] attained the capacity of being guided to their own improvement by conviction or persuasion . . . compulsion, either in the direct form or in that of pains and penalties for non-compliance, is no longer admissible as a means to their own good, and justifiable only for the security of others."[48] In Mill's estimation, as culturally insensitive as it was, a society could be properly prepared for the harm principle. Before that, however, forced rule by European powers was a reasonable arrangement for Mill.[49] Mill also claimed that there were "despotic" states—in his view, "the whole East"—which once were thriving but where "custom" had led to stagnation and subjugation by Europe.[50] Here, tradition (read as social, political, and religious conformity) had overcome individuality: "Custom is there, in all things, the final appeal; justice and right mean conformity to custom; the argument of custom no one, unless some tyrant intoxicated with power, thinks of resisting."[51] For such places, as with those he classified as populated by "barbarians," Mill believed that freedom was inappropriate. Mill practiced this theory as well, having very little concern as a politician for press freedoms in India even after vigorously defending press rights in Britain.[52]

Underlying his imperialistic sentiments and his callousness regarding racial, ethnic, and cultural differences, Mill's analysis reveals a belief that liberty is not always justified under all circumstances; it is never an end but rather the means in which individual lives can best flourish. In Mill's view, this was only possible in advanced democracies, and, even there, solely where culture and traditions favored certain conditions, like social equality, economic security, tolerance, and an educated populace.[53] In a person lacking maturity, in a society lacking culture, or in a society where change is regarded as immoral, liberty would do no good: "There is nothing for them but implicit obedience to an Akbar or a Charlemagne, if they are so fortunate to find one."[54] Mill's understanding was that liberty is not an inalienable right and that, in extraordinary circumstances, it must yield to coercion for the sake of human advancement.[55]

Think, for instance, of a combat zone or of an area experiencing a riot that necessitates the use of martial law; without confidence that other persons are willing to follow the rule of law, some other tenet besides the harm principle would be required. This is how this caveat could still reasonably be employed. Such a scenario also conforms with Mill's pronouncement that "all that makes existence valuable to anyone depends on the enforcement of restraints upon the actions of other people," because too few people would restrain themselves in a way to make the harm principle pragmatic.[56] But there is a more general point here that applies to all societies: one's liberty exists only if government can limit the ability of others to take action that would harm one's liberty.[57] Such restrictions on liberty need not be dramatic; for example, stoplights restrain our ability to drive with unfettered discretion on roadways, but they also create order that permits us to drive freely to the destination of our choice without excessive fear of collisions with other vehicles.

Mill's third caveat to the harm principle clarifies that even for capable persons living under a proper rule of law, there are "positive acts for the benefit of others which [one] may rightfully be compelled to perform," including requirements "to perform certain acts of individual beneficence."[58] This includes obligations to testify in court, to complete military service if conscripted, or to assist those who are in peril; all of these examples are responsibilities Mill thought must be undertaken to prevent harm from befalling our fellow citizens.[59] Additionally, Mill averred that parents must fulfill their obligations after "having undertaken the moral responsibility of a family."[60] Regarding these "most sacred duties of parents," Mill thought it necessary to educate and provide for one's children: "To bring a child into existence without a fair prospect of being able, not only to provide food for its body, but instruction and training for its mind, is a moral crime, both against the unfortunate offspring and against society; and that if the parent does not fulfil this obligation, the State ought to see it fulfilled."[61] Although he was a vocal critic of centralized, standardized education and a defender of individuals to make private choices as they see fit, Mill recognized that the consequences of actions must always be considered.[62] Thus, for Mill, the family was not solely a private sphere, untouchable by government under all circumstances.[63] Due to one's role as a citizen in society or because of responsibilities one has voluntarily taken on, there will be instances in which one can be compelled to act because of the harm caused by inaction.[64] But for Mill, this need for state intervention should be relatively rare: "A person may cause evil to others not only by his actions but by his inaction, and in either case he is justly accountable to them for the injury. The latter case, it is true, requires a much more cautious exercise of compulsion than the former. To make any one answerable for doing evil to others is the rule; to make him answerable for not preventing evil is, comparatively speaking, the exception."[65] What he placed in this category was a small set of actions one could be *compelled* to perform, which is different from a law requiring that one be *prohibited* from taking desired action.

This last caveat informs us that a person's action "is taken out of the self-regarding class and becomes amenable to moral disapprobation in the proper sense of the term" if a person violates "a distinct and assignable obligation to any other person or persons."[66] Mill examined this caveat (and presented an illustration of it) as follows: "When a person disables himself, by conduct purely self-regarding, from the performance of some definite duty incumbent on him to the public, he is guilty of a social offence. No person ought to be punished simply for being drunk; but a soldier or a policeman should be punished for being drunk on duty. Whenever, in short, there is a definite damage, or a definite risk of damage, either to an individual or to the public, the case is taken out of the province of liberty and placed in that of morality or law."[67] If one has agreed to take on certain responsibilities of citizenship, parenthood, or public employment, one agrees to limited restrictions on one's freedom. In the absence of those conditions, however, freedom should reign, because Mill, in his utilitarian calculus, saw the greater good to society in letting people act freely.[68] Indeed, according to Mill, if one engages in "conduct which neither violates any specific duty to the public, nor occasions perceptible hurt to any assignable individual except himself, the inconvenience is one which society can afford to bear, for the sake of the greater good of human freedom."[69]

All told, Mill's harm principle could be summed up as follows. First, he thought protected "conduct consists . . . in not injuring the interests of one another, or rather certain interests which, either by express legal provision or by tacit understanding, ought to be considered as rights."[70] Put another way, your right to swing your arm ends at another person's nose. One cannot personally define these rights, as it is a normative determination to be made by government for society.[71] Second, Mill thought that certain acts could be compelled in society if they involved "each person's bearing his share (to be fixed on some equitable principle) of the labors and sacrifices incurred for defending the society or its members from injury and molestation."[72] Mill thought it proper to protect a sizable amount of individual freedom, but this is limited by duties undertaken by citizens, parents, or public employees.

Mill devised the harm principle to understand the bounds of all liberties, but he had a special concern for expressive freedoms. He listed this freedom first in *On Liberty*, and a substantial portion of the book is devoted to it. The freedom of expression was a pressing issue for Mill and his family. Mill's father, James Mill—who had a tremendous influence over his son's education—took a then-radical position on the freedom of expression, first publishing an article in the *Edinburgh Review* in 1811 defending a broad interpretation of the freedom of the press and questioning the British state of the law on libel.[73] James Mill continued to publish on the importance of the freedom of expression throughout John's youth.[74] James Mill's zealousness for shielding the right to express unpopular opinions, including those challenging religious orthodoxy, was taught to John during his childhood.[75] John concluded a lengthy paragraph in his *Autobiography* on his father's approach to discussing ideas by expressing his own view of the necessity of having "a conscientious sense of the importance to mankind of the equal freedom of all opinions."[76] As a young man, his father taught him "to take the strongest interest in the Reformation, as the great and decisive contest against priestly tyranny for liberty of thought."[77] Later in his *Autobiography*, Mill wrote how he "held in common" with his father by the 1820s "an almost unbounded confidence in the efficacy of two things: representative government, and complete freedom of discussion."[78]

John Stuart Mill came of age in a time and place where the freedom of expression was a pressing issue of public policy. The freedom of speech was restricted to a significantly greater degree than it is today in either the United Kingdom or the United States, particularly for expression that questioned the prevailing religious orthodoxy.[79] During the mid-1800s there were high-profile cases of deists, secularists, atheists, and radical journalists in the United Kingdom being imprisoned for questioning the veracity of the Bible, reprinting Thomas Paine's *Age of Reason*, advocating for diminished salaries of clergy, and denying a belief in God.[80] Mill took a position on these debates long before penning *On Liberty* in 1859. Following in his father's footsteps, as early as 1823 Mill wrote editorials for the *Morning Chronicle* denouncing the prosecution of Robert Carlisle for his printing of blasphemous publications.[81] Mill remained immersed in these debates in publications during subsequent decades.[82] By the 1850s, he had refined his arguments on the freedom of expression after having participated in them for many years.[83]

In *On Liberty*, Mill explained that "the appropriate region of human liberty" includes, "first, the inward domain of consciousness, demanding liberty of conscience, in the most comprehensive sense, liberty of thought and feeling, absolute freedom of opinion and sentiment on all subjects, practical or speculative, scientific, moral, or theological."[84] This freedom is foundational because one's ability to live a fulfilling and enjoyable existence demands contemplation of the effects of one's decisions, including thoughtfully deliberating these decisions with others. Similarly, Mill proclaimed that the "liberty of expressing and publishing opinions may seem to fall under a different principle, since it belongs to that part of the conduct of an individual which concerns other people, but, being almost of as much importance as the liberty of thought itself, and resting in great part on the same reasons, is practically inseparable from it."[85] Mill understood the United States' First Amendment freedoms as foundational: the freedom of religion, the freedom of speech, and the freedom of the press. Mill confirmed his intent to include the freedom of the press in this first group of rights at the start of his chapter titled "Of the Liberty of Thought and Discussion": "The time, it is to be hoped, is gone by when any defense would be necessary of the 'liberty of the press' as one of the securities against corrupt or tyrannical governments."[86]

Mill boldly proclaimed that the freedoms of conscience, thought, speech, and press were to be protected according to the harm principle, going so far as to declare: "If all mankind minus one, were of one opinion, and only one person were of the contrary opinion, mankind would be no more justified in silencing that one person, than he, if he had the power, would be justified in silencing mankind."[87] For Mill, if beliefs and opinions were simply private property in the classical Lockean sense, "it would make some difference whether the injury was inflicted only on a few persons or on many."[88] If that were the case, then the greater harm would clearly be in the few silencing the many, as more "property" rights would be harmed. However, Mill did not understand expressive rights to be a form of property. Rather, he proclaimed that they were important to protect because they were socially utile.[89] Mill understood the great value in them because of the advantages that we obtain by listening to the ideas of others: "The peculiar evil of silencing the expression of an opinion is that it is robbing the human race, posterity as well as the existing generation—those who dissent from the opinion, still more than those who hold it. If the opinion is right, they are deprived of the opportunity of exchanging error for truth; if wrong, they lose, what is almost as great a benefit, the clearer perception and livelier impression of truth, produced by its collision with error."[90] Thus, the exchange of ideas provides benefits to all, even more so than in the personal fulfilment we might receive from expressing ourselves.

Mill in this passage echoed John Milton's famous defense of an unlicensed press in *Areopagitica* in 1644: "And though all the winds of doctrine were let loose to play upon the earth, so Truth be in the field, we do injuriously by licensing and prohibiting to misdoubt her strength. Let her and Falsehood grapple; who ever knew Truth put to the worse, in a free and open encounter?"[91] Mill's intellectual debt to Milton on the freedom of expression has been well documented.[92] Mill's opposition to speech restrictions is reminiscent of Milton's hostility to book licensing, both in his arguments and in the metaphors he used.[93] Although intellectually indebted to Milton, Mill was not as sanguine as Milton about truth's ability to prevail; he noted in *On Liberty* that "the dictum that truth always triumphs over persecution is one of those pleasant falsehoods which men repeat after one another till they pass into commonplaces, but which all experience refutes."[94] Mill cataloged how often Protestantism was repressed, and noted it was not inevitable that Christianity would survive the Roman Empire. Dogmatists and partisans will refuse to recognize truth and will work to suppress it. In a passage that resonates as much today as when Mill penned it, he observed,

> I acknowledge that the tendency of all opinions to become sectarian is not cured by the freest discussion, but is often heightened and exacerbated thereby; the truth which ought to have been, but was not, seen, being rejected all the more violently because proclaimed by persons regarded as opponents. But it is not on the impassioned partisan, it is on the calmer and more disinterested bystander, that this collision of opinions works its salutary effect. Not the violent conflict between parts of the truth, but the quiet suppression of half of it, is the formidable evil; there is always hope when people are forced to listen to both sides.[95]

While truth will not always prevail, Mill expected that if the freedom of expression is protected, the truth will resurface and, if circumstances are favorable, will likely gain a foothold and become accepted by good-faithed listeners. For both Milton and Mill, the freedom of expression was the most important right deserving protection, in part because it makes it possible for society to realize truth.[96]

Mill then cataloged the importance of protecting free expression, regardless of whether or not what the speaker says is true. He first declared that we "can never be sure that the opinion we are endeavoring to stifle is a false opinion; even if we were sure, stifling it would be an evil still."[97] The former is not difficult to see, as "the opinion which it is attempted to suppress by authority may possibly be true."[98] Those with government power to censor are not infallible, and they might wrongly think something true that is actually false.

According to Mill, to "refuse a hearing to an opinion because they are sure that it is false is to assume that *their* certainty is the same thing as *absolute* certainty. All silencing of discussion is an assumption of infallibility."[99] If government assumes that it is infallible and censors opinions it believes are wrong, everyone is deprived of an opportunity to hear the truth.[100] We have only reached a greater state of enlightenment because of opportunities to listen to, and discuss, different ideas: "Wrong opinions and practices gradually yield to fact and argument; but facts and arguments, to produce any effect on the mind, must be brought before it."[101] The freedom of speech ensures that we can learn from the mistakes of the past, which in turn makes a better future.[102]

Whether or not government or society at large considers an opinion obviously wrong, we ought to keep an open mind.[103] Mill cited the famed case of Socrates, who was executed for the views he expressed and for exposing ignorance.[104] Socrates is one of multiple illustrations given by Mill of the "propounder of a new truth," whom Mill believed carries out "as important of a service as a human being can render to his fellow creatures" by discovering for "the world something which deeply concerns it, and of which it was previously ignorant, to prove to it that it had been mistaken on some vital point of . . . interest."[105] Mill explained how public officials who ban the expression of others' views might even be more fervent in their censorship when silencing speech that is true: "Men are not more zealous for truth than they often are for error, and a sufficient application of legal or even social penalties will generally succeed in stopping the propagation of either."[106] Mill's goal was to seek truth, and he believed that censorship created too many risks of suppressing the truth.[107] His experience denouncing blasphemy prosecutions earlier in his life is evident in these passages of *On Liberty*.

According to Mill, some argue that there are social or religious beliefs so essential that admitting their falsity would devastate society, thus justifying the state's suppression of them. Mill rejected such calls for censorship:

There are, it is alleged, certain beliefs so useful, not to say indispensable, to well-being that it is as much the duty of governments to uphold those beliefs as to protect any other of the interests of society. In a case of such necessity, and so directly in the line of their duty, something less than infallibility may, it is maintained, warrant, and even bind, governments, to act on their own opinion confirmed by the general opinion of mankind. It is also often argued, and still oftener thought, that none but bad men would desire to weaken these salutary beliefs; and there can be nothing wrong, it is thought, in restraining bad men and prohibiting what only such men would wish to practice. This mode of thinking makes the justification of restraints on discussion not a question of the truth of doctrines, but of their usefulness. . . . The usefulness of an opinion is itself matter of opinion—as disputable, as open to discussion, and requiring discussion as much as the opinion itself.[108]

After explaining reasons to protect the freedom of speech because the view that is censored may be true, Mill described what he thought was a much more regular occurrence—"when the conflicting doctrines, instead of being one true and the other false, share the truth between them, and the nonconforming opinion is needed to supply the remainder of the truth of which the received doctrine embodies only a part."[109] Doctrines, especially ones that persist, almost always contain some value, Mill expounded: "Popular opinions, on subjects not palpable to sense, are often true, but seldom or never the whole truth. They are a part of the truth; sometimes a greater, sometimes a smaller part, but exaggerated, distorted, and disjoined from the truths by which they ought to be accompanied and limited."[110] Combining our partial truths in debate can lead us to understand more of what is true: "Truth, in the great practical concerns of life, is so much a question of the reconciling and combining of opposites, that very few have minds sufficiently capacious and impartial to make the adjustment with an approach to correctness, and it has to be made by the rough process of a struggle between combatants fighting under hostile banners."[111] According to Mill, "Only through diversity of opinion is there, in the existing state of human intellect, a chance of fair-play to all sides of the truth."[112] For Mill, even if someone's expression included a certain amount of false content, "since the general or prevailing opinion on any subject is rarely or never the whole truth, it is only by the collision of adverse opinions that the remainder of the truth has any chance of being supplied."[113] Mill believed that protecting both truth and falsity ensures that we understand every side of an issue and better comprehend what might be truth.[114]

Although Mill spoke generally of seeking truth (and protecting partial truths), he specifically applied this to politics and the shielding of different views during policy debates in a democracy. In a democratic system, "it is almost a commonplace that a party of order or stability and a party of progress or reform are both necessary elements of a healthy state of political life. . . . Each of these modes of thinking derives its utility from the deficiencies of the other."[115] Thus, the give-and-take of political debate needs protection, with the party in power prohibited from simply classifying the minority party's views as "false" by using the coercive power of the state to stifle the minority party's criticism. Instead, Mill understood that each side in political debate might be prone to expressing partial truths. Mill extended this thought process to those expressing marginal political ideas, as he believed that "opinions favorable to democracy and to aristocracy, to property and to equality, to co-operation and to competition, to luxury and to abstinence, to sociality and individuality, to liberty and discipline, and all the other standing antagonisms of practical life" should be "expressed with equal freedom."[116] For Mill, political freedom of expression is to be protected for the utilitarian reason of facilitating a better-functioning democratic policy-making process.[117]

Having discussed the problems of (1) censoring speech that may be true, and (2) censoring speech that contains some truth and some falsity, Mill explored what to do if (3) the "received opinion be not only true, but the whole truth."[118] Mill averred that if we really *knew* that an opinion was totally false, there would still be a problem in censoring it. A widely accepted view becomes mere dogma unless it "is suffered to be, and actually is, vigorously and earnestly contested"; then "it will, by most of those who receive it, be held in the manner of a prejudice, with little comprehension or feeling of its rational grounds. . . . The meaning of the doctrine itself will be in danger of being lost or enfeebled, and deprived of its vital effect on the character and conduct."[119] It is not enough to simply know the truth, as people must really understand it and be able to articulate why something is true; otherwise, they merely believe presumptions. Such beliefs, Mill explains, "will be held as a dead dogma, not a living truth."[120]

Furthermore, having to defend one's views improves society, increasing the likelihood that our beliefs are as close to the truth as possible: "He who knows only his own side of the case knows little of that. His reasons may be good, and no one may have been able to refute them. But if he is equally unable to refute the reasons on the opposite side, if he does not so much as know what they are, he has no ground for preferring either opinion."[121] Only through hearing an argument can we ascertain if it is false, or, perhaps, come to learn that our beliefs are true. Mill explained this using a metaphor: "Both teachers and learners go to sleep at their posts as soon as there is no enemy in the field."[122] We become intellectually lazy if we allow the government to ban expression of ideas widely held to be false. According to Mill, a well-lived life includes enthusiastically arguing with others, teaching them, learning from them, and using these opportunities to better understand what is true.[123] Accordingly, Mill thought it important to recognize "the necessity to the mental well-being of mankind (on which all their other well-being depends) of freedom of opinion, and freedom of the expression of opinion."[124]

This last line by Mill reveals another utilitarian reason to protect the freedom of expression. Much of the chapter "Of Thought and Discussion" focuses on protecting the freedom of expression to seek truth (including as it relates to promoting democratic governance by protecting discussion of policy proposals some think are false or immoral). However, Mill also thought that protecting the freedom of expression was one way to promote "mental well-being." Mill believed that "in things which do not primarily concern others, individuality should assert itself," as a way to support "human happiness."[125] Thought of in this way, Mill was arguing that it is essential to protect the freedom of expression because this aspect of personal autonomy helps people live their lives freely and experience as much happiness as possible, which will benefit society.[126] Thus, Mill defended the freedom of speech on three major grounds: advancing truth, facilitating the democratic process, and promoting personal autonomy.

With the harm principle, "everything must be free to be written and published without restraint."[127] Hence, Mill criticized anyone not willing to hear claims that were "pushed to an extreme."[128] This encompassed not just ideas, whether they be true or not, but also the mode of expressing them. Mill advocated protecting expression that was hate-filled, offensive, or insulting: we should "take some notice of those who say that the free expression of all opinions should be permitted on condition that the manner be temperate, and do not pass the bounds of fair discussion."[129] Mill's apprehension here was with the "impossibility of fixing where these supposed bounds are to be placed; for if the test be offence to those whose opinion is attacked, . . . experience testifies that this offence is given whenever the attack is telling and powerful, and that every opponent who pushes them hard, and whom they find it difficult to answer, appears to them . . . an intemperate opponent."[130] Calls for discussions to be calm, or for the use of certain language, or to not give offense, are subjective interpretations made by those who oppose the underlying ideas being expressed, and are impossible standards to police. "Invective, sarcasm, personality, and the like" have to be protected; Mill argued that dissidents who challenged the "prevailing opinion" are usually the persons condemned by a tyrannical majority for using these methods.[131] Indeed, Mill believed that intemperance may be necessary to shock the ruling orthodoxy.[132] Even if a speaker did "suppress facts or arguments, to misstate the elements of the case, or misrepresent the opposite opinion . . . law [cannot] presume to interfere with this kind of controversial misconduct."[133] While such methods may "justly incur severe censure," they should *not* be prohibited by law.[134] Mill says, it is "obvious that law and authority have no business with restraining" this type of expression, even if he concurrently advocated that we do our best to undertake a "real morality of public discussion."[135] We must each be free to draw our own conclusions about the appropriate methods of debate, rather than having government do that for us.[136]

Invective or offensive speech must be safeguarded, but Mill harmonized these sentiments on the freedom of speech with his harm principle. If expression causes actual harm, not just offense or moral anguish, then Mill believed that expression could be outlawed. Mill described how "even opinions lose their immunity when the circumstances in which they are expressed are such as to constitute their expression a positive instigation to some mischievous act."[137] From a Millian perspective, the context of speech matters.[138] Mill provided examples: "An opinion that corn dealers are starvers of the poor, or that private property is robbery, ought to be unmolested when simply circulated through the press, but may justly incur punishment when delivered orally to an excited mob assembled before the house of a corn dealer, or when handed about among the same mob in the form of a placard."[139] Immediate incitement to commit illegal action is not protected because there is no time for reasoned discussion before destructive activity takes place.[140] However, if reflective discussion can occur, then Mill thought promoting illegal conduct deserved protection.[141] Outside of circumstances when expression will lead directly to property damage or physical violence, Mill thought that "absolute freedom of opinion and sentiment on all subjects" must be protected.

While a significant portion of *On Liberty* focuses on the freedom of speech, Mill thought that free speech is more than a good in itself, as it is a necessary component to a choosing a life that reflects one's beliefs: "If people must be allowed, in whatever concerns only themselves, to act as seems best to themselves at their own peril, they must equally be free to consult with one another about what is fit to be so done; to exchange opinions, and give and receive suggestions."[142] Utilizing the harm principle, Mill asserted that if one "refrains from molesting others in what concerns them, and merely acts according to his own inclination and judgment in things which concern himself, the same reasons which show that opinion should be free prove also that he should be allowed, without molestation, to carry his opinions into practice at his own cost."[143] Mill understood the freedom of speech as essential because it not only enables one to investigate what is true and false; it is additionally the basis to determine what type of life one will live.[144] Thus, expressive freedoms enable one to live an independent and self-directed life. Such autonomy enables "experiments in living" that provide advantages to "society at large."[145] Even more to the point, "it is the privilege and proper condition of a human being, arrived at the maturity of his faculties, to use and interpret experience in his own way."[146]

Mill's advocacy for protection of free speech did not extend only to an individual right to express ideas about politics, religion, and other matters. Mill thought that "from this liberty of each individual follows the liberty, within the same limits, of combination among individuals; freedom to unite for any purpose not involving harm to others: the persons combining being supposed to be of full age, and not forced or deceived."[147] This freedom includes any cases where consenting adults act in concert, as long as what they do does not cause harm to third parties; examples Mill explored in *On Liberty* include the freedom of assembly and association, especially for expressive purposes: "If people must be allowed, in whatever concerns only themselves, to act as seems best to themselves at their own peril, they must equally be free to consult with one another about what is fit to be so done; to exchange opinions, and give and receive suggestions."[148] Mill decried puritanical attempts to make illegal "assemblages," including "for purposes of diversion," such as expressive reasons like playing music, dancing, and putting on theatrical performances.[149] Mill spoke positively in *On Liberty* of "voluntary associations" where "there are varied experiments and endless diversity of experience."[150] If the harm principle is maintained with these assemblies and associations, people have a right to participate, including for the purposes of expressing and discussing ideas, provided each individual's participation in the meeting or group is voluntary.[151] Mill wanted this associative and assembly right to be protected to the same degree as individual expression: "No society in which these liberties are not, on the whole, respected is free, whatever may be its form of government; and none is completely free in which they do not exist absolute and unqualified."[152] Mill thought it was essential that people have the right to join assemblies to advocate for and discuss ideas, and unless these groups caused direct harm to others, such associations should be protected without exception.[153] For these reasons, when we refer to Mill's notion of the freedom of expression, we mean it to encompass the freedom of speech (including religious expression), the freedom of the press, the right to assembly, and the freedom of association (including association for the purposes of petitioning the government).

Mill's protection for the freedom of expression (and its extension to expressive associations and gatherings) means that the "government cannot have too much of the kind of activity which does not impede, but aids and stimulates, individual exertion and development."[154] Mill thought it of utmost importance to defend the freedoms of speech, press, assembly, and association because of their value in advancing truth, facilitating the democratic process, and promoting the good that comes from protecting personal autonomy. Mill spent so many pages in *On Liberty* addressing the freedom of expression because it is the core of all human freedoms. It is necessary for one's ability to be a fully autonomous individual who makes informed choices when exercising other freedoms, spreading truth, and promoting democracy. However, as we shall see in the next chapter, the early years of the US Supreme Court did not reflect Mill's harm principle.

CHAPTER 2

Preventing Substantive Evils

The Supreme Court on Speech through World War I

John Stuart Mill's views on the freedom of expression did not find purchase among US Supreme Court justices in the nineteenth or early twentieth centuries. Until World War I, free speech cases comprised a comparatively small portion of the Supreme Court's docket, and the Supreme Court's decisions posited a rather crabbed view of free speech. The early Supreme Court rejected Millian arguments for the freedom of expression. This should not minimize the popular sentiment emphasizing free speech throughout US history. There is a long, well-documented record of efforts by various groups and persons to advance the freedom of expression before World War I.[1] These efforts failed to make legal headway, however, as evidenced by a string of political attempts to suppress speech, which includes passing the Sedition Act of 1798, restricting abolitionist speech in the antebellum South, squashing antiwar speech during the Civil War, enacting the Comstock Act of 1873, and issuing various restrictions on organized labor at the close of the nineteenth century.[2]

Early on, the Supreme Court largely avoided these free speech disputes. When introducing the Bill of Rights in 1789, James Madison proclaimed that if freedoms were enshrined in the Constitution, "independent tribunals of justice will consider themselves in a peculiar manner the guardians of those rights; they will be an impenetrable bulwark against every assumption of power in the legislative or executive."[3] Instead, for the first century of the

Supreme Court's existence, the justices had relatively little to say about the freedom of expression and the First Amendment. This was true for multiple reasons. First, in the late nineteenth and early twentieth centuries, the First Amendment had not been interpreted to limit the power of the states; protection of the freedom of expression was not incorporated to apply to state governments until *Gitlow v. New York* (1925).[4] State action that infringed on this right made infrequent appearances before the Supreme Court, and those few free speech claims concerned the Fourteenth Amendment's protection of "liberty." Furthermore, Congress did not provide the Supreme Court with much jurisdiction to hear First Amendment questions until after the Civil War; for instance, Congress failed to give the Supreme Court general federal question jurisdiction until 1875, which occurred during a period when the Supreme Court was incredibly backlogged.[5] Finally, besides the short-lived Sedition Act (repealed in 1801, just three years after its passage), Congress engaged in little control of expressive activities until it began regulating the use of the mails and banning expression deemed obscene or immoral in the 1870s.[6]

Toward the end of the nineteenth century, the Supreme Court finally issued rulings that interpreted the meaning of, or strongly implicated, the freedom of expression. Nevertheless, through the end of World War I, the Supreme Court's jurisprudence was decidedly different from Mill's philosophy. The often unanimous rulings of the Supreme Court into the 1910s offered a relatively narrow interpretation of the First Amendment. Only at the end of this decade did Justice Oliver Wendell Holmes Jr. begin to indicate any support for a view of the freedom of expression similar to Mill, and even then, that support was theoretical only. As David Rabban summarized, through the end of World War I, "no court was more unsympathetic to freedom of expression than the Supreme Court, which rarely produced even a dissenting opinion in a First Amendment case."[7]

This lack of sympathy to free expression claims stems from the English common law tradition that US courts were generally following. Without US precedents on point, US courts prior to World War I often adopted interpretations of the freedoms of speech and press consistent with the English common law.[8] That tradition was best explained by the English jurist Sir William Blackstone's *Commentaries on the Laws of England*. Blackstone stated that although one could not be restricted from expression before the fact, the government had the power to punish one for what one said after the fact: "The liberty of the press . . . consists in laying no *previous* restraints upon publication, and not in freedom from censure for criminal matter when published."[9] This understanding of the freedom of expression, by solely limiting the government's power to impose prior restraints on publication, permitted the government expansive power to ban expression it did not like *after* publication. As described by Blackstone, "blasphemous, immoral, treasonable, schismatical, seditious, or scandalous" expressions could be punished, even if the statements were true.[10] Mill's *On Liberty* rejected this English common law tradition that guided both British and US courts.[11]

Two of the earliest US Supreme Court decisions touching on free expression were *Ex Parte Jackson* (1877) and *In re Rapier* (1892). Both cases involved First Amendment challenges to a federal law that prohibited using the mails to advertise lotteries, making them the Supreme Court's first opportunities to interpret the Constitution's protection of commercial speech.[12] In both cases, the Supreme Court implied (without directly ruling) that advertising receives some First Amendment protection, but the Supreme Court also gave a rather narrow view to how much expression was protected. In *Jackson*, Justice Stephen Field reasoned for the Supreme Court that, regarding the freedom of the press, "liberty of circulating is as essential to that freedom as liberty of publishing; indeed, without the circulation, the publication would be of little value."[13] Nevertheless, Field held for a unanimous Supreme Court that "the object of Congress has not been to interfere with the freedom of the press, or with any other rights of the people; but to refuse its facilities for the distribution of matter deemed injurious to the public *morals*."[14] Field concluded for the Supreme Court that since Congress intended "that the mail should not be used to transport such corrupting publications and articles," then "we have no doubt" of "the constitutionality of the act."[15]

Likewise, in *Rapier*, a unanimous Supreme Court upheld the same law. Chief Justice Melville Fuller, following *Jackson*, reasoned that under the First Amendment, the "freedom of communication is not abridged" when "the government declines itself to become an agent in the circulation of printed matter which it regards as injurious."[16] Fuller reiterated in *Rapier* that what Congress can deem "injurious"—and hence what has no constitutional protection—includes that which is harmful "to the public *morals*."[17] The two decisions represent a view that the Constitution puts few limits on government power to restrict expression; commercial speech appeared to receive some constitutional protection, but all forms of expression could be constricted if deemed harmful to morality.[18] While Field's rationale that "liberty of circulating is as essential to that freedom as liberty of publishing" picks up a key idea in Mill's argument, neither case reflects Mill's maxim that morality is an illegitimate criterion to exclude ideas from being expressed, as he argued for "absolute freedom of opinion and sentiment on all subjects," including on questions of morality.[19]

Under the same guise that the First Amendment offered no protection to immoral expression, the Supreme Court in *Rosen v. United States* (1896) upheld the application of the Comstock Act to material deemed obscene, resulting in a thirteen-month prison sentence for Rosen. Writing for the Supreme Court, Justice John Marshall Harlan reasoned that government could use Victorian moral standards to dictate what ideas could be expressed: "Every one who uses the mails of the United States for carrying papers or publications must take notice of what, in this enlightened age, is meant by decency, purity, and chastity in social life, and what must be deemed obscene, lewd, and lascivious."[20] Harlan implicitly endorsed an expansive definition of obscenity, upholding this jury instruction: "The test of obscenity is whether the tendency of the matter is to deprave and corrupt the morals of those whose minds are open to such influence and into whose hands a publication of this sort may fall."[21] The jury instructions used by the trial judge in *Rosen* were derived from a UK decision, *Regina v. Hicklin* (1868).[22] Not only did this test for obscenity allow government to ban publications designated as immoral, but it also found that adults could not distribute such materials to other adults because of the possibility that children might obtain them, thus restricting adults to what is fit for children.[23] If it is anti-Millian to ban immoral expression, it is even more anti-Millian to ban expression among adults because of the effect it could have on children. Mill derided those who consider questions of public policy "as if the interest of children was everything, and that of grown persons nothing."[24] Harlan referred in his opinion to "the English precedents" on obscenity, demonstrating his acceptance of the *Hicklin* test and English common law.[25] Two justices dissented in *Rosen*, but their disagreement was over the specificity of the charge, and they appeared to also endorse the English common law test for obscenity.[26] Although the Supreme Court did not directly rule on the First Amendment in *Rosen*, the tacit approval of *Hicklin* led lower federal courts to consistently use that overly restrictive obscenity test for the next several decades.[27]

In *Robertson v. Baldwin* (1897), the Supreme Court continued to imply that the First Amendment did not protect speech the government declared to be immoral. The justices rejected a Thirteenth Amendment claim of involuntary servitude by seamen who had been arrested and forced back to work on a ship after deserting their labors before their contracts had expired.[28] Justice Henry Brown wrote for the Supreme Court: "The law is perfectly well settled that the first ten amendments to the Constitution, commonly known as the Bill of Rights, were not intended to lay down any novel principles of government, but simply to embody certain guaranties and immunities which we had inherited from our English ancestors, and which had from time immemorial been subject to certain well-recognized exceptions. . . . Thus, the freedom of speech and of the press (art. 1) does not permit the publication of libels, blasphemous or indecent articles, or other publications injurious to public morals or private reputation."[29] The Supreme Court interpreted the freedom of expression *not* from an individualistic perspective but as a restatement of eighteenth-century British law.[30] It was that Blackstonian common law understanding of freedom— and its substantial exceptions based on what offended majoritarian morality— to which Mill objected.[31]

The Supreme Court similarly decided *Davis v. Massachusetts* (1897), upholding the conviction of, and fine against, a reverend for preaching in a Boston public park, in violation of a city ordinance that required speakers to first obtain a mayoral-issued permit.[32] Writing for a unanimous Supreme Court, Justice Edward White emphasized the government's power to restrict expression on its own property: "The Fourteenth Amendment to the Constitution of the United States does not destroy the power of the States to enact police regulations as to the subjects within their control, and does not have the effect of creating a particular and personal right in the citizen to use public property in defiance of the constitution and laws of the State."[33] In his reasoning, Justice White quoted from the opinion of the Supreme Judicial Court of Massachusetts, which also upheld Davis's conviction; the opinion quoted by Justice White was written by Oliver Wendell Holmes Jr. when he was serving on the court below: "For the legislature absolutely or conditionally to forbid public speaking in a highway or public park is no more an infringement of the rights of a member of the public than for the owner of a private house to forbid it in his house. When no proprietary right interferes the legislature may end the right of the public to enter upon the public place by putting an end to the dedication to public uses. So it may take the less step of limiting the public use to certain purposes."[34] Neither Holmes nor White emphasized the freedoms of speech and religion. Both jurists accentuated government powers: if the government could ban people from entering government property altogether, it could allow people to enter government property but then restrict what they can say there.[35] Neither took a Millian approach to the freedom of expression. Indeed, Mill spoke disparagingly in *On Liberty* of the blasphemy prosecution of Thomas Pooley, who was imprisoned for expressing his opinions about religion on public property in a case where he lacked a government permit to do so.[36] The Supreme Court would abandon this narrower view of expression on public property for a more Millian jurisprudence in the 1930s, building on Millian reasoning that Holmes would adopt beginning in 1919.[37]

Just a few weeks before Holmes was appointed to the US Supreme Court, that tribunal decided *American School of Magnetic Healing v. McAnnulty* (1902). The case involved the postmaster general's seizure of mail addressed to a business selling "magnetic healing" literature; the postmaster general had determined that the business was defrauding the public.[38] Although challenged by the business on Fourth and Fifth Amendment grounds, the case had implications for the freedom of expression.[39] The Supreme Court overturned the postmaster general's decision by a vote of 6–2, with Justice Rufus Peckham writing for the Supreme Court that "there is no exact standard of absolute truth by which to prove the assertion false and a fraud."[40] Justice Peckham expounded on the point: "The claim of complainants cannot be the subject of proof as of an ordinary fact; it cannot be proved as a fact to be a fraud or false pretense or promise, nor can it properly be said that those who assume to heal bodily ills or infirmities by a resort to this method of cure are guilty of obtaining money under false pretenses."[41] Thus, the Supreme Court, similar to Mill, protected the expression of opinions, even if some believed them to be false. Reflecting a more contemporary debate, Peckham demonstrated the problem with conferring such a power on the postmaster general by asking a rhetorical question: "Vaccination is believed by many to be a preventive of smallpox, while others regard it as unavailing for that purpose. Under these statutes could the Postmaster General, upon evidence satisfactory to him, decide that it was not a preventive, and exclude from the mails all letters to one who practised it and advertised it as a method of prevention, on the ground that the moneys he received through the mails were procured by false pretenses?"[42] The Supreme Court's decision was an anomaly for this era, taking a Millian position, refusing the government the power to determine which speech is "false" and then ban it without proving some other sort of pressing justification, such as actual fraud.[43] The free speech triumph was ephemeral, though. As one historian put it, "*Magnetic Healing* was a complete victory for freedom of speech. . . . But the spirit of *Magnetic Healing* soon fell ill."[44]

Two years after *Magnetic Healing*, the Supreme Court decided *United States ex rel. Turner v. Williams* (1904), upholding a resident alien's exclusion from the country because he advocated anarchism.[45] Turner was a British national who possessed anarchist literature when he was arrested.[46] Arguing for the defense (which was financed by the Free Speech League), Clarence Darrow asserted that the deportation of Turner for his advocacy would violate the First Amendment.[47] Chief Justice Fuller disagreed, writing for a unanimous Supreme Court that Congress's decision to exclude or expel aliens was constitutional because the law "has no reference to . . . nor does [it] abridge the freedom of speech."[48] Instead, Fuller reasoned, the First Amendment applied to citizens only: "It is, of course, true that if an alien is not permitted to enter this country, or, having entered contrary to law, is expelled, he is in fact cut off from . . . speaking or publishing . . . in the country, but that is merely because of his exclusion therefrom. He does not become one of the people to whom these things are secured by our Constitution by an attempt to enter forbidden by law."[49] Fuller reasoned that Turner could be excluded because "even if Turner . . . only regarded the absence of government as a political ideal," when he "sought to attain it by advocating [anarchy] we cannot say that the inference was unjustifiable either that he contemplated the ultimate realization of his ideal by the use of force, or that his speeches were incitements to that end."[50] Fuller stated that even if "the word 'anarchists' should be interpreted as including aliens whose anarchistic views are professed as those of political philosophers innocent of evil intent," Congress still had the power to exclude such person, as Congress could determine that "the tendency of the general exploitation of such views is so dangerous to the public weal that aliens who hold and advocate them would be undesirable additions to our population."[51] Merely advocating anarchism—with no "evil intent" to engage in violence—was enough justification for the government to exclude Turner, who, the Supreme Court ruled, as an alien, did not possess the same constitutional rights as citizens.[52] Mill, though, thought it important to protect political debate of all stripes. He decried in *On Liberty* that the "despotism of custom is everywhere the standing hindrance to human advancement," arguing that where customary thought had ossified debate in a state, "if they are ever to be farther improved, it must be by foreigners."[53] Thus, similar to the *Davis* ruling that if the government can exclude someone from public property, it can restrict people's speech on that property, the Supreme Court in *Turner* ruled that if the government can exclude foreign nationals altogether, it can exclude foreign nationals because of their political expression. Justice Holmes participated in this case and voted with the majority.

Holmes had his first opportunity to author the opinion of the US Supreme Court in a free expression case in *Patterson v. Colorado* (1907). His ruling and reasoning in this case were far from Mill's philosophy. A newspaper publisher, Thomas Patterson, had been convicted of criminal contempt for printing articles and a political cartoon that characterized the Colorado Supreme Court as acting in an overtly partisan way.[54] Patterson believed the state supreme court's overturning of a gubernatorial election and a state constitutional amendment were invalid; since a petition for a rehearing in these matters was still pending before the Colorado Supreme Court, Patterson was charged with contempt on the theory that his publication could affect the outcome of decisions not yet finalized.[55] Essentially, though, Patterson was editorializing on the actions of public officials. Holmes, writing for a 7–2 US Supreme Court majority, upheld Patterson's conviction and fine.[56]

In *Patterson*, Justice Holmes declined to decide if the Fourteenth Amendment incorporated the First Amendment's freedom of expression.[57] Nevertheless, he declared that even if the First Amendment applied to states like Colorado, it would not bar Patterson's prosecution, as Holmes assumed that the "main purpose" of the First Amendment "is to prevent all such previous restraints upon publications as had been practiced by other governments."[58] Holmes interpreted the First Amendment so as to "not prevent the subsequent punishment of such as may be deemed contrary to the public welfare."[59] He concluded by stating that "the preliminary freedom extends as well to the false as to the true; the subsequent punishment may extend as well to the true as to the false."[60] Although Justice John Marshall Harlan in dissent proclaimed that the Constitution protects against more than prior restraints, Holmes's opinion commanded seven justices.[61] This decision permitted majoritarian preference to dictate what ideas could be expressed. The case affirmed what English common law, in the Blackstonian tradition, defined for the freedom of expression: the prohibition on prior restraint protects false speech, but the government may subsequently punish that false speech and, in pursuance of a vague notion of "public welfare," the government may punish *true* speech.[62] In *Patterson*, Holmes applied what became known as the bad tendency test, which allows for punishment of expression that would tend to produce an "evil" outcome.[63] Holmes upheld the punishment because the publication "would tend to obstruct the administration of justice."[64]

Justice Holmes's application of a Blackstonian understanding of the freedom of expression was even more explicit when he stated that his interpretation of the freedom of expression "was the law of criminal libel apart from statute in most cases, if not in all."[65] His opinion cited two state cases from the late eighteenth and early nineteenth centuries using Blackstone as authority.[66] Holmes's statement in *Patterson* limiting freedom of expression, whether true or false, to protection against prior restraints only reflected what Blackstone wrote in his *Commentaries* in the 1760s: "It is immaterial with respect to the essence of a libel, whether the matter of it be true or false; since the provocation, and not the falsity, is the thing to be punished criminally; though, doubtless, the falsehood of it may aggravate it's [sic] guilt, and enhance it's [sic] punishment."[67] Blackstone's *Commentaries* posited that under English common law, truth could be punished after the fact if it was deemed blasphemous, immoral, seditious, or scandalous.[68] Thus, much like *Rosen* opened the door for US courts to use the restrictive English court definition of obscenity from *Hicklin*, in *Patterson* Justice Holmes fully ushered into US Supreme Court jurisprudence Blackstone's crabbed view of the freedom of expression for even political speech.

The Blackstonian position held that neither truth nor falsity were as important as suppressing unorthodox ideas that challenged the status quo. This is diametrically opposed to Mill. The entire second chapter of *On Liberty* is a defense of individual choice, not because of an abstract commitment to rights but because the ability to choose your own "experiment of living" is what distinguishes individuals from "automatons in human form."[69] Freedom of expression is necessary because without access to diverse doctrines, faiths, and customs, individuals cannot lead lives borne out of genuine choices.

During the same year as *Patterson*, the Supreme Court decided *Halter v. Nebraska*, which involved a state law criminalizing as desecration the use of the US flag in advertising. The Supreme Court found the law compliant with the Fourteenth Amendment and upheld a fifty-dollar fine plus costs against the defendants. Writing for an 8–1 majority, Justice Harlan emphasized that "a State possesses all legislative power consistent with a republican form of government," including legislation to "provide not only for the health, morals and safety of its people, but for the common good, as involved in the well-being, peace, happiness and prosperity of the people."[70] Although a Millian understanding of freedom would agree with the need to restrict action to protect public health and safety, punishing expression deemed immoral surely stands in opposition to Mill's thought.[71] The Supreme Court in *Halter* permitted a blatant form of what is now termed "viewpoint discrimination," a restriction or punishment of speech because the government disagrees with the view expressed. Harlan defended the legislation on moral grounds and even seemed to encourage private actors to engage in violence against those expressing negative ideas about the US flag: "For that flag every true American has not simply an appreciation but a deep affection. . . . Hence, it has often occurred that insults to a flag have been the cause of war, and indignities put upon it, in the presence of those who revere it, have often been resented and sometimes punished on the spot."[72] This understanding of what is protected expression is markedly different from Mill, who criticized those who engaged in "fanatical moral intolerance."[73]

Justice Harlan in *Halter* wrote that "a State may exert its power to strengthen the bonds of the Union and therefore, to that end, may encourage patriotism and love of country among its people" by limiting expression related to the US flag.[74] He concluded: "As the statute in question evidently had its origin in a purpose to cultivate a feeling of patriotism . . . we are unwilling to adjudge that in legislation for that purpose the State erred in duty or has infringed the constitutional right of anyone."[75] In contrast, in *On Liberty*, Mill warned his readers that "patriotic feelings of their time and people" are capable of motivating some to overzealously restrict the freedoms of others.[76] That Justice Harlan, who penned a dissent in *Patterson*, wrote for the Supreme Court in *Halter* shows that no justice in the early twentieth century was consistently advocating for a broader, more Millian approach to the freedom of expression. While Justice Peckham dissented (without opinion), Justice Holmes again sided with the Blackstonian majority in upholding the regulation. Over the next several years, the freedom of expression fared no better, with the justices repeatedly and unanimously upholding antilabor injunctions.[77]

Two cases in 1915 showed the justices continuing to interpret the freedom of expression very narrowly. In an unanimous opinion written by Justice Joseph McKenna in *Mutual Film Corporation v. Industrial Commission of Ohio*, the justices upheld a law that prohibited public showings of any film, unless it was approved by a state censorship board as having a "moral, educational, or amusing and harmless character."[78] According to Justice McKenna, films "may be used for evil," including if "a prurient interest may be excited and appealed to."[79] He also postulated that "there are some things which should not have pictorial representation in public places and to all audiences."[80] McKenna dismissed the film company's argument that movies are "publications of ideas," instead reacting as follows: "We immediately feel that the argument is wrong or strained which extends the guaranties of free opinion and speech to the multitudinous shows which are advertised on the bill-boards of our cities and towns."[81] McKenna averred that if the freedom of expression protected the exhibition of movies, it would also (unreasonably in his mind) mean that the Constitution similarly protects expression in "the theatre, the circus, and all other shows and spectacles."[82] Since the state censorship board was exercising a prior restraint, Justice McKenna read the freedom of speech so narrowly as to not include movies as a medium worthy of constitutional protection: "The exhibition of moving pictures is a business pure and simple, originated and conducted for profit, like other spectacles, not to be regarded . . . we think, as part of the press of the country or as organs of public opinion."[83] *Mutual Film* affirmed the ability of states to use police power to censor films at will, something that was already being upheld in state courts and lower federal courts.[84]

The Supreme Court understood movies in *Mutual Film* as a form of entertainment that could easily incite immoral action; thus, they were not subject to protection by the freedoms of speech or press (although the justices would overrule this decision decades later).[85] The Supreme Court treated the case as essentially a question about regulating economic activities.[86] The fact that it was clearly a prior restraint on expression was of no consequence for the Supreme Court. In addition to opposing morality-based restrictions on expression, Mill thought that theatrical and other expressive recreational performances deserve protection.[87] In a case that took a narrow interpretation of the application of the freedom of speech to new technologies, Justice Holmes again sided with the majority.

Justice Holmes wrote the opinion of the Court in a case decided later that year, *Fox v. Washington*. Fox edited a magazine that published an article titled "The Nude and the Prudes," describing how a group of anarchist nude sunbathers was infiltrated by some "prudes" who alerted law enforcement, resulting in four of the group being arrested for indecent exposure. The article spoke positively of nudism and advocated a boycott of the businesses owned by the "prudes." For this, Fox was convicted of violating a criminal statute that prohibited the publication of printed matter "advocating, encouraging or inciting, or having a tendency to encourage or incite the commission of any crime, breach of the peace or act of violence, or which shall tend to encourage or advocate disrespect for law or for any court or courts of justice."[88]

In a short opinion for a unanimous Supreme Court, Justice Holmes upheld the law, declaring that it "does not appear and is not likely that the statute will be construed to prevent publications merely because they tend to produce unfavorable opinions of a particular statute or of law in general."[89] However, the facts of the case suggest that the law was being interpreted to allow the prosecution of unpopular views, as the article in question was simply advocating for public nudity and encouraging a business boycott.[90] Nevertheless, Holmes summarily declared that "the article encourages and incites a persistence in what we must assume would be a breach of the state laws against indecent exposure" before holding that the law in question "cannot be said to infringe the Constitution of the United States."[91] Like his *Patterson* opinion, Holmes's opinion for the Supreme Court in *Fox* expresses a bad tendency test approach to the freedom of expression, as the case upheld a law prohibiting expression that had a "tendency" to produce what were deemed by the Supreme Court to be adverse outcomes.[92] Holmes's opinion said of the statute that "there is no trouble with it for want of definiteness," even though the law made it criminal to "advocate disrespect for law or for any court or courts of justice," which is an extensive and vague restriction.[93] Allowing the state such discretion is expressly what Mill feared and why he argued for the harm principle.

The Supreme Court's narrow interpretation of the freedom of expression persisted as the United States entered World War I.[94] *Toledo Newspaper Co. v. United States* (1918) was perhaps the most consequential free expression decision issued by the Supreme Court during the war. A seven-member majority upheld a federal contempt citation and fine against the *Toledo News-Bee* for publishing articles critical of a judge's actions in a pending case between a city and a railroad company. For Chief Justice White and the majority, the inquiry in the case was something akin to the bad tendency test: the Supreme Court asked whether or not there was "any reasonable tendency" of the publication to produce the "evil" that would come from obstructing the "administration of justice."[95] In his narrow reading of the First Amendment, Chief Justice White denied that "the freedom of the press is the freedom to do wrong with impunity" or "to frustrate and defeat the discharge of those governmental duties upon the performance of which the freedom of all, including that of the press, depends."[96] In curt fashion, White proclaimed that "the right of the press to state public things and discuss them . . . is subject to the restraints which separate right from wrong-doing."[97] White's opinion for the Supreme Court failed to state what the wrongdoing was in this case.

Interestingly, Holmes and Justice Louis Brandeis dissented in *Toledo Newspaper*, although they did so based on statutory, not constitutional, interpretation.[98] Holmes briefly commented that criminal contempt must mean "something more than adverse comment or disrespect."[99] He declared that a publication could cause "an imminent possibility of obstruction" of justice, but it could be criminalized if "only immediate and necessary action is contemplated."[100] Without directly repudiating his opinions in *Patterson* or *Fox*, Holmes was beginning to draw away from them.[101] He was starting to rethink his approach to the freedom of expression, but he did not yet have a coherent and comprehensive alternative to the bad tendency test and the Blackstonian idea that the freedom of expression merely prohibited prior restraints. Indeed, Holmes referred to the language of the bad tendency test when he wrote in his *Toledo Newspaper* dissent that "a judge of the United States is expected to be a man of ordinary firmness of character, and I find it impossible to believe that such a judge could have found in anything that was printed even a *tendency* to prevent his performing his sworn duty."[102]

That Holmes's thinking about these issues had changed was more evident in his opinion of the Court one year later in *Schenck v. United States* (1919). Charles Schenck was convicted for distributing leaflets encouraging draft-eligible persons to resist the draft, in violation of the Espionage Act, which prohibited attempting to cause insubordination or refusal of military duty.[103] By Holmes's description, Schenck, the general secretary of the US Socialist Party, urged to draftees that "conscription was despotism in its worst form and a monstrous wrong against humanity in the interest of Wall Street's chosen few."[104]

Writing for a unanimous Supreme Court, Justice Holmes noted that the protection for the freedom of expression depends on the context, as "in many places and in ordinary times the defendants in saying all that was said in the circular would have been within their constitutional rights. But the character of every act depends upon the circumstances in which it is done."[105] Accordingly, Holmes offered a hypothetical situation to show that there are limits to the freedom of expression: "The most stringent protection of free speech would not protect a man in falsely shouting fire in a theatre and causing a panic."[106] While these comments by Holmes do not reflect the firmer commitment to protecting the freedom of speech that Mill expressed in *On Liberty*, Holmes formulated a new standard to judge whether expression has First Amendment protection, known as the clear and present danger test: "The question in every case is whether the words used are used in such circumstances and are of such a nature as to create a clear and present danger that they will bring about the substantive evils that Congress has a right to prevent."[107] Applying this test, Holmes found that Congress possessed the constitutional power to regulate the military; since the distribution of antidraft leaflets could obstruct military recruitment (an "evil" Holmes reasoned Congress was permitted to prevent), Holmes upheld Schenck's Espionage Act conviction.[108] On this point, Holmes wrote of the leaflets that "the documents would not have been sent unless it had been intended to have some effect, and we do not see what effect it could be expected to have upon persons subject to the draft except to influence them to obstruct the carrying of it out."[109]

By developing a First Amendment test where speech is protected unless it will produce a present, tangible harm, Justice Holmes was approaching what Mill argued in *On Liberty*, that expression could be punished "when delivered orally to an excited mob."[110] This emphasis on danger needing to be "present" had the potential to be comparable to not only Mill's thought but also the concept of imminence and immediacy that Holmes had begun referring to in *Toledo Newspaper*. Holmes even took a step away from the Blackstonian view of the First Amendment when he made the equivocal statement that "it well may be that the prohibition of laws abridging the freedom of speech is not confined to previous restraints, although to prevent them may have been the main purpose."[111] However, Holmes's application of the clear and present danger test to the facts in *Schenck* was still something more akin to the bad tendency test.[112] Schenck printed between fifteen thousand and sixteen thousand leaflets.[113] The leaflets contained the text of the Thirteenth Amendment (insinuating that the military draft was a form of slavery), made claims that World War I was being fought to serve the interests of wealthy capitalists, and advocated that readers not only resist the draft but also petition to repeal the draft law in effect.[114] Putting aside the question of how persuasive the leaflets may or may not have been, they were limited in both their numbers and area of distribution; there was no evidence that even a single draftee refused to report for duty after reading one. Thus, it is difficult to find how Schenck was, in fact, causing a clear and present danger.[115] More to the point, if being drafted and sent to a war zone really was a metaphorical "fire," Schenck was "shouting" his truth, making it expression that Mill thought deserved protection (and making Holmes's analogy rather inapt).[116] Even if Schenck's ideas were false, Mill advocated that such speech be protected short of immediate danger. Finally, Holmes proclaimed that how much was protected by the First Amendment "is a question of proximity and degree," a malleable approach that Mill rejected.[117] Overall, *Schenck* represents a transitional ruling; while some Millian sympathies were theoretically emerging in Holmes's opinion, the decision still endorsed Blackstonian practice, as evidenced by Holmes's application of the clear and present danger test to the facts of the case. This resulted in the anti-Millian outcome of sustaining a conviction for expression because it was critical of the government.[118]

Nevertheless, Holmes started moving toward a Millian position on free expression, at least in the abstract. It was not coincidence that Holmes was adopting Mill's views in 1919. Like Mill, he was drawn to publishing and advocating for free expression at a young age. While attending Harvard College, Holmes wrote for, and edited, *Harvard Magazine*, which published essays critical of the status quo, including articles that advocated for slavery abolition and the admission of women to the college. While Holmes was editor, the magazine was condemned for an article arguing for "free will in matters of religion." Holmes was admonished by the faculty during his senior year for his "repeated and gross indecorum" in the classroom of an instructor who was a strong defender of Unitarian orthodoxy. At Harvard, Holmes gained something of a reputation for supporting, and vigorously engaging in, the free exchange of radical ideas, particularly the questioning of religious ideas. Thus, in his formative years, he had similarities to Mill, who also strongly defended the free exchange of ideas and was critical of religious orthodoxy. More specifically, the seed for a Millian interpretation of the First Amendment seems to have been planted in Holmes as a young man. In the early 1860s (while at Harvard), he read several of Mill's works, including *On Liberty*. Mill's scientific approach to understanding social issues also appealed to a young Holmes. On graduation from Harvard Law School in 1866, Holmes took a trip to Europe, where he personally met with Mill on multiple occasions; Holmes wrote to his future wife, Fanny Dixwell, expressing great anticipation over his meetings with Mill.[119]

As a US Supreme Court justice in the early twentieth century, Holmes's affinity for Mill was rediscovered through the Harvard lecturer Harold Laski. Holmes met Laski in 1916. Holmes and Laski quickly became good friends, often writing to each other and meeting in person when they could. Laski was an adamant defender of the freedom of speech and adhered to Mill's philosophy on the subject. During World War I, Laski suggested to Holmes that he revisit *On Liberty*.[120] In early 1919, Holmes did just that. Writing to Laski on February 28, 1919, Holmes noted that he had "reread Mill on *Liberty*" and affectionately called Mill a "fine old sportsman."[121] Holmes's opinion in *Schenck* was released less than one week later, on March 3, 1919.[122] When one takes together Holmes's earlier studies and travels, his friendship with Laski, and his recent rereading of *On Liberty*, one can easily understand how Mill's ideas about the freedom of expression begin to appear in Holmes's writing. As an older man (Holmes turned seventy-eight in 1919), he still understood the need to debate ideas and make people defend their beliefs, and he remarked to Laski that "men to a great extent believe what they want to," and later opined, "I detest a man who knows that he knows," which showed that Holmes's thinking on these matters remained close to Mill's ideas in *On Liberty*.[123] Holmes put this thinking into the Supreme Court's First Amendment jurisprudence. Certainly, there would have been other philosophical and jurisprudential influences on the justices (including Blackstone), but through Holmes, Mill's thought was now part of the Supreme Court's precedents.

Nevertheless, Holmes's respect for longstanding Blackstonian precedents did not vanish overnight; he ultimately upheld Schenck's conviction for criticizing the war effort and advocating that draftees not report for duty. The companion cases to *Schenck* similarly saw Espionage Act convictions unanimously upheld. In *Sugarman v. United States* (decided the same day as *Schenck*), Justice Brandeis wrote the opinion of the Court, finding that no substantial federal question was raised by a defendant who was convicted for giving a speech urging draft resistance at a Socialist Party meeting; Sugarman had appealed his conviction on the grounds that the trial judge failed to provide certain jury instructions, including one explaining that the freedom of speech still applies during war.[124] One week later, Justice Holmes upheld in *Frohwerk v. United States* the conviction of a German-language newspaper editor for publishing articles critical of US entry into World War I; according to Holmes, citing *Schenck*, "The First Amendment while prohibiting legislation against free speech as such cannot have been, and obviously was not, intended to give immunity for every possible use of language."[125] Although Holmes in *Frohwerk* went on to proclaim that "we do not lose our right to condemn either measures or men because the Country is at war," he and his colleagues upheld Frohwerk's conviction and ten-year prison sentence because "it is impossible to say that it might not have been found that the circulation of the paper was in quarters where a little breath would be enough to kindle a flame and that the fact was known and relied upon by those who sent the paper out."[126] Finally, on the same day as *Frohwerk*, Holmes wrote for the Supreme Court in *Debs v. United States*, upholding the conviction and ten-year prison sentence for the former Socialist Party presidential candidate Eugene V. Debs for a speech he gave advocating socialism and opposing militarism. Although Debs's speech was to a general audience (not directed toward draftees like in *Schenck*), Holmes proclaimed for the Supreme Court that the conviction was constitutional; his language in *Debs* seemed to backtrack significantly from what he wrote just one week earlier: "One purpose of the speech . . . was to oppose not only war in general but this war, and . . . the opposition was so expressed that its natural and intended effect would be to obstruct recruiting. If that was intended and if, in all the circumstances, that would be its probable effect, it would not be protected by reason of its being part of a general program and expressions of a general and conscientious belief."[127] Holmes's opinion in *Debs* was something more akin to the bad tendency test, and it essentially allowed the government to criminalize pacifism.[128]

The results in *Schenck* and its companion cases notwithstanding, Holmes began to espouse a new vision of the First Amendment. *On Liberty* was published in 1859, long after the First Amendment was ratified in 1791 and long before *Schenck* was decided in 1919. Nevertheless, the lack of First Amendment free speech decisions by 1919 meant that a vacuum largely existed regarding the reasoning that could be applied to justify rulings in these cases. The bad tendency test was there, as was the jurisprudential influence of Blackstone, but there was little else in existing Supreme Court caselaw. This vacuum was ready to be filled with some reasoning, and Holmes started filling it with Millian thought. On rereading *On Liberty* at the behest of Harold Laski, he started to rethink his position on the freedom of speech. Although Holmes was not yet consistent in his expression of Mill's philosophy, in early 1919 the seed for a Millian vision of free speech had been planted; that seed would come to fruition, as least in the minds of Holmes and Brandeis, later that year.

CHAPTER 3

The Marketplace of Ideas

Holmes and Brandeis, the Great Dissenters

Justice Holmes's introduction of the clear and present danger test to First Amendment jurisprudence in *Schenck v. United States* in March 1919 began ushering Mill's political philosophy into US constitutional law. The *Schenck* test—in the abstract—was a much stronger protection of the freedom of speech than had been used previously by the US Supreme Court.[1] Still, writing for a unanimous Supreme Court in *Schenck*, Holmes applied that test narrowly, upholding Schenck's conviction for advocating resistance to the military draft. In companion cases, Holmes wrote language that was similar to the bad tendency test. But both Holmes and Justice Brandeis would soon become stronger advocates for a more Millian approach to the freedom of speech. Their adoption of that position solidified over the spring, summer, and fall of 1919, assisted by Holmes's friend Harold Laski and one of Laski's colleagues at Harvard Law School, Professor Zechariah Chafee.

As noted in the chapter 2, before Holmes wrote his opinion in *Schenck*, Laski—a devotee of Mill's position on free expression—convinced the justice to reread *On Liberty*.[2] Holmes began expressing remorse for his decisions in *Schenck* and *Debs* to Laski within one week after the final Espionage Act cases were announced. On March 16, 1919, Holmes wrote to Laski about those decisions: "I greatly regretted having to write them. . . . Of course I know that donkeys and knaves would represent us as concurring in the condemnation of Debs because he was a dangerous agitator. . . . The federal judges seem to me (again between ourselves) to have got hysterical about the war. I should think the President when he gets through with his present amusements might do some pardoning."[3] Clearly, Holmes thought that these prosecutions were excessive, even though he did not believe that he possessed the power to overturn them on the Supreme Court.

Others thought the prosecutions were excessive and that the Supreme Court should have struck them down. Holmes received letters from across the country protesting his decisions for upholding unconstitutional restrictions on the freedom of expression. These included complaints from the legal community, where Holmes's decisions were criticized by the University of Chicago law professor Ernst Freund and the federal judge Learned Hand. The most stinging—and consequential—condemnation came from Zechariah Chafee in June 1919. Chafee wrote an article for the *Harvard Law Review* entitled "Freedom of Speech in War Time" that denounced the restrictions the federal government placed on expression during World War I. Laski was a *Harvard Law Review* editor, and he eventually recommended that Holmes read the article; Laski also orchestrated a meeting between himself, Chafee, and Holmes in July 1919 to discuss "Freedom of Speech in War Time." The article's subject matter would have been discussed with Holmes, and he almost certainly read it in the summer of 1919.[4]

Chafee's "Freedom of Speech in War Time" began by offering his description of the Blackstonian theory of the First Amendment: "The government cannot interfere by a censorship or injunction *before* the words are spoken or printed, but can punish them as much as it pleases *after* publication, no matter how harmless or essential to the public welfare the discussion may be."[5] Chafee wrote critically of this legal theory, claiming that it "dies hard, but has no excuse for longer life."[6] When describing how the Blackstonian view developed in US law, Chafee addressed Holmes by name, both criticizing and praising him: "It was adopted by American judges in several early prosecutions for libel . . . whence Justice Holmes carried it into the United States Supreme Court. Fortunately he has now repudiated this interpretation of freedom of speech, but not until his dictum had had considerable influence, particularly in Espionage Act cases."[7] After recounting Holmes's *Schenck* analogy that the "most stringent protection of free speech would not protect a man in falsely shouting fire in a theatre and causing a panic," Chafee complained of its inaptness: "How about the man who gets up in a theater between the acts and informs the audience honestly but perhaps mistakenly that the fire exits are too few or locked? He is a much closer parallel to Schenck or Debs."[8] But after that criticism, Chafee cited *Schenck* positively, hinting, "Justice Holmes has not left us without some valuable suggestions pointing toward the ultimate solution of the problem of the limits of free speech."[9] Chafee spoke glowingly of Holmes's clear and present danger test from *Schenck*: "This portion of the opinion . . . substantially agrees with . . . the history and political purpose of the First Amendment."[10] According to Chafee, if that test had been applied properly by Holmes in *Debs*, the conviction should have been overturned.[11] Chafee had Holmes as his target audience before he and Laski met with the justice, as Chafee cited or referred to Holmes by name fourteen times in his article.[12]

Instead of claiming that Blackstone held the key to understanding the freedom of expression in the United States, Chafee turned to another familiar name: John Stuart Mill. According to Chafee, the "legal meaning of freedom of speech cannot properly be determined without a knowledge of the political and philosophical basis of such freedom. Four writings on this problem may be mentioned as invaluable: Plato's Apology of Socrates; Milton's Areopagitica; the second chapter of Mill On Liberty; and Walter Bagehot's essay, 'The Metaphysical Basis of Toleration.'"[13] Chafee emphasized Mill again later in the article: "Into the making of the constitutional conception of free speech have gone, not only men's bitter experience of the censorship and sedition prosecutions before 1791, but also the subsequent development of the law of fair comment in civil defamation, and the philosophical speculations of John Stuart Mill."[14] Chafee noted that "one of the most important purposes of society and government is the discovery and spread of truth on subjects of general concern."[15] If Chafee was writing his article with advice from Laski, the latter likely helped point Chafee toward Mill as a way of influencing Holmes, trying to persuade the justice to more fully embrace Mill's approach to free speech.

Laski's lobbying over several months and Chafee's *Harvard Law Review* article both emphasized a Millian understanding of the freedom of expression. One can assume that the July 1919 meeting between Laski, Chafee, and Holmes included discussion of this philosophy. Laski and Chafee understood Holmes's propensity for Millian, liberal thinking on the freedom of speech, and they relentlessly belabored these arguments to help him more consistently adopt this way of thinking in First Amendment cases. By the fall, Holmes had become concerned that his *Schenck* and *Debs* opinions did not go far enough to protect expression. Holmes wrote to Laski on October 26, 1919, a pithy and ominous line: "I fear we have less freedom of speech here than they have in England."[16] One month later, Holmes did something to change this in *Abrams v. United States.*

Jacob Abrams was part of a cohort of immigrant anarchists who distributed leaflets urging a general strike, to allegedly hamper US war efforts in World War I and against the Bolsheviks in the Russian Revolution: "Workers, our reply to the barbaric intervention has to be a general strike! An open challenge only will let the Government know that not only the Russian Worker fights for freedom, but also here in America lives the spirit of Revolution."[17] These leaflets also directly criticized the US president, Woodrow Wilson: "His shameful, cowardly silence about the intervention in Russia reveals the hypocrisy of the plutocratic gang in Washington and vicinity. . . . He is too much of a coward to come out openly and say: 'We capitalistic nations cannot afford to have a proletarian republic in Russia.'"[18] Abrams and his accomplices were convicted of violating the Espionage Act, for using "disloyal, scurrilous and abusive language about the form of Government of the United States," speaking in a way that would "bring the form of Government of the United States into contempt, scorn, contumely and disrepute," using language "intended to incite, provoke and encourage resistance to the United States in said war," and conspiring "by utterance, writing, printing and publication, to urge, incite and advocate curtailment of production of things and products, to wit, ordnance and ammunition, necessary and essential to the prosecution of the war."[19]

Behind the writing of Justice John Clarke, a 7–2 majority upheld the constitutionality of these convictions and the resultant twenty-year prison sentences. According to Justice Clarke, the leaflets were not protected by the First Amendment: "This is not an attempt to bring about a change of administration by candid discussion. . . . The manifest purpose of such a publication was to create an attempt to defeat the war plans of the Government of the United States."[20] Clarke continued, "The language of these circulars was obviously intended to provoke and to encourage resistance to the United States in the war . . . and, the defendants, in terms, plainly urged and advocated a resort to a general strike of workers in ammunition factories for the purpose of curtailing the production of ordnance and munitions necessary and essential to the prosecution of the war."[21] The Supreme Court's approach cut against Millian doctrine in two ways. First, there was no evidence provided that these circulars were threatening any direct harm. Second, Mill supported the right to engage in "criticizing institutions or the acts of persons or rulers," and Mill believed that even if one was attempting to instigate a civil war, prosecution could take place "only if an overt act has followed, and at least a probable connection can be established between the act and the instigation."[22] Calling for a general strike is quite distinct from actively instigating war, and even if it were comparable, no connection was shown between Abrams's leaflets and any act by any potential striker.

That having been said, *Abrams* interpreted the Constitution to protect more than prior restraints. Justice Clarke's statement that "this is not an attempt to bring about a change of administration by candid discussion" reveals that even the majority had begun to think that some discussion would be protected after the fact, even if the goal was to seek change in government through unconventional means. Nevertheless, the Supreme Court majority's characterization of the circulars as endangering the state used more of a bad tendency test to limit freedom of expression.[23]

In a dissent joined by Justice Brandeis, Justice Holmes engaged in a Millian analysis, explaining that "only the present danger of immediate evil or an intent to bring it about . . . warrants Congress in setting a limit to the expression of opinion. . . . Congress certainly cannot forbid all effort to change the mind of the country."[24] Holmes stated that "nobody can suppose that the surreptitious publishing of a silly leaflet by an unknown man, without more, would present any immediate danger that its opinions would hinder the success of the government arms."[25] The pamphlet was meant to invoke a change in government policy through direct action; this was not a harm to fellow citizens as much a criticism of the government's war aims and an attempt to motivate people to an antiwar cause. There was no threat of direct harm that could be caused by the pamphlet. In Mill's words, "the only purpose for which power can be rightfully exercised over any member of a civilized community, against his will, is to prevent harm to others."[26] To return to Holmes's *Schenck* analogy, Abrams was less an arsonist and more akin to Chafee's "honest but perhaps mistaken" speaker who questions the safety of the theater itself. And if we discard that problematic theater analogy from *Schenck*, it raises important questions in a Millian scheme, which protects expression regardless of whether the opinion being expressed is true or false. Following Mill's limits on when expression can be used as evidence of a conspiracy to engage in war-related activities, Holmes noted in *Abrams* that "it is evident from the beginning to the end that the only object of the paper is to help Russia and stop American intervention there against the popular government—not to impede the United States in the war that it was carrying on."[27]

The final paragraph of Holmes's *Abrams* dissent greatly reflected Millian philosophy. As explained by Holmes, such stringent limits on expression presume humans are infallible: "Persecution for the expression of opinions seems to me perfectly logical. If you have no doubt of your premises or your power and want a certain result with all your heart you naturally express your wishes in law and sweep away all opposition. To allow opposition by speech seems to indicate that you think the speech impotent, as when a man says that he has squared the circle, or that you do not care whole-heartedly for the result, or that you doubt either your power or your premises."[28] This is reminiscent of *On Liberty*, where Mill proclaimed that it is strange to "think that some particular principle or doctrine should be forbidden to be questioned because it is so *certain*, that is, because *they are certain* that it is certain."[29]

Continuing in *Abrams*, Holmes declared that "men have realized that time has upset many fighting faiths,"[30] which echoed Mill's claim that "every age [has] held many opinions which subsequent ages have deemed not only false but absurd; and it is as certain that many opinions, now general, will be rejected by future ages, as it is that many, once general, are rejected by the present."[31] For Holmes in *Abrams*, the learned observer will "come to believe even more than they believe the very foundations of their own conduct that the ultimate good desired is better reached by free trade in ideas—that the best test of truth is the power of the thought to get itself accepted in the competition of the market, and that truth is the only ground upon which their wishes safely can be carried out."[32] Given how Holmes was immersed in Mill's thought in 1919, this notion of ideas competing against each other is driven by passages in *On Liberty* like the one that proclaims, "Complete liberty of contradicting and disproving our opinion is the very condition which justifies us in assuming its truth for purposes of action; and on no other terms can a being with human faculties have any rational assurance of being right."[33] Likewise, Holmes would have been influenced by Mill's proposition that all ideas must be "fully, frequently, and fearlessly discussed," or else they "will be held as a dead dogma, not a living truth."[34] What Holmes described would eventually be called, for short, a "marketplace of ideas."[35]

As much as the marketplace of ideas analogy has come to be an enduring concept in US culture (going far beyond the legal realm), it is an oversimplification that subtly differs from what Mill argued.[36] Mill would find the analogy overly optimistic, as he was explicit that "men are not more zealous for truth than they often are for error."[37] Yet, Mill also made clear that the only way to obtain the truth is "by discussion and experience. Not by experience alone. There must be discussion to show how experience is to be interpreted. Wrong opinions and practices gradually yield to fact and argument; but facts and arguments, to produce any effect on the mind, must be brought before it."[38] For Mill, this is why we must protect the freedom of expression, so that truth has the chance to emerge: "The real advantage which truth has consists in this, that when an opinion is true, it may be extinguished once, twice, or many times, but in the course of ages there will generally be found persons to rediscover it, until some one of its reappearances falls on a time when from favorable circumstances it escapes persecution until it has made such head as to withstand all subsequent attempts to suppress it."[39] Holmes's analogy is derived from *On Liberty*, even if it is more sanguine than what Mill believed, which is that the free expression of ideas provides a framework so that the truth can eventually emerge, but with no promises that at any given debate—in any given era—it will appear.[40] Holmes's conclusion that the freedom of expression needs protecting to aid the search for truth also reflects the arguments of Chafee, another devotee of Mill.[41]

Although some might disagree with this marketplace of ideas approach to the First Amendment, Holmes proclaimed in *Abrams* that it "at any rate is the theory of our Constitution. It is an experiment, as all life is an experiment. Every year if not every day we have to wager our salvation upon some prophecy based upon imperfect knowledge."[42] Beyond his other statements in *On Liberty* explaining how "other people, in less enlightened times, have persecuted opinions now believed to be true," Mill also advocated that "while mankind are imperfect there should be different opinions, so is it that there should be different experiments of living."[43] As for Holmes in *Abrams*, he continued: "While that experiment is part of our system I think that we should be eternally vigilant against attempts to check the expression of opinions that we loathe and believe to be fraught with death, unless they so imminently threaten immediate interference with the lawful and pressing purposes of the law that an immediate check is required to save the country."[44] This recalls Mill advising in *On Liberty* that even false speech must be protected.[45] Mill had one exception to this rule: if the speech could lead to immediate violence. After *Debs* and *Frohwerk*, Holmes's sentiments had seemed in doubt, but in *Abrams*, there are multiple examples of Holmes asserting the need to protect advocacy unless there was "immediate" or "imminent" danger, similar to Mill's example of an agitator fulminating that corn dealers are starvers of the poor, "delivered orally to an excited mob" outside of the corn dealer's house.[46] This understanding of "clear and present danger" was much more protective of the freedom of expression than what Holmes ultimately proclaimed in *Schenck*.[47]

The Millian seed that was planted in Holmes's *Schenck* opinion had sprouted in his *Abrams* dissent. Throughout that dissent, one can read arguments that have their intellectual origins in *On Liberty*.[48] Justice Holmes became the linchpin at the right moment: he took a political philosophy about the freedom of speech that was expressed by an English thinker and used it to offer a definitive legal interpretation of the First Amendment to the US Constitution. Due to the power of precedent, Holmes's Millian thoughts in *Schenck* and *Abrams* would later be adopted by other justices, and they would become embedded in the Supreme Court's interpretation of the First Amendment. Mill's liberal thinking on the freedom of expression could take root in 1919 because Holmes posited it during a time when there was relatively little competing theory in First Amendment expression cases, because there had been relatively few such cases decided.

Other advocates of a more libertarian vision of the First Amendment took notice of the significance of Holmes's *Abrams* dissent. Holmes received many letters of support, including from Laski, Chafee, Hand, Walter Lippmann, and future Supreme Court justice Felix Frankfurter; the Harvard Law School dean Roscoe Pound characterized Holmes's *Abrams* dissent as "a document of human liberty to keep up the succession from the *Apology* of Socrates, the *Areopagitica*, and Mill *on Liberty* [sic]."[49] However, as much as Holmes and Brandeis were convinced by the validity of a Millian interpretation of the First Amendment, those arguments fell short for their colleagues, who adhered to existing First Amendment precedent; three justices approached Holmes at his home shortly before *Abrams* was to be announced, attempting to convince him not to publish his dissent.[50] Although the next decade would see the Supreme Court majority continually rejecting free speech claims, in the 1920s Holmes and Brandeis repeatedly dissented, advocating for a Millian vision of the First Amendment, something very different than what occurred on the Supreme Court prior to 1919.[51] These dissents eventually convinced a majority of the justices to change their approach to the freedom of expression in 1931.

In 1920 the Supreme Court interpreted the freedom of expression narrowly in a trio of cases, over three Brandeis dissents. In *Schaefer v. United States*, the Supreme Court by a vote of 6–3 upheld Espionage Act convictions and prison sentences for German-language newspaper publishers who printed articles critical of US involvement in World War I, including one article that stated that "'the American, who certainly cannot be called a coward' did 'not care to allow himself to be shot to satisfy British lust for the mastery of the world.'"[52] Another article, published on Independence Day, declared that "the Fourth of July celebration, which has long been an empty formality, will this year become a miserable farce" due to US involvement in World War I.[53] Justice Joseph McKenna cited *Schenck*, writing for the Supreme Court that the convictions were constitutional because the newspaper's "statements were deliberate and wil[l]fully false, the purpose being to represent that the war was not demanded by the people but was the result of the machinations of executive power, and thus to arouse resentment to it and what it would demand of ardor and effort."[54] Like Clarke in *Abrams*, this was another instance of the Supreme Court majority citing *Schenck* but applying something more like the bad tendency test.[55]

Brandeis's *Schaefer* dissent, joined by Holmes, emphasized how the majority was poorly utilizing *Schenck*'s clear and present danger test. Brandeis argued that the test "is a rule of reason. Correctly applied, it will preserve the right of free speech both from suppression by tyrannous, well-meaning majorities and from abuse by irresponsible, fanatical minorities."[56] In his dissent, Brandeis applied this new legal test to the facts of the case, personally finding that "no jury acting in calmness could reasonably say that any of the publications set forth in the indictment was of such a character or was made under such circumstances as to create a clear and present danger either that they would obstruct recruiting or that they would promote the success of the enemies of the United States."[57] Brandeis concluded his dissent with an exhortation: "Nor will this grave danger end with the passing of the war. The constitutional right of free speech has been declared to be the same in peace and in war. In peace, too, men may differ widely as to what loyalty to our country demands; and an intolerant majority, swayed by passion or by fear, may be prone in the future, as it has often been in the past, to stamp as disloyal opinions with which it disagrees. Convictions such as these, besides abridging freedom of speech, threaten freedom of thought and of belief."[58] Brandeis advocated using a test for incitement that is similar to Mill's standard and Holmes's articulations in *Abrams*. Brandeis also emphasized multiple times the need to restrain a tyrannical majority from suppressing speech (particularly as it applies to speech relating to democratic self-governance); this was at the forefront of Mill's mind when he wrote in *On Liberty*, "'The tyranny of the majority' is now generally included among the evils against which society requires to be on its guard."[59] Recall that for Mill, even an overwhelming majority had no right to tyrannize a sole dissenter: "If all mankind minus one, were of one opinion, and only one person were of the contrary opinion, mankind would be no more justified in silencing that one person, than he, if he had the power, would be justified in silencing mankind."[60] In his *Schaefer* dissent, Brandeis cited Chafee's "Freedom of Speech in War Time," an article that referred to Mill multiple times and used Millian thinking throughout.[61] Thus, Brandeis followed Holmes by penning his first free expression opinion using Millian reasoning in the year following *Schenck* and *Abrams*.[62]

One week after *Schaefer*, in *Pierce v. United States* (1920) the Supreme Court upheld more Espionage Act convictions, this time against a group of socialists for distributing pamphlets titled "The Price We Pay," which denounced World War I, the military draft, and capitalism. Writing for the majority, Justice Mahlon Pitney used a form of the bad tendency test, ruling that the jury could find that the pamphlet "would have a tendency to cause insubordination, disloyalty, and refusal of duty in the military and naval forces of the United States."[63] Pitney made clear that whether speech would cause harm was "a question for the jury to decide," thus deferring to majoritarian views on what expression is constitutionally protected, contravening Mill's advice from *On Liberty*.[64]

Brandeis (joined by Holmes) dissented in *Pierce*, attacking the majority's opinion for multiple reasons. One was its decision to agree with the government's allegations that the defendants spoke falsely when they claimed that "our entry into [World War I] was determined by the certainty that if the allies do not win, J. P. Morgan's loans to the allies will be repudiated, and those American investors who bit on his promises would be hooked."[65] In response, Brandeis explained, "The cause of a war—as of most human action—is not single. War is ordinarily the result of many cooperating causes, many different conditions, acts and motives. Historians rarely agree in their judgment as to what was the determining factor."[66] This is reminiscent of Mill, who argued that "on every subject on which difference of opinion is possible, the truth depends on a balance to be struck between two sets of conflicting reasons. Even in natural philosophy, there is always some other explanation possible of the same facts," and that many more explanations are available "when we turn to subjects infinitely more complicated, to morals, religion, politics, social relations, and the business of life."[67] It is for this reason that Mill, as well as Brandeis and Holmes, believed it improper to criminalize the expression of an opinion as false, as this can be impossible to prove. Brandeis in *Pierce* cited *Schenck*'s clear and present danger test before proclaiming that the defendants' speech should have been protected because the "statements like that here charged to be false are in essence matters of opinion and judgment, not matters of fact to be determined by a jury upon or without evidence."[68] This is a rejection of the bad tendency test; what should matter legally is not the opinion and judgment expressed in the tract but its likelihood to incite immediate danger. Brandeis had adopted a version of Mill's harm principle that reflected Mill's urging that "absolute freedom of opinion and sentiment on all subjects" should receive protection. Indeed, Brandeis's utilitarian comment from his concluding paragraph in *Pierce* could have been written by Mill: "The fundamental right of free men to strive for better conditions through new legislation and new institutions will not be preserved, if efforts to secure it by argument to fellow citizens may be construed as criminal incitement to disobey the existing law."[69]

He had joined Holmes's dissent in *Abrams*, but *Scheafer* and *Pierce* represented the first dissents where Brandeis explored the freedom of expression. He explained to his friend, the Harvard Law professor and future Supreme Court colleague Felix Frankfurter: "I have never been quite happy about my concurrence in [the] *Debs* and *Schenck* cases. I had not then thought the issues of freedom of speech out—I thought at the subject, not through it. Not until I came to write the *Pierce* and *Schaeffer* [sic] dissents did I understand it."[70] The opportunity to think "through" the subject by reading relevant Supreme Court caselaw in early 1919 was rather limited, given the dearth of relevant cases decided by that time. However, after reading and joining Holmes's dissent in *Abrams*, Brandeis adopted this liberal line of thinking shortly thereafter. There is not the same smoking gun for Brandeis as there was for Holmes, that he was influenced by Mill, because there is no direct evidence that Brandeis met Mill or that Brandeis even read *On Liberty*. Still, Brandeis's arguments in these cases reflect Mill's core reasoning from *On Liberty*.[71] Combining this with his close connection to Holmes and his citation of Chafee is strong circumstantial evidence that Brandeis was motivated by Millian arguments about protecting a free market of ideas, either directly or indirectly.[72]

Nine months after *Pierce*, the Supreme Court in *Gilbert v. Minnesota* (1920) upheld a conviction and one-year sentence of a man for violating the state's sedition law, which made it "unlawful for any person . . . to advocate or teach by word of mouth or otherwise that men should not enlist in the military or naval forces of the United States or the state of Minnesota."[73] Gilbert's conviction was for a speech that included this statement about World War I: "We were stampeded into this war by newspaper rot to pull England's chestnuts out of the fire for her. I tell you if they conscripted wealth like they have conscripted men, this war would not last over forty-eight hours."[74] According to Justice McKenna for the majority, "the asserted freedom is natural and inherent, but it is not absolute, it is subject to restriction and limitation."[75] Mill, a utilitarian, rejected that the freedom of expression was a natural right.[76] More to the point, the tone of McKenna's reasoning implies that there are significant limits on this freedom, which was not the case for Mill, who prescribed just a few instances where expression could be limited because of secondary harms. Justice McKenna found for the Supreme Court that "Gilbert's speech . . . was not an advocacy of policies or a censure of actions that a citizen had the right to make. . . . Every word that he uttered in denunciation of the war was false, was deliberate misrepresentation of the motives which impelled it, and the objects for which it was prosecuted."[77]

Justice Brandeis again dissented in *Gilbert*, contending that the law "abridges freedom of speech and of the press, not in a particular emergency, in order to avert a clear and present danger, but under all circumstances. The restriction imposed relates to the teaching of the doctrine of pacifism and the legislature in effect proscribes it for all time."[78] Brandeis argued that the "prohibition imposed by the Minnesota statute has no relation to existing needs or desires of the Government. . . . For the statute aims to prevent not acts but beliefs."[79] Just like Mill in *On Liberty*, Brandeis held that government power to restrict expression existed only when there would be immediate danger of direct harm to others: "There are times when those charged with the responsibility of Government, faced with clear and present danger, may conclude that suppression of divergent opinion is imperative; because the emergency does not permit reliance upon the slower conquest of error by truth. And in such emergencies the power to suppress exists."[80] In Millian and Holmesian fashion, Brandeis made an analogy similar to that of the marketplace of ideas, giving the truth a chance by letting ideas compete against each other: "Like the course of the heavenly bodies, harmony in national life is a resultant of the struggle between contending forces. In frank expression of conflicting opinion lies the greatest promise of wisdom in governmental action; and in suppression lies ordinarily the greatest peril."[81] Brandeis would have read this right more expansively and applied it to the states via the Fourteenth Amendment, something suggested by Justice Harlan in his *Patterson* dissent in 1907.[82] Although Justice Holmes concurred without opinion in *Gilbert* (possibly because it was a state case appealed to the US Supreme Court before the First Amendment was incorporated or because he thought a clear and present danger existed in the case), Holmes and Brandeis continued to join each other in dissent in other free expression cases in the early 1920s.[83]

When World War I ended, Brandeis's prediction in *Schaefer* was proven true; the "grave danger" against freedom of expression did not end. Instead, the Supreme Court's free speech cases focused more on state-level prosecutions for antisyndicalism, anticommunism, and antianarchy laws. Free speech cases remain an integral part of the Supreme Court's docket to the present day, showing the enduring importance of this topic and the ongoing controversies that surround it. During the height of the Supreme Court's reliance on the bad tendency test, a majority of justices upheld the conviction and prison sentence of Benjamin Gitlow in *Gitlow v. New York* (1925) after he was prosecuted for violating the state's criminal anarchy law, which prohibited speaking, writing, printing, or publishing anything "advocating, advising or teaching the doctrine that organized government should be overthrown by force, violence or any unlawful means."[84] Gitlow, a member of the Socialist Party, had published and helped distribute sixteen thousand copies of a document called "The Left Wing Manifesto." The manifesto advocated for a "Communist Revolution" through "mass action" to establish a "revolutionary dictatorship of the proletariat."[85] Writing for the Supreme Court, Justice Edward Sanford incorporated the freedom of speech to apply to the states: "For present purposes we may and do assume that freedom of speech and of the press—which are protected by the First Amendment from abridgment by Congress—are among the fundamental personal rights and 'liberties' protected by the due process clause of the Fourteenth Amendment from impairment by the States."[86] Sanford provided no reasoning as to why states were bound by the Fourteenth Amendment from infringing on the freedom of expression, but what was first proposed by Justice Harlan in *Patterson* and defended by Brandeis in *Gilbert* was now the law of the land.[87] This application of these First Amendment rights to the states would eventually have dramatic effects, broadening the reach of the freedom of expression substantially.

However, the freedom incorporated in *Gitlow* was narrowly construed by the Supreme Court. In the words of Justice Sanford, "A State in the exercise of its police power may punish those who abuse this freedom by utterances inimical to the public welfare, tending to corrupt public morals, incite to crime, or disturb the public peace."[88] Sanford wrote for the Supreme Court that "the general provisions of the statute may be constitutionally applied to the specific utterance of the defendant if its natural tendency and probable effect was to bring about the substantive evil which the legislative body might prevent."[89] Borrowing from Holmes's famous *Schenck* quote on falsely shouting fire in a crowded theater, Sanford made an analogy to justify an anti-Millian bad tendency approach: "A single revolutionary spark may kindle a fire that, smouldering for a time, may burst into a sweeping and destructive conflagration. It cannot be said that the State is acting arbitrarily or unreasonably when . . . it seeks to extinguish the spark without waiting until it has enkindled the flame or blazed into the conflagration."[90] Sanford's argument was a refutation of the clear and present danger test. For Sanford, the bad tendency test was superior because it considered all dangers to the public, not only in the immediate present but also into the foreseeable future. The Supreme Court used the test to uphold the prosecution of written expression that was simple advocacy and rhetoric; no threat of violence was present.[91]

Justice Holmes, joined again by Justice Brandeis, issued a short but stinging dissent in *Gitlow*. After citing his *Schenck* opinion and *Abrams* dissent, Holmes concluded that "there was no present danger of an attempt to overthrow the government by force on the part of the admittedly small minority who shared the defendant's views."[92] Holmes further explained his thinking on expression: "It is said that this manifesto was more than a theory, that it was an incitement. Every idea is an incitement. It offers itself for belief, and, if believed, it is acted on unless some other belief outweighs it or some failure of energy stifles the movement at its birth. The only difference between the expression of an opinion and an incitement in the narrower sense is the speaker's enthusiasm for the result."[93] Holmes's notion that "every idea is an incitement" does not mean that every idea is dangerous; rather, every idea offers an opportunity for discussion, and potentially, action at a later time.[94] As described by Mill in *On Liberty*, expressing all ideas should be protected unless that speech leads to direct and immediate harm to persons or property. Holmes's adoption of Millian philosophy is clearly seen in his rejection of Sanford's worry of a "revolutionary spark." In *Gitlow*, Holmes offered a revised understanding of a fire analogy, one that protects more expression than his

Schenck fire analogy: "Eloquence may set fire to reason. But whatever may be thought of the redundant discourse before us, it had no chance of starting a present conflagration. If, in the long run, the beliefs expressed in proletarian dictatorship are destined to be accepted by the dominant forces of the community, the only meaning of free speech is that they should be given their chance and have their way."[95] Holmes channeled Mill's notion that all opinions must be protected to ensure that we can find truth and achieve the best democratic ends, unless "the circumstances in which they are expressed are such as to constitute their expression a positive instigation to some mischievous act."[96] Holmes in *Gitlow* (like Mill) thought that advocating for what the majority deems to be an undesirable uprising deserves protection short of an immediate threat of violence.[97] Holmes expressed another Millian idea: some of what the majority believes to be true today may be ridiculed as absurd in the future because there are ideas held sacred in the past that we now find ridiculous. Similarly, Mill was "certain that many opinions, now general, will be rejected by future ages, as it is that many, once general, are rejected by the present."[98]

The next significant free speech case before the Supreme Court was *Whitney v. California* (1927), where the defendant was convicted of helping to establish the California Communist Labor Party in violation of the state's syndicalism law, which prohibited organizing an association to "advocate, teach or aid and abet criminal syndicalism."[99] On conviction, Charlotte Whitney was given a one- to fourteen-year prison sentence.[100] Writing for seven members of the Supreme Court, Justice Sanford upheld Whitney's conviction using the bad tendency test: "A State in the exercise of its police power may punish those who abuse this freedom [of speech] by utterances inimical to the public welfare, tending to incite to crime, disturb the public peace, or endanger the foundations of organized government and threaten its overthrow by unlawful means."[101] Sanford wrote that if peace or security are at issue, the government may determine that expression "should be penalized in the exercise of its police power. That determination must be given great weight. Every presumption is to be indulged in favor of the validity of the statute."[102] This level of deference to government authority to restrict expression—that *every* presumption should be *indulged* to try to find the law to be valid—is inimical to Mill's philosophy.

Brandeis (joined by Holmes) wrote a concurrence in *Whitney* instead of a dissent for reasons of judicial restraint. Brandeis believed that states had power to enact emergency legislation to prevent public dangers, and Whitney had failed to argue at trial that a danger was not present.[103] Brandeis's concurrence in *Whitney* read like a dissent, though, because he had drafted it as a dissent he had prepared for *Ruthenberg v. Michigan* (1927), a case that was dismissed because the defendant died after oral arguments at the Supreme Court.[104] Brandeis's *Whitney* concurrence represented the fullest, most developed defense of the freedom of speech to that point in the Supreme Court's history.[105] It was the culmination of Holmes and Brandeis's efforts at building a Millian defense of free expression over the eight years since *Schenck* and *Abrams*.

Brandeis began by describing the importance of the liberties in question: "The right of free speech, the right to teach and the right of assembly are, of course, fundamental rights."[106] This was the understanding held by Mill, who made the chapter "Of the Liberty of Thought and Discussion" his first substantive chapter in *On Liberty*. Brandeis's description of the proper standard for restricting speech was similar to the approach previously articulated by Mill and Holmes, with Brandeis citing *Schenck* for this proposition: "The necessity which is essential to a valid restriction [on expression] does not exist unless speech would produce, or is intended to produce, a clear and imminent danger of some substantive evil which the State constitutionally may seek to prevent."[107] Brandeis then offered a lengthy justification for this standard:

Those who won our independence believed that the final end of the State was to make men free to develop their faculties; and that in its government the deliberative forces should prevail over the arbitrary. They valued liberty both as an end and as a means. They believed liberty to be the secret of happiness and courage to be the secret of liberty. They believed that freedom to think as you will and to speak as you think are means indispensable to the discovery and spread of political truth; that without free speech and assembly discussion would be futile; that with them, discussion affords ordinarily adequate protection against the dissemination of noxious doctrine; that the greatest menace to freedom is an inert people; that public discussion is a political duty. . . . They knew that order cannot be secured merely through fear of punishment for its infraction; that it is hazardous to discourage thought, hope and imagination; that fear breeds repression; that repression breeds hate; that hate menaces stable government; that the path of safety lies in the opportunity to discuss freely supposed grievances and proposed remedies; and that the fitting remedy for evil counsels is good ones. Believing in the power of reason as applied through public discussion, they eschewed silence coerced by law—the argument of force in its worst form. Recognizing the occasional tyrannies of governing majorities, they amended the Constitution so that free speech and assembly should be guaranteed.

Fear of serious injury cannot alone justify suppression of free speech and assembly. Men feared witches and burnt women. It is the function of speech to free men from the bondage of irrational fears. To justify suppression of free speech there must be reasonable ground to fear that serious evil will result if free speech is practiced. There must be reasonable ground to believe that the danger apprehended is imminent. There must be reasonable ground to believe that the evil to be prevented is a serious one. Every denunciation of existing law tends in some measure to increase the probability that there will be violation of it. . . . But even advocacy of violation, however reprehensible morally, is not a justification for denying free speech where the advocacy falls short of incitement and there is nothing to indicate that the advocacy would be immediately acted on.[108]

This full-throated defense of the freedom of expression has Millian philosophy running throughout it.[109] Brandeis argued, like Mill, that society must have rules to curb "serious evil," but that coercion must be used only in an actual crisis. The limits Brandeis proposed are very similar to those set by Mill's harm principle, because the rationale Brandeis gives is a clear echo of Mill; Brandeis's claim that the state is in place to allow people to be "free to develop their faculties" is parallel to Mill's claim that freedom of expression and individuality are essential, if one is to flourish as a person: "It is only the cultivation of individuality which produces, or can produce, well-developed human beings."[110] Brandeis's idea that the freedom of speech is "indispensable to the discovery and spread of political truth" reminds one of Mill's notion that the freedom of speech must be protected because if "the opinion is right, [we] are deprived of the opportunity of exchanging error for truth; if wrong, [we] lose, what is almost as great a benefit, the clearer perception and livelier impression of truth, produced by its collision with error."[111] When Brandeis spoke of the proposition "that the greatest menace to freedom is an inert people" and "that public discussion is a political duty," he reminded his readers of Mill's rhetorical quip that "both teachers and learners go to sleep at their posts as soon as there is no enemy in the field."[112] When Brandeis wrote about the fear of "the occasional tyrannies of governing majorities," there is a clear connection to Mill, who called tyranny of the majority "among the evils against which society requires to be on its guard."[113] Brandeis recalled past evils where "men feared witches and burnt women," whereas Mill wrote that the suppression of opinion "made men burn magicians and heretics."[114] Brandeis advocated for the protection of expression—even speech seen by the majority as "reprehensible morally"—unless there is incitement, something similar to Mill's defense of protecting attacks on "any of the commonly received doctrines of morality" short of situations creating imminent violence.[115] Even though Brandeis wrote that he was reminding us of the thinking by "those who won our independence," his concurrence reflects not colonists who were immersed in Blackstonian theory but rather Mill's *On Liberty*.

Even if many abhor what Whitney advocated and how she questioned the prevailing political and economic order, Brandeis believed that she must be able to express those ideas as part of a search for truth; if government attempts to suppress such advocacy, it will often act irrationally and harm that search for truth.[116] As Mill put it, "If even the Newtonian philosophy were not permitted to be questioned, mankind could not feel as complete assurance of its truth as they now do."[117] Likewise, Brandeis wrote that if "there be time to expose through discussion the falsehood and fallacies, to avert the evil by the processes of education, the remedy to be applied is more speech, not enforced silence. Only an emergency can justify repression."[118] This reaffirms Mill, when he stated in *On Liberty* that "wrong opinions and practices gradually yield to fact and argument; but facts and arguments, to produce any effect on the mind, must be brought before it."[119]

After eight years of working together on a Millian approach to the First Amendment, Holmes and Brandeis had built their most comprehensive case in *Whitney*. But on the Supreme Court, no other justice joined them. And it looked like their interpretation of the First Amendment might be permanently in the minority. Although the justices unanimously overturned a syndicalism act conviction in *Fiske v. Kansas* (1927) because there had been no evidence presented that the Industrial Workers of the World, of which Fiske was a member, had ever advocated for criminal syndicalism, that case did not signal a thaw in the Supreme Court's icy approach to the freedom of speech.[120] Indeed, in *United States v. Schwimmer* (1929), the Supreme Court denied citizenship to a permanent resident, Rosika Schwimmer, because of the ideas she expressed: on the citizenship questionnaire asking if she would be "willing to take up arms in defense of this country," Schwimmer, a pacifist, responded, "I would not take up arms personally."[121] Holmes dissented from the ruling, again joined by Brandeis. After citing *Schenck*, Holmes wrote a succinct statement about Schwimmer's views: "Some of her answers might excite popular prejudice, but if there is any principle of the Constitution that more imperatively calls for attachment than any other it is the principle of free thought—not free thought for those who agree with us but freedom for the thought that we hate."[122] Holmes's sentiment of protecting all ideas in *Schwimmer* tracks that of Mill, who proclaimed in *On Liberty* that "everything must be free to be written and published without restraint."[123] Holmes's *Schwimmer* dissent, by emphasizing protection for even speech that excites "popular prejudice," also comports with Mill's notion that regardless of whether the majority agrees or is repelled by an idea, they have no right to exercise tyranny over the expression of ideas. Finally, protecting the right of Schwimmer to remain in the country is utile because it allows people whose ideas could improve the country to enter and remain here; as Holmes explained it, "Surely it cannot show lack of attachment to the principles of the Constitution that she thinks that it can be improved. I suppose that most intelligent people think that it might be."[124] Mill strongly believed in the need for ideas to cross borders through immigrants to prevent a country's intellectual stagnation.[125]

Thus, at the close of the 1920s, Mill's theory of free speech, which had not been expressed in Supreme Court opinions before 1919, was firmly adopted by Justice Holmes and Justice Brandeis. This was due to a confluence of factors, including Holmes's rereading of *On Liberty*, the lobbying of Harold Laski and Zechariah Chafee, and collaborating by Holmes and Brandeis. These two justices wrote several opinions that placed Millian philosophy into the Supreme Court's decisions at a time when there was very little competing First Amendment jurisprudence. Holmes and Brandeis were advocating this approach in dissents throughout the decade, but just two years after *Schwimmer*, these dissenting views would begin to command Supreme Court majorities.

CHAPTER 4

Preferred Freedoms

The Court Drifts toward Mill on Speech and Press . . . for a Time

During the 1930s and 1940s, the Supreme Court adopted the Millian approach to free expression in several (but not all) areas of First Amendment jurisprudence.[1] The free speech philosophy espoused by a majority of justices took a decidedly libertarian turn, following the views of Holmes and Brandeis.[2] This was engineered by Chief Justice Charles Evans Hughes, who mustered a majority to back the Mill-Holmes-Brandeis position on expression. After more than a decade in dissent—since Holmes's exhortation to free expression in *Abrams* in 1919—the free speech dam finally began to break in a pair of cases in 1931. Incredibly, 1931 was the first year that a citizen challenge of government restriction on expression was successful on First Amendment grounds, and it happened twice that year.[3]

The first of these two cases was *Stromberg v. California*, which dealt with a state law making it a felony to display a red flag as a sign of opposition to government or an invitation to anarchy or sedition. Yetta Stromberg, a nineteen-year-old supervisor at a children's communist summer camp, took part in a daily ceremony directing children in raising a red flag that was a reproduction of the Soviet Union's flag and the flag of the Communist Party of the United States. The daily ceremony also included a recitation of a pledge of allegiance to the flag and communist ideals. On conviction, Stromberg faced a sentence of up to ten years in prison.[4]

In his first term as chief justice, Hughes wrote for a 7–2 majority to overturn Stromberg's conviction. After affirming *Gitlow*'s holding that the freedom of speech limits state governments, Hughes determined that the California law was so vague that it criminalized peaceful criticism of the government: "The maintenance of the opportunity for free political discussion to the end that government may be responsive to the will of the people and that changes may be obtained by lawful means, an opportunity essential to the security of the Republic, is a fundamental principle of our constitutional system."[5] The decision marked a turning point, as the Hughes Court was signaling, using utilitarian reasoning, that dissent is essential to help our country find political truth.[6] Even if Stromberg's economic and political views were based on what Hughes and a majority of his colleagues thought was faulty logic, Hughes reasoned that her expression should be protected. Note the similarity to Mill's thinking in *On Liberty*: "Even if the world is in the right, it is always probable that dissentients have something worth hearing to say for themselves, and that truth would lose something by their silence."[7] Although the Supreme Court did not overrule its past decisions restricting expression, *Stromberg*'s protection of dissidents was a stark contrast to the conclusions reached a few years earlier in *Gitlow* (where a pro-communist pamphlet was held to be so dangerous that it warranted criminal action) and *Whitney* (where helping to organize a communist group was criminally punished).[8] The theory espoused by Hughes in *Stromberg* is in lockstep with Mill's, that "governments and nations have made mistakes" and that the freedoms of speech and press are protected to correct them.[9] This was precisely the thought that was articulated by Holmes's dissent in *Gitlow* and Brandeis's concurrence in *Whitney*.

The Supreme Court's other major First Amendment case in 1931 was *Near v. Minnesota*. Jay Near published articles in the *Saturday Press* that alleged "a Jewish gangster was in control of gambling, bootlegging and racketeering in Minneapolis, and that law enforcing officers and agencies were not energetically performing their duties."[10] The racist, antisemitic views expressed by Near's publication convinced the Hennepin County attorney to file an injunction under a state law that defined as a nuisance "a malicious, scandalous and defamatory newspaper, magazine or other periodical."[11] A trial judge found the *Saturday Press* to be a public nuisance and enjoined Near from publishing it. Chief Justice Hughes, writing for the Supreme Court's 5–4 majority in *Near*, overturned this injunction, holding that this prior restraint was unconstitutional.[12] This time, the Supreme Court's dissenters invoked Blackstonian ideals, following previous decisions like *Mutual Film*, wanting to uphold this prior restraint because they thought it was a nuisance.[13] For the majority, Hughes offered a description of what the Minnesota law did: "Public authorities may bring the owner or publisher of a newspaper or periodical before a judge upon a charge . . . of publishing scandalous and defamatory matter—in particular that the matter consists of charges against public officers of official dereliction—and unless the owner or publisher is able and disposed to bring competent evidence to satisfy the judge that the charges are true and are published with good motives and for justifiable ends, his newspaper or periodical is suppressed."[14] Hughes concisely characterized this as "the essence of censorship."[15] Hughes's conclusion was Millian, as it emphasized the right to directly criticize the government, something Mill assumed should be protected.[16]

To be sure, some elements of Hughes's decision in *Near* were distinctly Blackstonian: he held that "chief purpose of the [constitutional] guaranty" of the freedom of the press was "to prevent previous restraints," and he cited *Patterson* when reasoning that the "preliminary freedom, by virtue of the very reason for its existence, does not depend, as this Court has said, on proof of truth."[17] Nevertheless, Hughes explained how the Blackstonian approach "cannot be deemed to exhaust the conception of the liberty guaranteed by State and Federal Constitutions."[18] Hughes moved the Supreme Court closer to Millian philosophy when he reasoned that "charges of reprehensible conduct may create resentment and the disposition to resort to violent means of redress, but this well-understood tendency did not alter the determination to protect the press against censorship and restraint upon publication."[19] This is significant, because the orthodox Blackstonian position held that generating offense against majoritarian moral sentiment *was* an acceptable ground to criminalize speech.[20] Hughes opened the door to an understanding of press freedom reminiscent of Mill, who not only permitted "invective, sarcasm, personality, and the like" but also acknowledged that when the majority decides expression warrants censorship because it is "offensive," the scales are always tipped toward the prevailing opinion.[21] Although *Gitlow* spoke in dicta of the assumption that the freedom of the press was incorporated, *Near* was the first case involving the press where this right was incorporated.[22] Mill clearly intended for written materials to have as much protection as the spoken word, remarking in *On Liberty* that the freedom of "publishing opinions . . . [has] as much importance as the liberty of thought itself, and . . . is practically inseparable from it."[23]

Both Holmes and Brandeis voted with the majority in *Stromberg* and *Near*. They, along with Mill, certainly influenced the new chief justice. Like Holmes before him, Hughes was a devotee of Mill.[24] In his home office, Chief Justice Hughes hung the portraits of just two historical figures: Edward White (the chief justice when Hughes was an associate justice on the Supreme Court) and John Stuart Mill.[25] Hughes placed Mill on his wall to remind himself of his commitment to a classically liberal worldview.[26] Nevertheless, when Hughes was an associate justice on the Supreme Court from 1910 to 1916, he showed no affinity for protecting the freedom of expression, voting with the majority to uphold restrictions on expression in every case he heard during those years, including in *Mutual Film* and *Fox*. By the time Hughes was appointed chief justice in 1930, though, Holmes and Brandeis had laid the jurisprudential groundwork in their dissents and concurrences for a Millian turn. Beginning in 1931, Hughes embraced that view as the leader of the Supreme Court. With now three justices—including a chief justice—advocating for this position on the freedom of speech, Mill's sway over the Supreme Court grew as the 1930s progressed.[27]

For instance, in *DeJonge v. Oregon* (1937), the justices unanimously overturned a state syndicalism conviction and seven-year prison sentence for conducting a Communist Party meeting; DeJonge had spoken at the meeting in protest of various government policies and practices, including local jail conditions, police response to a strike, and police raids on communists. Writing for the Supreme Court in *DeJonge*, Hughes emphasized that "the right of peaceable assembly is a right cognate to those of free speech and free press, and is equally fundamental."[28] Mill held a similar view, opining to his readers that one has a right to engage in liberty—placing on the same level expressing opinions and "combining among individuals," for this purpose—unless we create "an excited mob" at a place where those assembled will "do harm to others."[29] Mill wanted this protection to apply even to those espousing the view that "private property is robbery," meaning he thought communists should be protected.[30] Following Mill's distinction between core liberties and harms, Hughes explained that "rights may be abused by using speech or press or assembly in order to incite to violence and crime. The people through their legislatures may protect themselves against that abuse. But the legislative intervention can find constitutional justification only by dealing with the abuse. The rights themselves must not be curtailed."[31] According to Hughes, the "greater the importance of safeguarding the community from incitements to the overthrow of our institutions by force and violence, the more imperative is the need to preserve inviolate the constitutional rights of free speech, free press and free assembly in order to maintain the opportunity for free political discussion, to the end that government may be responsive to the will of the people."[32] Like Mill, Hughes understood the important connection between First Amendment rights and the democratic process.

In *Lovell v. Griffin* (1938) Chief Justice Hughes wrote for a unanimous Supreme Court, overturning a fifty-day jail sentence and a fifty-dollar fine for a Jehovah's Witness who sold pamphlets and magazines door-to-door without permission from the city manager. After affirming that freedoms of speech and press are fundamental, Hughes penned that the "liberty of the press is not confined to newspapers and periodicals. It necessarily embraces pamphlets and leaflets. These indeed have been historic weapons in the defense of liberty."[33] Barring incitement, Mill advocated for an ecumenical interpretation of freedom of expression, including outside of newspapers and periodicals.[34] Like Hughes, Mill understood that freedom of expression was intimately tied to other freedoms, particularly the freedom to bring ideas to fruition through action: "The same reasons which show that opinion should be free prove also that he should be allowed, without molestation, to carry his opinions into practice at his own cost."[35] Mill thought that the ability to express one's ideas and associate with those who concur empowers one to live a happy life that is autonomously chosen.[36] Like Holmes and Brandeis before him, Hughes was showing throughout his tenure as chief justice that he had adopted Mill's understanding of free expression.

Justice Owen Roberts, likewise, ruled in accordance with a Millian approach in free expression cases during the Great Depression.[37] In *Schneider v. State* (1939), the Supreme Court reviewed ordinances restricting the distribution of handbills in public, justified on the grounds that such laws reduced littering. Justice Roberts ruled for an 8–1 Supreme Court that these ordinances were unconstitutional. Roberts wrote of the narrow, harm-causing restrictions that may be placed on the relevant freedoms: "Although a municipality may enact regulations in the interest of the public safety, health, welfare or convenience, these may not abridge the individual liberties secured by the Constitution to those who wish to speak, write, print or circulate information or opinion."[38] Roberts clarified that laws aimed at promoting majoritarian views cannot infringe on free expression rights: "Mere legislative preferences or beliefs respecting matters of public convenience may well support regulation directed at other personal activities, but be insufficient to justify such as diminishes the exercise of rights so vital to the maintenance of democratic institutions."[39] This statement is reminiscent of Mill's arguments that the freedom of expression serves the utilitarian purpose of promoting democratic self-governance.[40] According to Roberts, "The streets are natural and proper places for the dissemination of information and opinion; and one is not to have the exercise of his liberty of expression in appropriate places abridged on the plea that it may be exercised in some other place."[41]

That same year, in a 5–2 decision, Justice Roberts wrote for the Supreme Court in *Hague v. CIO* that it was unconstitutional for a city to ban labor organizations from holding meetings and distributing literature. According to Roberts, "Citizenship of the United States would be little better than a name if it did not carry with it the right to discuss national legislation and the benefits, advantages, and opportunities to accrue to citizens therefrom."[42] As Roberts explained, "Streets and parks . . . have immemorially been held in trust for the use of the public and, time out of mind, have been used for purposes of assembly, communicating thoughts between citizens, and discussing public questions."[43] Roberts's reasoning in *Hague* is quintessentially Millian in arguing for the protection of free public discussions of ideas and the search for truth.[44] *Hague* and *Schneider* effectively nullified *Davis v. Massachusetts*, which had let the government restrict expression on public property under the non-Millian rationale that parks and streets are simply government possessions where expression can be tightly controlled by the legislature.[45] *Davis* was not formally overruled, but the reasoning behind it had been replaced in *Hague* and *Schneider* by something more Millian.[46]

Two non–First Amendment cases from the late 1930s demonstrate the Supreme Court's continued movement toward the Millian philosophy of Holmes and Brandeis. In *Palko v. Connecticut* (1937)—a case asking about the incorporation of the Fifth Amendment right against double jeopardy—Justice Benjamin Cardozo wrote for the Supreme Court that the "freedom of thought, and speech . . . is the matrix, the indispensable condition, of nearly every other form of freedom."[47] Mill believed that "the same reasons which show that opinion should be free prove also that he should be allowed, without molestation, to carry his opinions into practice at his own cost," meaning Cardozo's statement reflects Mill's belief that protecting the freedom of speech is a pathway to ensuring people can best live their lives freely.[48] Similarly, in *United States v. Carolene Products* (1938), Justice Harlan Fiske Stone wrote for the Supreme Court that although economic regulations would be presumed constitutional, "there may be narrower scope for operation of the presumption of constitutionality when legislation appears on its face to be within a specific prohibition of the Constitution, such as those of the first ten amendments."[49] In support of this proposition, Stone cited multiple First Amendment cases, including *Stromberg*.[50] Stone emphasized there may need to be "more exacting judicial scrutiny . . . on restraints upon the dissemination of information[,] on interferences with political organizations [and] prohibition of peaceable assembly."[51] On this point, Stone cited the Millian opinions of *Near*, *Stromberg*, Brandeis's concurrence in *Whitney*, and Holmes's dissent in *Gitlow*.[52] Stone went on to indicate that "prejudice against discrete and insular minorities may be a special condition . . . which may call for a correspondingly more searching judicial inquiry," thus implying a more active role for the courts to protect minorities from the tyranny of the majority, a primary focus of Mill's *On Liberty*.[53] In a case not answering any direct questions on the freedom of expression, Justice Stone inserted a significant amount of Millian analysis. He did not cite Mill, but his employment of Millian theory referenced several important Millian Supreme Court opinions from the prior twenty years. In fact, an early draft of Stone's *Carolene Products* opinion did not mention First Amendment rights; he added a discussion of them at the behest of the Mill devotee Charles Evans Hughes, again showing Hughes's influence over his colleagues.[54] The citations to prior Holmes and Brandeis opinions demonstrate that the older majority rulings were slowly being abandoned by the justices throughout the 1930s. The Holmes and Brandeis dissents were now being incorporated into majority opinions, giving their Millian jurisprudence new life as binding precedent.

As the 1940s dawned, it appeared that the Supreme Court had firmly adopted a Millian understanding of the freedom of expression. The jurisprudence expressed in Supreme Court opinions fit Mill's theory, and since 1931 there had been a string of cases where the Supreme Court was striking down restrictions on expression. In the 1940s the justices often expressed Millian philosophy on speech and press issues, but the Supreme Court started to become less consistent in its use of Mill's theory in the early years of World War II. This retrenchment in the face of war would have disappointed but not surprised Mill. The emergence of a crisis to justify restrictions on speech was how Mill framed the opening of the second chapter of *On Liberty*, titled "Of the Liberty of Thought and Discussion." Mill noted that "liberty of the press" is never questioned, "except during some temporary panic when fear of insurrection drives ministers and judges from their propriety."[55]

Confounding this crisis, retirements from the Supreme Court opened the door to a brief period of inconsistency regarding the freedoms of speech and press. In the decade after Holmes retired in 1932, the Supreme Court would lose two other defenders of a Millian approach; Brandeis remained a justice until 1939, and Hughes resigned in 1941. To be sure, though, there were still several cases supporting a broader, more Millian interpretation of expressive rights in the early 1940s. For instance, there was a series of cases upholding the rights of labor picketers. This was best exemplified by *Thornhill v. Alabama* (1940), where the Supreme Court by an 8–1 vote overturned a law making it illegal to "loiter" around or "picket" a business. Writing for the majority, Justice Frank Murphy used Millian reasoning to describe the freedoms of speech and press: "The safeguarding of these rights to the ends that men may speak as they think on matters vital to them and that falsehoods may be exposed through the processes of education and discussion is essential to free government."[56] Murphy continued this utilitarian analysis, emphasizing Millian arguments like the search for truth and the promotion of democratic governance:

"Noxious doctrines . . . may be refuted and their evil averted by the courageous exercise of the right of free discussion. Abridgment of freedom of speech and of the press, however, impairs those opportunities for public education that are essential to effective exercise of the power of correcting error through the processes of popular government."[57] We all learn through discussing these ideas, and the process of discussion helps to ensure that we will find truth. In this vein, recall Mill's pithy point: "Both teachers and learners go to sleep at their post, as soon as there is no enemy in the field."[58]

Murphy then applied the clear and present danger test in *Thornhill*, explaining that the modes of expression prohibited by the law "may enlighten the public on the nature and causes of a labor dispute. The safeguarding of these means is essential to the securing of an informed and educated public opinion with respect to a matter which is of public concern."[59] Following Mill's argument that the majority should not be able to restrict views it dislikes, Murphy wrote that "the group in power at any moment may not impose penal sanctions on peaceful and truthful discussion of matters of public interest merely on a showing that others may thereby be persuaded to take action inconsistent with its interests."[60] Murphy's opinion cited a host of opinions containing Millian reasoning, including *Carolene Products, Schneider, Hague, Near, DeJonge,* and *Stromberg*.[61] *Thornhill* cited Holmes's *Schenck* opinion in holding that "the danger of injury to an industrial concern is neither so serious nor so imminent as to justify the sweeping proscription of freedom of discussion embodied in" the law at issue.[62] Almost every First Amendment labor dispute decided by the Supreme Court in the early 1940s reached a Millian outcome, and during this period the Supreme Court did not uphold a labor injunction in the absence of a specific clear and present danger.[63]

One labor case particularly showed how, without the presence of Holmes and Brandeis, some of the justices in the early 1940s struggled with whether to use the clear and present danger test and how much expression should be protected in the marketplace of ideas. In *Bridges v. California* (1941), the Supreme Court by a vote of 5–4 overturned contempt of court convictions for (1) a labor leader threatening to strike if an adverse court order were enforced and (2) newspapers that published editorials criticizing judicial decisions. In the majority opinion, Justice Hugo Black's philosophical underpinnings were similar to those of Mill, emphasizing that the freedom of expression promotes other freedoms: "The First Amendment does not speak equivocally. It prohibits any law 'abridging the freedom of speech, or of the press.' It must be taken as a command of the broadest scope that explicit language, read in the context of a *liberty-loving society*, will allow."[64] Justice Black declined to use the Blackstonian common law approach of *Patterson*, instead applying *Schenck's* clear and present danger test: "'Clear and present danger' is an appropriate guide in determining the constitutionality of restrictions upon expression where the substantive evil sought to be prevented by the restriction is 'destruction of life or property, or invasion of the right of privacy.'"[65] Black showed his commitment to Mill's specificity, referring to Brandeis's *Whitney* concurrence to critique the test's subjectivity, especially regarding "when a danger shall be deemed clear [and] how remote the danger may be and yet be deemed present."[66] Nevertheless, Black applied the test, emphasizing that "the substantive evil must be extremely serious and the degree of imminence extremely high before utterances can be punished."[67] Similar to Mill's idea that "invective" deserves protection in debate, Black concluded for the Supreme Court that "it is a prized American privilege to speak one's mind, although not always with perfect good taste, on all public institutions."[68] Black's *Bridges* opinion also quoted from Holmes's *Abrams* dissent and Brandeis's dissent in *Schaefer* to explore the meaning of the clear and present danger test.[69]

As much as Black's majority opinion in *Bridges* embraced Millian philosophy, an anti-Millian approach to free expression was gaining traction on the Supreme Court. Justice Frankfurter's dissent, joined by three other justices, relied on *Patterson* and Blackstone. Frankfurter emphasized state power, not freedom, opining about the majority opinion that "to find justification for such deprivation of the historic powers of the states is to misconceive the idea of freedom of thought and speech as guaranteed by the Constitution."[70] After citing Blackstone, Frankfurter quoted *Patterson*, remarking that the case "has never been questioned by any member of the Court."[71] Although Frankfurter cited the clear and present danger test, he used it to restrict expression, like Holmes originally did in *Schenck*.[72] Frankfurter went farther in his *Bridges* dissent, arguing of "clear and present danger" that "the phrase itself is an expression of tendency," thus interpreting the test as something more like the bad tendency test.[73] As much as Mill's theory had garnered precedential value through a series of Supreme Court decisions in the 1930s, without explicitly overruling the older Blackstonian cases, they retained precedential value that justices who rejected Mill could still cite.

The majority opinion in *Bridges* notwithstanding, the Supreme Court's approach to various areas of expression after Hughes's retirement in the early 1940s was either non-Millian or a very narrow interpretation of Millian theory. In *Valentine v. Chrestensen* (1942), the justices unanimously upheld a New York City ban on distributing handbills with commercial advertising, under the guise that although "the streets are proper places for the exercise of the freedom of communicating information and disseminating . . . the Constitution imposes no such restraint on government as respects purely commercial advertising."[74]

The Supreme Court summarily concluded that since the handbills at issue included an advertisement, they "are matters for legislative judgment."[75]

Mill was concerned about economic transactions being other-regarding activity that could cause harm to others.[76] According to Mill, anyone who "undertakes to sell any description of goods to the public does what affects the interest of other persons, and of society in general; and thus his conduct, in principle, comes within the jurisdiction of society."[77] For Mill, the "principle of individual liberty is not involved in the doctrine of free trade," meaning government has the power to regulate the economy to ensure it does not restrict other freedoms.[78] As Mill was writing to defend individual autonomy, he had little to say about commercial speech, and what he does say suggests that, as a matter of commerce, it might not be subject to the same level of protection as other speech. Those points notwithstanding, at no place in *On Liberty* does Mill explicitly proclaim that there is a commercial speech exception to his general comments about the freedom of expression. Mill questioned the motives of "the instigator [who] derives a personal benefit from his advice, when he makes it his occupation," but this was largely in the context of "dealers . . . promoting intemperance" in the traditional vices of alcohol, gambling, and prostitution.[79] There is no evidence that Mill thought commercial *advertising* could be subject to the level of regulation he thought was permissible for commercial *transactions*. Thus, *Valentine* was anti-Millian, and it was a contradiction of the Supreme Court's ruling a few years earlier in *Lovell*. It ignored labor speech rulings like *Thornhill*, which protected expression on economic questions.[80] Indeed, this non-Millian *Valentine* opinion did not cite a single Supreme Court precedent in reaching its conclusion, instead harkening back to the thinking from the *Davis* decision that had been discredited just a few years earlier.[81] It was not until *Bigelow v. Virginia* (1975) that the Supreme Court ruled some forms of commercial speech were protected by the First Amendment. Since Mill's views on commercial regulation reflected the prevailing view in English common law and were a bit ambiguous on the subject, it is not surprising that a court adopting Millian thought in free expression cases was late to recognize the importance of freedom of commercial expression compared with political speech, where Mill's advocacy was clearer.[82]

Similar to *Valentine*, in *Chaplinsky v. New Hampshire* (1942) the Supreme Court interpreted the freedom of expression narrowly, for the first time declaring that what it termed "fighting words" were not protected by the First Amendment: "The test is what men of common intelligence would understand would be words likely to cause an average addressee to fight. . . . The English language has a number of words and expressions which by general consent are 'fighting words' when said without a disarming smile. . . . Such words, as ordinary men know, are likely to cause a fight."[83] According to a unanimous Supreme Court, "such utterances are no essential part of any exposition of ideas, and are of such slight social value as a step to truth that any benefit that may be derived from them is clearly outweighed by the social interest in order and morality."[84] Although some Millian and Holmesian notion of protecting speech that is in furtherance of the search for truth in the marketplace of ideas is present here, not protecting speech because it contains invective or is deemed immoral runs counter to *On Liberty*.[85] *Chaplinsky* carved out major categories of expression—including "the lewd and obscene, the profane, the libelous, and the insulting or 'fighting' words"—from constitutional protection, opposing a Millian interpretation of the First Amendment, as Mill wanted to protect the "freedom of opinion and sentiment on *all* subjects," whether those expressions are "practical or speculative."[86] Although Mill's theory permits the punishment of expression that will directly and immediately cause violence, the Supreme Court's painting with such broad brushstrokes in *Chaplinsky* emboldens authorities to penalize much more speech than necessary.[87] This included the words uttered by Chaplinsky, who criticized law enforcement and local government, as he was prosecuted for stating to a police officer, "You are a God damned racketeer and a damned Fascist and the whole government of Rochester are Fascists or agents of Fascists."[88] Even justices who advocated Millian theory during this era—like Black, Stone, and Murphy—joined the Supreme Court's *Chaplinsky* opinion, showing that the World War II Court was not acting consistently in First Amendment cases.

Another example of the Supreme Court interpreting the freedom of expression narrowly in the early 1940s occurred in *NBC v. United States* (1943). Justice Frankfurter, not typically an advocate of Millian philosophy, ruled for a 5–2 majority that the FCC's content-based regulations on radio broadcasting—requiring broadcasts to serve "public interest, convenience, or necessity"—were constitutional.[89] According to Frankfurter, "Radio inherently is not available to all. That is its unique characteristic, and that is why, unlike other modes of expression, it is subject to governmental regulation."[90] If one applied that thinking to print media (where a physical printing press is not within the economic grasp of many to own, the amount of available paper may be limited, etc.), it could be used to justify significant restrictions on newspapers, periodicals, and books.[91] Both Mill and his predecessor John Milton opposed that type of press regulation.[92] Nevertheless, Frankfurter concluded for the Supreme Court that "denial of a station license on that ground" of not serving public interest, convenience, or necessity "is not a denial of free speech."[93] Protecting speech on a vague notion of whether it is "convenient" certainly falls short of Mill's standard. This lack of Millian philosophy in cases involving broadcasting is something that reemerged in several other important Supreme Court decisions in latter decades.

No other area of First Amendment law encapsulates the Supreme Court's struggle with free speech in the early 1940s more than cases involving Jehovah's Witnesses. On the one hand, *Cantwell v. Connecticut* (1940) unanimously overturned a ban on canvassing without a permit (applied to Jehovah's Witnesses), because, as explained by Justice Roberts, "the system of licensing still leaves that system one of previous restraint which, in the field of free speech and press, we have held inadmissible."[94] As we explored in earlier chapters, the idea of prior restraints certainly runs counter to Mill's philosophy and even Blackstone's. *Cantwell* also involved a government official determining if one's cause was religious or not. Roberts wrote for the Supreme Court that giving an official power to "withhold his approval if he determines that the cause is not a religious one" could easily constitute "censorship of religion as the means of determining its right to survive," which "is a denial of liberty."[95] Mill absolutely opposed government attempts to restrict religious speech or punish speakers from minority religions, as he decried the religiously based prosecutions of Socrates and Jesus Christ for impiety and blasphemy.[96]

On the other hand, after *Cantwell*, the Supreme Court issued a series of decisions upholding restrictions on speech by Jehovah's Witnesses, a minority religious group that suffered significant persecution and discrimination during this era.[97] In *Jones v. Opelika* (1942), Justice Stanley Reed upheld for a 5–4 majority a Jehovah's Witness's conviction for selling Bibles without a license. Although Justice Reed spoke to the importance of free expression, he used a balancing test in the case, emphasizing "the right to employ the sovereign power explicitly reserved to the State by the Tenth Amendment to ensure orderly living."[98] While Reed held for the Supreme Court that "ordinances absolutely prohibiting the exercise of the right to disseminate information are, *a fortiori*, invalid," the *Opelika* majority sustained regulations of religious expression that were struck down in *Lovell* and *Cantwell*.[99]

In response, each of the four dissenters in *Opelika* wrote an opinion. Chief Justice Stone complained that "the only activities involved are the dissemination of ideas, educational and religious, and the collection of funds for the propagation of those ideas."[100] Stone articulated a position similar to Mill in *On Liberty* and Brandeis in *Whitney*, declaring of First Amendment rights that "the Constitution, by virtue of the First and the Fourteenth Amendments, has put those freedoms in a preferred position."[101] Similarly, Justice Murphy emphasized the need to protect the freedom of expression for the utilitarian reasons of effective democratic self-governance and happiness related to personal autonomy: "Those historic privileges . . . are so essential to our political welfare and spiritual progress."[102] Murphy cautioned against the tyranny of the majority: "The protection of the Constitution must be extended to all, not only to those whose views accord with prevailing thought but also to dissident minorities who energetically spread their beliefs."[103] Murphy continued his Millian approach, writing that "freedom of speech, freedom of the press, and freedom of religion all have a double aspect—freedom of thought and freedom of action. Freedom to think is absolute of its own nature . . . but even an aggressive mind is of no missionary value unless there is freedom of action."[104] Thus, Murphy connected the freedom of thought and the freedom of expression to the freedom to act, something Mill did in *On Liberty* by proclaiming that a consequence of the freedom of expression is that one "should be allowed, without molestation, to carry his opinions into practice."[105] Nevertheless, these Millian views were expressed solely in dissent in *Opelika*.

Then, much like the Supreme Court suddenly changed to a more Millian position in 1931, the Supreme Court's brief struggles over free speech abruptly ended in 1943, as a majority of justices embarked again on a more libertarian understanding of the freedom of expression. More than anything else, this was due to the resignation of the more conservative Justice James Byrnes and his replacement by the more liberal Justice Wiley Rutledge in February 1943.[106] It was also due to a reevaluation by the justices of this freedom in light of violations of human rights in Nazi Germany during World War II.[107] Thus, 1943 markedly shifted the Supreme Court's First Amendment jurisprudence back to a more Millian position. And for several years, it appeared that the shift was again permanent.

This began with several cases affecting the rights of Jehovah's Witnesses.[108] These included a summary reversal of *Opelika* and a majority opinion by Justice William Douglas in *Murdock v. Pennsylvania* emphasizing the Millian concept articulated by the chief justice in *Opelika* that expressive rights have particular primacy: "Freedom of press, freedom of speech, freedom of religion are in a preferred position."[109] The most noteworthy of the 1943 cases involving Jehovah's Witnesses was *West Virginia v. Barnette*, where the justices overruled *Minersville School District v. Gobitis* (1940). Justice Frankfurter had written for the Supreme Court in *Gobitis*, upholding the expulsion from public schools of Jehovah's Witness children who refused to salute the US flag. According to Frankfurter, courts needed to defer state legislatures on educational policy, even when First Amendment rights are at stake: "It is not our province to choose among competing considerations in the subtle process of securing effective loyalty to the traditional ideals of democracy."[110]

In *Barnette*, the Supreme Court overturned the expulsion of public school students who refused to say the Pledge of Allegiance and salute the US flag.

Writing for the 6–3 majority, Justice Jackson began by relying on another Supreme Court opinion steeped in Millian philosophy: Chief Justice Hughes's decision in *Stromberg*.[111] He clarified that the standard to be applied was a familiar one: "Censorship or suppression of expression of opinion is tolerated by our Constitution only when the expression presents a clear and present danger of action of a kind the State is empowered to prevent and punish."[112] Jackson approached this test like Holmes in *Abrams*, not Holmes in *Schenck*: "It would seem that involuntary affirmation could be commanded only on even more immediate and urgent grounds than silence. But here the power of compulsion is invoked without any allegation that remaining passive during a flag salute ritual creates a clear and present danger that would justify an effort even to muffle expression."[113] Jackson emphasized the Millian notion that we must avoid the tyranny of the majority when he remarked that "very purpose of a Bill of Rights was to withdraw certain subjects from the vicissitudes of political controversy, to place them beyond the reach of majorities and officials and to establish them as legal principles to be applied by the courts. One's right to life, liberty, and property, to free speech, a free press, freedom of worship and assembly, and other fundamental rights may not be submitted to vote."[114] Like Mill, Jackson reasoned that while there should be more government power to regulate economic interests, "freedoms of speech and of press, of assembly, and of worship may not be infringed on such slender grounds. They are susceptible of restriction only to prevent grave and immediate danger to interests which the State may lawfully protect."[115]

Jackson explained in *Barnette* that "struggles to coerce uniformity of sentiment in support of some end thought essential to their time and country have been waged by many good as well as by evil men," which was similar to Mill when he cautioned that those trying to restrict the freedom of speech historically were "not bad men . . . but rather the contrary; men who possessed in a full, or somewhat more than a full measure, the religious, moral, and patriotic feelings of their time and people."[116] Mill spoke about this attitude leading to the executions of dissidents like Socrates and Jesus Christ, another point explained by Jackson in *Barnette*: "Those who begin coercive elimination of dissent soon find themselves exterminating dissenters. Compulsory unification of opinion achieves only the unanimity of the graveyard."[117] Due to this danger, Jackson resolved that the government cannot compel people what to say: "If there is any fixed star in our constitutional constellation, it is that no official, high or petty, can prescribe what shall be orthodox in politics, nationalism, religion, or other matters of opinion or force citizens to confess by word or act their faith therein."[118] Jackson concluded with Millian sentiment that the Constitution requires the free market of ideas and individual autonomy:

"To believe that patriotism will not flourish if patriotic ceremonies are voluntary and spontaneous instead of a compulsory routine is to make an unflattering estimate of the appeal of our institutions to free minds. We can have intellectual individualism and the rich cultural diversities that we owe to exceptional minds only at the price of occasional eccentricity and abnormal attitudes."[119] All told, *Barnette* strongly reaffirmed the Supreme Court's earlier commitment to Millian philosophy in free expression cases.[120] Like Mill's *On Liberty*, Jackson's opinion in *Barnette* maintains the right of dissent to ensure full debate on public matters to ultimately lead society to a better place.[121]

The Supreme Court's libertarian position on the freedom of expression continued during the height of World War II.[122] One of the more consequential decisions was the Supreme Court's only Espionage Act case during World War II, *Hartzel v. United States* (1944). The justices by a vote of 5–4 overturned a five-year prison sentence for mailing approximately six hundred copies of an antisemitic, racist exhortation that criticized the Allies' war effort. Writing for the majority, Justice Murphy applied the clear and present danger test, quoting Holmes's *Abrams* dissent to demonstrate that the Supreme Court's emphasis was on protecting, not restricting expression: "Legislation, being penal in nature and restricting the right to speak and write freely, must be construed narrowly and 'must be taken to use its words in a strict and accurate sense.'"[123] This demonstrates that the Supreme Court had adopted the more Millian understanding of the clear and present danger test that Holmes advocated in *Abrams*. Mindful that the country was "engaged in a total war for national survival," Murphy nonetheless proclaimed for the Supreme Court that "an American citizen has the right to discuss these matters either by temperate reasoning or by immoderate and vicious invective."[124] This Millian statement—using some of the same words as Mill (who wrote of the right to engage in "intemperate discussion" and use "invective") when defending the right to speak this way—was a bold one for the Supreme Court to make during the war.[125] It showed that the justices were willing to protect dissenters during World War II in ways the Supreme Court did not during and after World War I.[126]

Even stronger evidence of the Supreme Court's adoption of a Millian approach to free expression during World War II was its application to those who were not natural-born citizens. The justices by a vote of 5–3 overturned a decision to strip citizenship from a naturalized citizen in *Baumgardner v. United States* (1944). Wilhelm Baumgardner, an immigrant from Germany, had his citizenship revoked because of remarks in support of Hitler and the Nazi Party. But according to Justice Frankfurter for the majority, Baumgartner's country of origin (which was at war with the United States) and the fact that he was a naturalized citizen (as opposed to a natural-born citizen) did not diminish his free expression rights: "Under our Constitution, a naturalized citizen stands on an equal footing with the native citizen in all respects, save that of eligibility to the Presidency."[127] Writing with a very different tone than he typically did in First Amendment cases, Frankfurter, himself an immigrant from Austria-Hungary, announced one of his strongest defenses of free expression during his Supreme Court tenure: "American citizenship is the right to criticize public men and measures—and that means not only informed and responsible criticism but the freedom to speak foolishly and without moderation."[128] This reminds one of Mill's advice to protect invective. Frankfurter's *Baumgartner* opinion echoed Mill's commitment to the discussion of all ideas: "Our trust in the good sense of the people on deliberate reflection goes deep. For such is the contradictoriness of the human mind that the expression of views which may collide with cherished American ideals does not necessarily prove want of devotion to the Nation."[129] This was one of multiple cases during World War II where the Supreme Court ruled against citizenship revocation or alien deportation that was based on the subject's expression.[130] Sentiment in these cases that free expression rights attach to all persons, not just natural-born citizens, comports with Mill's theory, as he stated in *On Liberty* that if "all mankind minus one were of one opinion, and only one person were of the contrary opinion, mankind would be no more justified in silencing that one person than he, if he had the power, would be justified in silencing mankind."[131] This statement by Mill was not qualified by borders or citizenship status.

The peak of Supreme Court Millianism during World War II occurred in *Thomas v. Collins* (1945). An injunction was issued against the labor leader R. J. Thomas, prohibiting him from speaking at a labor meeting because he had not obtained an organizer's card from the state. Recalling not only Mill but also Brandeis's *Whitney* concurrence, Justice Rutledge wrote for a 5–4 majority about "the preferred place given in our scheme to the great, the indispensable, democratic freedoms secured by the First Amendment. That priority gives these liberties a sanctity and a sanction not permitting dubious intrusions."[132] Accordingly, Rutledge reminded his readers of the same idea used by Mill, Holmes, Brandeis, and Hughes: "Any attempt to restrict those liberties must be justified by clear public interest, threatened not doubtfully or remotely, but by clear and present danger."[133] On the question of the timing of a threat, Rutledge confirmed that it must be "public danger, actual or impending" for expression to be punishable.[134] Put another way later in the opinion, restrictions on expression, "without greater or more *imminent* danger to the public interest . . . is incompatible with the freedoms secured by the First Amendment."[135] Rutledge confirmed that this Millian approach had become a cornerstone of US constitutional law because of relevant past dissents: "The

First Amendment is a charter for government, not for an institution of learning. 'Free trade in ideas' means free trade in the opportunity to persuade to
action, not merely to describe facts. Cf. *Abrams v. United States*, and *Gitlow v.
New York*, dissenting opinions of Mr. Justice Holmes."[136] In a sweeping statement, Rutledge declared that "the rights of free speech and a free press are
not confined to any field of human interest," which was reminiscent of Mill's
quote that the freedom of speech should extend to "all subjects, practical or
speculative, scientific, moral, or theological."[137] Although just three years
earlier the Supreme Court had held in *Valentine* that commercial speech was
not protected by the First Amendment, Rutledge emphasized in *Thomas* that
"the idea is not sound therefore that the First Amendment's safeguards are
wholly inapplicable to business or economic activity," thus opening the door
to the justices eventually expanding commercial speech rights in the future.[138]
Thomas represents an affirmation of Mill's philosophy on the freedom of expression, including the marketplace of ideas analogy, as channeled through
Holmes's dissents decades earlier.[139] Minority opinions espousing Millian philosophy from 1919 and the 1920s were being adopted in majority opinions,
extending Mill's thoughts into Supreme Court jurisprudence in the future.

For the next few years, the Supreme Court largely adhered to the preferred
freedoms approach, emphasizing the marketplace of ideas analogy and applying the clear and present danger test in the vein of Mill, Holmes, Brandeis,
and Hughes.[140] The preferred freedoms approach presumed that restrictions
on the freedom of expression were unconstitutional, thus elevating the status
of First Amendment rights above other constitutional claims.[141] This "special
status" for the freedoms of speech and press was supported by the Supreme
Court beginning in *Carolene Products*, and that case's application of more scrutiny to restrictions on these rights stemmed from Holmes's and Brandeis's
opinions on expression after World War I.[142] Ultimately, the intellectual origins of this approach lie in Mill's *On Liberty*.[143] Indeed, Mill listed the "freedom of opinion and sentiment," including the "liberty of expressing and
publishing opinions," first among the rights he thought should be safeguarded,
and he wanted these freedoms to be protected absolutely.[144]

Even when the Supreme Court upheld restrictions on expression during this
period, they arguably used exceptions articulated by Mill.[145] In *United Public
Workers of America v. Mitchell* (1947), a 4–3 majority upheld the application of
the Hatch Act to federal employees, prohibiting them from taking "any active
part in political management or in political campaigns."[146] Justice Reed, writing for the majority, noted that when "actions of civil servants in the judgment
of Congress menace the integrity and the competency of the service, legislation to forestall such danger and adequate to maintain its usefulness is

required."[147] Mill was aware of the tension between private belief and public service, understanding that there are legitimate reasons to restrict expression for government employees: "Whenever, in short, there is a definite damage, or a definite risk of damage, either to an individual or to the public, the case is taken out of the province of liberty and placed in that of morality or law."[148] In this sense, one could argue, as Reed declared for the Supreme Court, that "Congress may reasonably desire to limit party activity of federal employees so as to avoid a tendency toward a one-party system."[149] However, Mill also emphasized that one had to be working for this exception to apply: "No person ought to be punished simply for being drunk; but a soldier or a policeman should be punished for being drunk *on duty*."[150] It is one thing for a public employee to express one's political convictions after work, but quite another to use one's governmental position to promote it. Mill dreaded a majoritarian rule that would silence public employees from being able to express their opinions on their own time, effectively forcing them to be apolitical.[151] Thus, Justice Black dissented, citing the more Millian decision of *Thornhill*. Black decried that public employees could be punished for "expressing political views" and opined that "laws which restrict the liberties guaranteed by the First Amendment should be narrowly drawn to meet the evil aimed at and to affect only the minimum number of people imperatively necessary to prevent a grave and imminent danger to the public."[152] Although some Millian sentiment was expressed by both the majority and the dissent in *Mitchell*, the dissent was much closer to what Mill supported in *On Liberty*.

In the late 1940s, the Supreme Court majority took Millian stances and struck down government action in several important cases, most notably in *Terminiello v. Chicago* (1949).[153] The Supreme Court overturned a breach of the peace conviction of the suspended priest Arthur Terminiello for an inflammatory speech containing antisemitic and racist rhetoric that he gave to a large, angry crowd. In his speech to an "inflamed mob," Terminiello referred to those protesting him as "'slimy scum,' 'snakes,' 'bedbugs,' and the like."[154] As deplorable as Terminiello's speech was, Justice Douglas affirmed for a 5–4 majority that Mill's marketplace of ideas and promotion of democratic self-governance, channeled through previous Supreme Court decisions, was controlling: "The vitality of civil and political institutions in our society depends on free discussion. As Chief Justice Hughes wrote in *DeJonge v. Oregon*, it is only through free debate and free exchange of ideas that government remains responsive to the will of the people and peaceful change is effected. The right to speak freely and to promote diversity of ideas and programs is therefore one of the chief distinctions that sets us apart from totalitarian regimes."[155] Douglas explained that the freedom of speech is "protected against censorship or punishment, unless shown likely to produce a clear and present danger of a serious substantive evil that rises far above public inconvenience, annoyance, or unrest."[156] As in many cases decided in the 1940s, the Supreme Court majority had adopted an understanding of "clear and present danger" similar to Holmes and Brandeis, and by extension, Mill and his corn dealer hypothetical.[157] In what looked like it might have been an implicit overruling of *Chaplinsky*, Douglas proclaimed in Millian fashion that "a function of free speech under our system of government is to invite dispute. It may indeed best serve its high purpose when it induces a condition of unrest, creates dissatisfaction with conditions as they are, or even stirs people to anger. Speech is often provocative and challenging. It may strike at prejudices and preconceptions and have profound unsettling effects as it presses for acceptance of an idea."[158] Finally, Douglas, like Mill, implied that this is approach is necessary to avoid a tyrannical majority dictating which ideas are acceptable: "There is no room under our Constitution for a more restrictive view. For the alternative would lead to standardization of ideas either by legislatures, courts, or dominant political or community groups."[159] Douglas's *Terminiello* opinion placed him among the justices who adopted a Millian interpretation of the First Amendment, such as Holmes, Brandeis, Hughes, Black, and Stone.

However, the Supreme Court's Millian approach during this era had developed some cracks by the late 1940s, as the Supreme Court was more frequently issuing divided decisions with multiple justices dissenting, particularly Justice Frankfurter.[160] Perhaps most surprisingly, in *Terminiello* Justice Jackson dissented, wanting to uphold the speaker's conviction, and he put the situation in dire terms: "There is danger that, if the Court does not temper its doctrinaire logic with a little practical wisdom, it will convert the constitutional Bill of Rights into a suicide pact."[161]

The growing number of dissents reflected changes with Supreme Court personnel. Chief Justice Stone, the author of the *Carolene Products* opinion and a Millian dissent in *Opelika*, died and was replaced in 1946 by Chief Justice Fred Vinson, who would prove to be more deferential to government attempts to regulate expression.[162] Among the justices who remained on the Supreme Court, Justice Frankfurter was an advocate of judicial restraint who had dissented in Millian decisions like *Barnette*, but Justice Jackson had written the rousing majority opinion that strongly defended the freedom of speech in that case. While prosecuting war criminals at Nuremberg, the once devoted civil libertarian Jackson saw how Soviet leaders controlled their representatives at those proceedings; he also closely analyzed how the Nazis rose to power in Germany through mesmerizing speeches.[163] It was due to this that Jackson emphasized in his *Terminiello* dissent that the "drive by totalitarian groups to undermine the prestige and effectiveness of local democratic governments is advanced whenever either of them can win from this Court a ruling which paralyzes the power of these officials. . . . The group of which Terminiello is a part claims that his behavior, because it involved a speech, is above the reach of local authorities."[164] As Jackson saw it, inflammatory speeches needed to be suppressed because "fascist and communist groups . . . resort to these terror tactics to confuse, bully and discredit . . . freely chosen governments. Violent and noisy shows of strength discourage participation of moderates in discussions so fraught with violence, and real discussion dries up and disappears."[165] Jackson thought the *Terminiello* decision would enable this: "Terminiello's victory today certainly fulfills the most extravagant hopes of both right and left totalitarian groups, who want nothing so much as to paralyze and discredit the only democratic authority that can curb them in their battle for the streets."[166] Unlike Holmes, who moved more toward Mill the longer he served on the US Supreme Court, Jackson had moved away from that understanding of free speech. His vote was in the minority in *Terminiello*, but it would soon be part of a non-Millian majority.

A shift away from Millianism was suggested by the Supreme Court's ruling in *Kovacs v. Cooper* (1949), decided a few months before *Terminiello*. In *Kovacs*, a 5–4 majority upheld a conviction for using sound amplification equipment to give a speech in violation of a Trenton, New Jersey, ordinance that prohibited "loud and raucous noises."[167] Writing for the Supreme Court, Justice Reed offered an assessment that was far from Millian: "The police power of a state extends beyond health, morals and safety, and comprehends the duty, within constitutional limitations, to protect the well-being and tranquility of a community. A state or city may prohibit acts or things reasonably thought to bring evil or harm to its people."[168] Although Mill thought it was necessary to protect health and safety and prevent actual harm, restricting expression for moral and related reasons runs against *On Liberty*.[169] Promoting a more limited notion of free expression, Reed explained that "it is an extravagant extension of due process to say that because of it a city cannot forbid talking on the streets through a loud speaker in a loud and raucous tone."[170] Furthermore, even though Reed's judgement alluded to the "preferred position of freedom of speech," he noted that the right could be restricted if others found it to be a mere "nuisance."[171]

More consequential than Justice Reed's majority opinion in *Kovacs* was Justice Frankfurter's lengthy concurrence, which was largely devoted to dismantling the idea of First Amendment "preferred freedoms": "I deem it a mischievous phrase, if it carries the thought, which it may subtly imply, that any law touching communication is infected with presumptive invalidity. . . .

I say the phrase is mischievous because it radiates a constitutional doctrine without avowing it."[172] Frankfurter offered an extensive recounting of the past cases that used the phrases "preferred freedoms" or "preferred position," or that led to that doctrinal development.[173] These cases were all written from a Millian perspective, including *Carolene Products, Thornhill, Schneider, Bridges, Opelika, Murdock, Barnette,* and *Thomas.*[174] Instead of a Millian preferred freedoms approach, Frankfurter called for "striking a wise balance between liberty and order."[175] Frankfurter thought that this more balanced approach was proper and stemmed from the opinions of Justice Holmes, although Frankfurter did not cite any Holmes opinions to this point. Interestingly, Frankfurter cited Justice Holmes as supporting what really are Millian ideas: "Mr. Justice Holmes . . . realized that the progress of civilization is to a considerable extent the displacement of error which once held sway as official truth by beliefs which in turn have yielded to other beliefs. . . . For him the right to search for truth was of a different order than some transient economic dogma. And without freedom of expression, thought becomes checked and atrophied."[176] Nevertheless, after explaining these Millian ideals expressed by Holmes, Frankfurter supported upholding the conviction in *Kovacs* because "these are matters for the legislative judgment controlled by public opinion."[177] As in his *Bridges* dissent, Frankfurter cited Holmes but then advocated a test for expression that allowed local majorities to control expression.

Justice Black dissented in *Kovacs,* emphasizing that the decision contradicted other recent judgments, as the Supreme Court had "placed use of loud speakers in public streets and parks on the same constitutional level as freedom to speak on streets without such devices, freedom to speak over radio, and freedom to distribute literature."[178] As Black explained, the mode of expression at issue deserves protection for the same reasons that older methods of communication needed protection: "Public speaking is done by many men of divergent minds with no centralized control over the ideas they entertain so as to limit the causes they espouse. . . . Transmission of ideas through public speaking is also essential to the sound thinking of a fully informed citizenry."[179] Although Mill did not live in an age of electronic enhancement of communication, the theory Black uses here—to ensure people of different views can express ideas unpopular with a ruling majority—bears imprints of Mill. Black further appealed to a Millian utilitarian idea of protecting expression to further democratic self-governance: "It is of particular importance in a government where people elect their officials that the fullest opportunity be afforded candidates to express and voters to hear their views."[180] Finally, Black made reference to the marketplace analogy when he explained the need to protect "all information that may be disseminated or received through this new avenue for trade in ideas."[181] Black's Millian exhortation notwithstanding, the majority's ruling and Frankfurter's long concurrence called into question the more libertarian preferred freedoms approach that the majority of justices had been using.

Kovacs, decided in January 1949, was just one case, and a majority of justices would apply Millian reasoning in *Terminiello* in May 1949. Holmes and Brandeis's dissents had laid a solid Millian groundwork that had been adopted first by Hughes and then by several other justices. However, a mounting group of justices started to question this libertarian position on the freedom of expression, with the Supreme Court issuing some deeply divided decisions. As the decade closed, the Millian vision of expression, first brought to the Supreme Court by Holmes, was in some doubt. The Supreme Court's First Amendment caseload continued to be large, as free speech questions consistently arose, so the direction taken by the justices would have a ripple effect throughout the country. Two shocking deaths in 1949 would divert the Supreme Court away from its libertarian approach to expression.

CHAPTER 5

No Law Means No Law
The Court Retrenches but Black and Douglas Carry On

As the 1940s turned to the 1950s, the popularity of Mill's philosophy precipitously declined on the US Supreme Court. Although the adoption of a libertarian approach to free expression occurred in earnest throughout the 1930s and 1940s, the Supreme Court became increasingly divided on how to decide these types of First Amendment questions in *Terminiello* and *Kovacs*. Fatal events over the summer of 1949 altered the Supreme Court's approach to the freedom of expression.

On July 19, 1949, Justice Frank Murphy died. Murphy had authored several opinions that espoused a Millian approach to the freedom of expression, including *Thornhill* and *Hartzel*.[1] Murphy's successor, Tom Clark, regularly deferred to the executive branch.[2] On September 10, 1949, Justice Wiley Rutledge died. Rutledge had authored the pro–free speech opinion of the Court in *Thomas v. Collins* that used Millian rhetoric and cited Holmes's *Abrams* and *Gitlow* dissents in support of the marketplace of ideas analogy. Rutledge's vacancy was filled by Sherman Minton, who exhibited a preference to uphold restrictions on expression by politically unpopular speakers.[3] On a closely divided Supreme Court, these personnel changes caused a retrenchment on free expression protections during the Cold War, similar to how the Red Scare in the 1920s prevented most justices from taking a more libertarian approach.[4] Many of the older, Blackstonian precedents that had been criticized and distinguished in the 1930s and 1940s had not been explicitly overruled; in the 1950s those older precedents were used by justices who were less libertarian in their understanding of free speech. However, just as Holmes and Brandeis opposed anti-Millian majorities during the first Red Scare, Hugo Black and William Douglas continued to keep alive Mill's view of these rights during the second Red Scare. These two justices would later be joined in several key cases by Chief Justice Earl Warren and Justice William Brennan.

American Communications Association v. Douds (1950) was the first case demonstrating the Supreme Court's move toward anti-Millianism. The justices by a vote of 5–1 upheld a federal law requiring labor representatives to file affidavits declaring that they were not members of the Communist Party. Writing for the Supreme Court, Chief Justice Vinson appeared at first to support a Millian version of the First Amendment, as he cited Justices Holmes and Brandeis, particularly Brandeis's concurrence in *Whitney*.[5] But then Vinson distinguished the situation in *Douds*, reasoning that "the question with which we are here faced is not the same one that Justices Holmes and Brandeis found convenient to consider in terms of clear and present danger."[6] Vinson did not think the more protective test was applicable: "When the effect of a statute or ordinance upon the exercise of First Amendment freedoms is relatively small and the public interest to be protected is substantial, it is obvious that a rigid test requiring a showing of imminent danger to the security of the Nation is an absurdity."[7] Citing previous decisions that were less protective of expression, Vinson proclaimed that "the right of the public to be protected from evils of conduct, even though First Amendment rights of persons or groups are thereby in some manner infringed, has received frequent and consistent recognition by this Court."[8] Vinson clarified that he rejected the Millian position on free speech: "Legitimate attempts to protect the public, not from the remote possible effects of noxious ideologies, but from present excesses of direct, active conduct, are not presumptively bad because they interfere with and, in some of its manifestations, restrain the exercise of First Amendment rights."[9] Vinson saw the disputed law as an economic regulation and was willing to defer to Congress, even though it chilled advocacy of certain political ideas and restricted associational freedom.[10]

In a concurring opinion, Justice Jackson was bolder in his disdain for protecting free speech rights, continuing the approach he had begun in his *Terminiello* dissent. According to Jackson in *Douds*, if "the statute before us required labor union officers to forswear membership in the Republican Party, the Democratic Party or the Socialist Party, I suppose all agree that it would be unconstitutional," but "the Communist Party is something different in fact from any other substantial party we have known, and hence may constitutionally be treated as something different."[11] The justice who wrote for the Supreme Court in *Barnette* that the Constitution protects one from being compelled to express political ideas now explained in *Douds* that "I suppose no one likes to be compelled to exonerate himself from connections he has never acquired," but the "public welfare . . . outweighs any affront to individual dignity."[12] His experience prosecuting war criminals in Nuremburg continued to weigh on Jackson's opinion of First Amendment rights, causing him to defer to the exercise of government power on questions like this.[13]

Justice Black's dissent in *Douds* appealed to Mill's notion that the freedom of thought and the expression of all ideas should be absolutely protected, declaring that "'freedom to think is absolute of its own nature.' . . . But people can be, and in less democratic countries have been, made to suffer for their admitted or conjectured thoughts."[14] Black accentuated Millian themes, including the history of political and religious persecution of minorities by majorities around the world: "Not the least of the virtues of the First Amendment is its protection of each member of the smallest and most unorthodox minority. Centuries of experience testify that laws aimed at one political or religious group . . . generate hatreds and prejudices which rapidly spread beyond control."[15] Black called attention to how oaths like the one in *Douds* were used to stifle the Huguenots in France, those deemed to be "heretics" during the Spanish Inquisition, and various religious groups in England.[16] Mill likewise found the use of oaths (particularly religious oaths) to determine who would be truthful to be based on faulty premises, as they encourage people to lie or are the basis to persecute those who object to taking them.[17] Black expressed concern, like Mill, about how ideas need continual discussion and how threats of censorship take many forms: "Freedom to think is inevitably abridged when beliefs are penalized by imposition of civil disabilities. [This law] was passed to exclude certain beliefs from one arena of the national economy."[18] Black argued something akin to Mill's harm principle, discussing "the wisdom of the basic constitutional precept that penalties should be imposed only for a person's own conduct, not for his beliefs or for the conduct of others with whom he may associate."[19] Black quoted at length from Chief Justice Hughes's Millian exhortation in *DeJonge v. Oregon* (1937), which stressed the need to protect free expression, even when facing threats of government overthrow, so that the government responds to the will of the people.[20]

Like Holmes and Hughes before him, Black admired John Stuart Mill and had read Mill's writings.[21] During the 1950s, Black developed and adhered to an absolutist approach to protecting the freedom of expression.[22] His *Douds* dissent was the first of many during this decade keeping Mill's spirit alive on the Supreme Court. Justice Black's views, however, were in the minority. Following *Douds*, a majority of the Supreme Court continued to largely defer to governmental constraints on expression and association for the next several years.[23] Often, this was over the dissents of Black and Douglas. For instance, the Supreme Court upheld five injunctions against labor picketers in the early 1950s, and in none of them did the majority use the clear and present danger test, thus significantly withdrawing the protection for protest that had been put in place just a few years earlier.[24]

The Supreme Court's backpedaling was most evident in *Dennis v. United States* (1951), where a 6–2 majority upheld the constitutionality of the Smith Act, which made it illegal "to knowingly or willfully advocate, abet, advise, or teach the duty, necessity, desirability, or propriety of overthrowing or destroying any government in the United States by force or violence."[25] The Supreme Court sustained five-year prison sentences and $10,000 fines against American Communist Party members, with Chief Justice Vinson making it clearer than in *Douds* that the Supreme Court no longer viewed First Amendment rights as preferred freedoms, instead concluding that "the societal value of speech must, on occasion, be subordinated to other values and considerations."[26] Although he offered a detailed history of free speech cases and even cataloged the famous dissents and concurrences of Holmes and Brandeis, Vinson's description of the clear and present danger test in *Dennis* read more like a clear and *probable* danger test, asking "whether the gravity of the evil, discounted by its *improbability*, justifies such invasion of free speech as is necessary to avoid the danger."[27] Vinson's application of the test was very deferential to governmental restrictions, as the defendants in the case were convicted solely for the ideas they advocated; as Vinson admitted, "Petitioners' activities did not result in an attempt to overthrow the Government by force and violence."[28] The *Dennis* decision revealed a significant problem with the clear and present danger test, as the Supreme Court used it to easily uphold criminal penalties on minority groups for advocating disfavored political ideas in the absence of concrete threats.[29] Although the test was, in theory, a significant move toward Millian libertarianism, Holmes misapplied it originally in *Schenck* to unduly restrict expression.[30] Holmes quickly realized this in his *Abrams* dissent, pushing further to emphasize protecting speech unless a dangerous threat was "imminent" or "immediate," rather than the more amorphous "present," or, as was eventually the case in *Dennis*, simply probable.[31] Brandeis's *Whitney* concurrence similarly explained the need to protect speech short of an imminent threat.[32] The Supreme Court in *Dennis* did not protect the First Amendment as proclaimed by Holmes and Brandeis, as there was no threat of imminent violence in Dennis's advocacy.[33]

Concurring opinions in *Dennis* were similarly crabbed. Frankfurter, who worked to bury the preferred freedoms doctrine in *Kovacs*, wrote a lengthy concurrence in *Dennis*, giving a history of government restrictions on speech before surmising that a balancing test should be used for the freedom of expression: "The demands of free speech in a democratic society as well as the interest in national security are better served by candid and informed weighing of the competing interests."[34] Frankfurter quoted Sir William Haley's reference of Mill's "famous dictum" that "if all mankind minus one were of one opinion, and only one person were of the contrary opinion, mankind would be no more justified in silencing that one person, than he, if he had the power, would be justified in silencing mankind."[35] Even though Frankfurter was indirectly using what appears to have been the first quote of Mill's *On Liberty* in a US Supreme Court free expression decision (Frankfurter quoted Haley, who quoted Mill), Frankfurter was not referencing Mill to defend a Millian view of free expression. Frankfurter may have personally agreed with Mill's philosophy, but he advocated judicial restraint as a justice, including in *Dennis*: "Much that should be rejected as illiberal, because repressive and envenoming, may well be not unconstitutional. The ultimate reliance for the deepest needs of civilization must be found outside their vindication in courts of law."[36] Mill promoted a free expression culture in private institutions because "there needs protection also against the tyranny of the prevailing opinion and feeling, against the tendency of society to impose, by other means than civil penalties, its own ideas and practices as rules of conduct on those who dissent from them."[37] However, in the same passage in *On Liberty*, Mill indicated that this was *in addition to* government actors fulfilling their roles to protect this vital freedom, proclaiming that "protection . . . against the tyranny of the magistrate" was essential too.[38] In this sense, Frankfurter's use of Mill in *Dennis* was misplaced.

Indeed, rather than declaring support for Mill's views, Frankfurter's opinion cited Alexander Meiklejohn to attack a Millian, absolutist vision of free expression.[39] Frankfurter wrote favorably of Meiklejohn's self-governing theory of free speech, which would protect "a citizen who is planning for the general welfare" but not "a merchant advertising his wares, . . . a paid lobbyist fighting for the advantage of his client," those working in commercial "radio," or even academics conducting "scholarship."[40] Putting aside how many major areas of expression could be banned if the Supreme Court adopted Frankfurter and Meiklejohn's position, it was inapplicable in *Dennis*, as the defendants were citizens "planning for the general welfare" by promoting their political views.

Like Frankfurter, Jackson in *Dennis* deferred to legislatures on expression regulation. According to Jackson, the clear and present danger test should not be used in cases involving advocacy of communism because the test "was an innovation by Mr. Justice Holmes in the *Schenck* case, reiterated and refined by him and Mr. Justice Brandeis in later cases, all arising before the era of World War II revealed the subtlety and efficacy of modernized revolutionary techniques used by totalitarian parties."[41] Jackson also approvingly quoted Meiklejohn, including his argument that the clear and present danger test "annuls the most significant purpose of the First Amendment. It destroys the intellectual basis of our plan of self-government."[42] Jackson concluded in *Dennis* that "an individual cannot claim that the Constitution protects him in advocating or teaching overthrow of government by force or violence."[43] Frankfurter and Jackson, by espousing Meiklejohn's self-governing theory of free speech, were taking a middle approach on expression: they were not fully backtracking to Blackstone's position like some of their colleagues, but they were also repudiating a Millian protection for speech seeking truth or expressing personal autonomy.

Justices Black and Douglas adhered to a Millian version of free speech in *Dennis*, carrying on Holmes's and Brandeis's arguments. Writing in dissent, Black explained that the "petitioners were not charged with an attempt to overthrow the Government. They were not charged with overt acts of any kind designed to overthrow the Government. They were not even charged with saying anything or writing anything designed to overthrow the Government."[44] Instead, the "charge was that they agreed to assemble and to talk and publish certain ideas at a later date. . . . No matter how it is worded, this is a virulent form of prior censorship of speech and press."[45] Understanding the potential for harm, Black made clear that the issue was previously settled by the Supreme Court's adoption of the vision of Holmes and Brandeis (and, by extension, Mill): "Undoubtedly a governmental policy of unfettered communication of ideas does entail dangers," but "the benefits derived from free expression were worth the risk."[46] Black connected free expression to other rights: "I have always believed that the First Amendment is the keystone of our Government, that the freedoms it guarantees provide the best insurance against destruction of all freedom."[47] In *On Liberty*, this is precisely what Mill argued following the chapter titled "Of Thought and Discussion," as he opened the next chapter by remarking that "the same reasons which show that opinion should be free prove also that he should be allowed, without molestation, to carry his opinions into practice at his own cost."[48] Thus, Black, like Mill, connected the freedom of expression to the safeguarding of other rights.

Douglas also provided a forceful dissent in *Dennis*:

> Free speech has occupied an exalted position because of the high service it has given our society. Its protection is essential to the very existence of a democracy. . . . When ideas compete in the market for acceptance, full

and free discussion exposes the false, and they gain few adherents. Full and free discussion even of ideas we hate encourages the testing of our own prejudices and preconceptions. Full and free discussion keeps a society from becoming stagnant and unprepared for the stresses and strains that work to tear all civilizations apart.

Full and free discussion has . . . been the safeguard of every religious, political, philosophical, economic, and racial group amongst us. We have counted on it to keep us from embracing what is cheap and false; we have trusted the common sense of our people to choose the doctrine true to our genius and to reject the rest.[49]

Douglas succinctly proclaimed that "free speech is the rule, not the exception. The restraint to be constitutional must be based on more than fear, on more than passionate opposition against the speech, on more than a revolted dislike for its contents. There must be some immediate injury to society that is likely if speech is allowed."[50]

Douglas's *Dennis* dissent clearly links to Mill, through Holmes and Brandeis. Douglas denoted the clear and present danger test multiple times in his *Dennis* dissent.[51] Douglas mentioned Holmes: "There have been numerous First Amendment cases before the Court raising the issue of clear and present danger since Mr. Justice Holmes first formulated the test in *Schenck v. United States*."[52] And Douglas referenced Brandeis, after discussing his libertarian view of the First Amendment: "The classic statement of these conditions was made by Mr. Justice Brandeis in his concurring opinion in *Whitney v. California*."[53] Even more than Black, Douglas channeled Mill through Holmes and Brandeis, using several of Mill's significant arguments, including that the freedom of speech facilitates democratic government, leads to the discovery of truth, keeps our arguments sharp, and prevents us from "falling asleep" at our posts. Although the Supreme Court was now entering a dark period regarding the freedom of speech, the opinions of Black and Douglas kept alive the Millian flame that had been lit by Holmes and Brandeis. Like Black, Douglas was an admirer of Mill and clearly familiar with his writings; Douglas would cite Mill in an article where Douglas argued that "it is precisely the unpopular views, the minority views, which we need to hear. We do not learn by hearing what we already agree with. We need to hear ideas with which we may disagree."[54]

The majority of the justices abandoned this Millian approach in the early 1950s. Some of this could be attributed to Cold War paranoia, but the decisions upholding speech restrictions extended well beyond communists and labor unions.[55] In *Feiner v. New York* (1951), the Supreme Court by a vote of 6–3 sustained the disorderly conduct conviction of a man who gave a speech supportive of equal rights for African Americans. As Chief Justice Vinson described it for the Supreme Court, Feiner made some "derogatory" remarks toward public officials and rhetorically encouraged African Americans in the audience to "rise up" and "fight" for their rights.[56] According to Vinson, the speech, given to approximately seventy-five people, "stirred up a little excitement," with at least one member of the crowd threatening violence, so police officers on the scene "stepped in to prevent it from resulting in a fight" by demanding that Feiner cease speaking; when Feiner refused, he was arrested, subsequently convicted of disorderly conduct, and sentenced to thirty days in jail.[57] Vinson held that Feiner's conviction was constitutional because of "the imminence of greater disorder coupled with petitioner's deliberate defiance of the police officers."[58] *Feiner* was another case incompatible with decisions from a few years earlier, most notably *Terminiello*, but it is explained by personnel changes on the Supreme Court that pushed it away from a libertarian view on free speech.[59]

Black and Douglas dissented, chiding the *Feiner* majority for upholding what is now known as "a heckler's veto."[60] As put by Justice Black, "I reject the implication of the Court's opinion that the police had no obligation to protect petitioner's constitutional right to talk," and if police "in the name of preserving order . . . ever can interfere with a lawful public speaker, they first must make all reasonable efforts to protect him."[61] For Black, the holding in *Feiner* meant "that as a practical matter, minority speakers can be silenced in any city. Hereafter, despite the First and Fourteenth Amendments, the policeman's club can take heavy toll of a current administration's public critics. Criticism of public officials will be too dangerous for all but the most courageous."[62] Likewise, according to Justice Douglas,

> Public assemblies and public speech occupy an important role in American life. One high function of the police is to protect these lawful gatherings so that the speakers may exercise their constitutional rights. When unpopular causes are sponsored from the public platform, there will commonly be mutterings and unrest and heckling from the crowd. When a speaker mounts a platform it is not unusual to find him resorting to exaggeration, to vilification of ideas and men, to the making of false charges. But those extravagances . . . do not justify penalizing the speaker by depriving him of the platform or by punishing him for his conduct.[63]

Both Black and Douglas explained that it is the government's duty to protect speakers, especially those espousing minority viewpoints, even if the speech employs what Mill termed "invective, sarcasm, personality and the like."[64] As

Mill noted in *On Liberty*, what a society considers offensive usually tracks majoritarian inclinations and beliefs: "The rules which obtain among themselves appear to them self-evident and self-justifying. This all but universal illusion is one of the examples of the magical influence of custom, which is not only, as the proverb says, a second nature but continually mistaken for the first."[65] Just as Mill put the onus on his readers to make an effort to listen and engage in dialogue with speakers they find disagreeable, the final paragraph of Douglas's *Feiner* dissent rebuked not the speaker but the "unsympathetic audience and the threat of one man to haul the speaker from the stage."[66]

The Supreme Court's narrow interpretation of the freedom of speech did not just restrict the expression of those, like Feiner, who advocated for racial equality. The Supreme Court also upheld the constitutionality of a group libel law that punished the expression of racists. In *Beauharnais v. Illinois* (1952), at issue was a Chicago ordinance making it illegal to produce any publication that "portrays depravity, criminality, unchastity, or lack of virtue of a class of citizens, of any race, color, creed or religion."[67] Beauharnais was convicted of distributing a leaflet attempting to recruit whites into the White Circle League of America, which was petitioning the Chicago government to racially segregate the city; Beauharnais's racist leaflet claimed that "if persuasion and the need to prevent the white race from becoming mongrelized by the negro will not unite us, then the aggressions . . . rapes, robberies, knives, guns and marijuana of the negro, surely will."[68] Writing for a 5–4 Supreme Court, Justice Frankfurter deemed the speech to be false, and hence, not protected by the First Amendment, with no need for the government to show imminent harm: "Libelous utterances not being within the area of constitutionally protected speech, it is unnecessary . . . to consider the issues behind the phrase 'clear and present danger.' Certainly no one would contend that obscene speech, for example, may be punished only upon a showing of such circumstances. Libel, as we have seen, is in the same class."[69] Unwillingness to protect opinion, whether true or false, runs counter to Mill's well-known aphorism. Rather than follow Mill's advice of having counterspeech be the antidote to such falsehoods, the majority again deferred to legislative power to restrict expression, with Frankfurter even admitting this may be an ineffective solution to the problem: "It would be out of bounds for the judiciary to deny the legislature a choice of policy. . . . That the legislative remedy might not in practice mitigate the evil, or might itself raise new problems . . . is the price to be paid for the trial-and-error inherent in legislative efforts to deal with obstinate social issues."[70]

Justice Black maintained a Millian position in his *Beauharnais* dissent—and explicitly denied the efficacy of Frankfurter's judicial restraint—by claiming that "no legislature is charged with the duty or vested with the power to de-cide what public issues Americans can discuss. In a free country that is the in-dividual's choice, not the state's. . . . I reject the holding that either state or nation can punish people for having their say in matters of public concern."[71] Echoing Mill's emphasis on protecting expression to better ensure democratic self-governance, Black maintained that "state experimentation in curbing free-dom of expression is startling and frightening doctrine in a country dedicated to self-government by its people."[72] Since Beauharnais was advocating a posi-tion on a divisive public policy issue of the early 1950s, Black believed, follow-ing Mill, that Beauharnais had the right to express his views, even if he was clearly wrong: "Beauharnais is punished for publicly expressing strong views in favor of segregation. . . . To say that a legislative body can, with this Court's approval, make it a crime to petition for and publicly discuss proposed legisla-tion seems as farfetched to me as it would be to say that a valid law could be enacted to punish a candidate for President for telling the people his views."[73] In closing, Black made it clear that he supported a Millian position on free speech, perhaps more than even Holmes or Brandeis: "I think the First Amend-ment, with the Fourteenth, 'absolutely' forbids such laws without any 'ifs' or 'buts' or 'whereases.'"[74]

Even this decision was too much for Justice Jackson, who thought the clear and present danger test should have been applied: "Mr. Justice Holmes formu-lated for the Court as 'the question in every case' the 'clear and present dan-ger' test. He and Mr. Justice Brandeis adhered to it as a 'rule of reason,' dissenting when they thought the rest of the Court apostate."[75] Jackson noted the philosophical connections between Holmes, Brandeis, and Hughes: "Jus-tices Holmes and Brandeis in 1931 joined Chief Justice Hughes, who spoke for the Court, in striking down a state Act because it authorized restraint by injunction previous to publication."[76] Nevertheless, *Beauharnais*, combined with other early 1950s decisions allowing major restrictions on expression, demonstrated that the Supreme Court had largely retreated on this issue dur-ing this era.[77]

It was not as though the Supreme Court was upholding *every* governmen-tal regulation of, and prohibition on, expression during the early to mid-1950s.[78] For instance, *Burstyn v. Wilson* (1952) overturned a state ban on showing "sac-rilegious" films (finding rescinding a license for showing such films to be an unconstitutional prior restraint), finally establishing that movies receive con-stitutional protection. The Supreme Court rejected the reasoning of the 1915 *Mutual Film Corp.* decision: "It cannot be doubted that motion pictures are a significant medium for the communication of ideas."[79] By the early 1950s, films exhibited increasing similarities to traditional print media, in part due to the rise of newsreels, leading the justices to finally find them to be constitutionally protected.[80] Mill understood the importance of unconventional ideas, especially ones that acted as a foil to social custom. He wrote, "There is no reason that all human existence should be constructed on some one or small number of patterns," warning that "unless there is a corresponding diversity in their modes of life, they neither obtain their fair share of happiness, nor grow up to the mental, moral, and aesthetic stature of which their nature is capable."[81] Mill foresaw that a rapidly mobilizing society, linked by "improvements in the means of communication" and an "increase in commerce and manufacturing," would lead to a growing conformity in thought, belief, and living.[82] Reflecting Mill's point about the necessity of unorthodox artistic expression like music, dance, and theater performances, the Supreme Court in *Burstyn* reasoned that movies "may affect public attitudes and behavior in a variety of ways, ranging from direct espousal of a political or social doctrine to the subtle shaping of thought which characterizes all artistic expression. The importance of motion pictures as an organ of public opinion is not lessened by the fact that they are designed to entertain as well as to inform."[83] Moving away from *Valentine*'s proclamation that there is no constitutional protection for "purely commercial advertising," the Supreme Court in *Burstyn*, following Mill, explained, "That books, newspapers, and magazines are published and sold for profit does not prevent them from being a form of expression whose liberty is safeguarded by the First Amendment."[84] The Supreme Court reversed course from its pre–World War I approach to film: over no dissents, the justices ruled that "expression by means of motion pictures is included within the free speech and free press guaranty of the First and Fourteenth Amendments. To the extent that language in the opinion in *Mutual Film Corp.* is out of harmony with the views here set forth, we no longer adhere to it."[85] However, the freedom of expression during this time remained under a less protective standard, and it was applied unevenly, allowing some controversial ideas to be expressed while many others were not.[86]

To that point, the Supreme Court decided *Poulos v. New Hampshire* (1953), where it upheld the conviction of Jehovah's Witnesses for holding a religious meeting in a public park without a license, even though the parties in question had properly applied for a license (which was denied).[87] The facts of *Poulos* were reminiscent of *Davis v. Massachusetts* (1897), where the Supreme Court upheld a conviction for preaching in a public park without a permit. *Davis* had been effectively nullified in 1939 by the Millian decisions *Hague* and *Schneider*. However, those cases did not explicitly overrule *Davis*. Without being overruled, older Blackstonian precedents were being used by a less libertarian Supreme Court majority to restrict expressive rights in the 1950s. In response,

Justice Douglas's *Poulos* dissent, joined by Justice Black, referred to "the preferred position granted freedom of speech, freedom of press, freedom of assembly, and freedom of religion," citing *Thomas v. Collins*.[88] Similar to Mill's absolutism comments from *On Liberty*, Douglas averred that the "command of the First Amendment (made applicable to the States by the Fourteenth) is that there shall be *no* law which abridges those civil rights. The matter is beyond the power of the legislature to regulate, control, or condition."[89] Douglas rejected the Blackstonian understanding that the First Amendment protected *only* prior restraints: "A legislature that undertakes to license or censor the right of free speech is imposing a prior restraint, odious in our history."[90] Douglas's emphasis on individual autonomy was evident when he remarked that "a man has the right to make his speech, print his handbill, compose his newspaper, and deliver his sermon without asking anyone's permission."[91] Douglas specifically referred to the "market place of ideas" in a concurring opinion in a different case in 1953, which was the first use of that exact phrase in a justice's opinion.[92] But the majority of justices were not subscribing to Millian philosophy on the First Amendment.

By the latter 1950s, Millian thought had begun to recover lost ground. Two of the newer Eisenhower nominees, Chief Justice Warren (appointed in 1953) and Justice Brennan (appointed in 1956), started moving the Supreme Court closer to its free expression position from the 1930s and 1940s. The venerable pair Black and Douglas still consistently adhered to Millian philosophy. This was not true in all cases.[93] Still, the Supreme Court began protecting the freedom of expression to a greater degree and espousing Millian philosophy more, most notably when one of these four justices wrote for the Supreme Court and they could convince a one more colleague to join this group of four.[94]

A good example was *Roth v. United States* (1957), where the Supreme Court first delineated a comprehensive test for obscenity. Justice Brennan confirmed that obscenity was *not* protected by the First Amendment, but he also provided a narrower definition of obscenity than what had been adopted by US courts following nineteenth-century precedents like *Hicklin* and *Rosen*: "The early leading standard of obscenity allowed material to be judged merely by the effect of an isolated excerpt upon particularly susceptible persons. Some American courts adopted this standard, but later decisions have rejected it and substituted this test: whether to the average person, applying contemporary community standards, the dominant theme of the material taken as a whole appeals to prurient interest."[95] Brennan reasoned that "all ideas having even the slightest redeeming social importance—unorthodox ideas, controversial ideas, even ideas hateful to the prevailing climate of opinion—have the full protection of the guaranties" of the First Amendment.[96] Brennan used consequentialist reasoning about the need to protect the freedom of expression, similar to what Mill argued: "The fundamental freedoms of speech and press have contributed greatly to the development and wellbeing of our free society and are indispensable to its continued growth. Ceaseless vigilance is the watchword to prevent their erosion by Congress or by the States."[97] Writing about the subject matter of the case, Brennan remarked that "the portrayal of sex, e.g., in art, literature and scientific works, is not itself sufficient reason to deny material the constitutional protection. . . . Sex, a great and mysterious motive force in human life, has indisputably been a subject of absorbing interest to mankind through the ages; it is one of the vital problems of human interest and public concern."[98] As Mill criticized puritanical restrictions on expressive activities, Brennan thought that sexual expression had some First Amendment protection.[99] Nevertheless, much like Holmes's *Schenck* opinion boldly stated a more libertarian free speech theory while applying that theory narrowly in the case, Brennan ruled that the expression of certain sexual ideas can be "excludable [from constitutional protection] because they encroach upon the limited area of more important interests," and he relied on how "implicit in the history of the First Amendment is the rejection of obscenity as utterly without redeeming social importance."[100] For the majority, Brennan upheld convictions for mailing or selling sexually oriented books, photographs, and magazines. Although *Roth* narrowed the obscenity category of unprotected expression, it maintained that obscenity was unprotected by the First Amendment, effectively ignoring free speech protections based on personal autonomy, falling short of *On Liberty*'s standard.[101] During the same term that the Supreme Court decided *Roth*, it upheld government restrictions on obscenity possession in several cases, although the justices did begin overturning obscenity convictions on various grounds in the late 1950s and early 1960s.[102]

Justice Douglas's dissent (joined by Justice Black) articulated various concerns he had with the *Roth* obscenity standard, many of which reflected Millian themes. Douglas scolded his colleagues for agreeing to a standard that could easily result in morality-based majority tyranny: "Any test that turns on what is offensive to the community's standards is too loose, too capricious, too destructive of freedom of expression to be squared with the First Amendment."[103] Douglas continued: "Under that test, juries can censor, suppress, and punish what they don't like, provided the matter relates to 'sexual impurity' or has a tendency 'to excite lustful thoughts.' This is community censorship in one of its worst forms. It creates a regime where, in the battle between the literati and the Philistines, the Philistines are certain to win."[104] Underscoring the Millian theme that expression should not be banned because it is deemed immoral, Douglas wrote, "If the First Amendment guarantee of freedom of speech and press is to mean anything in this field, it must allow protests even against the moral code that the standard of the day sets for the community. In other words, literature should not be suppressed merely because it offends the moral code of the censor."[105] Douglas used the same absolutist thinking that Mill proclaimed in *On Liberty*: "The First Amendment, its prohibition in terms absolute, was designed to preclude courts as well as legislatures from weighing the values of speech against silence. The First Amendment puts free speech in the preferred position."[106] Douglas concluded, "Freedom of expression can be suppressed if . . . it is so closely brigaded with illegal action as to be an inseparable part of it. . . . I have the same confidence in the ability of our people to reject noxious literature as I have in their capacity to sort out the true from the false in theology, economics, politics, or any other field."[107] As Mill rhetorically asked in *On Liberty*, "Who can compute what the world loses in the multitude of promising intellects combined with timid characters, who dare not follow out any bold, vigorous, independent train of thought, lest it should land them in something which would admit of being considered irreligious or immoral?"[108] Even though Douglas's views were confined to a dissenting opinion, with some espousal of Millian thought by Brennan's opinion of the Court, Mill's influence among the justices was again rising.

With a growing contingent of justices accepting Millian thought, during the late 1950s and early 1960s the Supreme Court issued some rulings that were more protective of the freedom of expression, but also standards (like the obscenity test in *Roth*) that fell short of Mill's vision in *On Liberty* or the jurisprudence articulated by Holmes, Brandeis, and Hughes. This inconsistency was true for the expressive rights of union members and state regulation of movies, where the Supreme Court oscillated, sometimes adopting a libertarian Millian position and sometimes retreating to the Blackstonian position.[109] In other areas, the Supreme Court took a Millian position more consistently, including in cases where the defendant had criticized the judicial system or protested racial segregation.[110]

As encouraging as some of these decisions were, into the early 1960s the Supreme Court was largely still upholding government attempts to suppress the views of those deemed subversives, including requiring them to testify about their views in front of legislative bodies and take loyalty oaths. While the Supreme Court was using the clear and present danger test in the cases where Millian justices like Black or Douglas could command a majority, in cases involving communist expression, the Cold War Supreme Court was still very deferential to government regulation, often upholding convictions through the use of a vague balancing test, similar to what the Supreme Court did in *Dennis*.[111] Nowhere was this more apparent than in *Barenblatt v. United*

States (1959), where a 5–4 majority sustained the contempt conviction of Lloyd Barenblatt, a Vassar College psychology instructor, after he objected to questions by the House Un-American Activities Committee (HUAC) asking if he had ever been a member of the Communist Party. Justice John Marshall Harlan II wrote for the majority, explaining a distinctly non-Millian approach to the freedom of expression: "Where First Amendment rights are asserted to bar governmental interrogation, resolution of the issue always involves a balancing by the courts of the competing private and public interests at stake in the particular circumstances shown."[112] Similar to Justice Jackson, Justice Harlan held that the rules were different because of the views expressed: "This Court in its constitutional adjudications has consistently refused to view the Communist Party as an ordinary political party, and has upheld federal legislation aimed at the Communist problem which in a different context would certainly have raised constitutional issues of the gravest character."[113] Harlan held firm on this position, even though the activity being investigated was teaching and advocacy: "We think that investigatory power in this domain is not to be denied Congress solely because the field of education is involved."[114] The Supreme Court determined in *Barenblatt* that since Congress possessed power to investigate communist activity, the balance was in favor of the government, and the First Amendment was not violated.[115] Clearly, when it came to communist expressive activities, the Supreme Court in the 1950s applied a different, non-Millian approach.

Appealing to Millian themes, Justice Black offered a stinging dissent in *Barenblatt*. He decried the majority's reliance on "a balancing test to decide if First Amendment rights shall be protected," concluding, "I do not agree that laws directly abridging First Amendment freedoms can be justified by a congressional or judicial balancing process."[116] Black challenged the idea that views could be silenced because someone interpreted them as detrimental to national security: "I cannot agree with the Court's notion that First Amendment freedoms must be abridged in order to 'preserve' our country. That notion rests on the unarticulated premise that this Nation's security hangs upon its power to punish people because of what they think, speak or write about, or because of those with whom they associate for political purposes."[117] Black distinguished the freedom that must be protected in a democratic society versus one that is autocratic: "Despotic governments cannot exist without stifling the voice of opposition to their oppressive practices. The First Amendment means . . . that the only constitutional way our Government can preserve itself is to leave its people the fullest possible freedom to praise, criticize or discuss, as they see fit, all governmental policies and to suggest, if they desire, that even its most fundamental postulates are bad and should be changed."[118]

There is similarity between this and what Mill wrote in *On Liberty*, when he argued that the rule of despotism was a mark of barbarism, but that advanced societies adopt democratic rule and a willingness to discuss ideas: "As soon as mankind have attained the capacity of being guided to their own improvement by conviction or persuasion . . . compulsion, either in the direct form or in that of pains and penalties for non-compliance, is no longer admissible as a means to their own good, and justifiable only for the security of others."[119] For Mill, actual security concerns would justify restricting speech (e.g., exciting a mob assembled outside the home of the corn dealer), but positing ideas, even purportedly "dangerous" ones, should be protected if they are advanced for the purpose of discussion and debate.[120] Or, as Black put it in *Barenblatt*, "Our Constitution assumes that the common sense of the people and their attachment to our country will enable them, after free discussion, to withstand ideas that are wrong."[121]

Notably, in *Barenblatt*, Black cited Mill's *On Liberty* at two points in his dissent. First, Black cataloged historical instances of those in power in the United States persecuting what government deemed to be subversive views, including the passage of the Alien and Sedition Acts in the 1790s, attacks on Masons in the 1830s, antebellum hatred toward abolitionists, and legislative efforts to suspend duly elected socialists in the 1920s.[122] In summarizing these tragedies, Black referenced *On Liberty* to support the point that "history should teach us then, that in times of high emotional excitement minority parties and groups which advocate extremely unpopular social or governmental innovations will always be typed as criminal gangs and attempts will always be made to drive them out."[123] The passage Black cited from *On Liberty* is a footnote where Mill stated that "there ought to exist the fullest liberty of professing and discussing, as a matter of ethical conviction, any doctrine, however immoral it may be considered," with Mill asserting about tyrannicide that "the instigation to it, in a specific case, may be a proper subject of punishment, but only if an overt act has followed, and at least a probable connection can be established between the act and the instigation."[124]

Black cited *On Liberty* in another *Barrenblatt* footnote, this time for the proposition that "sincerity and patriotism do not, unfortunately, insure against unconstitutional acts. Indeed, some of the most lamentable and tragic deaths of history were instigated by able, patriotic and sincere men."[125] Mill used the executions of Socrates and Jesus Christ as examples to prove the need to protect the freedom of expression, as both men were sentenced to death for the blasphemous ideas they expressed, and, as explained by Mill, in both cases the executions were carried out by those who thought they were doing good: "These were, to all appearance, not bad men . . . but rather the contrary; men who possessed in a full, or somewhat more than a full measure, the religious, moral, and patriotic feelings of their time and people."[126] Thus, Black explicitly connected his understanding of First Amendment freedoms to Mill's *On Liberty*. However, these exhortations to Mill and citations to *On Liberty* fell one vote short of convincing the Supreme Court. Also dissenting in *Barenblatt* were Chief Justice Warren and Justices Douglas and Brennan.

These four dissenters' convictions notwithstanding, the Supreme Court continued to uphold most contempt convictions for refusing to testify and most loyalty oaths against communists and others deemed subversive in the late 1950s and early 1960s, usually in 5–4 decisions.[127] For instance, in *Konigsberg v. State Bar of California* (1961), by a vote of 5–4 the Supreme Court used another balancing test to uphold the exclusion from the California bar of an attorney who refused to say whether he was a member of the Communist Party. In his opinion of the Court, Justice Harlan declared, "We reject the view that freedom of speech and association, as protected by the First and Fourteenth Amendments, are 'absolutes.'"[128] Harlan explained that in addition to categories of expression like fighting words and obscenity that are outside of First Amendment protection, laws regulating expression have been upheld "when they have been found justified by subordinating valid governmental interests, a prerequisite to constitutionality which has necessarily involved a weighing of the governmental interest involved."[129]

In his *Konigsberg* dissent, Justice Black took a Millian approach, emphasizing "the First Amendment's unequivocal command that there shall be no abridgment of the rights of free speech and assembly" before citing Holmes and Brandeis:

> The Court attempts to justify its refusal to apply the plain mandate of the First Amendment in part by reference to the so-called "clear and present danger test" forcefully used by Mr. Justice Holmes and Mr. Justice Brandeis, not to narrow but to broaden the then prevailing interpretation of First Amendment freedoms. I think very little can be found in anything they ever said that would provide support for the "balancing test" presently in use. Indeed, the idea of "balancing" away First Amendment freedoms appears to me to be wholly inconsistent with the view, strongly espoused by Justices Holmes and Brandeis, that the best test of truth is the power of the thought to get itself accepted in the competition of the market. The "clear and present danger test" was urged as consistent with this view in that it protected speech in all cases except those in which danger was so imminent that there was no time for rational discussion.[130]

Black emphasized core themes used by Mill, Holmes, and Brandeis, including protecting the freedom of expression as a path to finding truth, relying on the marketplace of ideas, and restricting expression only if there is imminent threat of harm. As for the Supreme Court's employment of a balancing test, Black argued that it "rests upon the notion that some ideas are so dangerous that Government need not restrict itself to contrary arguments as a means of opposing them even where there is ample time to do so."[131] After stressing the Millian notion that we must allow for discussion of all ideas unless there is threat of immediate harm, Black admitted that the clear and present danger test no longer protected as much expression as he believed should be the case, even if it did advance protections of free expression more than had been the case earlier.[132] Instead, Black advocated an absolutist approach to expression, which is similar to Mill in *On Liberty*, where he used absolutist language.[133]

In *Scales v. United States* (1961), a 5–4 majority upheld the Smith Act conviction of Julius Scales for being a member of the Communist Party. Justice Harlan's majority opinion dismissively announced that "little remains to be said concerning the claim that the statute infringes First Amendment freedoms. It was settled in *Dennis* that the advocacy with which we are here concerned is not constitutionally protected speech."[134] But as Justice Black observed in dissent, the majority was far from the more Millian approach he advocated: "The Court relies upon its prior decisions to the effect that the Government has power to abridge speech and assembly if its interest in doing so is sufficient to outweigh the interest in protecting these First Amendment freedoms."[135] Just as Mill thought anything short of his standard of protection would unduly restrict expressive rights, Black in *Scales* believed that "this case re-emphasizes the freedom-destroying nature of the 'balancing test' presently in use by the Court."[136]

Justice Douglas also targeted the Supreme Court's retraction from vigilantly protecting these rights in *Scales*, commenting that upholding the Smith Act, "legalize[s] today guilt by association, sending a man to prison when he committed no unlawful act."[137] Mill supported protection for associational rights no less than the freedom of speech—and thought the two rights are inextricably linked—because "voluntary associations" provide for "varied experiments and endless diversity of experience" from which one can learn.[138] After citing Millian authorities—including *Barnette*, Charles Evans Hughes, and Zechariah Chafee—Douglas explained that "in recent years we have been departing . . . from the theory of government expressed in the First Amendment. We have too often been 'balancing' the right of speech and association against other values in society to see if we, the judges, feel that a particular need is more important than those guaranteed by the Bill of Rights."[139] Mill advocated for a standard more protective of expression than balancing, requiring a threat of imminent violence to suppress speech. It is particularly problematic from a Millian standpoint that the speech of communists was repeatedly suppressed in the 1950s and early 1960s: the communists prosecuted in these cases were essentially asserting the claim that "private property is robbery," something Mill specified should be protected expression unless it is "delivered orally to an excited mob" outside the house of a corn dealer.[140]

Even in the handful of contempt and loyalty oath convictions overturned during this period, a majority of justices employed something other than a Millian approach by upholding the constitutionality of the Smith Act.[141] Thus, in the early 1960s, the Supreme Court majority was still where it was in the early 1950s, far from the views expressed by Holmes and Brandeis in the 1920s and by Hughes and other justices in the 1930s. However, Black and Douglas consistently maintained that philosophy in dissent, citing key 1920s dissents and Supreme Court majority opinions from the 1930s and 1940s. By the latter 1950s, Black and Douglas were frequently joined by Warren and Brennan in dissent. Black remained particularly absolutist in his free speech jurisprudence, putting him perhaps closest to Mill's philosophy of justices who served during this era. In 1962, Black was interviewed about his understanding of the freedom of expression: "The beginning of the First Amendment is that 'Congress shall make no law.' I understand that it is rather old-fashioned and shows a slight naivete to say that 'no law' means no law. It is one of the most amazing things about the ingeniousness of the times that strong arguments are made, which *almost* convince me, that it is very foolish of me to think 'no law' means no law. But what it *says* is 'Congress shall make no law.' . . . I believe [the Amendment] means what it says."[142] Such absolutism—although also stemming from a textualist understanding of the First Amendment—reflects Mill's proclamation that we are entitled to "absolute freedom of opinion and sentiment on all subjects, practical or speculative, scientific, moral, or theological."[143] Black was the first Supreme Court justice to favorably cite *On Liberty* in a First Amendment opinion (in his *Barenblatt* dissent). Black spent years with Douglas, and then Warren and Brennan, dissenting on these questions, but things were about to change. By the mid-1960s, just as Cold War tensions were starting to ease internationally, the Supreme Court was on the cusp of returning to the more Millian First Amendment heritage that it had proclaimed decades earlier. The older Blackstonian precedents were about to be overruled, and the Supreme Court would take a dramatic Millian trajectory, even in cases involving communism and sexually oriented expression.

CHAPTER 6

Imminent Lawless Action

The Latter Warren Court Moves toward Mill on Free Speech

Felix Frankfurter's retirement in 1962 was a watershed moment for the Supreme Court's free speech jurisprudence. Outside of his *Baumgardner* opinion, Frankfurter espoused something quite different from Mill's understanding of free speech. Frankfurter regularly deferred to government power over expression. His animus toward the preferred freedoms doctrine in *Kovacs v. Cooper* arrested the Millian philosophy advanced by the Hughes and Stone Courts.[1] With his departure, the Supreme Court was poised to become more Millian on First Amendment questions. After the appointment of Arthur Goldberg, five justices—including Black, Douglas, Warren, and Brennan—routinely applied a Millian approach to important expression questions. Brennan embraced this philosophy more than in the past. This shift on the Supreme Court was spurred on by cases on civil rights protests and a thaw in Cold War relations. In the 1960s, the Supreme Court came full circle on incitement, finally adopting the Mill-Holmes-Brandeis standard. This movement toward Mill narrowed the definitions of multiple categories of unprotected speech (including libel and obscenity), protected offensive speech, and safeguarded speech by public employees. While the justices did not fully adopt Millian theory at the end of the Warren Court, it moved further in that direction than even the Hughes and Stone Courts.

Multiple cases in the mid-1960s demonstrated that the Supreme Court had begun to shift back toward Mill on free expression cases involving civil rights.[2]

NAACP v. Button (1963) overturned a Virginia law that broadened the definition of solicitation, with the law aiming to restrict the ability of civil rights organizations to seek clients challenging racial segregation. As Justice Brennan wrote for a 6–3 majority in *Button*, "The Constitution protects expression and association without regard to the race, creed, or political or religious affiliation of the members of the group which invokes its shield, or to the truth, popularity, or social utility of the ideas and beliefs which are offered."[3] Brennan declared that "abstract discussion is not the only species of communication which the Constitution protects; the First Amendment also protects vigorous advocacy, certainly of lawful ends, against governmental intrusion."[4]

This was a crucial evolution of the Supreme Court's understanding of free expression. Mill contended that rights are not simply dictates from pure reason or divine fiat but rather are justified by the role they play in an individual's life. Mill understood the freedom of speech as a fundamental right because it not only permits one to explore what is right and wrong; it is also the foundation from which one can decide which actions to pursue in life.[5] Mill argued that freedom of expression is the foundation of a constellation of rights designed to allow for human flourishing. In particular, Mill advocated the right to live in accordance with the ideas expressed in a society that embraced freedom of speech.[6] As Mill stated in *On Liberty*, if one "refrains from molesting others in what concerns them, and merely acts according to his own inclination and judgment in things which concern himself, the same reasons which show that opinion should be free prove also that he should be allowed, without molestation, to carry his opinions into practice."[7] This same sentiment by Brennan went against earlier Supreme Court decisions that protected discussion of abstract ideas but not advocacy.[8] Instead, Brennan's opinion in *Button* recalled the more Millian decisions of the preferred freedoms era, quoting *Thomas v. Collins* to explain that "'free trade in ideas' means free trade in the opportunity to persuade to action, not merely to describe facts."[9] Like Mill, Brennan proclaimed that speech restrictions must be narrow and specifically tailored: "Broad prophylactic rules in the area of free expression are suspect."[10] *Button* rejected not only Blackstone's theory of expression but also the middle position of Meiklejohn, who argued in *Free Speech and Its Relation to Self-Government* that the First Amendment did *not* protect either "a merchant advertising his wares" or "a paid lobbyist fighting for the advantage of his client."[11] A lawyer soliciting business and then working on behalf of a client would fall into these categories, so by overturning the law, the Supreme Court was showing preference for Mill over Meiklejohn.

Civil rights were also at the center of the Supreme Court's foundational libel decision, *New York Times v. Sullivan* (1964), with Justice Brennan's opinion of the Court containing a great deal of Millian rhetoric. Sullivan, the police commissioner in Montgomery, Alabama, sued the *New York Times* for an advertisement titled "Heed Their Rising Voices." The ad detailed a civil rights protest that was suppressed by Montgomery police; the ad was largely true, but there were some minor factual errors, including an allegation that the protestors sang "My Country 'Tis of Thee," when they actually sang the national anthem. Sullivan won a $500,000 jury award against the *Times* in Alabama state court. Brennan reversed the decision for a unanimous Supreme Court, declaring that "debate on public issues should be uninhibited, robust, and wide-open, and that it may well include vehement, caustic, and sometimes unpleasantly sharp attacks on government and public officials."[12] In emphasizing the need for the marketplace of ideas, not government, to determine truth, Brennan wrote that "authoritative interpretations of the First Amendment guarantees have consistently refused to recognize an exception for any test of truth—whether administered by judges, juries, or administrative officials."[13] In Millian fashion, Brennan reasoned that "erroneous statement is inevitable in free debate, and . . . it must be protected if the freedoms of expression are to have the 'breathing space' that they 'need . . . to survive.'"[14] To Mill's point that often statements contain both truth and falsity, Brennan explained that the First Amendment protects expression "even though the utterance contains 'half-truths' and 'misinformation.'"[15] He made the Millian connection between protecting false speech and ensuring true speech could emerge when he reasoned that libel law must protect more than just true expression, or else a chilling effect would emerge: "Allowance of the defense of truth, with the burden of proving it on the defendant, does not mean that only false speech will be deterred."[16]

To defend his Millian interpretation of the First Amendment, Brennan cited and quoted Mill's *On Liberty* in two footnotes in *Sullivan*. First, Brennan quoted this passage by Mill: "To argue sophistically, to suppress facts or arguments, to misstate the elements of the case, or misrepresent the opposite opinion . . . all this, even to the most aggravated degree, is so continually done in perfect good faith, by persons who are not considered, and in many other respects may not deserve to be considered, ignorant or incompetent, that it is rarely possible, on adequate grounds, conscientiously to stamp the misrepresentation as morally culpable; and still less could law presume to interfere with this kind of controversial misconduct."[17] Brennan then reasoned as follows, again quoting *On Liberty*: "Even a false statement may be deemed to make a valuable contribution to public debate, since it brings about 'the clearer perception and livelier impression of truth, produced by its collision with error.'"[18] Although Mill was arguing in these passages about the need to debate opinions and beliefs, not facts, Brennan applied Mill's arguments to facts that are deployed in discussions about beliefs and opinions—in this case, facts used in an appeal for civil rights.[19] With this understanding of free expression, Brennan held for the Supreme Court the standard for libel in cases involving public officials: "The constitutional guarantees require, we think, a federal rule that prohibits a public official from recovering damages for a defamatory falsehood relating to his official conduct unless he proves that the statement was made with 'actual malice'—that is, with knowledge that it was false or with reckless disregard of whether it was false or not."[20] Ensuring citizens can criticize their government is something Mill would have lauded as a positive development.[21] Mill was a longtime critic of overly burdensome libel laws, as was his father, James Mill.[22] Brennan's arguments and quotations from *On Liberty* make *Sullivan* one of the most Millian Supreme Court opinions.

One could argue that Brennan's *Sullivan* opinion was influenced by Alexander Meiklejohn. In a prominent 1965 *Harvard Law Review* article titled "The Supreme Court and the Meiklejohn Interpretation of the First Amendment," Brennan wrote that *Sullivan* "presented a classic example of an activity that Dr. Meiklejohn called an activity of 'governing importance' within the powers reserved to the people and made invulnerable to sanctions imposed by their agency-governments."[23] Brennan stated of *Sullivan*'s lack of protection for false statements made with actual malice that Meiklejohn "might have approved that qualification."[24] Although Meiklejohn clearly had some influence over the Supreme Court, as proven by Frankfurter and Jackson's *Dennis* concurrences, Brennan's discussion of Meiklejohn in his *Harvard Law Review* article is not evidence that Brennan was influenced by Meiklejohn in any significant way in *Sullivan*. First, the article was based on a lecture Brennan gave on April 14, 1965, at Brown University; its title was the "Alexander Meiklejohn Lecture."[25] Meiklejohn, who earned his undergraduate degree from Brown before serving on the faculty and as a dean at Brown, died on December 17, 1964.[26] Thus, Brennan's article was based on a lecture that served as something of a memorial speech for Meiklejohn at the deceased's alma mater, rather than an after-the-fact explanation of who had influenced the Supreme Court's *Sullivan* decision. Brennan's equivocal statement that Meiklejohn "*might* have approved" of what the Supreme Court decided in *Sullivan* reflects this.[27] Furthermore, Brennan's discussion of Meiklejohn regarding *Sullivan* was to contrast Meiklejohn's views not with Mill's but with those held more broadly by Justice Black.[28] Mill, like Meiklejohn, thought it important to protect speech integral to self-government, in addition to wanting to protect it as a means to truth and to further personal autonomy. Brennan did not cite or quote Meiklejohn in his *Sullivan* opinion, instead citing and quoting Mill, whose philosophy was evident throughout the opinion. In these ways, Brennan's *Sullivan* opinion reflects Millian thought, even if Brennan had clearly read Meiklejohn's book, too.

Indeed, with his opinion of the Court in *Sullivan*, Brennan joined the pantheon of justices—including Holmes, Brandeis, Hughes, Black, and Douglas—with a direct connection to Mill and the freedom of expression. Brennan reasoned, like Mill, that truth, democratic self-government, and autonomy are best achieved by preventing the government from regulating the expression of ideas.[29] Brennan shifted over his career from a more paternalistic understanding of the freedom of expression to a more libertarian one, which included acceptance of Millian protection of free speech.[30] The next year, Brennan made the first use of the phrase "marketplace of ideas" (with "marketplace" written as one word, as opposed to two) in a justice's opinion, concurring in *Lamont v. Postmaster General* (1965): "The dissemination of ideas can accomplish nothing if otherwise willing addressees are not free to receive and consider them. It would be a barren marketplace of ideas that had only sellers and no buyers."[31] The use of "marketplace of ideas" is now a well-accepted phrase in the Supreme Court's free speech jurisprudence, and it reflects Holmes's phraseology of "free trade in ideas" and "competition of the market" that he used to encapsulate Millian thought in his *Abrams* dissent.[32]

Nevertheless, Brennan's establishment of the actual malice standard in *Sullivan* did not go far enough for some of his colleagues. Black, joined by Douglas, declared that the actual malice standard restricted too much expression, arguing instead that "the *Times* and the individual defendants had an absolute, unconditional constitutional right to publish in the *Times* advertisement their criticisms of the Montgomery agencies and officials."[33] According to Black, even narrowly drawn libel laws allowed for the threat of public officials using civil suits to silence their critics.[34] The only way to prevent this "deadly danger to the press" was "by granting the press an absolute immunity for criticism of the way public officials do their public duty."[35] Likewise, Goldberg was joined by Douglas in averring that "the First and Fourteenth Amendments to the Constitution afford to the citizen and to the press an absolute, unconditional privilege to criticize official conduct despite the harm which may flow from excesses and abuses."[36] As Goldberg argued, "That the Constitution affords the citizen and the press an absolute privilege for criticism of official conduct does not leave the public official without defenses against unsubstantiated opinions or deliberate misstatements," because public officials can use their own freedom of expression to communicate with other media outlets, who in turn can use their freedom of the press to publish the truth.[37] Thus, three justices embraced Mill as much as, if not more than, Brennan in *Sullivan*.[38]

Sullivan represented a major step toward Mill's admonition that we possess "absolute freedom of opinion and sentiment on all subjects, practical or speculative, scientific, moral, or theological," with respect to expression about public officials.[39] Given that southern politicians had filed additional libel lawsuits against major media outlets for their reporting on civil rights demonstrations, *Sullivan* represented another Millian proposition: the legal system should not be used to suppress expression or reporting on government.[40] This helps explain why Mill was an opponent of overly burdensome libel laws, especially when utilized by government officials. Throughout the remainder of the Warren Court, the justices continued narrowing the definition of libel, strengthening expressive protections.[41] This built a consequentialist jurisprudence by protecting the press's ability to engage in criticism of public officials and public figures.[42] And it followed the utilitarian John Stuart Mill, who believed that protecting free expression promoted democracy.[43]

Another area of First Amendment jurisprudence where the justices took an increasingly Millian turn in the 1960s was obscenity and sexually oriented expression. Brennan again emerged as the Millian leader, authoring several Supreme Court opinions on this subject after *Roth*. It began with *Jacobellis v. Ohio* (1964), where six justices overturned the conviction of a movie theater manager for showing the French film *The Lovers*, which the state had deemed obscene. Writing a plurality opinion, Justice Brennan affirmed that "motion pictures are within the ambit of the constitutional guarantees of freedom of speech and of the press," thus continuing adherence to *Burstyn* and *not* returning to the non-Millian *Mutual Film Corp.* decision.[44] Brennan's opinion in *Jacobellis* specifically upheld the *Roth* standard, itself a move toward a Millian vision on free expression.[45] Brennan's overturning of the conviction in *Jacobellis* moved closer toward Mill, as it confirmed that local authorities could not impose their own definition(s) of obscenity: "The constitutional status of an allegedly obscene work must be determined on the basis of a national standard."[46] Brennan explained the reasoning behind requiring a national standard and not permitting enforcement of local moral norms:

> It can hardly be assumed that all the patrons of a particular library, bookstand, or motion picture theater are residents of the smallest local "community" that can be drawn around that establishment. Furthermore, to sustain the suppression of a particular book or film in one locality would deter its dissemination in other localities where it might be held not obscene, since sellers and exhibitors would be reluctant to risk criminal conviction in testing the variation between the two places. It

would be a hardy person who would sell a book or exhibit a film any-
where in the land after this Court had sustained the judgment of one
"community" holding it to be outside the constitutional protection.[47]

Brennan's focus on eschewing power of local officials to control what ideas
can be expressed in their community incorporates an important Millian idea.
In *On Liberty*, Mill decried local "despotism of custom" as "the standing hindrance to human advancement" that is promoted by "the spirit of liberty."[48]
The *Jacobellis* case also began to emphasize some language from *Roth* that did
not previously appear to be a part of the obscenity test; in *Jacobellis*, Brennan
highlighted that "a work cannot be proscribed unless it is 'utterly' without social importance."[49] This altered how lower courts understood the *Roth* test,
and its refocusing protected more sexually oriented expression.[50]

Several other justices in *Jacobellis* showed their affinity for a libertarian approach to obscenity.[51] But the three justices who dissented in *Jacobellis* were
willing to uphold local burdens on expression, which showed that not all justices were fully embracing Mill's philosophy. Nevertheless, in the mid-1960s
the Supreme Court was shifting toward Mill on obscenity, which was evident
in several other cases.[52] In particular, the Supreme Court's change to its obscenity test in *Jacobellis* and *Memoirs v. Massachusetts* (1966), that a "book cannot be proscribed unless it is found to be *utterly* without redeeming social
value," moved the Supreme Court closer to Mill.[53] This new emphasis would
expand the protections for sexually oriented expression over the next few
years.[54] True to form, though, in a concurrence, Douglas took the more Millian position on the issue in *Memoirs*: "The First Amendment, written in terms
that are absolute, deprives the States of any power to pass on the value, the
propriety, or the morality of a particular expression."[55]

Although not every obscenity case decided by the Supreme Court during
this era included a majority or plurality of justices applying more Millian principles, by the late 1960s, the Supreme Court was trending toward a Millian position on obscenity.[56] This was most evident in *Redrup v. New York* (1967), where
the Supreme Court overturned the conviction of a newsstand clerk who was
arrested for selling two books, *Lust Pool* and *Shame Agent*, to an undercover police officer.[57] In a short per curiam opinion, the Supreme Court explained that
the justices have adhered to different standards for judging obscenity, ranging
from Black's and Douglas's absolutism to the *Roth-Memoirs* test.[58] According
to the Supreme Court, under none of these tests were the materials in the case
obscene. The opinion in *Redrup* noted that there was not "a specific and limited
state concern for juveniles," "any suggestion of an assault upon individual privacy so obtrusive as to make it impossible for an unwilling individual to avoid

exposure to it," or "evidence of . . . 'pandering.'"[59] Thus, short of material that involved minors or that was invasive into a nonconsenting person's home or life, the Supreme Court held that sexually oriented expressions involving consenting adults were constitutionally protected. Including *Redrup*, the Supreme Court summarily reversed thirty-two obscenity convictions over the next several years, bringing the Supreme Court very close to Mill's libertarianism on this subject.[60] Furthermore, this decision was motivated by an understanding of the importance of freedom of expression in "experiments of living" according to the harm principle and an acknowledgment of the Millian ideal that citizens ought to be free to live according to their own moral and aesthetic standards. Rather than deferring to local notions of morality, the Supreme Court's approach to obscenity reflected personal autonomy, where expression was protected unless it involved children or nonconsenting adults.

Where the Supreme Court upheld a conviction in the late 1960s involving sexually oriented expression, in *Ginsberg v. New York* (1968), the justices did so because it involved minors. Justice Brennan wrote for the Supreme Court, sustaining the conviction of a store owner who sold nonobscene pornographic magazines to a sixteen-year-old boy, because "it was not irrational for the legislature to find that exposure to material condemned by the statute is harmful to minors."[61] As elaborated by Brennan, "the well-being of its children is of course a subject within the State's constitutional power to regulate," and "the State has an interest to protect the welfare of children and to see that they are safeguarded from abuses which might prevent their growth into free and independent well-developed men and citizens."[62] Brennan limited minors' access to certain sexually explicit materials for their own well-being. The Supreme Court found expressive activity that was not protected by the First Amendment, but it did so by relying on one of Mill's well-known caveats to the harm principle: children's freedoms can be restricted for their own personal good and long-term development into fully functioning, free adults.[63]

This more Millian approach was evident in the mid- to late 1960s when the Supreme Court examined restrictions on films generally.[64] In *Interstate Circuit v. Dallas* (1968), Justice Thurgood Marshall wrote for eight of the nine justices, striking down a film censorship ordinance for being unconstitutionally vague in determining if a movie was "not suitable for young persons."[65] Marshall, like Brennan in *Jacobellis*, affirmed in *Interstate Circuit* the *Burstyn* precedent: "Motion pictures are, of course, protected by the First Amendment."[66] In finding the law was too vague, Marshall accepted Mill's notion that full expressive rights do not apply to minors, writing that "a State may regulate the dissemination to juveniles of, and their access to, material objectionable as to them, but which a State clearly could not regulate as to adults."[67] However,

Marshall also affirmed that minors have some expressive rights: "It is . . . essential that legislation aimed at protecting children from allegedly harmful expression—no less than legislation enacted with respect to adults—be clearly drawn and that the standards adopted be reasonably precise so that those who are governed by the law and those that administer it will understand its meaning and application."[68] Mill believed that rights apply to a lesser degree for the young: "Those who are still in a state to require being taken care of by others must be protected against their own actions as well as against external injury."[69] Mill thought these freedoms could apply to minors to a lesser degree, to protect minors from harm; beyond that, there is no evidence in *On Liberty* that Mill thought the state should possess power to continually take *all* rights away from the young.[70] The Supreme Court's decision in *Interstate Circuit* was Millian, finding that expressive rights can be restricted more for minors, but they cannot be abolished altogether.

As US-Soviet relations began to thaw in the mid-1960s, the Supreme Court's position on communist expression and loyalty oaths also became more libertarian.[71] Unlike in the 1950s and early 1960s, when it consistently upheld loyalty oaths for public employees, the Supreme Court by the mid- to late 1960s was consistently striking them down.[72] The Supreme Court ruled that loyalty oaths were particularly troublesome for university instructors, finding that such requirements trampled on academic freedom. In *Keyishian v. Board of Regents* (1967), a 5–4 Supreme Court held unconstitutional a loyalty oath requiring public university instructors to affirm that they were not members of the Communist Party. Justice Brennan wrote for the majority that "academic freedom . . . is of transcendent value to all of us and not merely to the teachers concerned. That freedom is therefore a special concern of the First Amendment, which does not tolerate laws that cast a pall of orthodoxy over the classroom."[73] Making use of the "marketplace of ideas" phrase for the first time in a majority opinion of the Supreme Court, Brennan explained for his colleagues that "the classroom is peculiarly the 'marketplace of ideas.' The Nation's future depends upon leaders trained through wide exposure to that robust exchange of ideas which discovers truth out of a multitude of tongues, [rather] than through any kind of authoritative selection."[74] Brennan described how the loyalty oath law's "stifling effect on the academic mind from curtailing freedom of association . . . is manifest."[75]

Brennan again channeled Mill, in his consequentialist protection for free expression rights to produce benefits for all of society. His repeated use of the "marketplace of ideas" analogy placed him squarely in the Millian tradition ushered into First Amendment jurisprudence by Holmes. Brennan's eschewing of convention dictating what can be discussed is quite similar to Mill's rebuke of a "ban placed on all inquiry which does not end in the orthodox conclusions" that was applied to heretics.[76] Regarding teachers, Mill was strongly committed to the free exchange of ideas in the classroom, as Mill noted that it is not a "fair means" for those opposing progress to be "silencing teachers."[77] Furthermore, Mill fought against accepting dogma as truth, and he thought that teachers need freedom to explore different ideas to adequately reveal to their students varying perspectives: "If the teachers of mankind are to be cognizant of all that they ought to know, everything must be free to be written and published without restraint."[78] Thus, through Justice Brennan the Supreme Court was espousing a Millian perspective in *Keyishian*.

These loyalty oath cases, whether decided on freedom of association or freedom of speech grounds, collectively demonstrated a willingness to protect the First Amendment rights of those with subversive views. As much as Mill himself stated in *On Liberty* that a person's freedom may be restricted if one "disables himself, by conduct purely self-regarding, from the performance of some definite duty incumbent on him to the public," Mill clarified that these restrictions apply only if "there is a definite damage, or a definite risk of damage, either to an individual or to the public."[79] The Supreme Court majority in cases like *Keyishian* affirmed that joining with others to carry into action subversive views might not be protected for public employees under narrow circumstances, but simply holding those views should not disqualify one from service as a public employee, and the illegal subversive activity had to be specifically and narrowly defined by the government.[80]

The Supreme Court by the late 1960s was interpreting greater free expression rights for public employees outside of the loyalty oath context. This was most prominent in *Pickering v. Board of Education* (1968), where the justices held that the First Amendment was violated when a school district fired a teacher for his letter to the editor criticizing the relative allocation of funding for athletic programs and classroom instruction. Justice Marshall explained for an 8-1 majority, quoting from *Keyishian*, that even though "the State has interests as an employer in regulating the speech of its employees that differ significantly from those it possesses in connection with regulation of the speech of the citizenry in general . . . the theory that public employment which may be denied altogether may be subjected to any conditions, regardless of how unreasonable, has been uniformly rejected."[81] Like Brennan in *Keyishian*, Marshall concluded for the Supreme Court in *Pickering* that the protection of an individual public employee's autonomy served a greater good, as he emphasized that there was a "public interest in having free and unhindered debate on matters of public importance," which is "the core value of the Free Speech Clause of the First Amendment."[82] This was relevant in the case, because "teachers are, as a class, the members of a community most likely to have informed and definite opinions as to how funds allotted to the operation of the schools should be spent," which is of importance to the public "in a society that leaves such questions to popular vote."[83] As explained by Marshall, a "teacher's exercise of his right to speak on issues of public importance may not furnish the basis for his dismissal from public employment" because "the threat of dismissal from public employment is . . . a potent means of inhibiting speech."[84]

Even more than *Keyishian*, *Pickering* demonstrated Mill's idea that while a public employee's freedom can be restricted if there would be "definite damage, or a definite risk of damage, either to an individual or to the public," in the absence of such damage, public employees should retain the right—like everyone else—to speak on public matters to help contribute to the pursuit of truth.[85] Indeed, if a public employee speaks on "issues of public importance," that would qualify as Mill's "definite duty incumbent on him to the public." Even if the public employee were mistaken, such speech would cause no "definite damage" and should be protected for what Mill called "the sake of the greater good of human freedom."[86] Protecting teachers' expression furthers individual autonomy, learning how public funds are spent helps the search for truth, and protecting the teacher's editorial in *Pickering* fosters democracy (for the voters who can read the teacher's editorial). Themes Mill argued for appear throughout Marshall's *Pickering* opinion.

In many other cases in the mid to late 1960s, the Supreme Court took a more Millian approach.[87] Admittedly, though, the justices did not find that expression was protected in *every* case in these years.[88] One example was *Adderley v. Florida* (1966), where the Supreme Court upheld by a vote of 5–4 the conviction of university students for protesting the racial segregation of inmates at a county jail; those students were protesting the jail's segregation because other students—who had been arrested for protesting racial segregation—were housed at that jail. The Supreme Court took the anti-Millian stance that this was a simple trespass case, declaring that "the State, no less than a private owner of property, has power to preserve the property under its control for the use to which it is lawfully dedicated."[89] The majority in *Adderley* found no right to protest on the property outside of a county jail. This was reminiscent of Chief Justice White's reasoning in *Davis v. Massachusetts*, where the Supreme Court compared the state's power to control public property to a person's power to control who can enter their house.[90] Writing for four dissenters in *Adderley*, Justice Douglas decried that "by allowing these orderly and civilized protests against injustice to be suppressed, we only increase the forces of frustration which the conditions of second-class citizenship are generating amongst us."[91] For Douglas, "the right to petition for the redress of grievances has an ancient history and is not limited to writing a letter or sending a telegram to a congressman; it is not confined to appearing before the local city council, or writing letters to the President or Governor or Mayor."[92] Similar to Mill's idea that the freedom of expression protects lively and antagonistic protesting (short of inciting "an excited mob assembled before the house of a corn dealer"), Douglas explained that "conventional methods of petitioning may be, and often have been, shut off to large groups of our citizens. . . . Their methods should not be condemned as tactics of obstruction and harassment as long as the assembly and petition are peaceable."[93] This was the heart of Mill's desire to protect personal autonomy: in a free society, individuals must be free to choose what they think will be the most effective ways of communicating their ideas to others. Otherwise, the government will rationalize as illegitimate the methods used by dissidents.

In *United States v. O'Brien* (1968), the Supreme Court also took a narrow view of the freedom of expression by devising a test for symbolic speech test that deferred to the government's regulatory power. The justices did this even though the first free speech claim where a litigant was successful before the Supreme Court was *Stromberg v. California*, which involved flying a flag, where the Supreme Court drew no distinction between the protections for symbolic speech and pure speech.[94] In upholding O'Brien's conviction for burning his draft card while protesting the Vietnam War, the chief justice applied a test weaker than the strong protections advocated by Mill: "A government regulation is sufficiently justified if it is within the constitutional power of the Government; if it furthers an important or substantial governmental interest; if the governmental interest is unrelated to the suppression of free expression; and if the incidental restriction on alleged First Amendment freedoms is no greater than is essential to the furtherance of that interest."[95] Warren, an advocate of Millian views in many other cases in the 1960s, was dismissive of O'Brien's claim, characterizing the prosecution as merely placing "incidental limitations on First Amendment freedoms."[96] Trivializing creative ways to engage in expression of ideas runs counter to Mill's advice in *On Liberty* and Justice Douglas's dissent in *Adderley*. Unsurprisingly, Douglas dissented in *O'Brien* as well.[97] The majority in *O'Brien* included some of the more Millian justices like Black and Brennan. Nevertheless, exceptions like *Adderley* and *O'Brien* aside, by the late 1960s the decisions of the Supreme Court were largely Millian.[98]

Nineteen sixty-nine—the last year of Warren's chief justiceship—was the most Millian year yet on the Supreme Court, serving as a culmination of a more libertarian approach to the freedom of expression in several key areas.[99]

One decision that demonstrated a commitment to Millian principles was *Brandenburg v. Ohio* (1969), where the justices unanimously overturned the syndicalism conviction of a Ku Klux Klan leader who at a rally had used racial slurs, made antisemitic statements, and threatened to take "revengeance" against various federal officials if they continued to promote civil rights. In a brief per curiam opinion, the Supreme Court announced a new test for incitement: "The constitutional guarantees of free speech and free press do not permit a State to forbid or proscribe advocacy of the use of force or of law violation except where such advocacy is directed to inciting or producing imminent lawless action and is likely to incite or produce such action."[100] This sweeping statement, after fifty years of jurisprudence that began with *Schenck*, brought all sitting justices in line with Mill's prescription that expression should be protected unless "the circumstances in which they are expressed are such as to constitute their expression a positive instigation to some mischievous act," as "when delivered orally to an excited mob."[101] *Brandenburg* formally overruled *Whitney v. California*, validating the Millian approach taken by Justice Brandeis in his famous concurrence.[102] By overruling *Whitney*, the justices made it unlikely that a Supreme Court in the future would favorably cite that Blackstonian decision.

The per curiam opinion in *Brandenburg* positively cited earlier Millian decisions, including *DeJonge* and *Stromberg*, that were supported by Holmes, Brandeis, and Hughes.[103] *Brandenburg*'s emphasis on imminence reflected the spirit of the clear and present danger test as used by Holmes and Brandeis in their 1920s dissents, without the same verbiage that had been twisted by the Supreme Court in cases like *Dennis* and *Schenck* to uphold convictions for mere advocacy.[104] *Brandenburg* brought to fruition, more so than ever before, a Millian understanding of free expression.[105] By overturning the clear and present danger test, the Warren Court ensured that this more malleable standard was unavailable for less libertarian justices to misinterpret. In a concurring opinion, Justice Douglas forthrightly made the connection to Mill and those earlier Millian decisions, citing Holmes's free speech opinions eight times and Brandeis's free speech opinions four times.[106] Douglas's concurrence also laid to rest the idea that the clear and present danger test could serve the goals originally laid out by Holmes, as it had been manipulated by the Supreme Court too many times in the past: "I see no place in the regime of the First Amendment for any 'clear and present danger' test, whether strict and tight as some would make it, or free-wheeling as the Court in *Dennis* rephrased it."[107] Douglas used his *Brandenburg* concurrence to opine on the Supreme Court's anti-Millian *O'Brien* decision, which Douglas characterized as being inconsistent with the First Amendment.[108] Douglas closed his concurrence by pithily summarizing the stances held by Mill, Holmes, and Brandeis: "The quality of advocacy turns on the depth of the conviction; and government has no power to invade that sanctuary of belief and conscience."[109]

This Millian approach was also apparent in *Watts v. United States* (1969), where the Supreme Court reversed the conviction of a draft-age man who gave a speech explaining that he would not submit to military conscription, instead insisting, "I am not going. If they ever make me carry a rifle the first man I want to get in my sights is L.B.J."[110] After affirming in a per curiam opinion that an actual threat of violence against the president's life would *not* be protected speech, the Supreme Court determined that "the kind of political hyperbole indulged in by petitioner" is protected expression, as the "language of the political arena . . . is often vituperative, abusive, and inexact."[111] Watts's expression was simply "a kind of very crude offensive method of stating a political opposition to the President."[112] Similarly, Mill wrote in *On Liberty* that "intemperate discussion, namely invective, sarcasm, personality, and the like" should be protected forms of expression.[113] A Millian outcome was achieved in *Watts*, and whichever justice wrote the opinion was using some of the same reasoning as Mill.

Just as he did in *Brandenburg*, Douglas concurred in *Watts*, arguing that the "charge in this case is of an ancient vintage" and recounting that the federal statute Watts was accused of violating originated from an English law that made it illegal to "compass or imagine the Death of . . . the King."[114] Douglas recited cases and laws through five centuries in which hyperbole about the English king—and later, the president of the United States—led to criminal convictions of speakers who, based on the context, had no real intent of attempting to kill their chief executive.[115] Douglas concluded his concurrence: "Suppression of speech as an effective police measure is an old, old device, outlawed by our Constitution."[116] Mill agreed with that sentiment. Mill thought that prosecutions for tyrannicide were just "only if an overt act has followed, and at least a probable connection can be established between the act and the instigation," a position that protects the exaggerated statement uttered by Watts.[117]

In *Street v. New York* (1969), the Supreme Court by a vote of 5–4 overturned Sidney Street's conviction for violating a state law making it a crime to "mutilate, deface, defile, or defy, trample upon, or cast contempt upon either by words or act" the US flag. Street's conviction was based on him stating, "We don't need no damn flag," on hearing about an assassination attempt on James Meredith.[118] Although Street also burned a US flag, it is not clear that he was prosecuted for anything beyond his statement.[119] Justice Harlan wrote for the Supreme Court that the conviction could not stand because "the public

expression of ideas may not be prohibited merely because the ideas are themselves offensive to some of their hearers."[120] Harlan then quoted from the
Millian opinion in *Barnette*: "We have no doubt that the constitutionally guaranteed 'freedom to be intellectually . . . diverse or even contrary,' and the 'right
to differ as to things that touch the heart of the existing order,' encompass the
freedom to express publicly one's opinions about our flag, including those
opinions which are defiant or contemptuous."[121] Harlan concluded that "we
are unable to sustain a conviction that may have rested on a form of expression, however distasteful, which the Constitution tolerates and protects."[122]
Certainly, Mill supported protecting one's ability to express unpopular ideas
that run counter to "the religious, moral, and patriotic feelings of their time."[123]
O'Brien, just one year earlier, had been this type of case—prosecuting persons
who used novel, symbolic methods to express what are deemed "unpatriotic"
stances against government policy. The justices' inconsistency in these two
cases shows that as much as Millian thought was manifesting itself on the Supreme Court, it was not fully touching every decision. This type of case
would come to the Supreme Court again in the future, though, and the approach the justices eventually adopted was more *Street*'s than *O'Brien*'s.

Regarding the freedom of speech and public school students, *Tinker v. Des
Moines* (1969) overturned the suspension of students who silently protested
the Vietnam War by wearing black armbands bearing peace symbols. In a 7–2
decision, Justice Abe Fortas penned for the Supreme Court that "First Amendment rights, applied in light of the special characteristics of the school envi-
ronment, are available to teachers and students. It can hardly be argued that
either students or teachers shed their constitutional rights to freedom of speech
or expression at the schoolhouse gate."[124] This is not an unfettered speech
right, though; Fortas ruled that students' expressive rights are protected unless
there is "a showing that the students' activities would materially and substantially disrupt the work and discipline of the school."[125] Thus, Fortas distinguished the protected wearing of symbols in the case—which he characterized
as involving "direct, primary First Amendment rights akin to 'pure speech'"—
with "aggressive, disruptive action" that would not be protected.[126] Indeed,
Tinker was unconstitutionally punished for what Fortas described as "a silent,
passive expression of opinion."[127] Even regarding punishment of children in
public schools, Fortas held that "for the State . . . to justify prohibition of a particular expression of opinion, it must be able to show that its action was
caused by something more than a mere desire to avoid the discomfort and un-
pleasantness that always accompany an unpopular viewpoint."[128] Like Mill,
Fortas eschewed government punishment of a speaker because of their viewpoint.[129] He noted that while students expressing opposition to the Vietnam

War were disciplined by school officials, students were permitted to wear other symbols in school, including the Iron Cross (a Nazi representation) and buttons supporting candidates in national political campaigns.[130] The Supreme Court in *Tinker* and *Street* was willing to protect a much greater amount of symbolic speech in 1969 than it did just one year earlier in *O'Brien*, but neither case overruled *O'Brien*, which indicated that some dissonance still existed.[131] The case safeguarded antiwar protest, demonstrating that speech during wartime was protected like in *Hartzel* during World War II, not subject to punishment like in *Schenck* at the end of World War I.

Interestingly, Justice Black dissented in *Tinker*. This justice who typically displayed Millian sentiment on expression approached this case differently: "I have never believed that any person has a right to give speeches or engage in demonstrations where he pleases and when he pleases."[132] Although Mill (and Black's colleagues) would not necessarily disagree with that sentence, Black exhibited a different tone on expression in *Tinker* than he typically did. Black dismissed Fortas's conclusion that students have expressive rights in public schools: "Nor are public school students sent to the schools at public expense to broadcast political or any other views to educate and inform the public."[133] Instead, Black emphasized the need for student discipline, arguing that "children are to be seen not heard," and that "taxpayers send children to school on the premise that at their age they need to learn, not teach."[134]

To Black's point, Mill wrote that his harm principle "is meant to apply only to human beings in the maturity of their faculties," and he thought that the freedoms for "children or young persons below the age which the law may fix as that of manhood or womanhood" could be limited for the purpose of protecting them "against their own actions as well as against external injury."[135] In that sense, there is an argument that Mill's theory might support the suspensions in *Tinker*. However, if the liberty to be exercised would not cause harm to the young person or others, Mill's protection of freedom would appear to apply even to high school students, especially if exercising their freedom of expression.[136] Even though later in *On Liberty* Mill said of young people that "society has had absolute power over them during all the early portion of their existence; it has had the whole period of childhood and nonage in which to try whether it could make them capable of rational conduct in life," at no point did Mill explain when that period of nonage ends.[137] Put another way, it could end before students reach high school age, thus including the students in *Tinker* under the full harm principle.[138] In this way, although Black (a devotee of Mill) could have been taking something of a Millian position by affording students no free speech rights in public school, the greater weight of Mill's statements was in line with the *Tinker* majority: students have free speech rights in school as long as they are not materially and substantially disruptive of the educational process, which would include something that could harm themselves or their classmates. Either way, both the majority in *Tinker* and Black in dissent were arguing over Millian principles.

Finally, Mill was on the justices' minds in *Red Lion Broadcasting v. FCC* (1969). There, the justices unanimously upheld the fairness doctrine, which required radio and television broadcasters to present and give fair coverage to both sides when discussing public issues. Writing for a unanimous Supreme Court, Justice Byron White held that under the First Amendment, "it is the right of the viewers and listeners, not the right of the broadcasters, which is paramount."[139] Citing *Sullivan* and Holmes's dissent in *Abrams*, White used Holmes's famous analogy: "It is the purpose of the First Amendment to preserve an uninhibited marketplace of ideas in which truth will ultimately prevail, rather than to countenance monopolization of that market, whether it be by the Government itself or a private licensee."[140] Indeed, Mill cautioned that "social tyranny" in private society restricting expression was a threat to the free exchange of ideas.[141] White then discussed how it was consistent "with the First Amendment goal of producing an informed public capable of conducting its own affairs to require a broadcaster to permit answers to personal attacks occurring in the course of discussing controversial issues, or to require that the political opponents of those endorsed by the station be given a chance to communicate with the public."[142] In support of this reasoning, White's footnote at the end of that sentence states:

> The expression of views opposing those which broadcasters permit to be aired in the first place need not be confined solely to the broadcasters themselves as proxies. "Nor is it enough that he should hear the arguments of adversaries from his own teachers, presented as they state them, and accompanied by what they offer as refutations. That is not the way to do justice to the arguments, or bring them into real contact with his own mind. He must be able to hear them from persons who actually believe them; who defend them in earnest, and do their very utmost for them." J. Mill, *On Liberty* 32 (R. McCallum ed. 1947).[143]

This Mill quote shows the philosopher's growing influence on the Supreme Court. Beyond this statement where Mill expressed that the listener would best learn both sides of an argument from those who hold competing views, Mill thought that the best hope for people to break free from dogmatic sectarianism beliefs was "when people are forced to listen to both sides" of an issue; thus, the Supreme Court was approaching the fairness doctrine's constitutionality from a Millian perspective.[144]

All told, the mid- to late 1960s saw the largest transformation of the Supreme Court to a more Millian approach since the 1930s and 1940s, and this latter period surpassed the earlier one in terms of the sheer volume of cases and areas of expression at issue. Like the earlier period, not every decision used Millian reasoning or reached a Millian outcome, but in many cases this did occur. This return to Mill occurred because of personnel changes on the Supreme Court, a thaw in the Cold War, and the justices' sympathy toward the free speech plight of civil rights protestors. Whether they were the familiar "subversive" cases involving communists and other political radicals or cases on newer questions about civil rights, the Supreme Court's docket remained packed with free expression cases, including some involving obscenity, libel, public school students, and public employees. The issues had changed, but the underlying questions raised by Mill's *On Liberty* had continuing relevance. The main types of cases approaching the justices would change again, but debates over Millian jurisprudence would continue in the 1970s.

CHAPTER 7

No Such Thing as a False Idea

The Burger Court Holds Relatively Steady on Mill

The US Supreme Court's march toward a Millian approach to free expression slowed starting in 1969, as Chief Justice Earl Warren was succeeded by Chief Justice Warren Burger. Over the next several years, Justices Fortas, Black, Harlan, and Douglas were replaced by Harry Blackmun, Lewis Powell, William Rehnquist, and John Paul Stevens. However, unlike the retrenchment on free expression that engulfed the early Cold War Court in the 1950s, two decades later, the Supreme Court was merely plateauing (and only occasionally taking a step backward) on its climb toward a more libertarian understanding of free expression. Most of the gains from 1963 to 1969 were maintained, and in some respects the Supreme Court became more Millian, due to the efforts of Justices Brennan and Marshall. These two justices led the Supreme Court to enough Millian outcomes to sustain this jurisprudence. Whereas the court in the 1950s made use of older cases that had not been explicitly overruled, decisions like *Brandenburg* in the 1960s overturned many of those older, non-Millian decisions. Thus, the more Millian precedents were cemented in place, although a fractured Burger Court would find exceptions to them to sometimes halt their expanse. There was no steady advance toward Mill like what had occurred at the end of the Warren Court, but enough of the prior developments were sustained during the Burger Court to allow for a greater renewal to begin in the late 1980s during the Rehnquist Court.

The first few years of the Burger Court looked similar to the last years of the Warren Court. The addition of Chief Justice Burger, who was decidedly less Millian than his predecessor, made little immediate impact on the Supreme Court's First Amendment jurisprudence.[1] In the 1969 to 1970 term, no cases challenging restrictions on free expression were upheld, and most rulings were unanimous.[2] Following the resignation of Abe Fortas (who held Millian positions on free expression) in 1969, President Nixon appointed Harry Blackmun to the Supreme Court in 1970. Eventually, with Brennan's convincing, Blackmun would become more Millian on a variety of issues, but earlier in his career Blackmun's views on the First Amendment were far from the philosophy of *On Liberty*.[3] The deepening divisions on the Supreme Court over whether to continue with a Millian approach became evident in several different types of cases, even though Millian philosophy and outcomes tended to prevail.[4]

Offensive speech was at issue in *Cohen v. California* (1971), where the Supreme Court by a vote of 5–4 overturned a breach-of-the-peace conviction of a man who wore a jacket bearing the words "Fuck the Draft" while walking the corridors of a county courthouse. For the majority, Justice Harlan found that the speech was *not* an example of *Chaplinsky's* fighting words and instead appealed to the Millian theme that invective needs to be permitted in public discourse, even if the expression was "crude."[5] Harlan reasoned that the tyranny of the majority should not restrict expression, denying "a governmental power to force persons who wish to ventilate their dissident views into avoiding particular forms of expression."[6] He explained why Cohen's expression was protected by the First Amendment, in language that would have made Mill proud:

> The constitutional right of free expression is powerful medicine in a society as diverse and populous as ours. It is designed and intended to remove governmental restraints from the arena of public discussion, putting the decision as to what views shall be voiced largely into the hands of each of us, in the hope that use of such freedom will ultimately produce a more capable citizenry and more perfect polity and in the belief that no other approach would comport with the premise of individual dignity and choice upon which our political system rests. . . .
>
> To many, the immediate consequence of this freedom may often appear to be only verbal tumult, discord, and even offensive utterance. These are, however, within established limits, in truth necessary side effects of the broader enduring values which the process of open debate permits us to achieve. That the air may at times seem filled with verbal cacophony is, in this sense not a sign of weakness but of strength. . . .

Surely the State has no right to cleanse public debate to the point where it is grammatically palatable to the most squeamish among us. . . . While the particular four-letter word being litigated here is perhaps more distasteful than most others of its genre, it is nevertheless often true that one man's vulgarity is another's lyric. Indeed, we think it is largely because governmental officials cannot make principled distinctions in this area that the Constitution leaves matters of taste and style so largely to the individual. . . .

Much linguistic expression serves a dual communicative function: it conveys not only ideas capable of relatively precise, detached explication, but otherwise inexpressible emotions as well. In fact, words are often chosen as much for their emotive as their cognitive force. . . . We cannot indulge the facile assumption that one can forbid particular words without also running a substantial risk of suppressing ideas in the process. Indeed, governments might soon seize upon the censorship of particular words as a convenient guise for banning the expression of unpopular views.[7]

These passages from *Cohen* explore Millian themes related to democracy, truth, and autonomy.[8] The opinion emphasized the importance of allowing the speaker to use emotion when arguing, something highlighted in *On Liberty*.[9] The case demonstrates Mill's prescription that everyone should remain "open to criticism of [their] opinions and conduct."[10] *Cohen* protected expression critical of the US war effort, in the same type of case Holmes had used to usher Millian philosophy into First Amendment jurisprudence. Earlier in his career, Harlan had not been the most Millian justice, upholding restrictions on expressive activities in cases like *Barenblatt*, *Konigsberg*, and *Scales*. Toward the end of his career, though, Harlan's First Amendment jurisprudence began looking more like Mill's thought, writing for the Supreme Court in both *Street* and *Cohen*. Harlan especially connected the freedom of speech to deliberative democracy, one of Mill's major reasons for protecting expression.[11] Harlan's bold statement in *Cohen* stands alongside Holmes's *Abrams* dissent, Brandeis's *Whitney* concurrence, and Jackson's opinion in *Barnette* as one of the most sweeping defenses of a Millian version of the First Amendment. Harlan's focus in *Cohen* on protecting the emotive aspects of expression matches Mill's sentiment that censoring expression for its emotional content restricts the speaker's message (thus harming listeners' ability to seek truth) and the autonomy of the speaker.[12] *Cohen* imitated Mill's desire to protect speech for both its rational and emotional aspects.[13]

As strong as Harlan's arguments were, four justices disagreed. In dissent, Justice Blackmun characterized the event as follows: "Cohen's absurd and immature antic, in my view, was mainly conduct and little speech."[14] Blackmun said this even though Cohen's prosecution was for pure political speech that was clearly communicative. Still, a five-justice majority was consistently allowing for more of Mill's "invective" and narrowing the fighting words doctrine in the early 1970s, including overturning, as vague and overbroad, a state law that made it illegal to use "opprobrious words or abusive language, tending to cause a breach of the peace,"[15] and vacating a disorderly conduct conviction for using the word "motherfucker" at a school board meeting.[16]

A Millian majority likewise held together in the 1970s on overturning prior restraints against the press, even in the face of growing divisions.[17] The most famous of these cases was *New York Times v. United States* (1971), where a 6–3 majority sustained the right of newspapers to print excerpts from the Pentagon Papers, which were stolen, classified documents detailing the history of US policy making in the Vietnam War. The per curiam opinion of the Court tersely explained that "'any system of prior restraints of expression comes to this Court bearing a heavy presumption against its constitutional validity.' The Government 'thus carries a heavy burden of showing justification for the imposition of such a restraint,'" which was not met in the case.[18] This was to be expected, as even the conventional Blackstonian common law tradition forbade prior restraints.[19]

Millian philosophy surfaced in each of the six concurring opinions in the *New York Times* case. For example, Justice Black again exhibited his absolutist sentiment: "I believe that every moment's continuance of the injunctions against these newspapers amounts to a flagrant, indefensible, and continuing violation of the First Amendment."[20] Black emphasized the connection between democracy and free expression when he explained that the press needed protection "to fulfill its essential role in our democracy. The press was to serve the governed, not the governors."[21] Justice Douglas quoted at length from *Near*, one of the Supreme Court's first Millian majority opinions, before pithily remarking, "Secrecy in government is fundamentally anti-democratic, perpetuating bureaucratic errors. Open debate and discussion of public issues are vital to our national health."[22] Justice Brennan penned a concurrence averring that the "First Amendment stands as an absolute bar to the imposition of judicial restraints" in this type of case.[23] Brennan posited something quite similar to Mill's harm principle regarding the rare situation when a prior restraint would be constitutional: "Only governmental allegation and proof that publication must inevitably, directly, and immediately cause the occurrence of an event kindred to imperiling the safety of a transport already at sea can support even the issuance of an interim restraining order."[24] Again, though, this decision was split, with Burger, Harlan, and Blackmun dissenting.

As for defamation, the early Burger Court expanded the very Millian *Sullivan* decision.[25] This was most evident in *Rosenbloom v. Metromedia* (1971), where the Supreme Court extended the actual malice standard of *Sullivan* to private persons if there was public interest in a news story's subject matter. Rosenbloom was arrested on obscenity charges, and a Metromedia radio station characterized him "and his business associates as 'smut distributors' and 'girlie-book peddlers.'"[26] However, Rosenbloom was acquitted, and he subsequently sued Metromedia for libel. Writing for the Supreme Court, Justice Brennan overturned that verdict, declaring, like Mill, that the freedom of expression should apply to a broad array of subjects: "Self-governance in the United States presupposes far more than knowledge and debate about the strictly official activities of various levels of government. The commitment of the country to the institution of private property . . . places in private hands vast areas of economic and social power that vitally affect the nature and quality of life in the Nation."[27] Just as Mill believed in "absolute freedom of opinion and sentiment on all subjects, practical or speculative, scientific, moral, or theological," Brennan found for the Supreme Court in *Rosenbloom* that "if a matter is a subject of public or general interest, it cannot suddenly become less so merely because a private individual is involved. . . . The public's primary interest is in the event."[28] This remains true, according to Brennan, even though we must sometimes tolerate lies: "We are aware that the press has, on occasion, grossly abused the freedom it is given by the Constitution. All must deplore such excesses. . . . But . . . this free society, dependent as it is for its survival upon a vigorous free press, has tolerated some abuse."[29]

Brennan's focus on protecting even false speech as a path to self-governance is Millian. Although there is a harm in the Millian sense in making defamatory false statements about a private person, if the *Sullivan* standard is applied to unintentionally false statements where there is a genuine public interest, *Rosenbloom* promotes the search for truth in Mill's marketplace of ideas. Thus, Brennan was following Mill, who sought to protect a liberal idea of expression that reaffirms personal autonomy while also limiting that expression for legitimate utilitarian reasons.[30] However, in *Rosenbloom*, Brennan's opinion commanded a plurality of only three justices, meaning that it could be revisited, which occurred in 1974.

In other areas, the Supreme Court's approach to free expression questions was already yielding more mixed results after Blackmun's appointment. Although the justices had consistently struck down loyalty oaths in the later 1960s in cases like *Keyishian*, the Supreme Court in the early 1970s did not find all proofs of loyalty unconstitutional.[31] Eventually, the justices would signal the death knell for these types of loyalty oaths, bringing the Supreme Court more into line with *On Liberty*, but that would not happen for several more years.[32] Similarly, following Blackmun's appointment, the Supreme Court began to chip away at the very strong protections that existed under its obscenity rulings in the mid- to late 1960s, although no significant changes would develop in this area until 1973.[33]

Those developments were spurred on by personnel changes. In 1972, Lewis Powell was appointed to fill the seat of Hugo Black, and William Rehnquist was confirmed to fill the position voided by John Marshall Harlan. Black was a strong devotee of Mill's philosophy on many First Amendment questions; although Harlan was not a consistent follower of Mill, later in his career he expressed that philosophy more regularly, especially in *Cohen*. As a new justice, Powell held some Millian sentiments, but Rehnquist did not. Thus, a partial shift away from Mill was underway. However, the establishment of key 1960s precedents ensured that this backsliding was relatively minor compared to what the Supreme Court did two decades earlier. And in some areas, those key precedents led to expansion of a Millian approach in First Amendment caselaw in the mid-1970s.

Regarding obscenity and expressions about sex, the partial shift began almost immediately after Powell's and Rehnquist's appointments.[34] *Miller v. California* (1973) designed the test that the Supreme Court continues to use for obscenity today. Chief Justice Burger wrote for a 5–4 Supreme Court, upholding an obscenity conviction for brochures that advertised books and a film. These brochures had "pictures and drawings very explicitly depicting men and women in groups of two or more engaging in a variety of sexual activities, with genitals often prominently displayed."[35] Burger replaced the *Memoirs* test with the following one for obscenity, asking "(a) whether the average person, applying contemporary community standards would find that the work, taken as a whole, appeals to the prurient interest; (b) whether the work depicts or describes, in a patently offensive way, sexual conduct specifically defined by the applicable state law; and (c) whether the work, taken as a whole, lacks serious literary, artistic, political, or scientific value."[36] In contrast to *Memoirs*'s focus on whether or not a work was *utterly* without redeeming value, the Supreme Court in *Miller* required a more specific finding for a work to *not* qualify as obscene, and this would be determined locally by a jury.[37] Allowing local notions of morality to determine if expression is protected runs against Mill in two ways. First, Mill thought that sexual activities deserved legal protection, mentioning in *On Liberty* that "fornication, for example, must be tolerated," and, although he personally believed it to be immoral, he defended the practice of polygamy in reaction to US suppression of Mormonism.[38] More fundamentally, Mill argued that appealing to the sentiments of the community will inevitably lead to the suppression of minority views. Mill noted of cultural chauvinism that the "practical principle which guides them to their opinions on the regulation of human conduct is the feeling in each person's mind that everybody should be required to act as he, and those with whom he sympathizes, would like them to act."[39] Mill argued that these unsupported "standards" are often more pernicious, by employing the example of "planters and Negros" to demonstrate how "custom" is used to shield class interests and maintain social dominance.[40]

One of the Supreme Court's more Millian justices, Douglas, complained in dissent of the majority moving away from *Memoirs*: "The idea that the First Amendment permits punishment for ideas that are 'offensive' to the particular judge or jury sitting in judgment is astounding. No greater leveler of speech or literature has ever been designed. To give the power to the censor, as we do today, is to make a sharp and radical break with the traditions of a free society."[41] Reflecting Mill's notion that we must protect "liberty of tastes and pursuits," Douglas chided the *Miller* majority for creating a less protective test: "We deal with tastes and standards of literature. What shocks me may be sustenance for my neighbor. What causes one person to boil up in rage over one pamphlet or movie may reflect only his neurosis. . . . We deal here with a regime of censorship."[42] Douglas even alluded to the emotional and moral components of the case, value judgments that he thought the judiciary should never impose: "Obscenity cases usually generate tremendous emotional outbursts. They have no business being in the courts."[43] Like Mill, Douglas recalled the history of the majorities suppressing speech: "The tendency throughout history has been to subdue the individual and to exalt the power of government."[44] Although *Miller* ushered in a broader definition of obscenity, the test's focus on "applying contemporary community standards" meant that if society adopts a more Millian attitude toward sexual expression, then obscenity could be narrowed, particularly due to technological advancements that make it easier to distribute such material nationwide.[45] The long-term effect of this eventually created a Millian result in what the First Amendment shields from prosecution today.

Paris Adult Theatre I v. Slaton (1973) was a companion to *Miller* where the same 5–4 majority held that the First Amendment does not protect the showing of obscene films to consenting adults. In *Paris I*, Chief Justice Burger wrote, "For us to say that our Constitution incorporates the proposition that conduct involving consenting adults only is always beyond state regulation, is a step we are unable to take" and cited Mill's *On Liberty* as an approach the Supreme Court was *not* adopting.[46] Thus, Burger directly repudiated Mill.[47] However, in response, Justice Brennan—the author of the *Roth* decision and many other obscenity opinions of the Court—refused to continue using such tests, remarking, "I have concluded that the time has come to make a significant departure from that approach."[48] Brennan expressed concern over the chilling effect caused by the Supreme Court changing obscenity standards.[49] He proclaimed that precedents of the Supreme Court before *Miller* "rejected as wholly inconsistent with the philosophy of the First Amendment, the notion that there is a legitimate state concern in the control [of] the moral content of a person's thoughts."[50] Taking a Millian tone, Brennan argued that "a legitimate, sharply focused state concern for the morality of the community cannot . . . justify an assault on the protections of the First Amendment."[51] Brennan instead advocated for a type of harm principle–based, free speech approach to obscenity, similar to that espoused by Justices Black and Douglas: "I would hold . . . that at least in the absence of distribution to juveniles or obtrusive exposure to unconsenting adults, the First and Fourteenth Amendments prohibit the State and Federal Governments from attempting wholly to suppress sexually oriented materials on the basis of their allegedly 'obscene' contents."[52] Brennan's shift on obscenity in *Paris I* showed his commitment to the free flow of ideas, reflecting a Millian understanding of the First Amendment.[53] Nevertheless, Brennan remained one vote short of achieving this Millian approach to obscenity. Beginning with *Miller* and *Paris I*, the Supreme Court issued several other 5–4 obscenity opinions that were non-Millian.[54]

Nevertheless, the Supreme Court's new limits for sexually oriented expression in the 1970s did not create a carbon copy of the Supreme Court's retrenchment on First Amendment rights in the 1950s. This was shown by *Jenkins v. Georgia* (1974), where Justice Rehnquist wrote for a unanimous Supreme Court that under the *Miller* test's community standards prong, "nudity alone is not enough to make material legally obscene," thus holding that the film *Carnal Knowledge*, which included sex scenes, was protected by the First Amendment.[55] More to the point, Rehnquist denied that juries could simply impose by law any morality-based limits on sexual expression, reasoning that "it would be a serious misreading of *Miller* to conclude that juries have unbridled discretion in determining what is 'patently offensive.'"[56] The opinion of the Court in *Jenkins* did not go far enough for Justice Douglas (who argued in *Jenkins* that no obscenity prosecution was constitutional) or Justice Brennan (who believed that the *Miller* test continued to chill protected expression), but it signaled that obscenity would continue to be defined relatively narrowly rather than continually being re-expanded.[57] Other mid-1970s cases struck down restrictions on sexually oriented expression.[58] The line had been (temporarily) moved regarding what was obscene, but it had not been pushed too far back from where it was under *Memoirs*.

Libel was another area of First Amendment law where the justices slightly diminished protections of expression. The most significant libel decision was *Gertz v. Robert Welch, Inc.* (1974), where a 5–4 Supreme Court overturned *Rosenbloom*, holding that a private person does not have to show *Sullivan*'s actual malice to win compensatory damages in a defamation suit. Granted, Justice Powell wrote for the Supreme Court a Millian statement: "Under the First Amendment there is no such thing as a false idea. However pernicious an opinion may seem, we depend for its correction not on the conscience of judges and juries but on the competition of other ideas."[59] Powell's free speech rhetoric seemed like it could have been written by Mill himself: "The erroneous statement of fact [is] inevitable in free debate. . . . And punishment of error runs the risk of inducing a cautious and restrictive exercise of the constitutionally guaranteed freedoms of speech and press."[60] Nevertheless, Powell's further comments were not Millian in practice, similar to how Justice Holmes used Millian language in *Schenck* but upheld a significant speech restriction. According to Powell, "There is no constitutional value in false statements of fact," and "absolute protection for the communications media" would be unsuitable because it "requires a total sacrifice of the competing value served by the law of defamation."[61] Unlike Brennan in *Rosenbloom*, who evaluated in a Millian, utilitarian way the competing harm of defamation against the threat of chilling speech on matters of public concern, Powell focused on the status of the person being defamed.[62]

Thus, a divided Supreme Court upheld a libel award against a magazine publisher for stating some inaccuracies about an attorney who was "well known in some circles" but "had achieved no general fame or notoriety in the community."[63] This was to the chagrin of Justice Brennan, who, as he did in obscenity cases, explained why libel laws can lead to dangerous self-censorship: "I cannot agree . . . that free and robust debate—so essential to the proper functioning of our system of government—is permitted adequate 'breathing space,' when, as the Court holds, the States may impose all but strict liability for defamation if the defamed party is a private person."[64] The dissent's concerns are reminiscent of Mill over a century earlier when he was critical of British libel laws.[65] In the mid-1970s the Supreme Court did not uphold all libel laws—for instance, in finding protection for the "rhetorical hyperbole" of calling a nonunion employee a "scab."[66] No doubt, Mill, who defended the ability to use intemperate language in public debate, would have agreed.[67] Thus, as was the case with obscenity, the Supreme Court's libel jurisprudence in the mid- to late 1970s narrowed protected expression a bit but largely maintained the late 1960s to early 1970s framework.[68]

With President Nixon's four appointees on the Supreme Court, a chasm was opening between Mill's theory and the majority's jurisprudence in cases involving noncitizens and prisoners. In *Kleindienst v. Mandel* (1972), a 6–3 majority held that the First Amendment was not violated when the attorney general refused to permit the foreign journalist and Marxist scholar Ernest Mandel to enter the country to meet with US academics, effectively meaning that the First Amendment did not apply to noncitizens attempting to enter the country. For the Supreme Court, Justice Blackmun emphasized the power of government, not individual liberty: "The power to exclude aliens is inherent in sovereignty, necessary for maintaining normal international relations and defending the country against foreign encroachments and dangers—a power to be exercised exclusively by the political branches of government."[69] The aging Justice Douglas delivered a dissent reminiscent of Mill and Holmes: "Thought control is not within the competence of any branch of government. Those who live here may need exposure to the ideas of people of many faiths and many creeds to further their education."[70] Douglas cited the Millian decisions *Thomas* and *Brandenburg*. Justice Marshall dissented, citing *Terminiello* and Brandeis's *Whitney* concurrence. For Marshall, "there can be no doubt that by denying the American appellees access to Dr. Mandel, the Government has directly prevented the free interchange of ideas guaranteed by the First Amendment."[71] Since Mandel was excluded for the expression of ideas and posed no direct harm, Marshall averred that "government has no legitimate interest in stopping the flow of ideas. It has no power to restrict the mere advocacy of communist doctrine, divorced from incitement to imminent lawless action."[72] *Kleindienst* stands out as a case revealing a residual 1950s anticommunist bias employed against foreigners.[73] And this was during the same era that the Supreme Court struck down a loyalty oath in the last such case brought before it, in 1974, effectively ending such anticommunist oaths for US citizens.[74] Denying a foreigner the right to enter the country to discuss ideas with other academics runs counter to Mill's advocacy of protecting free expression, as Mill criticized the denial of equal rights to "a foreigner" after he expressed his beliefs.[75]

In the mid-1970s, the Supreme Court began using an intermediate standard of scrutiny to decide if prisoners' mail should be censored, balancing freedom of expression against possible prisoner threats.[76] While one could argue that this was Millian in form, it is not Millian in spirit. The Supreme Court's growing aversion to the free expression rights of prisoners was evident in *Pell v. Procunier* (1974) and *Saxbe v. Washington Post* (1974), where a split Supreme Court held that neither prisoners' free speech rights nor the media's freedom of the press were violated by state and federal rules prohibiting face-to-face interviews of inmates. As the majority clarified in *Pell*, the "Constitution does not . . . require government to accord the press special access to information not shared by members of the public generally."[77] Although the Supreme Court acknowledged in *Saxbe* that lawyers and clergy do have a special constitutional right of access to prisons, a majority of justices would not extend such a right to the press.[78] As explained in Douglas's *Pell* dissent, such restrictions on the media run counter to Millian thought on the public's right to learn information and discuss public issues: "The prohibition here is . . . offensive to First Amendment principles; it flatly prohibits interview communication with the media on the government's penal operations by the only citizens with the best knowledge and real incentive to discuss them."[79] Douglas used Millian utilitarian thinking on the freedom of the press promoting democratic self-government: "It is important to note that the interest it protects is not possessed by the media themselves," as what was violated was "the right of the people, the true sovereign under our constitutional scheme, to govern in an informed manner."[80] These decisions continued to provide a lower level of First Amendment protection of expression at jails and prisons, something the Supreme Court began with *Adderley*, although the level of protection provided in the 1970s was reduced even further in the 1980s.[81] From a Millian perspective, this prejudicial attitude toward inmates represents a glaring lacuna in judicial reasoning, a gap that still exists today. That these decisions were about limiting rights of inmates and expression at jails and prisons was evident by examining other mid-1970s free press cases, which, outside of the libel context, were decidedly more Millian.[82]

Although there were several areas of First Amendment jurisprudence where the Supreme Court was balancing Millian thought against other concerns, in some areas the majority of justices remained committed to Mill's philosophy. The Supreme Court was more consistently moving toward a position that the government cannot regulate, or discriminate against, speech based on content.[83] This became increasingly clear in cases involving offensive speech or advocacy of illegality. For instance, in *Hess v. Indiana* (1973), the Supreme Court overturned a disorderly conduct conviction for a man who, when ordered by law enforcement to clear off of a street during a protest, stated to a sheriff, "We'll take the fucking street again [or later]."[84] The per curiam opinion in *Hess* alluded to the pro-Millian standard from *Brandenburg*, which even the three dissenters in *Hess* did not question. *Lewis v. New Orleans* (1974) upheld the fighting words doctrine from *Chaplinsky*, but the justices struck down an ordinance prohibiting "obscene or opprobrious language" applied to a driver who said "you goddamn motherfucking police" during a traffic stop.[85] In the 6–3 decision, Brennan wrote for the majority that this "speech, although vulgar or offensive . . . is protected by the First and Fourteenth Amendments."[86] This is similar to Mill's argument that law and authority have no business restraining "vituperation" when employed in the expression of ideas.[87] Similarly, following the *Street* precedent, the Supreme Court overturned multiple convictions for offensive use of the US flag.[88]

The justices also broke new ground in advancing a more Millian approach to expression in the years immediately following the Powell and Rehnquist appointments. One was with public university students. In *Healy v. James* (1972), the Supreme Court held that "state colleges and universities are not enclaves immune from the sweep of the First Amendment."[89] Instead, in ruling that a chapter of Students for a Democratic Society (a leftist organization) was unconstitutionally denied official college recognition, the justices reasoned that "the precedents of this Court leave no room for the view that, because of the acknowledged need for order, First Amendment protections should apply with less force on college campuses than in the community at large. . . . The college classroom with its surrounding environs is peculiarly the 'marketplace of ideas.'"[90] In overturning the college's decision in *Healy*, the Supreme Court affirmed that dissident students with ideas considered radical by the majority have a right to espouse and discuss those ideas on campus, in a parallel to Mill's criticism that UK universities stifled open inquiry.[91] Mill thought it was a "deep-seated error" and "inveterate prejudice" that universities in his time believed that teaching "means to inculcate our own opinions, and that our business is not to make thinkers or inquirers, but disciples."[92]

Healy was followed by *Papish v. Board of Curators of the University of Missouri* (1973), where the Supreme Court reaffirmed *Healy*'s notion that public university students have free speech rights unless they are materially and substantially disruptive of campus activities: "The mere dissemination of ideas—no matter how offensive to good taste—on a state university campus may not be shut off in the name alone of 'conventions of decency.'"[93] In overturning the expulsion of a student for distributing a newspaper that was deemed to contain offensive content, the Supreme Court in *Papish* asserted that "the First Amendment leaves no room for the operation of a dual standard in the academic community with respect to the content of speech."[94] These two cases first applied free expression rights to public university students, which Mill would have approved, given his statements in *On Liberty* that offensive speech should be protected and that students (especially if adults) should be able to learn from the speech of others, which was confirmed by another of his concerns: "A person who derives all his instruction from teachers or books, even if he escape the besetting temptation of contenting himself with cram, is under no compulsion to hear both sides."[95]

Commercial speech was another area where the Supreme Court started to move toward Mill during this time. Recall *Valentine v. Chrestensen* (1942), where the justices unanimously held that commercial speech was not protected by the First Amendment. In *Bigelow v. Virginia* (1975), the Supreme Court signaled that it was rethinking this approach. The Supreme Court ruled in *Bigelow* that a law prohibiting advertising abortion services was unconstitutional. As Blackmun, author of the *Roe v. Wade* (1973) decision, held in *Bigelow*, "Commercial advertising enjoys a degree of First Amendment protection," and in this case the advertisement "contained factual material of clear 'public interest.'"[96] Blackmun proclaimed that "the relationship of speech to the marketplace of products or of services does not make it valueless in the marketplace of ideas."[97] This insight revealed that the boundary that earlier Supreme Courts (and to a certain extent Mill himself) had drawn between expression and commerce is far more permeable than the justices initially believed.[98] That a message has a commercial aim does not necessarily mean that it cannot also have content that is in the public interest, a position that the Supreme Court would eventually adopt.[99] Thus, the justices began to expand protections for commercial speech, pushing it more toward Mill, who preferred that information having a public interest be protected in the marketplace of ideas.[100] However, given the tie here to the constitutional right to abortion and the justices' commitment in the 1970s to protecting that right, it was unclear how much commercial speech was protected by the First Amendment.[101]

Justice Douglas retired in 1975 after suffering a stroke. He was one of the Supreme Court's most ardent supporters of a Millian approach to free expression.[102] There were several key First Amendment cases argued to the Supreme Court before Douglas's successor, John Paul Stevens, was appointed. Like the previous few years, these cases that were released in 1976 were mixed in how Millian they were.

The Supreme Court's first ruling on campaign finance and the First Amendment, *Buckley v. Valeo* (1976), employed a libertarian philosophy. The justices held that government restrictions on contributions to campaigns and candidates are constitutional but restrictions on expenditures are unconstitutional. One could argue whether the outcome of the case was Millian, due to the fact that Mill never wrote directly on this issue.[103] But the per curiam opinion in *Buckley* spoke to Millian themes: "The First and Fourteenth Amendments guarantee freedom to associate with others for the common advancement of political beliefs and ideas."[104] That Millian sentiment continued: "The First Amendment denies government the power to determine that spending to promote one's political views is wasteful, excessive, or unwise. In the free society ordained by our Constitution it is not the government but the people—individually as citi-

zens and candidates and collectively as associations and political committees—
who must retain control over the quantity and range of debate on public issues
in a political campaign."[105] The Supreme Court also indirectly adhered to the
harm principle in upholding contribution limits, which prevent "the reality or
appearance of improper influence stemming from the dependence of candidates on large campaign contributions. The contribution ceilings thus serve the
basic governmental interest in safeguarding the integrity of the electoral process
without directly impinging upon the rights of individual citizens and candidates
to engage in political debate and discussion."[106] The justices built on this Millian
foundation for cases dealing with campaign finance and campaign expression
through the remainder of the Burger Court.[107] In the small number of other free
expression cases argued before the Supreme Court after Douglas's departure
but before Stevens's appointment, the results were mixed, with some decisions being more Millian than others.[108]

The appointment of John Paul Stevens in late 1975 would produce some
short-term shifts away from Mill, with the Millian torch being carried by Justices Brennan and Marshall. Nevertheless, the Supreme Court maintained free
speech protections in several important areas and even expanded First Amendment rights in some contexts. Stevens did not have much of a Millian outlook
initially but would later in his career.

In the mid-1970s to early 1980s, the Supreme Court continued to reexam-
ine protections for sexual expression. In *Young v. American Mini Theatres* (1976),
Justice Stevens wrote for a 5–4 Supreme Court in upholding a zoning ordinance
prohibiting adult theaters from opening within one thousand feet of buildings
with "regulated uses" or within five hundred feet of a residential district. For
the majority, Stevens noted that for sexually oriented expression, "the State
could prohibit the distribution or exhibition of such materials to juveniles and
unconsenting adults."[109] The majority opinion explained further that sexual
expression received scant constitutional protection: "Even though we recognize that the First Amendment will not tolerate the total suppression of erotic
materials that have some arguably artistic value, it is manifest that society's
interest in protecting this type of expression is of a wholly different, and lesser,
magnitude than the interest in untrammeled political debate."[110] Although Stevens for the majority examined a Millian variable—harm to others—when
proclaiming of "crime" that "it is this secondary effect which these zoning ordinances attempt to avoid, not the dissemination of 'offensive' speech," Justice Potter Stewart's dissent took the more Millian approach: "The kind of
expression at issue here is no doubt objectionable to some, but that fact does
not diminish its protected status."[111] Stewart argued, "That the 'offensive'
speech here may not address 'important' topics—'ideas of social and political

significance,' in the Court's terminology—does not mean that it is less worthy of constitutional protection."[112] This case illustrates a problem that Mill himself struggled with, and one where it may be difficult to fully discern his views.[113] Using the harm principle as a guide, Stevens's rationale appears quite weak. While Stevens attempted to distinguish restrictions based on content from the secondary harms sexual expression may produce, he did not demonstrate that these secondary harms presented an imminent threat. Mill, in the closing chapter of *On Liberty*, considered limiting the liberty of those "with an interest opposed to what is considered the public weal, and whose mode of living is grounded on the counteraction of it."[114] Mill argued that there is "considerable force" in arguments that the state should have power to rightly restrict commercial enterprises whose existence works to undermine important social institutions.[115] Mill refused to endorse such a view, but he did not refute it either.[116] Whatever one thinks of this reasoning, it is important to see that in both decision and dissent, Millian rationales exist, demonstrating Mill's growing influence over the Supreme Court's First Amendment jurisprudence. This growth was inconsistent though, as sexually oriented expression cases during this period often had anti-Millian results.[117]

The Supreme Court maintained anti-Millian restrictions on expression in several areas after the appointment of Stevens. This included narrowly defining who is a public figure (and hence who needs to prove actual malice under *Sullivan*), and continuing to restrict First Amendment rights for prisoners in the vein of *Pell* and *Saxbe*.[118] The most noteworthy anti-Millian decision of the late 1970s was *FCC v. Pacifica Foundation* (1978), where the justices by a vote of 5–4 upheld a federal ruling against a radio station for broadcasting George Carlin's "Filthy Words" monologue. The opinion of the Court, instead of emphasizing the freedom of speech, stressed the categories of expression not protected by the First Amendment, including fighting words, libel, and obscenity.[119] Even after affirming that offensive expression receives constitutional protection, Justice Stevens underscored that "the content of Pacifica's broadcast was 'vulgar,' 'offensive,' and 'shocking.'"[120] According to Stevens for the majority, "indecent material presented over the airwaves confronts the citizen, not only in public, but also in the privacy of the home, where the individual's right to be left alone plainly outweighs the First Amendment rights of an intruder."[121]

As Justice Brennan put it in his dissent in *Pacifica*, such non-Millian analysis by the majority was misplaced: "The Court's balance . . . fails to accord proper weight to the interests of listeners who wish to hear broadcasts the FCC deems offensive. It permits majoritarian tastes completely to preclude a protected message from entering the homes of a receptive, unoffended minority."[122] Brennan instead "place[d] the responsibility and the right to weed worthless and offensive communications from the public airways where it belongs and where, until today, it resided: in a public free to choose those communications worthy of its attention from a marketplace unsullied by the censor's hand."[123] Brennan decried the majority's attempt to silence the expressive autonomy of the minority: "The Court's decision [is] another of the dominant culture's inevitable efforts to force those groups who do not share its mores to conform to its way of thinking, acting, and speaking."[124] Brennan's arguments echoed Mill's famous statement in *On Liberty* that "if all mankind minus one were of one opinion, and only one person were of the contrary opinion, mankind would be no more justified in silencing that one person than he, if he had the power, would be justified in silencing mankind."[125] Brennan's dissent demonstrated why *Pacifica* was one of the most anti-Millian decisions of the Burger Court.

At the same time the Supreme Court was upholding restrictions on broadcast expression, it continued to expand commercial speech protections. In *Bates v. State Bar of Arizona* (1977), Justice Blackmun wrote for a 5–4 majority in striking down a bar association rule prohibiting advertising of legal services, finding that rule unconstitutional because "the disciplinary rule serves to inhibit the free flow of commercial information and to keep the public in ignorance."[126] Even though the interests at stake were largely economic, Blackmun explained that "advertising, though entirely commercial, may often carry information of import to significant issues of the day."[127] Blackmun used Millian reasoning in presuming that competent adult clients of attorneys could generally be trusted to sort through lawyers' advertising, as he chided the Arizona state bar for "assum[ing] that the public is not sophisticated enough to realize the limitations of advertising, and that the public is better kept in ignorance than trusted with correct but incomplete information. We suspect the argument rests on an underestimation of the public."[128] Blackmun clarified, though, that the justices "do not hold that advertising by attorneys may not be regulated in any way," offering multiple examples of how commercial speech could be restricted more than noncommercial expression and declaring that "advertising that is false, deceptive, or misleading of course is subject to restraint."[129]

Although the Supreme Court's jurisprudence on commercial speech in the 1970s was moving more toward Mill's philosophy, it still upheld bans on false statements that could contribute to public debate.[130] Thus, the justices unevenly upheld and struck down commercial speech regulations during this period.[131] Although Mill questioned in *On Liberty* how much it is in the public interest to permit those who "derive a personal benefit" as a part of their occupation to "promote what society and the State consider to be an evil," such arguments were applied by Mill only partially—at best—to traditional vices like drinking and gambling, not the practice of law or medical services, which were the bulk of commercial speech regulations before the Supreme Court in the mid- to late 1970s.[132]

In *Central Hudson Gas and Electric v. Public Service Commission* (1980), the Supreme Court confirmed that commercial speech deserved constitutional protection, albeit a lower level of protection than political speech. In the 8–1 decision, Justice Powell for the majority wrote that "commercial expression not only serves the economic interest of the speaker, but also assists consumers and furthers the societal interest in the fullest possible dissemination of information. . . . We have rejected the 'highly paternalistic' view that government has complete power to suppress or regulate commercial speech."[133] Recalling Mill's idea that there is utility in protecting partial truths that help us reach full truth, Powell reasoned that "even when advertising communicates only an incomplete version of the relevant facts, the First Amendment presumes that some accurate information is better than no information at all."[134] Powell declared that the "First Amendment's concern for commercial speech is based on the informational function of advertising," showing utilitarian concern with the dissemination of ideas in the marketplace.[135] Like Holmes's original use of Mill in *Schenck* and Powell's opinion in *Gertz*, though, sweeping Millian rhetoric was masked by a constitutional test that deferred to the government's regulatory power. For commercial speech to be protected by the First Amendment, "it at least must concern lawful activity and not be misleading. Next, we ask whether the asserted governmental interest is substantial. If both inquiries yield positive answers, we must determine whether the regulation directly advances the governmental interest asserted, and whether it is not more extensive than is necessary to serve that interest."[136] The Supreme Court, while moving toward Mill, fell short of realizing the full function that protecting false speech can serve for seeking truth through commercial speech.[137]

Even this deferential test was too much for Justice Rehnquist, who in dissent thought the Supreme Court was making a mistake by providing *any* constitutional protection for commercial speech: "The Court's asserted justification for invalidating the New York law is the public interest discerned by the Court to underlie the First Amendment in the free flow of commercial information. Prior to [1976], however, commercial speech was afforded no protection."[138] Rehnquist understood why the majority was protecting more commercial speech, making the connection to Mill through Holmes's *Abrams* dissent: "The view apparently derives from the Court's frequent reference to the 'marketplace of ideas.' . . . This notion was expressed by Mr. Justice Holmes in his dissenting opinion in *Abrams v. United States*, wherein he stated that 'the best test of truth is the power of the thought to get itself accepted in the competition of the market. . . .' *See also*, e.g., . . . J. Mill, *On Liberty* (1858)."[139] Rehnquist's opinion explicitly recognized that Mill's influence was gaining traction in commercial speech cases, although the ultimate test of judging regulations of this expression remained short of what Mill promoted.

Regarding compelled speech, the Supreme Court remained true to its *Barnette* precedent (one of the Supreme Court's most Millian decisions) in *Wooley v. Maynard* (1977), where Chief Justice Burger wrote for a 6–3 majority to find unconstitutional New Hampshire's requirement that the state motto "Live Free or Die" be placed on all state license plates. Burger's admission that the "right to speak and the right to refrain from speaking are complementary components of the broader concept of individual freedom of mind" fit with Mill's conception that freedom of thought is essential to personal autonomy.[140] Articulating Millian concerns about morality and majority tyranny, Burger reasoned that the "First Amendment protects the right of individuals to hold a point of view different from the majority and to refuse to foster, in the way New Hampshire commands, an idea they find morally objectionable."[141] The decision evinces that Mill's ideas were starting to have enduring appeal among the justices, particularly when used by Burger. Compelled speech was one of multiple areas of First Amendment law where the Supreme Court took a Millian approach in the late 1970s and early 1980s.[142]

Sandra Day O'Connor, who filled the seat vacated by Justice Stewart's retirement in 1981, was the last justice appointed during the Burger Court. During Burger's final years as chief justice, the Supreme Court treaded through freedom of expression cases, rarely breaking new ground, and in some cases slightly contracting expressive rights that were boldly proclaimed during the Warren Court.

The Supreme Court had a mixed record on public employee speech rights in the 1970s, upholding *Pickering*, but also chipping away at it.[143] That continued in *Connick v. Myers* (1983), where a 5–4 majority emphasized government interests, finding no First Amendment violation when an assistant district attorney was fired for circulating a questionnaire to fellow employees about internal office issues. The majority defined public employee speech rights more narrowly than in *Pickering*, declaring that "the Government, as an employer, must have wide discretion and control over the management of its personnel and internal affairs."[144] For Justice Brennan in dissent, this decision ran counter to the spirit of *Pickering*, and his reasoning was more Millian than the majority's. Brennan believed that Myers's speech was on matters of public concern, and the questionnaire's "distribution did not adversely affect the operations of the District Attorney's Office or interfere with Myers' working relationship with her fellow employees."[145] Protecting public employees' speech to promote the utilitarian good of democratic self-governance was on Brennan's mind: "The Court's decision today inevitably will deter public employees from making critical statements about the manner in which government agencies are operated for fear that doing so will provoke their dismissal. As a result, the public will be deprived of valuable information with which to evaluate the performance of elected officials. . . . Protecting the dissemination of such information is an essential function of the First Amendment."[146] Although the *Connick* majority used some Millian reasoning, Brennan in dissent argued closer to Mill's sentiments. The seed for a diminishing of *Pickering's* protection for public employee speech was planted in that case's emphasis on merely shielding expression on matters of public concern, as this allows less Millian justices in a case like *Connick* to define expression as being outside of matters of public concern, a more malleable standard than Mill's own, as he believed that public employee speech should be protected unless there would be definite damage, or risk of such damage, to the public, meaning harm to vital or essential interests.[147] Mill expressed concerns with powerful officials chilling expression by determining for themselves what is in the public interest.[148]

Tinker's protection for K–12 public student expression was eroded in *Bethel School District v. Fraser* (1986), where a divided Supreme Court upheld the suspension of a high school student who gave an assembly speech that included sexual innuendo. The Supreme Court emphasized the Millian exception that children did not warrant the same rights of self-expression as adults; Chief Justice Burger's opinion of the Court echoed this, proclaiming that "the constitutional rights of students in public school are not automatically coextensive with the rights of adults in other settings."[149] The majority deferred to public schools' authority to restrict student expression, holding that the "determination of what manner of speech in the classroom or in school assembly is inappropriate properly rests with the school board."[150] In a dissent, Justice Marshall explained that even in schools, "where speech is involved, we may not unquestioningly accept a teacher's or administrator's assertion that certain pure speech interfered with education."[151] Sticking with the standard from *Tinker*, Marshall in *Bethel* argued that "the School District had not demonstrated any disruption of the educational process."[152] The Millian emphasis on protecting liberty was expressed succinctly in Justice Stevens's dissent: "I believe a strong presumption in favor of free expression should apply whenever an issue of this kind is arguable."[153] Although Mill argued in *On Liberty* that "those who are still in a state to require being taken care of by others must be protected against their own actions as well as against external injury," he also limited this exception to those not "in the maturity of their faculties" who were in "the early portion of their existence."[154] Thus, high school students might instead be considered to have fuller rights in Mill's scheme.[155] Either way, even Chief Justice Burger in upholding the restriction on student speech expressed Millian themes, although not to the same degree as Justices Marshall and Stevens. Other cases during the late Burger Court that affected the rights of students in public schools were more Millian.[156]

Of course, Mill did not oppose *all* restrictions on expression involving young people—for instance, if expression caused harm or violated one of his noted exceptions in *On Liberty. New York v. Ferber* (1982) clearly fits one of those exceptions. In *Ferber*, the Supreme Court held that child pornography may be banned without meeting the requirements of the *Miller* test because of the government interest in protecting children who are abused when such materials are produced. As Justice White emphasized in a unanimous decision, "The use of children as subjects of pornographic materials is harmful to the physiological, emotional, and mental health of the child."[157] As explained by White, since child pornography "bears so heavily and pervasively on the welfare of children engaged in its production . . . it is permissible to consider these materials as without the protection of the First Amendment."[158] This is Millian in two respects. First, the Supreme Court emphasized something like Mill's harm principle, that it is proper to interfere with another person's actions "to prevent harm to others."[159] Those producing these materials, who are causing substantial, direct harm to children, can be prosecuted and punished because what they are doing falls outside of what Mill defined as freedom. Second, multiple times in *On Liberty* Mill discussed the corresponding need to limit the actions of children who are not "in the maturity of their faculties" because they cannot fully appreciate the consequences of those actions; they are "in a state to require being taken care of by others," so they "must be protected against their own actions as well as against external injuries."[160] Children under the age of maturity are not capable of legal consent because they cannot fully understand all of the ramifications of their actions, meaning they must be protected against such harms being perpetrated on them by malicious adults.[161]

With the exception of *Ferber*, the Supreme Court's decisions on obscenity and related questions were largely anti-Millian during the last several years of the Burger Court.[162] The best example of this was in *Renton v. Playtime Theatres* (1986), where a 7–2 Supreme Court, following *Young*, upheld an ordinance banning adult movie theaters from being located "within 1,000 feet of any residential zone, single- or multiple-family dwelling, church, park, or school" as a valid, content-neutral time, place, and manner restriction.[163] The Supreme Court deferred to local governments on restricting this type of expression.[164] Justice Rehnquist wrote for the majority in *Renton* about local governments'

interests in suppressing vaguely defined "secondary effects of adult theaters."[165]
This concern could conceivably be aimed at the types of dangers Mill emphasized with the harm principle. Indeed, preventing secondary effects would be
taking a more Millian approach than being concerned with enforcing standards
of public morality.[166] However, Rehnquist and the majority provided no definition of what these "secondary effects" are. This, combined with the ordinance in question not targeting similar businesses that might produce harmful
effects, led Justice Brennan in dissent to argue that the ordinance was "discriminating against adult theaters based on the content of the films they exhibit."[167]
Brennan concluded that the municipality "has not shown that locating adult
movie theaters in proximity to its churches, schools, parks, and residences will
necessarily result in undesirable 'secondary effects,' or that these problems
could not be effectively addressed by less intrusive restrictions."[168] The last few
years of the Burger Court also saw a majority of justices continue applying a
lower, less-than-Millian level of protection for symbolic speech, and the Supreme Court's record remained mixed in libel cases.[169]

On the other hand, the Supreme Court's decisions on public forums—
including as they relate to incitement, picketing, and protesting—were more
protective of free expression during this time. In *NAACP v. Claiborne Hardware*
(1982), the justices unanimously held that the nonviolent portions of a boycott are protected by the First Amendment, even if some participants engaged
in violence. Justice Stevens wrote for the Supreme Court that "speech does
not lose its protected character . . . simply because it may embarrass others
or coerce them into action."[170] Reflecting Mill's protection of invective, Stevens reasoned in *Claiborne Hardware* that the "emotionally charged rhetoric
of . . . speeches did not transcend the bounds of protected speech set forth in
Brandenburg."[171] Stevens stated that "strong and effective extemporaneous rhetoric cannot be nicely channeled in purely dulcet phrases. An advocate must
be free to stimulate his audience with spontaneous and emotional appeals for
unity and action in a common cause. When such appeals do not incite lawless
action, they must be regarded as protected speech."[172] As in Mill's corn dealer
scenario, the Supreme Court protected emotionally charged speech short of
incitement, regardless of viewpoint.[173] This echoes Mill, who decried viewpoint discrimination due to "the mischief of denying a hearing to opinions
because we, in our own judgment, have condemned them."[174] Other public
forum decisions in the early to mid-1980s were of a similar caliber.[175]

A more Millian approach was developing for commercial speech until the
last term of the Burger Court, as the justices struck down multiple restrictions
on advertising from 1982 through 1985.[176] The Supreme Court's steady march
toward Mill on commercial speech halted in *Posadas de Puerto Rico Associates v.*

Tourism Company (1986), where Justice Rehnquist wrote for a 5–4 majority in upholding a ban on gambling advertising, even where gambling was legal, using the deferential *Central Hudson* test. Rehnquist—who opposed constitutional protections for commercial speech and rejected Millian theory in *Central Hudson*—characterized the expression in question disparagingly, writing that "this case involves the restriction of pure commercial speech which does no more than propose a commercial transaction."[177] This rationale permitted Rehnquist to uphold a ban on expression that "concerns a lawful activity and is not misleading or fraudulent," due to government concerns that more advertising could lead to immoral activity.[178] Granted, Mill questioned in *On Liberty* whether gambling should be made legal, and if it is legal, Mill indicated that the state may be able to impose restrictions on "promoting intemperance."[179] However, Mill's arguments in this section of *On Liberty* were rather tepid, arguing in multiple places in this passage that "there are arguments on both sides," and simply that there was "considerable force" in some of the arguments justifying prohibition.[180] Thus, at best, Mill might have questioned the level of protection for such activity. At worst, such restrictions run directly counter to Mill's harm principle and his antipaternalistic approach expressed throughout *On Liberty*.

Justice Brennan in dissent reflected this latter interpretation of Mill: "I see no reason why commercial speech should be afforded less protection than other types of speech where . . . the government seeks to suppress commercial speech in order to deprive consumers of accurate information concerning lawful activity."[181] As Brennan explained, "No differences between commercial and other kinds of speech justify protecting commercial speech less extensively where . . . the government seeks to manipulate private behavior by depriving citizens of truthful information concerning lawful activities."[182] Brennan's dissent was antipaternalistic on free expression, similar to Mill's views on the subject.[183]

At the end of the Burger Court, First Amendment jurisprudence held largely steady from where it was when Chief Justice Warren retired. The justices remained fractured on some of its most contentious areas of free expression, with Millian and non-Millian justices largely in a standoff during the 1970s and into the 1980s. Changes in Supreme Court personnel resulted in some small advances toward a Millian approach, but these were balanced by decisions where the Supreme Court slightly backed away from earlier, established protections. This equilibrium was a result of bold Warren Court rulings that formally overturned earlier non-Millian decisions. As chapter 8 demonstrates, the Supreme Court's expansion of Millian thought continued to a greater degree soon after Chief Justice Burger's retirement in 1986.

CHAPTER 8

A Bedrock Principle

Brennan Leads the Rehnquist Court Closer to Mill

The Rehnquist Court's early jurisprudence largely mirrored that of the Burger Court's latter years. After William Rehnquist was elevated to chief justice and Antonin Scalia took his associate justice seat, Millian theory was applied in key areas of First Amendment jurisprudence. However, as with the end of the Burger Court, the early Rehnquist Court still fell short of Mill's prescriptions in various areas, especially sexually oriented expression, symbolic speech, and commercial speech. Nevertheless, Brennan and Marshall remained steadfast in adhering to jurisprudence that bore great resemblance to the philosophy in *On Liberty*. Blackmun and Stevens became more Millian. Personnel changes would solidify more precedents, reflecting traditions begun by Holmes and Brandeis. The nature of free expression questions continued to change—particularly as new media, like cable television and the Internet, were used by a larger percentage of the public—and free speech questions remained in need of Supreme Court resolution. More and more, those questions were resolved by resorting to Millian reasoning.

The Rehnquist Court's first term, 1986 to 1987, decided several important expressive freedom cases. Even in decisions where the majority espoused no Millian philosophy, dissenters often did, and in several others the majority was Millian.[1] For instance, in *Turner v. Safley* (1987), a 5–4 majority held that regulations of First Amendment rights of prisoners (to engage in correspondence) should receive only rational basis review, thus lowering the level of protection for inmates that had been established by the Burger Court in the 1970s.[2] In *Turner*, Justice O'Connor's opinion of the Court reasoned that it was proper "to accord deference to the appropriate prison authorities" because "running a prison is an inordinately difficult undertaking."[3] O'Connor upheld extensive restrictions on inmate communication, reasoning that "the correspondence regulation does not deprive prisoners of *all* means of expression."[4]

Granted, there are major security difficulties in running a prison, especially when it comes to concerns about violence and inmate escape. But in dissent, Justice Stevens rebuked the majority for upholding a prison regulation that infringed on fundamental rights. Stevens noted that "security is logically furthered by a total ban on inmate communication, not only with other inmates but also with outsiders who conceivably might be interested in arranging an attack within the prison or an escape from it," but such a rule would not be constitutional for furthering that interest.[5] Stevens wrote of "the exchange of mail" and "the satisfaction, solace, and support it affords to a confined inmate."[6] The majority elevated vague institutional concerns about the individual right to engage in expression that may promote happiness and even the development of intelligence and virtue; the *Turner* dissent invoked Millian arguments.[7] The majority's focus on discipline over expressive rights strayed far from what Mill advocated, particularly without a showing of harm existing in any of the communications at issue in the case.

In *Pope v. Illinois* (1987), both the majority and dissent started moving closer toward Mill on regulation of sexually oriented expression. Justice White wrote for a 5–4 majority that the *Miller* test's third prong requires a "reasonable person," not merely "an ordinary member of any given community," to decide whether a work, taken as a whole, lacks serous literary, artistic, political, or scientific value.[8] According to White, requiring anything less would risk that "a jury member could consider himself bound to follow prevailing local views."[9] The Supreme Court confirmed in *Pope* something that decisions from the late 1970s began to suggest, that determinations of value in obscenity cases should reflect a national, not a local, standard.[10] This was a subtle move toward Mill, who opposed provincial notions of morality dictating what people can think and say. However, by allowing a jury to determine if a work is protected based on what a "reasonable person" would think, the Supreme Court in *Pope* still made it easy for juries to suppress unorthodox or cutting-edge sexually oriented expression.[11] Stevens's dissent demonstrated a more Millian approach: "The difficulties inherent in the Court's 'reasonable person' standard reaffirm my conviction that government may not constitutionally criminalize mere possession or sale of obscene literature, absent some connection to minors or obtrusive display to unconsenting adults."[12] Like he did in his *Paris Adult Theatre I* dissent, Justice Brennan reiterated in *Pope* his "view that *any* regulation of such material with respect to consenting adults suffers from the defect that the concept of 'obscenity' cannot be defined with sufficient specificity and clarity . . . to prevent substantial erosion of protected speech."[13] In both *Turner* and *Pope*, the four dissenters taking the more Millian approach were Brennan, Marshall, Blackmun, and Stevens.

In other cases during 1986 to 1987, most or all of those four justices were able to convince at least one or two more of their colleagues to form a Millian majority.[14] In *Rankin v. McPherson* (1987), a 5–4 Supreme Court affirmed the right of public employees to speak on matters of public concern, ruling unconstitutional the firing of a deputy constable for casually remarking about the 1981 assassination attempt of President Ronald Reagan, "If they go for him again, I hope they get him."[15] Justice Marshall steered the majority more toward *Pickering* and away from the more deferential *Connick* decision on public employee rights: "Vigilance is necessary to ensure that public employers do not use authority over employees to silence discourse, not because it hampers public functions but simply because superiors disagree with the content of employees' speech."[16] This echoes Mill's emphasis on protecting dissent to improve society.[17] Furthermore, the Supreme Court clarified that the burden was on the government to prove that firing an employee for their expression was justifiable.[18] Marshall's opinion of the Court reflected Mill's notion that public employees should have liberties restricted only if "there is a definite damage, or a definite risk of damage, either to an individual or to the public," with Marshall reasoning that the deputy constable spoke on matters of public concern, and while her "statement was made at the workplace, there is no evidence that it interfered with the efficient functioning of the office."[19] With *Rankin* as precedent, the Supreme Court announced Millian rulings on public employee speech rights throughout Rehnquist's tenure as chief justice.[20]

Houston v. Hill (1987) followed *Lewis v. New Orleans*, continuing to chip away at *Chaplinsky*'s fighting words doctrine by striking down as overbroad an ordinance making it illegal to "oppose, molest, abuse or interrupt any policeman in the execution of his duty."[21] Hill sued the city after he was acquitted of violating that ordinance for shouting "Why don't you pick on somebody your own size?" to a police officer who was speaking to another person; when the officer inquired if Hill was speaking to him, Hill responded, "Yes, why don't you pick on somebody my size?"[22] As Justice Brennan wrote for the Supreme Court, "The First Amendment protects a significant amount of verbal criticism and challenge directed at police officers," just as Mill believed that the freedom of speech includes protecting "intemperate discussion, namely invective, sarcasm, personality, and the like."[23] As Brennan put it forthrightly, "The freedom of individuals verbally to oppose or challenge police action without thereby risk-ing arrest is one of the principal characteristics by which we distinguish a free nation from a police state."[24] Brennan, like Mill, concluded that although the justices were "mindful that the preservation of liberty depends in part upon the maintenance of social order . . . the First Amendment recognizes, wisely we think, that a certain amount of expressive disorder not only is inevitable in a society committed to individual freedom, but must itself be protected if that freedom would survive."[25] *Hill* appeared to deny that the fighting ords doc-trine could be applied to speech directed at police.[26] Since *Chaplinsky* also in-volved speech to a police officer, *Hill* narrowed the anti-Millian doctrine's application.

Lewis Powell, who sometimes joined the Brennan-Marshall-Blackmun-Stevens group, retired in the summer of 1987. Since President Reagan's initial nominee to replace Powell, Robert Bork, was rejected by the Senate, Anthony Kennedy was not confirmed to replace Powell until February 1988.[27] Thus, there were several First Amendment cases heard between Powell's retirement and Kennedy's investiture. In *Hazelwood School District v. Kuhlmeier* (1988), a 5–3 Supreme Court held that a public high school principal may constitutionally excise articles deemed inappropriate (in this case, articles about divorce and teenage pregnancy) from a school-sponsored newspaper. As Justice White wrote for the majority, the school may decide that "readers or listeners are not exposed to material that may be inappropriate for their level of maturity."[28] White appealed to one of Mill's arguments used to justify restricting young people's freedoms, that a school may censor material that is "unsuitable for immature audiences."[29] However, this narrowing of student speech rights that began in *Bethel* was noticed in dissent by Justice Brennan, who characterized the principal's actions as viewpoint discrimination: "Official censorship of stu-dent speech on the ground that it addresses 'potentially sensitive topics' is . . . impermissible."[30] Mill supported young people being introduced to different ideas, which was relevant in *Hazelwood*.[31] Furthermore, Mill wanted to see lib-erties protected so that people could learn from their mistakes for utilitarian reasons, meaning that high school students should have opportunities to learn how to become future professional journalists, which will benefit society.[32] As Brennan explained, "Public education serves vital national interests in prepar-ing the Nation's youth for life in our increasingly complex society and for the duties of citizenship in our democratic Republic. The public school conveys to our young the information and tools required not merely to survive in, but to contribute to, civilized society."[33] Brennan's dissent reflected more of Mill's analysis than the majority opinion, even though one could argue that one of Mill's key exceptions to the harm principle applied.

The Supreme Court's other expressive freedom cases heard between Powell's retirement and Kennedy's appointment were more Millian in tone.[34] This was best exemplified when the justices unanimously found that parodies of public figures were protected by the First Amendment in *Hustler Magazine v. Falwell* (1988). The author of the Supreme Court's opinion, Chief Justice Rehnquist, who was not a devotee of Mill's philosophy, cited Holmes's *Abrams* dissent and quoted its line relevant to the marketplace of ideas to support his opinion: "The heart of the First Amendment is the recognition of the fundamental importance of the free flow of ideas and opinions on matters of public interest and concern."[35] Rehnquist wrote for his colleagues that "even though falsehoods have little value in and of themselves, they are nevertheless inevitable in free debate, and [to] impose strict liability on a publisher for false factual assertions would have an undoubted 'chilling' effect on speech . . . that does have constitutional value."[36] This is Millian in tone, although Mill would have gone further than Rehnquist, arguing that even falsehoods have value in an open society, even if that protection will not always lead to truth prevailing.[37] And, just as Mill advocated for protection of invective due to the subjectivity of determining when speech is impolite, Rehnquist rejected a First Amendment standard that would allow sanctioning "outrageous" speech: "'Outrageousness' in the area of political and social discourse has an inherent subjectiveness about it which would allow a jury to impose liability on the basis of the jurors' tastes or views, or perhaps on the basis of their dislike of a particular expression."[38] Instead, Rehnquist extended the *Sullivan* standard to this case, concluding that "such a standard is necessary to give adequate 'breathing space' to the freedoms protected by the First Amendment."[39]

With Kennedy's appointment in 1988, Brennan was progressively able to lay the groundwork for a more consistent Millian understanding of the First Amendment. In several cases, he built a coalition of at least five justices who were willing to apply Mill's theory. This was not true for every decision, but it started to become more consistent, just as it was on the Supreme Court in the mid- to late 1960s.

The most important decision of the early Rehnquist Court that ushered Mill's philosophy into the Supreme Court's precedents was *Texas v. Johnson* (1989), as it involved speech critical of the most prominent "symbol of nationhood and national unity."[40] A 5–4 Supreme Court struck down a state flag desecration statute applied to a political protestor who burned the US flag, with Justice Brennan writing for the majority (and Kennedy providing the fifth vote) that Texas was engaged in unconstitutional viewpoint discrimination: "If there is a bedrock principle underlying the First Amendment, it is that the government may not prohibit the expression of an idea simply because society finds the idea itself offensive or disagreeable."[41] Brennan cited *Brandenburg*, proclaiming that the "First Amendment does not guarantee that other concepts virtually sacred to our Nation as a whole—such as the principle that discrimination on the basis of race is odious and destructive—will go unquestioned in the marketplace of ideas. We decline, therefore, to create for the flag an exception to the joust of principles protected by the First Amendment."[42] Like Mill, Brennan believed that people of all perspectives should be free to discuss their ideas, even if they are upsetting.[43] Brennan also built off of Holmes's free speech jurisprudence in this regard.[44] Brennan emphasized Millian thinking when he proclaimed the importance of protecting more than reasoned expression: "The emotive impact of speech on its audience is not a 'secondary effect' unrelated to the content of the expression itself."[45] Instead of restricting expression, Brennan conveyed that our response should be more speech: "The way to preserve the flag's special role is not to punish those who feel differently about these matters. It is to persuade them that they are wrong."[46]

Brennan's *Johnson* opinion eviscerated *O'Brien*'s symbolic speech test—a test deferential to government interests—by adding an additional constitutional check. The opinion reordered *O'Brien* by adding a precursor test. After *Johnson*, the Supreme Court first determines if the government's interest is related "to the suppression of free expression." If this is the case, the *O'Brien* test is set aside, and the justices instead apply a heightened standard of review.[47] The case made the *O'Brien* test applicable in relatively rare circumstances. Instead, Brennan placed more emphasis in *Johnson* on some of the Supreme Court's greatest Millian opinions, citing to and quoting from Holmes's *Abrams* dissent, Brandeis's *Whitney* concurrence, *Barnette*, and *Brandenburg*.[48] Brennan, like Mill, emphasized the connection between the freedom of expression and democratic self-governance.[49] This was one of several cases where the Supreme Court's Millian approach was becoming more evident at the end of the 1980s and the beginning of the 1990s.[50]

Some key limitations remained, though. On questions of obscenity and sexual expression, the Supreme Court was issuing opinions that were more Millian than in the mid-1970s through the mid-1980s, even as *Miller* was maintained.[51] In *Sable Communications v. FCC* (1989), the justices ruled that although obscene messages may be banned through dial-a-porn services (thus continuing to adhere to *Miller*), adults may not be banned from accessing indecent speech through such services. Justice White wrote for the majority that "there is a compelling interest in protecting the physical and psychological well-being of minors. This interest extends to shielding minors from the influence of literature that is not obscene by adult standards."[52] This affirmed something akin to Mill's harm principle and Mill's restriction on certain liberties for children. Furthermore, White reasoned that, for adults, "sexual expression which is indecent but not obscene is protected by the First Amendment," concluding that the law in question had "the invalid effect of limiting the content of adult telephone conversations to that which is suitable for children to hear."[53] In a partial concurrence and dissent in *Sable*, Justice Brennan wrote for Justices Marshall and Stevens that the ban on obscene messages should have also been struck down: "The exaction of criminal penalties for the distribution of obscene materials to consenting adults is constitutionally intolerable."[54] For the dissent, the only consideration was whether the material involved children or was distributed to nonconsenting adults: "This criminal statute curtails freedom of speech far more radically than the Government's interest in preventing harm to minors could possibly license."[55] Even more than the *Sable* majority, this reflects the harm principle and Mill's idea that children "must be protected against their own actions as well as against external injuries," while adults should remain free to express themselves to each other.[56]

Regarding commercial speech, the Burger Court's decision in *Posadas* looked like it might signal a retrenchment on First Amendment protections, as it was more deferential to government interests than *Central Hudson*.[57] It was not clear if the Rehnquist Court would continue to adhere to *Posadas*. In some cases, the Supreme Court was striking down more restrictive regulations on commercial speech, but even in these cases, the justices were using the deferential *Central Hudson* test, falling short of Millian standards.[58] Reliance on *Central Hudson* and *Posadas* led the Supreme Court in *Board of Trustees v. Fox* (1989) to uphold a public university's prohibition of commercial speech, which resulted in an arrest of a woman holding a "Tupperware party" in a college dorm room. For the 6–3 majority, Justice Scalia affirmed that "communications can constitute commercial speech notwithstanding the fact that they contain discussions of important public issues," which runs contrary to Mill's philosophy of protecting the discussion of all ideas.[59] The Supreme Court in *Fox* considered speech combining commercial and noncommercial elements to be commercial speech, thus affording it a lower level of protection.[60] Scalia wrote regarding the *Central Hudson* test that the justices "reject the contention that the test we have described is overly permissive."[61]

Justice Blackmun, demonstrating how much he adopted Mill's philosophy in his later years on the Supreme Court, wrote for Justices Brennan and Marshall in dissent in *Fox*, emphasizing a harm principle argument: "A public university cannot categorically prevent these fully protected expressive activities from occurring in a student's dorm room. The dorm room is the student's residence for the academic term, and a student surely has a right to use this residence for expressive activities that are not inconsistent with the educational mission of the university or with the needs of other dorm residents."[62] For the Millian dissenters, the *Central Hudson* test was overly restrictive, as it upheld a rule that would also prohibit students from meeting in their dorm rooms with paid doctors, lawyers, tutors, music teachers, or speech therapists.[63] Blackmun argued that "it cannot plausibly be asserted that music, art, speech, writing, or other kinds of lessons are inconsistent with the educational mission of the university."[64] If commercial speech contains cultural elements or public affairs aspects, it helps foster democratic self-government or improves society more generally, and Mill would have advocated for its protection.[65]

With regard to cases involving noncommercial solicitation or speech in public forums, the record was mixed at this time.[66] For instance, in *Ward v. Rock Against Racism* (1989) the Supreme Court upheld a New York City rule requiring musical performances at the Central Park bandshell to use city-provided sound equipment and a city-employed sound technician. Citing the non-Millian precedent *Kovacs*, Justice Kennedy wrote for the 6–3 majority that "government ha[s] a substantial interest in protecting its citizens from unwelcome noise."[67] This emphasis on order over expression was opposed by Justice Marshall, who argued in dissent that the rule was a prior restraint: "Government's exclusive control of the means of communication enables public officials to censor speech in advance of its expression."[68] Although Mill never opined on the use of sound amplification equipment, Marshall made connections to restrictions on expression that were familiar to Mill when he chided the majority for setting a precedent that could have far-reaching consequences: "After today's decision, a city could claim that bans on handbill distribution or on door-to-door solicitation are the most effective means of avoiding littering and fraud."[69]

Nevertheless, in *Ward* the Supreme Court was developing a more protective intermediate scrutiny test for content-neutral regulations: "The government may impose reasonable restrictions on the time, place, or manner of protected speech, provided the restrictions are justified without reference to the content of the regulated speech, that they are narrowly tailored to serve a significant governmental interest, and that they leave open ample alternative channels for communication of the information."[70] Justices Brennan, Marshall, and Stevens dissented in *Ward*, but the test the majority used would eventually be applied in a more Millian fashion during the Roberts Court in cases like *McCullen v. Coakley* (2014). Additionally, in *Ward*, Justice Kennedy proclaimed for the Supreme Court that "music is one of the oldest forms of human expression" that "is protected under the First Amendment."[71] Mill would have approved of that statement, writing in *On Liberty* about the need to protect the "diversity of taste" regarding many pursuits, including music.[72]

The Supreme Court's record was also mixed on its use of Millian philosophy in cases involving campaign expression.[73] The Supreme Court's march toward applying Mill's philosophy to campaign finance took an interesting turn in *Austin v. Michigan Chamber of Commerce* (1990), as some elements of Millian philosophy were displayed by both the majority and dissent. The majority in *Austin* upheld state bans on nonprofit corporations using treasury funds to support or oppose candidates in elections. The Supreme Court affirmed *Buckley* in ruling that "the use of funds to support a political candidate is 'speech'; independent campaign expenditures constitute political expression at the core of our electoral process and of the First Amendment freedoms."[74] The *Austin* majority upheld the regulation to prevent what Mill would have been concerned about as other-regarding activity relating to the world of trade—"the corrosive and distorting effects of immense aggregations of wealth that are accumulated with the help of the corporate form and that have little or no correlation to the public's support for the corporation's political ideas."[75] However, for Justice Kennedy in dissent, the *Austin* majority minimized free expression concerns and promoted censorship: "It is an unhappy paradox that this Court, which has the role of protecting speech and of barring censorship from all aspects of political life, now becomes itself the censor."[76] Justice Scalia was more pointed in drawing connections to Millian concerns with majority tyranny: "The Court today endorses the principle that too much speech is an evil that the democratic majority can proscribe. I dissent because that principle is contrary to our case law and incompatible with the absolutely central truth of the First Amendment: that government cannot be trusted to assure, through censorship, the 'fairness' of political debate."[77] In 1989 and 1990, there was little evidence of Millian thought from the majority in cases involving libel and inmates.[78]

These latter cases notwithstanding, on his retirement in 1990, Justice Brennan had left an indelible mark on the Supreme Court's jurisprudence. The first justice to quote Mill in a First Amendment opinion of the Court had established numerous precedents that reached Millian outcomes and used Millian philosophy. His eloquent dissents also provided Millian arguments for justices to review in future cases. Brennan belongs with the Supreme Court's most Millian justices, including Holmes, Brandeis, Hughes, Black, and Douglas. Brennan's personal influence would continue after his retirement, as he maintained an office at the Supreme Court building for several more years. David Souter, the justice who took Brennan's seat, regularly sought the retired justice's advice, which helped move him—like Blackmun and Stevens before him—more toward Mill's philosophy during his tenure on the Supreme Court.[79] Brennan also habitually dined with O'Connor after his retirement, which may have persuaded her to take a more Millian approach in First Amendment cases.[80]

When Souter joined the Supreme Court in 1990, Millianism was growing.[81] Millian principles were so established that more opinions addressed Millian reasoning, including when the Supreme Court ultimately upheld restrictions on expression. *Barnes v. Glen Theatre* (1991) was a 5–4 decision in which Chief Justice Rehnquist's plurality opinion ruled that states may prohibit nude dancing at businesses. Rehnquist's opinion applied the *O'Brien* test, and Rehnquist emphasized that the law in question was constitutional because it "furthers a substantial government interest in protecting order and *morality*," something Mill would have found unpersuasive.[82] However, Rehnquist's plurality opinion also contained more pro-expression pronouncements, including for the first time an assertion that this form of sexual expression receives some constitutional protection: "Nude dancing of the kind sought to be performed here is expressive conduct within the outer perimeters of the First Amendment."[83] More importantly, Justice Souter's concurrence stressed the need to concentrate on something akin to the harm principle by proclaiming that a "zoning ordinance designed to prevent the occurrence of harmful secondary effects" could be upheld as constitutional.[84] Souter defined specific instances of harmful secondary effects as "prostitution, sexual assault, and associated crimes."[85] Souter's conception of secondary effects was more exact than the vague notion of secondary effects referred to by older decisions like *Young* and *Renton*. Souter also identified crimes that clearly violate the harm principle, such as sexual assault. This emphasis on harms to public safety, rather than moral objections, reflects Souter's classically liberal utilitarian thinking, similar to Mill.[86]

Admittedly, Mill had some reservations about appeals to secondary effects. In his final chapter of *On Liberty*, "Applications," he expressed ambivalence regarding the regulation of gambling houses and brothels, especially if the practice is driven by popular morality.[87] Although Mill did not speak of prostitution in *On Liberty*, he later said that "with the exception of sheer brutal violence, there is no greater evil that this propensity [of men] can produce than prostitution. Of all modes of sexual indulgence consistent with personal freedom and safety of women, I regard prostitution as the very worst."[88] Characteristically for Mill, though, he worried that considering secondary effects would be filtered through a populist lens, and the regulation would be broadened to unjustly burden nonconformists. Mill appeared before a royal commission to denounce the Contagious Disease Acts, which were laws designed to protect soldiers and sailors from venereal disease by empowering police to physically examine women they believed were infected.[89] For Mill, secondary effects could not justify regulating human activities, particularly speech, unless those effects were narrowly construed and directly reflected the harm principle. The Supreme Court's older appeals to secondary effects in *Young* and *Renton* were far from Millian, but the more specific harms identified by Souter in *Barnes* reach closer to Mill's arguments.

Among the four *Barnes* dissenters, the sentiment was Millian as well, but it emphasized another argument from *On Liberty*, by letting the individual decide what art to consume: "That the performances in the Kitty Kat Lounge may not be high art, to say the least, and may not appeal to the Court, is hardly an excuse for distorting and ignoring settled doctrine. The Court's assessment of the artistic merits of nude dancing performances should not be the determining factor in deciding this case."[90] The dissenters advocated protecting the expression at issue by appealing to personal autonomy and not permitting majoritarian morality to dictate the bounds of acceptable art. The dissent channeled Mill by citing cases like *Cohen*, *Texas v. Johnson*, and *Sable*, showing the power of precedent to keep Millian thought alive on the Supreme Court.[91]

What might appear to be an anti-Millian decision in *Masson v. New Yorker Magazine* (1991) also took the Supreme Court closer to Mill. The justices unanimously held that "deliberate alteration" of language in quotation marks in a news story could be evidence of actual malice if the "alteration results in a material change in the meaning conveyed by the statement."[92] For the Supreme Court, Justice Kennedy proclaimed that "in general, quotation marks around a passage indicate to the reader that the passage reproduces the speaker's words verbatim."[93] However, Justice Kennedy reasoned that "quotations do not always convey that the speaker actually said or wrote the quoted material. . . . Writers and reporters by necessity alter what people say, at the very least to eliminate grammatical and syntactical infelicities. If every alteration constituted the falsity required to prove actual malice, the practice of journalism . . . would require a radical change, one inconsistent with our precedents and First Amendment principles."[94] Furthermore, "an interviewer who writes from notes often will engage in the task of attempting a reconstruction of the speaker's statement. . . . If a speaker makes an obvious misstatement, for example by unconscious substitution of one name for another, a journalist might alter the speaker's words but preserve his intended meaning."[95] Thus, Kennedy's opinion of the Court bolstered the protection publishers have against libel claims, which he explained as follows: "If an author alters a speaker's words but effects no material change in meaning, including any meaning conveyed by the manner or fact of expression, the speaker suffers no injury to reputation that is compensable as a defamation."[96] As Kennedy put it, "Minor inaccuracies do not amount to falsity so long as the substance, the gist, the sting, of the libelous charge be justified."[97] The practical effect of the decision defends the press more, as it protects reporters who quote sources in good faith, publishing a quote that is wrong but substantially true.[98] Reporters engaged in the endeavors Kennedy described are searching for truth, just as Mill advocated. Mill would have gone farther, arguing for the protection of speech even when it is "exaggerated, distorted, and disjoined from the truths."[99] Nevertheless, this growing protection of free speech in *Masson* represented Millian thinking, which was also manifested in the decision's reliance on *Sullivan*.[100] Millian thinking was evident in multiple free press cases during the Rehnquist Court.[101] These cases created practical protections for the press within the spirit of Mill's pronouncement that "the 'liberty of the press' [is] one of the securities against corrupt or tyrannical government."[102] Indeed, when he wrote *On Liberty*, Mill had long understood the freedom of the press as helping to prevent governments from being tyrannical.[103]

Assuredly, there were cases right after Souter's appointment where the majority did not exhibit Millian philosophy.[104] Nevertheless, the tide was turning more toward Mill, even after Brennan's departure. The retirement in 1991 of Justice Marshall, who displayed consistent Millian thinking, might be expected to decelerate the Supreme Court's march toward Mill. Instead, the appointment of Clarence Thomas continued the Supreme Court on its Millian path. This is true even though Thomas has taken some anti-Millian positions since the beginning of the Roberts Court, particularly in cases involving expressive rights of younger people in *Morse v. Frederick* (2007) and *Mahanoy Area School District v. B.L.* (2021), and in his questioning of *Sullivan*'s validity in a series of opinions starting in 2019.

The most noteworthy freedom of expression decision in Thomas's first term was *R.A.V. v. St. Paul* (1992), where the justices unanimously struck down a bias-motivated crime ordinance that prohibited the use of a Nazi swastika or burning cross that "arouses anger, alarm or resentment in others on the basis of race, color, creed, religion or gender."[105] The justices overturned a juvenile's conviction under this ordinance for burning a cross, with Scalia writing for the Supreme Court that even if a law restricts fighting words, the law cannot engage in viewpoint or content discrimination: "The First Amendment does not permit St. Paul to impose special prohibitions on those speakers who express views on disfavored subjects."[106] As Scalia explained, "The reason why fighting words are categorically excluded from the protection of the First Amendment is not that their content communicates any particular idea, but that their content embodies a particularly intolerable (and socially unnecessary) *mode* of expressing *whatever* idea the speaker wishes to convey."[107] Scalia colorfully summarized this point by stating that "St. Paul has no such authority to license one side of a debate to fight freestyle, while requiring the other to follow Marquis of Queensberry rules."[108] Although the Supreme Court did not overrule *Chaplinsky*, *R.A.V.* effectively buried the fighting words doctrine. In *Gooding v. Wilson* (1972), the Supreme Court overturned an ordinance aimed at banning fighting words for being overbroad, meaning it restricts *more* speech than may be constitutionally proscribed; in *R.A.V.*, the Supreme Court overturned an ordinance discriminating on the basis of content for not prohibiting *enough* expression.[109] Even though *Chaplinsky* still survives as precedent, the practical difficulty of being able to construct a constitutional "goldilocks" fighting words law that prohibits enough but not too much expression essentially means that the Millian position on speech now reigns in this area of First Amendment law. The justices implicitly recognize this, as the Supreme Court has not upheld a fighting words conviction since *Chaplinsky* in 1942.[110] As a follow-up to *R.A.V.*, the Supreme Court in *Wisconsin v. Mitchell* (1993) unanimously upheld a penalty enhancement for bias-motivated conduct—in this case, a physical assault.[111] To protect expression in *R.A.V.* but hold that a bias-motivated penalty enhancement in an assault case is constitutional in *Mitchell* mirrors Mill's harm principle. As Mill succinctly put it in *On Liberty*, "No one pretends that actions should be as free as opinions."[112] Other public forum cases in the 1991 and 1992 terms revealed flashes of Millian thinking.[113]

After Justice Thomas's appointment, commercial speech protections remained unclear, continuing the confusion from the *Posadas* case. The justices struck down some overly burdensome restrictions on commercial speech in the early 1990s.[114] But in *United States v. Edge Broadcasting* (1993), the Supreme Court held constitutional a federal law banning the broadcasting in nonlottery states of state-run lottery advertisements. Justice White's opinion of the Court emphasized that "the Constitution . . . affords a lesser protection to commercial speech than to other constitutionally guaranteed expression."[115] Instead of accentuating expressive freedom, like Mill, the majority stressed government power to ban speech deemed an immoral evil: "The activity underlying the relevant advertising—gambling—implicates no constitutionally protected right; rather, it falls into a category of 'vice' activity."[116] Recalling the more Millian decision in *Bigelow*, Justice Stevens argued in dissent in *Edge Broadcasting* that a federal law banning such advertising "is about paternalism, and informational protectionism. It is about one State's interference with its citizens' fundamental constitutional right to travel in a state of enlightenment, not government-induced ignorance."[117] Stevens then elaborated on his Millian understanding of the law at issue:

> The Federal Government has not regulated the content of such advertisements to ensure that they are not misleading, nor has it provided for

the distribution of more speech, such as warnings or educational information about gambling. Rather, the United States has selected the most intrusive, and dangerous, form of regulation possible—a ban on truthful information regarding a lawful activity imposed for the purpose of manipulating, through ignorance, the consumer choices of some of its citizens. Unless justified by a truly substantial governmental interest, this extreme, and extremely paternalistic, measure surely cannot withstand scrutiny under the First Amendment.[118]

Mill was aware of the complexities that occur when an ideal theory is exposed to the complexities of the lived world. In *On Liberty*'s final chapter, "Applications," Mill argues that "trade is a social act" that has social ramifications, and some business practices can legitimately be regulated.[119] Releasing untreated chemicals into the local water source puts everyone in the community at risk, even those who do not benefit from the business and who certainly did not consent to undertake these risks; Mill cited regulating dangerous occupations, requiring warning labels for dangerous products, enforcing sanitary codes, and creating laws against fraudulent advertising as legitimate restraints.[120] He drew a sharp distinction between these regulations and ones that paternalistically restrict buyers from purchasing goods or services society deemed immoral or risky.[121]

Mill had a more complicated view on advertising addictive products (like alcohol) or activities (like gambling): "The interest, however, of these dealers in promoting intemperance is a real evil and justifies the State in imposing restrictions and requiring guarantees which, but for that justification, would be infringements of legitimate liberty."[122] Nonetheless, while he supported some restraints on promoting these products, Mill never called for total bans on this speech, and he generally found total bans on expression to be flawed. The *Edge Broadcasting* decision strayed from Mill, who wished to see more regulation for expression promoting vices than for other types of expression, but also eschewed the paternalism of complete bans. In this case, even more than in *Young* or *Posadas*, the link between harm to the public weal and the legal restrictions on advertising was tenuous. Although the Supreme Court majority was not ready to adopt that line of Millian thinking in 1993, that would change several years later.

Justice White, who inconsistently exhibited Mill's philosophy, retired in 1993. Ruth Bader Ginsburg was then elevated to the Supreme Court. Several cases over the next term demonstrated that Ginsburg's addition continued the Supreme Court's drift toward Mill, with some caveats.[123] In *Ladue v. Gilleo* (1994), Justice Stevens wrote a unanimous decision, striking down an ordinance prohibiting the posting of most types of signs, including political signs, on residential properties. The law allowed nonprofit organizations and commercial establishments to post signs not permitted on residential properties. The sign Gilleo was banned from displaying on her front lawn read "Say No to War in the Persian Gulf, Call Congress Now."[124] While Stevens wrote that municipalities have the power to stop the "'unlimited' proliferation of residential signs," he applied strict scrutiny to the law in *Ladue*.[125] Strict scrutiny requires that "a State . . . assert a compelling state interest [and] demonstrate that its law is necessary to serve the asserted interest."[126] Strict scrutiny's emphasis on protecting expression is the modern iteration of the older preferred freedoms approach to the First Amendment, which demonstrates the Supreme Court's return to its Millian roots of the 1930s and 1940s.[127] In *Ladue*, Stevens wrote: "Signs that react to a local happening or express a view on a controversial issue both reflect and animate change in the life of a community. . . . They may not afford the same opportunities for conveying complex ideas as do other media, but residential signs have long been an important and distinct medium of expression."[128] Mill would agree: in *On Liberty* he discussed that an opinion on a "placard" should generally be permitted, except in instances such as "when handed about among [a] mob."[129] Such sentiment dovetails with the Supreme Court's admonition that residential signage is protected within narrowly proscribed limits. Mill's placement of free expression within the larger notion of freedom was captured by Stevens in *Ladue*: "A special respect for individual liberty in the home has long been part of our culture and our law; that principle has special resonance when the government seeks to constrain a person's ability to *speak* there."[130] Mill emphasized the exercise of free expression in the political realm, which was the type of speech at issue in *Ladue*.

Similarly, in *Turner Broadcasting v. FCC I* (1994), Justice Kennedy wrote for the Supreme Court about the need to protect speech unless actual harm results, thus arguing something like Mill's harm principle: "When the Government defends a regulation on speech as a means to redress past harms or prevent anticipated harms, it must do more than simply posit the existence of the disease sought to be cured. It must demonstrate that the recited harms are real, not merely conjectural, and that the regulation will in fact alleviate these harms in a direct and material way."[131] In *Turner Broadcasting*, the Supreme Court refused to extend the greater regulatory power that government has for broadcast radio and television to cable television, and Kennedy began questioning the Supreme Court's historical deference to government for broadcast media regulation: "The rationale for applying a less rigorous standard of First Amendment scrutiny to broadcast regulation, whatever its validity in the cases elaborating it, does not apply in the context of cable regulation."[132] Kennedy stated that cable television expression must be left to the marketplace of ideas, regardless of the consequences: "The mere assertion of dysfunction or failure in a speech market, without more, is not sufficient to shield a speech regulation from the First Amendment standards applicable to nonbroadcast media."[133] Although Mill never wrote of cable television regulations, he advocated for the full protection of the free expression of ideas in newer media in his day, and he eschewed notions that government should be empowered to "fix" speech markets by deeming them "dysfunctional." The case also reflects Mill's concern with ensuring that actual harm must occur for individual autonomy to be restricted.[134] Kennedy was now becoming a leader in promoting a libertarian understanding of the First Amendment; starting in the 1994 term, for the next several years he took the speech-protective position more often than any other justice.[135]

Other cases in the 1993 term exhibited less Millianism.[136] Notably, *Madsen v. Women's Health Center* (1994) ruled unconstitutional some court-ordered buffer zones at an abortion clinic but upheld others (such as a thirty-six-foot buffer zone around clinic entrances). Even though the injunction was aimed at restricting speech by anti-abortion protestors, Chief Justice Rehnquist held for the Supreme Court that "the fact that the injunction covered people with a particular viewpoint does not itself render the injunction content or viewpoint based. Accordingly, the injunction issued in this case does not demand the level of heightened scrutiny."[137] In downplaying the free speech interests in *Madsen*, Rehnquist stressed the government's "strong interest in ensuring the public safety and order."[138] In direct contradiction to *Cohen*'s statement that filling the air "with verbal cacophony" is a "strength" of a free society, Rehnquist in *Madsen* proclaimed that "the First Amendment does not demand that patients at a medical facility undertake Herculean efforts to escape the cacophony of political protests."[139] According to Justice Scalia in dissent, the Supreme Court inappropriately applied a lower standard of scrutiny, finding "the injunction in the present case was content based (indeed, viewpoint based)," meaning that the injunction was trying to stifle an anti-abortion viewpoint.[140] Scalia elaborated that the "danger of content-based statutory restrictions upon speech is that they may be designed and used precisely to suppress the ideas in question rather than to achieve any other proper governmental aim. But that same danger exists with injunctions. . . . The injunction was sought against a single-issue advocacy group by persons and organizations with a business or social interest in suppressing that group's point of view."[141] Echoing Mill's idea that one person is not justified in silencing everyone else, Scalia proclaimed that the "right to free speech should not lightly be placed within the control of a single man or woman."[142] Nevertheless, even *Madsen* struck down a three-hundred-foot "no-approach zone" around the clinic.[143] That the case involved a specific injunction, not a statute, made it a poor case to judge the Supreme Court's direction on the freedom of expression in public forums. The Roberts Court would eventually move more toward Mill in cases involving public protests.

In the summer of 1994 Justice Blackmun retired, and soon thereafter, Stephen Breyer was appointed to the Supreme Court. No new justice would be appointed until 2005, making 1994 to 2005 one of the longest periods of personnel consistency in the Supreme Court's history. These nine justices would also forge a consistent expansion of Millian philosophy in almost every type of expression case.

Commercial speech was one area of First Amendment jurisprudence where the justices took a significant Millian turn in the latter years of the Rehnquist Court. From 1994 through 2005, in only one case did the justices uphold a restriction on commercial speech, and that was a 5–4 case involving attorney direct solicitation regulations.[144] The remainder of Rehnquist Court rulings saw majorities employ more Millian reasoning to commercial advertising.[145] This was apparent in *44 Liquormart v. Rhode Island* (1996), where the justices unanimously ruled that a state ban on alcohol advertising violated the First Amendment. In the opinion of the Court, Justice Stevens signaled that the Supreme Court was applying the *Central Hudson* test for commercial speech differently, giving more scrutiny to the government's asserted interest and whether its restrictions on expression advance that interest: "Precisely because bans against truthful, nonmisleading commercial speech rarely seek to protect consumers from either deception or overreaching, they usually rest solely on the offensive assumption that the public will respond 'irrationally' to the truth. The First Amendment directs us to be especially skeptical of regulations that seek to keep people in the dark for what the government perceives to be their own good."[146] Stevens emphasized that legitimate restrictions must prohibit real harms to other persons: "Bans that target truthful, nonmisleading commercial messages rarely protect consumers from such harms. Instead, such bans often serve only to obscure an underlying governmental policy that could be implemented without regulating speech. In this way, these commercial speech bans not only hinder consumer choice, but also impede debate over central issues of public policy."[147]

In a concurring opinion in *44 Liquormart*, Justice Thomas went further, advocating that the Supreme Court overrule *Central Hudson* and review regulations of commercial speech the same way it reviews regulations of noncommercial expression.[148] Thomas wrote with a Millian concern for paternalism, as when "the government's asserted interest is to keep legal users of a product or service ignorant in order to manipulate their choices in the marketplace."[149] For

Thomas, the *Central Hudson* test "invites judges to decide whether they themselves think that consumption of a product is harmful enough that it *should* be discouraged," and concluded, like Mill, "that informed adults are the best judges of their own interests."[150] Even though Mill thought that the government should have power to limit the "real evil" of allowing businesses to promote "intemperance," as noted above, he also eschewed letting the government impose "restrictions and requiring guarantees" that were greater than necessary and that were made out of a sense of morality.[151] Thus, the majority and Thomas's concurrence were appealing to Millian philosophy as applied to the freedom of expression. As explained by the dissent in *Fox*, restricting commercial speech often raises questions about public affairs in addition to advertising products or services.[152] Here, advertising alcohol raises questions about the morality of consuming alcohol, and if the ads had mentioned political concerns about the ad ban (e.g., an advertisement that asks consumers, "Don't you think it's unfair that the government won't let us advertise our low, low prices?!?!"), then the mixing of political and commercial speech would be difficult to untangle. Mill's solution to preventing a majority from imposing its morality was to prohibit it from imposing restrictions on speech for trumped-up reasons.

The Rehnquist Court's growing Millian approach to commercial speech is best encapsulated in *Greater New Orleans Broadcasting Association v. United States* (1999), where the justices unanimously overturned a complete ban on broadcasting gambling advertisements, effectively overruling *Posadas*. The Supreme Court's approach to *Central Hudson* by the late 1990s was emphasizing protection for commercial expression. As Stevens wrote in the opinion of the Court in *Greater New Orleans*, the justices presumed that "the speaker and the audience, not the Government, should be left to assess the value of accurate and nonmisleading information about lawful conduct."[153] By the close of the twentieth century, the Supreme Court "had rejected the argument that the power to restrict speech about certain socially harmful activities was as broad as the power to prohibit such conduct."[154] As for a government ban on gambling advertisements, the *Greater New Orleans* decision embraced the harm principle, chastising the federal government for "permitting a variety of speech that poses the same risks the Government purports to fear, while banning messages unlikely to cause any harm at all."[155] *44 Liquormart* and *Greater New Orleans* together represented a shift, with the justices indicating that they were giving more scrutiny to commercial speech regulations, particularly if those restrictions were undertaken for moral reasons.[156] For Mill, allowing businesses to provide truthful advertising about lawful activities to competent adults would be much more proper than a complete ban on such expression: "(Unless he is a child, or delirious, or in some state of excitement or absorption incompatible with the full use of the reflecting faculty), he ought, I conceive, to be only warned of the danger; not forcibly prevented from exposing himself to it."[157]

Regarding obscenity and sexual expression, the Supreme Court in the late 1990s and early 2000s moved as close to Mill as it had in the late 1960s. *Reno v. ACLU* (1997) struck down vague and content-based restrictions on "indecent" online speech in the Communications Decency Act (CDA); the CDA also prohibited obscenity online with reference to one prong of the *Miller* test only. Writing for the Supreme Court, Justice Stevens used Millian reasoning, referring to harm and the need to impose restrictions related to children, but affirming protection of expressive rights for adults: "It is true that we have repeatedly recognized the governmental interest in protecting children from harmful materials. But that interest does not justify an unnecessarily broad suppression of speech addressed to adults. As we have explained, the Government may not 'reduce the adult population . . . to . . . only what is fit for children.'"[158] In emphasizing a Millian principle that speech promotes democracy, Stevens spoke of "the vast democratic fora of the Internet," proclaiming how the "interest in encouraging freedom of expression in a democratic society outweighs any theoretical but unproven benefit of censorship."[159] Stevens rejected the government's argument in *Reno* that indecent and offensive expression online deters people from using the Internet: "The dramatic expansion of this new marketplace of ideas contradicts the factual basis of this contention. The record demonstrates that the growth of the Internet has been and continues to be phenomenal. As a matter of constitutional tradition, in the absence of evidence to the contrary, we presume that governmental regulation of the content of speech is more likely to interfere with the free exchange of ideas than to encourage it."[160] Stevens used the Millian marketplace of ideas analogy in his *Reno* opinion. Stevens had moved from the justice who penned the opinion of the Court in *Pacifica* in 1978 (upholding regulation of indecent speech in broadcast media) to become a convert to Millian philosophy. *Reno* was a signal that the Supreme Court would be as skeptical of government restrictions on speech online as it was for restrictions on print media or pure speech.[161] The justices struck down another portion of the CDA that applied to cable television, using reasoning similar to *Reno*.[162] The Supreme Court understood newer media to have as much protection as older media. The only exception remained broadcast media, where extensive restrictions contrasted with the freedom of pure speech, print media, cable television, and the Internet. Mill wanted expression in the media to have the same high level of protection as pure speech. Mill witnessed the world's first mass media as newspapers, particularly the affordable, accessible, and rapidly expanding "penny press." This development was not contained to England; in 1833 the

Morning Post debuted in New York City. Less than a decade later, it was joined by *The Sun*, the *New York Herald*, and the *New York Tribune*.[163]

A 5–4 majority upheld a ban on completely nude dancing in *Erie v. Pap's A.M.* (2000). According to Justice O'Connor's opinion of the Court, "Even if Erie's public nudity ban has some minimal effect on the erotic message by muting that portion of the expression that occurs when the last stitch is dropped, the dancers . . . are free to perform wearing pasties and G-strings. Any effect on the overall expression is *de minimis*."[164] Although the majority allowed for restrictions on erotic expression, the constraints were relatively minor, and the majority found them constitutional *not* for moral reasons but due to specific secondary harms Justice Souter raised in his *Barnes* concurrence. According to O'Connor, the Supreme Court was giving due consideration to the municipality's concerns with curbing secondary effects like "violence, . . . prostitution and other serious criminal activity."[165] Justice Souter—who originated this analytical approach of essentially considering the harm principle for sexually explicit expression in his *Barnes* concurrence—wrote a partial dissent in *Erie*, arguing that the city had not proven its case: "The record before us now does not permit the conclusion that Erie's ordinance is reasonably designed to mitigate real harms."[166]

Justice Stevens also dissented, arguing that the majority used this harm analysis as cover to censor protected speech.[167] Stevens indicated, in Millian fashion, that he would have protected this expression to a greater degree, decrying how the regulation allowed nudity in other settings, making it a form of content discrimination: "It is clear beyond a shadow of a doubt that the Erie ordinance was a response to a more specific concern than nudity in general, namely, nude dancing."[168] Appealing to Mill, Stevens argued that for sexually oriented expression, the state should not "limit the size of the market in such speech."[169] Although the majority and Souter both emphasized protecting the expression in question up to the point of it causing harm, there is a question whether the majority was using this as a post hoc rationalization.[170] Nevertheless, Souter applied this Millian principle, and the majority was at least appealing to it. *Erie* was not the only sexually oriented expression case during this period where the Supreme Court majority applied a secondary effects analysis, rather than one based on majoritarian morality.[171]

Ashcroft v. Free Speech Coalition (2002) declared that virtual child pornography that is neither obscene nor actual child pornography is protected expression. Recall the Supreme Court's upholding of child pornography prohibitions in *Ferber* on the Millian idea that such expression causes physiological, emotional, and mental harms to children who are abused in their production. However, Justice Kennedy found unconstitutional in *Free Speech Coalition* a federal ban on virtual child pornography that either uses adults who appear to be children or uses computer-enhanced images of adults. In a narrow reading of the *Miller* test, Kennedy emphasized something like Mill's harm principle when he explained how virtual "images do not involve, let alone harm, any children in the production process."[172] Kennedy held that "where the speech is neither obscene nor the product of sexual abuse, it does not fall outside the protection of the First Amendment. . . . Some works in this category might have significant value" in a literary, artistic, political, or scientific sense.[173] Kennedy opined in *Free Speech Coalition* that "First Amendment freedoms are most in danger when the government seeks to control thought or to justify its laws for that impermissible end. The right to think is the beginning of freedom, and speech must be protected from the government because speech is the beginning of thought."[174] Kennedy understood the inextricable link between freedom of speech and other liberties. This connection between thought, speech, and other freedoms is remarkably similar to Mill's proclamation that "the same reasons which show that opinion should be free prove also that he should be allowed, without molestation, to carry his opinions into practice."[175] Finally, Kennedy's embrace of the preferred status for speech was highlighted in his opinion of the Court that "First Amendment cases draw vital distinctions between words and deeds, between ideas and conduct."[176] This is reminiscent of Mill's proclamation in *On Liberty* that "no one pretends that actions should be as free as opinions."[177]

Reno v. ACLU, *Ashcroft v. Free Speech Coalition*, and other cases during the latter years of the Rehnquist Court collectively demonstrate that without overruling *Miller*, the Supreme Court was applying that test to be more protective of expression.[178] Justice Brennan's *Paris Adult Theatre I* dissent—arguing that consenting adults should be able to view, and participate in the production of, sexually oriented expression that the majority may deem immoral—is now effectively the law of the land. Due to technological changes since *Miller*, the "community standards" prong of that test must accommodate the national community's willingness to accept such materials, a significant Millian turn spurred on by contemporary Supreme Court decisions.[179] Because of these decisions, obscenity prosecutions involving consenting adults are very rare, with prosecutions of sexually explicit material instead focused almost exclusively on child pornography, something that Mill's philosophy would certainly find prohibitable due to its infliction of actual harm on minors.[180]

In its latter years the Rehnquist Court also showed a greater willingness to apply Mill's philosophy to most questions of campaign-related speech. Justice Stevens cited Mill's *On Liberty* in *McIntyre v. Ohio Elections Commission* (1995) when striking down a statute banning anonymous campaign literature. Writing for the majority, Stevens held that "the interest in having anonymous works enter the marketplace of ideas unquestionably outweighs any public interest in requiring disclosure as a condition of entry. . . . An author's decision to remain anonymous, like other decisions concerning omissions or additions to the content of a publication, is an aspect of the freedom of speech protected by the First Amendment."[181] According to Stevens, "Under our Constitution, anonymous pamphleteering is not a pernicious, fraudulent practice, but an honorable tradition of advocacy and of dissent. Anonymity is a shield from the tyranny of the majority. *See* generally J. Mill, *On Liberty* and *Considerations on Representative Government.*"[182] Citing Holmes's *Abrams* dissent, Stevens employed the logic of utilitarianism in his judgment that "political speech by its nature will sometimes have unpalatable consequences, and, in general, our society accords greater weight to the value of free speech than to the dangers of its misuse."[183] He emphasized the Millian-Holmesian theme of free speech markets when he reasoned in *McIntyre*, "In the field of literary endeavor, the interest in having anonymous works enter the marketplace of ideas unquestionably outweighs any public interest in requiring disclosure as a condition of entry."[184]

Steven's opinion of the Court was over the objection of Justice Scalia, who chastised the majority for its use of Mill's philosophy on this First Amendment issue: "Preferring the views of the English utilitarian philosopher John Stuart Mill, to the considered judgment of the American people's elected representatives from coast to coast, the Court discovers a hitherto unknown right-to-be-unknown while engaging in electoral politics. I dissent from this imposition of free-speech imperatives that are demonstrably not those of the American people today, and that there is inadequate reason to believe were those of the society that begat the First Amendment or the Fourteenth."[185] Regardless of Justice Scalia's rejection of Mill's philosophy in *McIntyre*, the opinion of the Court approvingly cited *On Liberty* when interpreting the freedom of expression, and Scalia understood this connection.

Several latter Rehnquist Court campaign speech cases exhibited a Millian approach, with the most noteworthy one being *McConnell v. FEC* (2003).[186] A 5–4 majority upheld a Bipartisan Campaign Reform Act (BCRA) ban on soft-money contributions and a ban on electioneering communications (i.e., advertisements) by corporations and labor unions for thirty days before a primary and sixty days before a general election. Applying closely drawn scrutiny—a standard deferential to government regulation—in upholding the ban, the majority minimized any free speech concerns by concluding that the soft-money ban entailed "only a marginal impact on the ability of contributors, candidates, officeholders, and parties to engage in effective political speech."[187] The Supreme Court upheld the electioneering communications prohibition because corporations and labor unions could engage in political discussions before elections as long as they did not discuss candidates: "Corporations and unions may finance genuine issue ads during those time frames by simply avoiding any specific reference to federal candidates."[188] While the *McConnell* majority demonstrated Mill's concern with needing to regulate trade and the influence of wealth in the corporate form, it simultaneously ignored some of Mill's prescriptions in protected expression, particularly political speech.

In *McConnell*, Justice Scalia took an approach different from his *McIntyre* dissent. Scalia's *McConnell* dissent was Millian by advocating that strict scrutiny be applied to BCRA. Scalia characterized the *McConnell* decision as "a sad day for the freedom of speech" because it "smile[s] with favor upon a law that cuts to the heart of what the First Amendment is meant to protect: the right to criticize the government."[189] For Scalia, it was unconstitutional for the government to single out groups of associated persons and censor them from commenting on candidates running for public office, seizing on Mill's idea that we protect free speech as a path to democratic governance: "A candidate should not be insulated from the most effective speech that the major participants in the economy and major incorporated interest groups can generate."[190] Protecting the right to criticize the government, invoked by Scalia, was something Mill spoke about favorably in *On Liberty*.[191] Likewise, Mill's notion that individuals should be able to band together in "combination among individuals" comports with Scalia's analysis.[192] No such sentiment was discussed by the majority in *McConnell*. Regardless of how Mill might have decided a campaign finance case or whether he would have even thought of campaign finance as a category of "speech" like the contemporary Supreme Court does, his claims were evident in Scalia's arguments in *McConnell*.

If one uses the Millian standards developed by Holmes, there are concerns with the latter Rehnquist Court decisions involving protests outside of abortion clinics.[193] For instance, *Hill v. Colorado* (2000) upheld a law prohibiting persons outside a health care facility from knowingly approaching within eight feet of another person to engage in protest, education, or counseling. According to Justice Stevens for the 6–3 majority, the ban was constitutional because it ensured "avoidance of potential trauma to patients associated with confrontational protests."[194] Instead of speakers' rights, Stevens emphasized the "unwilling listener's interest in avoiding unwanted communication" and used a balancing test to uphold the speech restrictions.[195] It is possible to read Mill as supportive of this ruling if one considers the negative effects of social tyranny, although that discussion goes beyond the points from *On Liberty* that Holmes introduced into US constitutional law.[196]

Seizing on the Holmesian version of Mill, Justice Kennedy dissented in *Hill*, alleging the law unfairly targeted self-styled "sidewalk counselors," and he scolded the majority for upholding "a law which bars a private citizen from passing a message, in a peaceful manner and on a profound moral issue, to a fellow citizen on a public sidewalk."[197] Kennedy argued, "It should be a profound disappointment to defenders of the First Amendment that the Court today refuses to apply the same structural analysis when the speech involved is less palatable to it."[198] Kennedy stressed the need for tolerance of those with opposing moral views, a proposition also supported by Mill.[199] Finally, Kennedy explained the law should have been declared unconstitutional for frustrating the search for truth:

> There runs through our First Amendment theory a concept of immediacy, the idea that thoughts and pleas and petitions must not be lost with the passage of time. In a fleeting existence we have but little time to find truth through discourse. No better illustration of the immediacy of speech, of the urgency of persuasion, of the preciousness of time, is presented than in this case. Here the citizens who claim First Amendment protection seek it for speech which, if it is to be effective, must take place at the very time and place a grievous moral wrong, in their view, is about to occur.[200]

Kennedy's impassioned libertarian defense of free speech notwithstanding, the majority concluded that private individuals have a right against encountering invective in *Hill*. The Rehnquist Court majority failed to apply Holmes's version of Millian reasoning to expression cases involving abortion, not only in *Hill*, but also in *Madsen*, *Rust v. Sullivan* (1991), and *Schenck v. Pro-Choice Network* (1997). Outside of regulations on abortion protests, though, when the case involved public forums and solicitation cases, the latter Rehnquist Court majority applied the libertarian standard promoted by Holmes.[201]

As the new millennium dawned, there were a small number of areas of the First Amendment where Millian thought was absent for a majority of the justices. For instance, they continued to devalue expressive protections for inmates, following the deferential test from *Turner v. Safley*.[202] Overall, however, the last few years of the Rehnquist Court saw a growing attunement to Millian philosophy. *Virginia v. Black* (2003) exemplifies this better than any other latter Rehnquist Court case. *Black* held that hateful expression, including cross burning, is protected unless it constitutes a true threat. Citing Holmes's *Abrams* dissent, Brandeis's *Whitney* concurrence, and *Texas v. Johnson*, Justice O'Connor wrote for a 7–2 majority that the "hallmark of the protection of free speech is to allow 'free trade in ideas'—even ideas that the overwhelming majority of people might find distasteful or discomforting."[203] Although O'Connor paid homage to *Chaplinsky*'s fighting words doctrine, she carved out an exception to find that speech is not protected only where there is actual harm caused by a true threat, defined by the Supreme Court as "those statements where the speaker means to communicate a serious expression of an intent to commit an act of unlawful violence to a particular individual or group of individuals."[204] O'Connor implemented something very similar to Mill's harm principle, reasoning that "when a cross burning is directed at a particular person not affiliated with the Klan, the burning cross often serves as a message of intimidation, designed to inspire in the victim a fear of bodily harm. . . . The history of violence associated with the Klan shows that the possibility of injury or death is not just hypothetical."[205]

To show the narrowness of this exception to protected speech, though, O'Connor clarified in *Black* that "a State [may] choose to prohibit only those forms of intimidation that are most likely to inspire fear of bodily harm."[206] O'Connor reasoned that banning all cross burnings would risk chilling speech of persons "engaging only in lawful political speech at the core of what the First Amendment is designed to protect. As the history of cross burning indicates, a burning cross is not always intended to intimidate. Rather, sometimes the cross burning is a statement of ideology."[207] O'Connor's opinion speaks to several ideas expressed by Mill in *On Liberty*, including the harm principle's ban on only true damage to others, safeguarding the free exchange of ideas to reach a greater good, and protecting "intemperate discussion, namely invective, sarcasm, personality, and the like."[208] The key difference between the prohibitable cross burning and the protected one is that the former aims to terrorize individuals, whereas the latter is a dramatic (albeit hateful) statement against the social ideal of equality. O'Connor's reasoning that the constitutional defect in the Virginia law was that it "does not distinguish between a cross burning at a public rally or a cross burning on a neighbor's lawn. It does not treat the cross burning directed at an individual differently from the cross burning directed at a group of like-minded believers."[209] This is reminiscent, like *Brandenburg*, of Mill's statement that context matters: "An opinion that corn dealers are starvers of the poor . . . ought to be unmolested when simply circulated through the press, but may justly incur punishment when delivered orally to an excited mob assembled before the house of a corn-dealer."[210] Three justices in *Black* would have gone farther than O'Connor. Justice Souter, joined by Justices Kennedy and Ginsburg, argued that cross burning bans are directed at silencing the messages of hate groups, so Souter would have found any such bans to be a content-based violation of the First Amendment.[211]

Cases like *Black* show how the justices toward the end of the Rehnquist Court grappled with the nuances of Mill's philosophy. Sometimes, the types of free expression questions were similar to the ones the Supreme Court had been facing for decades, including those related to campaigning and sexually oriented communications. Others were new, such as those asking how the First Amendment applies to the Internet. Overall, though, the enduring questions raised by Mill—and elaborated on by Holmes and earlier justices—remained at the forefront of the Supreme Court's jurisprudence. Mill's thinking was becoming more evident in almost all areas of free speech caselaw, with particular gains during the Rehnquist Court in obscenity and commercial speech cases. That movement toward Mill would continue as personnel changes arrived at the Supreme Court again beginning in 2005.

CHAPTER 9

Special Protection

The Roberts Court's First Amendment Embrace of Mill

The death of William Rehnquist in September 2005 and Sandra Day O'Connor's retirement in January 2006 led to the appointments of Chief Justice John Roberts and Justice Samuel Alito. Rehnquist was not a consistent proponent of Millian philosophy, often dissenting in First Amendment cases where the majority struck down laws enforcing morality; in *Central Hudson*, Rehnquist chastised the majority for adopting Millian philosophy. Roberts, however, has frequently used Millian reasoning in free expression cases. Alito was not a consistent Millian thinker when he arrived on the Supreme Court, but he began drifting toward a more libertarian position on expression in the 2010s.[1] O'Connor was not the most consistent supporter of Mill in her tenure as a justice, either. Thus, after these personnel changes, the Supreme Court's expanded embrace of Millian theory in First Amendment cases continued unabated. Due to the growing number of Millian precedents, it has become common on the Roberts Court for both the opinion of the Court and any dissenting opinions to apply Millian arguments in freedom of expression cases, even if the majority does not reach Millian conclusions. Although there remain noted exceptions to the Supreme Court's use of Mill, including in broadcasting and with regard to the rights of prisoners and foreigners, in almost all free expression cases today, Mill's influence is evident.

The sheer number of cases decided by the Supreme Court had begun to slow in the latter years of the Rehnquist Court, and the Roberts Court has maintained a lower caseload. Indeed, the Roberts Court routinely issues full opinions in less than half the number of cases per term than the Burger Court did in its last years.[2] This overall reduction in opinions has affected First Amendment cases.[3] Nevertheless, the enduring issues involving the freedom of expression means new cases continue to be brought to the Supreme Court every year, with new questions about offensive speech and campaign finance, as well as emerging questions for developing technology, such as expression on social media. The number of cases has shrunk in recent years, but the justices' embrace of Mill has accelerated.

The early Roberts Court's adoption of Mill's rhetoric—including emphasizing the harm principle, democratic utilitarianism, and the marketplace of ideas—occurred in multiple campaign finance cases.[4] This includes *FEC v. Wisconsin Right to Life* (2007), where the Supreme Court ruled that BCRA's ban on corporate treasury funded political advertisements was unconstitutional as applied to a nonprofit group planning to run advertisements within thirty days before a primary, with the ads advocating that viewers contact members of the Senate and advise them how to vote on judicial nominations. In striking down this application of the law, Chief Justice Roberts applied strict scrutiny and wrote for the 5–4 Supreme Court with Millian sentiment: "The First Amendment requires us to err on the side of protecting political speech rather than suppressing it."[5] Roberts explained that the type of issue ad contemplated in the case "conveys information and educates."[6] Espousing Mill's idea that we must protect the freedom of expression to ensure democratic self-government, Roberts concluded for the majority that "discussion of issues cannot be suppressed simply because the issues may also be pertinent in an election. Where the First Amendment is implicated, the tie goes to the speaker, not the censor."[7] Other justices were more forthright in expressing Millian theory in *Wisconsin Right to Life*. In a concurrence, Justice Scalia connected the freedom of speech to "decisionmaking in a democracy" before arguing that BCRA, by threatening people with prosecution, will cause speakers "simply to abstain from protected speech—harming not only themselves but society as a whole, which is deprived of an uninhibited marketplace of ideas."[8] In dissent, Justice Souter embraced Millian sentiment as well, warning of corporations using their "financial muscle to gain advantage in the political marketplace when they turn from core corporate activity to electioneering."[9]

The appearance of Millian thought in the majority, concurrence, and dissent in *Wisconsin Right to Life* emphasized First Amendment concepts that can be traced back through precedents to Holmes's original introduction of Millian theory into the Supreme Court's jurisprudence. Roberts's opinion of the Court used quotes from *Buckley v. Valeo* that were requotes of core Millian decisions like *Thomas v. Collins* and *New York Times v. Sullivan* about protecting free discussion of ideas.[10] In this and similar cases, Scalia emphasized, similar to Mill, the need to protect people's ability to openly declare their preferences to ensure democratic debate of public issues.[11] *Wisconsin Right to Life* was the first Supreme Court case to chip away at the ruling in *McConnell*, with the justices overruling it a few years later.[12]

Mill placed a premium on protecting political speech, so that society could best find political truths and then act in concert with like-minded people to advocate enacting those ends into policy. The question that *Wisconsin Right to Life* exposes is how to best protect speech. Roberts and Scalia argued it was best to move away from *McConnell*, seeing restraints on corporations funding political advertisements as an illegitimate restriction on the free flow of ideas and the freedom of expressive association. Souter argued that limiting corporate funding of political messaging was constitutional to protect the marketplace of ideas, maintaining that corporate-funded speech will carry the day by outspending, not outarguing, competing views.

As for government workers, a 5–4 decision in *Garcetti v. Ceballos* (2006) held that a public employee's speech, even on matters of public concern, may be subject to discipline unless one is speaking as a private citizen (not pursuant to official work duties). In *Garcetti*, a deputy district attorney was reassigned and denied a promotion after he informed a defense attorney about serious misrepresentations in a sheriff's deputy's affidavit used to obtain a search warrant. Justice Kennedy wrote for the Supreme Court, emphasizing one of Mill's exceptions to liberty—when one is performing, as Mill put it, "some definite duty incumbent on him to the public."[13] According to Kennedy, "When a citizen enters government service, the citizen by necessity must accept certain limitations on his or her freedom. Government employers, like private employers, need a significant degree of control over their employees' words and actions; without it, there would be little chance for the efficient provision of public services."[14] Kennedy noted that the First Amendment rights of public employees speaking as citizens on matters of public concern can be restricted if it is "necessary for their employers to operate efficiently and effectively."[15] Certainly, this reflects Mill's prescription that public employee freedoms can be limited if "there is a definite damage, or a definite risk of damage, either to an individual or to the public."[16] Still, Mill's emphasis on limiting public employee speech when there is *definite* damage or risk of damage constitutes a much narrower restriction on expression than expression that causes a public institution to operate less "efficiently" or "effectively," particularly given the potentially vague ways these terms could be defined.

Indeed, one can question how well the majority applied Millian reasoning to the facts of *Garcetti*. As Justice Souter explained in dissent, if Ceballos's "speech undercut effective, lawful prosecution, there would have been every reason to rein him in or fire him; a statement that created needless tension among law enforcement agencies would be a fair subject of concern."[17] But for Souter, there was no real harm or definite damage to the public in this case, and the relevant "First Amendment safeguard rests on . . . the value to the public of receiving the opinions and information that a public employee may disclose."[18] Justice Breyer wrote a dissent arguing that although the speech rights of public employees are subject to more restrictions than those of the general public, "where professional and special constitutional obligations are both present, the need to protect the employee's speech is augmented, [and] the need for broad government authority to control that speech is likely diminished."[19] Both Souter and Breyer mirrored Mill's concern with government silencing whistleblower employees, as this is "the peculiar evil of silencing the expression of an opinion [that] is robbing the human race, posterity as well as the existing generation," of truth.[20] Both the majority and dissents in *Garcetti* expressed Millian themes, although the dissenters' application of this philosophy appears closer to what Mill advocated in *On Liberty*.[21]

Mill's theory was also used by both the majority and dissent in *Morse v. Frederick* (2007), a case upholding the suspension of a public school student for unfurling at a school-sponsored event a banner that stated "BONG HiTS 4 JESUS."[22] Undoubtedly, Mill provided an exception to the harm principle allowing for more restrictions on the freedom of "children, or of young persons below the age which the law may fix as that of manhood or womanhood. Those who are still in a state to require being taken care of by others, must be protected against their own actions as well as against external injury."[23] Writing for a five-member majority in *Morse*, Chief Justice Roberts echoed these Millian concerns, citing *Bethel* for the proposition that students' rights in public schools can be curtailed. Roberts explained that "a principal may . . . restrict student speech at a school event, when that speech is reasonably viewed as promoting illegal drug use," because "drug abuse can cause severe and permanent damage to the health and well-being of young people."[24] Advocating for an even greater level of restriction on young people's rights, Justice Thomas in concurrence wrote: "In the earliest public schools, teachers taught, and students listened. Teachers commanded, and students obeyed. Teachers did not rely solely on the power of ideas to persuade; they relied on discipline to maintain order."[25]

However, Justice Stevens in dissent in *Morse* convincingly argued that the majority's position was highly paternalistic, claiming that high school students have reached an age where they can sufficiently think for themselves to have earned expressive freedoms: "Admittedly, some high school students (including those who use drugs) are dumb. Most students, however, do not shed their brains at the schoolhouse gate, and most students know dumb advocacy when they see it."[26] Stevens believed that the majority was "deaf to the constitutional imperative to permit unfettered debate, even among high-school students, about the wisdom of the war on drugs or of legalizing marijuana for medicinal use."[27] Indeed, as much as Mill's exception to the harm principle would justify restrictions on teenagers' *use* of marijuana, denying teenagers the ability to express *opinions* on a public issue misemphasizes the point of Mill's caveat by denying teenagers the chance to be challenged by different ideas.[28] Mill's failure to discuss the child exception in his chapter "Of Thought and Discussion" may be evidence that he did not think the exception should even apply to expressive freedoms, thus justifying full protection of speech rights for young people while simultaneously restricting their other freedoms.[29] In this vein, Stevens appears to have been applying something like Mill's harm principle to the student in the case, arguing that "the First Amendment protects student speech if the message itself neither violates a permissible rule nor expressly advocates conduct that is illegal and harmful to students. This nonsense banner does neither, and the Court does serious violence to the First Amendment in upholding—indeed, lauding—a school's decision to punish Frederick for expressing a view with which it disagreed."[30] As in *Garcetti*, both the majority and dissent were using Millian thinking in *Morse*, with the dissent reaching a conclusion more consistent with that philosophical vision. Both the majority and the dissent wrote approvingly of one of the Warren Court's most Millian decisions, *Tinker*, meaning that the power of precedent was carrying Mill's thought into twenty-first-century caselaw.[31] *Morse* was not the only early Roberts Court case that grappled with questions of young people and the harm principle.[32]

In rare cases during the early Roberts Court, there was no Millian analysis presented by the majority in free speech decisions. For instance, *Beard v. Banks* (2006) continued a long line of cases narrowly interpreting the rights of inmates, upholding restrictions on prisoners' access to reading materials, using the very deferential *Turner v. Safley* test. As the Supreme Court again averred in *Beard*, even for First Amendment questions, "courts owe substantial deference to the professional judgment of prison administrators."[33] The dissent in *Beard* carried the Millian sentiment, as explained Justice Stevens: "It is indisputable that this prohibition on the possession of newspapers and photographs infringes upon respondent's First Amendment rights. The State may not, consistently with the spirit of the First Amendment, contract the spectrum of available knowledge. The right of freedom of speech and press includes not only the right to utter or to print, but the right to distribute, the right to receive, the right to read and freedom of inquiry, freedom of thought."[34] Stevens charged that the prison rule upheld by the majority "comes perilously close to a state-sponsored effort at mind control" because "the complete prohibition on secular, nonlegal newspapers, newsletters, and magazines prevents prisoners from receiv[ing] suitable access to social, political, esthetic, moral, and other ideas, which are central to the development and preservation of individual identity, and are clearly protected by the First Amendment."[35] Note how Stevens's analysis strikes on Millian themes regarding utilitarianism, the freedom of thought, the free exchange of ideas, and personal autonomy. Although the justices in the *Beard* majority were using Millian reasoning in other cases, they maintained the Supreme Court's long practice of not approaching inmate free speech cases this way. Indeed, since *Turner*, the Supreme Court has not struck down a prison policy on First Amendment grounds, showing a complete lack of Millian reasoning by the majority of justices in this area of free expression caselaw.[36]

In 2009, David Souter retired, and he was replaced by Sonia Sotomayor. Both showed a willingness to apply Millian thinking to First Amendment questions. In Sotomayor's first year on the Supreme Court, several cases highlighted the ubiquity of Millian philosophy. The justices' uses of Millian arguments were in great alignment in *United States v. Stevens* (2010), where an 8–1 Supreme Court overturned a federal ban on depictions of animal cruelty for being an overbroad content restriction. Eschewing the creation of another category of unprotected expression (like defamation, incitement, obscenity, or child pornography), Chief Justice Roberts explained in the opinion of the Court that the "statute does not address underlying acts harmful to animals, but only portrayals of such conduct."[37] Accordingly, Roberts wrote that there is a difference between expressing ideas and engaging in the underlying conduct that causes harm: "As the Government notes, the prohibition of animal cruelty itself has a long history in American law. . . . But we are unaware of any similar tradition excluding *depictions* of animal cruelty from 'the freedom of speech' codified in the First Amendment, and the Government points us to none."[38] Roberts appealed to something like the harm principle, in that the government has constitutional power to ban harmful conduct but not expression, outside of narrow circumstances.

Roberts also recognized that, although many are outraged by it, the expression at issue in *Stevens* should be debated in the marketplace of ideas, as "there is an enormous national market for hunting-related depictions."[39] Roberts reasoned for the majority that the "First Amendment's guarantee of free speech does not extend only to categories of speech that survive an ad hoc balancing of relative social costs and benefits. The First Amendment itself re-flects a judgment . . . that the benefits of its restrictions on the Government outweigh the costs."[40] This free speech liberalism that emphasized utilitarian consequentialism has the imprint of Mill. The majority in *Stevens* refused to allow the federal law in question to be upheld as a type of obscenity regula-tion, continuing to narrow the definition of that form of unprotected expres-sion.[41] The Supreme Court signaled that it was reluctant to create a new category of unprotected expression or to balance free speech rights against some vague notion of majoritarian morality.[42] Only Justice Alito dissented in *Stevens*, with the other eight justices all supporting a jurisprudence that gave less deference to government regulatory power over expression.[43]

The other relevant decisions of the Supreme Court in its 2009 to 2010 term were more closely divided, but in each case, the majority and the dissent exhib-ited at least some Millian thinking. In *Christian Legal Society v. Martinez* (2010), the Supreme Court upheld a public university's denial of official student organization status to a chapter of the Christian Legal Society for violating a state law barring discrimination based on religion and sexual orientation; the organization required its members to sign a "statement of faith," and its bylaws excluded from membership any students who engaged in what the organization referred to as "unrepentant homosexual conduct."[44] Justice Ginsburg wrote for the 5–4 majority, emphasizing the need for viewpoint neutrality and how the state had met that standard: "If restrictions on access to a limited public forum are viewpoint discriminatory, the ability of a group to exist outside the forum would not cure the constitutional shortcoming. But when access barriers are viewpoint neutral, our decisions have counted it significant that other available avenues for the group to exercise its First Amendment rights lessen the burden created by those barriers."[45] Ginsburg explained that it is "hard to imagine a more viewpoint-neutral policy than one requiring *all* student groups to accept *all* comers."[46] In a Millian sense, the government tried to allow for the expres-sion of all viewpoints and encourage students of all views to congregate into education-based organizations to discuss ideas with each other. As Justice Gins-burg explained, the university's "all-comers policy, to the extent it brings to-gether individuals with diverse backgrounds and beliefs, 'encourages tolerance, cooperation, and learning among students'"—precisely what Mill argued.[47] Promoting tolerance, particularly religious tolerance that was at the heart of the *Christian Legal Society* decision, was a focus of Mill in *On Liberty*.[48]

In his *Christian Legal Society* dissent, Justice Alito quoted from Holmes's *Schwimmer* dissent to explain his belief that the majority was allowing the state to discriminate on the basis of viewpoint: "The proudest boast of our free speech jurisprudence is that we protect the freedom to express 'the thought that we hate.' Today's decision rests on a very different principle: no freedom for expression that offends prevailing standards of political correctness in our country's institutions of higher learning."[49] Thus, Alito was also appealing to a long-standing Millian argument that had been adopted into US constitutional jurisprudence. Mill emphasized that all liberties, including expressive freedoms, consist of rights to exercise them in "combination among individuals" and "freedom to unite for any purpose not involving harm to others."[50] As Alito described it, "A group's First Amendment right of expressive association is burdened by the forced inclusion of members whose presence would affec[t] in a significant way the group's ability to advocate public or private viewpoints."[51]

The use of Millian reasoning and citing relevant jurisprudence dating back to Holmes also occurred in *Holder v. Humanitarian Law Project* (2010), where a 6–3 Supreme Court held that the federal government may ban a US organization from giving support to groups designated by the US State Department as foreign terrorist organizations. The majority ruled this way even though that support would be in the form of training on how to peacefully resolve disputes. Roberts's opinion of the Court emphasized that the Humanitarian Law Project could be banned from engaging in what was, first, a form of "material support" to foreign terrorist organizations that could cause harm, as Roberts explained these foreign organizations are "deadly groups" that have injured and killed thousands of people.[52] For Roberts, any relevant speech that the Humanitarian Law Project wished to engage in is prohibitable because this type of speech involves "training and advising a designated foreign terrorist organization on how to take advantage of international entities," which "might benefit that organization in a way that facilitates its terrorist activities."[53] This line of reasoning by Roberts appears be a retrograde notion, with the entire weight of the argument resting on a highly improbable harm that *might* happen, harkening back to the bad tendency test. The justification for banning material on peaceful conflict resolution due to a nonspecific, possible future harm is a far cry from the imminent lawless action test.[54] As with incarcerated persons, this ruling stands in conflict with the Supreme Court's overall deep commitment to the freedom of expression.

The weaknesses of the majority's arguments in *Holder* were indicated by Justice Breyer. He cited Holmes's dissent in *Abrams* when explaining, "Here the plaintiffs seek to advocate peaceful, *lawful* action to secure *political* ends; and they seek to teach others how to do the same. No one contends that the plaintiffs' speech to these organizations can be prohibited as incitement under *Brandenburg*. . . . Not even the 'serious and deadly problem' of international terrorism can require *automatic* forfeiture of First Amendment rights."[55]

Indeed, Mill advocated an exception to the general rule of free speech only in cases of actual incitement (such as described in *Brandenburg*), and he admonished governments for trying to justify overregulating citizens by putting them "in constant peril of being subverted by foreign attack or internal commotion."[56] Breyer chided the majority for its use of something like a bad tendency test in *Holder*, explaining that "the risk that those who are taught will put otherwise innocent speech or knowledge to bad use is omnipresent, at least where that risk rests on little more than (even informed) speculation. Hence to accept this kind of argument without more . . . would automatically forbid the teaching of any subject in a case where national security interests conflict with the First Amendment."[57] The dissent called for protecting political advice that causes no direct harm.[58] The connection to foreign speakers—by members of the Humanitarian Law Project helping to enable the speech of foreigners—helps to explain the majority's refusal to fully apply Millian theory, as it extended an exception the Supreme Court has long held for such speakers' expressive rights. The majority's refusal again to apply Millian reasoning to cases involving foreign persons was even more problematic in *Holder*, though, as it directly restricted speech by US citizens, which was not the case in older decisions upholding restrictions on foreigners' speech, such as in *Kleindienst*. Again, expressive rights were diluted for no other reason than their connection to a person's foreign status, directly conflicting with Millian libertarianism.

A Millian rationale was also advanced in one of the Supreme Court's most controversial campaign finance decisions, *Citizens United v. FEC* (2010). A 5–4 majority struck down BCRA's prohibition on labor unions and corporations making independent political expenditures by engaging in electioneering communications. *Citizens United* overruled relevant portions of *Austin* and *McConnell*, finding that a BCRA ban on the release of the critical documentary *Hillary: The Movie* within thirty days of a primary or within sixty days of a general election violated the First Amendment. Justice Kennedy explained for the majority that strict scrutiny is appropriate for restrictions on political speech, which is expression "that is central to the meaning and purpose of the First Amendment."[59] Given Mill's focus on protecting "political discussion," one can argue that the majority's approach reflects *On Liberty*'s philosophy.[60] Speaking about the utilitarian function of free expression in a democracy, Kennedy opined that "speech is an essential mechanism of democracy, for it is the means to hold officials accountable to the people. The right of citizens to inquire, to hear, to speak, and to use information to reach consensus is a precondition to enlightened self-government and a necessary means to protect it."[61] In a Millian mindset, Kennedy stated: "Premised on mistrust of governmental power, the First Amendment stands against attempts to disfavor certain subjects or viewpoints. . . . We find no basis for the proposition that, in the context of political speech, the Government may impose restrictions on certain disfavored speakers."[62]

Kennedy wrote for the Supreme Court in *Citizens United* that "First Amendment protection extends to corporations."[63] Kennedy understood corporations, labor unions, and other associations as constituting ways for like-minded people to join together to express ideas.[64] Kennedy's opinion overruled *Austin*, a decision that, he wrote, "interferes with the 'open marketplace' of ideas protected by the First Amendment," again appealing to that Holmesian-Millian analogy.[65] As for BCRA, Kennedy proclaimed that the "purpose and effect of this law is to prevent corporations, including small and nonprofit corporations, from presenting both facts and opinions to the public."[66]

The legal fiction that corporations are "persons" dates back in US jurisprudence to *Santa Clara County v. Southern Pacific Railroad Company* (1886), where the Supreme Court assumed that the Equal Protection Clause of the Fourteenth Amendment applied to corporations.[67] The Supreme Court's ruling in *First National Bank of Boston v. Bellotti* (1978) added First Amendment rights to corporations, which were legally considered corporate "persons."[68] Before *Bellotti*, corporate expression was subordinate to the free speech rights of human "persons" and was regulated by the legislature to insulate the political process from the wealth and influence that corporations could bring to bear. This was seized on by Justice Stevens in dissent in *Citizens United*, where he explained why some rights available to human "persons" remain deniable to corporations: "The distinction between corporate and human speakers is significant. Although they make enormous contributions to our society, corporations are not actually members of it. . . . The financial resources, legal structure, and instrumental orientation of corporations raise legitimate concerns about their role in the electoral process. Our lawmakers have a compelling constitutional basis, if not also a democratic duty, to take measures designed to guard against the potentially deleterious effects of corporate spending in local and national races."[69] Like the majority in *Austin*, Stevens's *Citizens United* dissent expressed Millian concern about the influence of those engaging in trade, through the corporate form, over political discussions. Perhaps one difference for the majority in *Citizens United* was that the corporation at issue (Citizens United) was *nonprofit*, raising fewer of these Millian concerns than the organization at issue in *Austin* (the Chamber of Commerce), which represented mostly *for-profit* businesses.[70] Nevertheless, the *Citizens United* ruling applied to both nonprofit and for-profit corporations.

The multiplication of conflicting Millian thoughts reflects the utilitarian basis of Mill's view of liberty. He valued freedom of expression instrumentally;

this approach tends to expand the possibilities of living and governing. As Mill positively described it in *On Liberty*, "With individuals and voluntary associations . . . there are varied experiments, and endless diversity of experience. What the State can usefully do . . . is to enable each experimentalist to benefit by the experiments of others, instead of tolerating no experiments but its own."[71] While it remains a serious question whether Mill would have been opposed to campaign finance regulations such as those in BCRA, the majority in *Citizens United* used Millian rhetoric to strike down a statute on First Amendment grounds.[72] The case also cited numerous Millian precedents, including *Reno, Turner Broadcasting, Sullivan,* and *Buckley*.[73]

Justice Stevens retired in the summer of 2010, leading to the appointment of Elena Kagan. Like Stevens in his later years, Kagan embraced Millian philosophy that by the early twenty-first century had been reiterated in numerous Supreme Court precedents. She routinely joined opinions that reached Millian outcomes. One excellent example was the 8–1 decision in *Snyder v. Phelps* (2011). The Supreme Court overturned a multimillion-dollar civil verdict against Fred Phelps and the Westboro Baptist Church for intentional infliction of emotional distress for picketing near a military funeral with homophobic signs that alleged that God was punishing the country for its acceptance (including in the military) of gays and lesbians.[74]

Citing *Texas v. Johnson*, Chief Justice Roberts wrote for the majority in *Snyder* that since Phelps's "speech was at a public place on a matter of public concern, that speech is entitled to 'special protection' under the First Amendment. Such speech cannot be restricted simply because it is upsetting or arouses contempt."[75] This emphasis is Millian and reminiscent of the "preferred freedoms" approach that the Holmes-inspired Supreme Court was using in the 1930s and 1940s. The trial judge in *Snyder* instructed the jury that the church's speech was not protected if its picketing was found by the jury to be "outrageous," but Roberts quoted from the Millian *Hustler Magazine* decision to explain how "outrageousness" "is a highly malleable standard with 'an inherent subjectiveness about it which would allow a jury to impose liability on the basis of the jurors' tastes or views, or perhaps on the basis of their dislike of a particular expression.'"[76] Following a Millian line of thinking that intemperate discussion and invective should be protected, Roberts proclaimed for the Supreme Court that even hateful and offensive speech receives constitutional protection: "Speech is powerful. It can stir people to action, move them to tears of both joy and sorrow, and—as it did here—inflict great pain. On the facts before us, we cannot react to that pain by punishing the speaker. As a Nation we have chosen a different course—to protect even hurtful speech on public issues to ensure that we do not stifle public debate."[77]

One could question whether the type of psychological pain at issue in *Snyder* was a type of "harm" in Mill's scheme. Mill's focus in *On Liberty* was on the difference between physical or property harms and moral harms. A discussion of psychological pain was lacking in *On Liberty*, and there is no evidence that Mill believed that another person's emotional or psychological well-being was a sufficient reason for the government to use the law to stop someone from speaking.[78] One can see that the Supreme Court, after focusing on prohibitable harms being physical or property-based in many past precedents, refused to broaden the notion of harm to include psychological pain in *Snyder*. Roberts's opinion instead revealed a strong defense of the freedom of expression, which was not dissimilar from that expressed by Mill in *On Liberty* when he defended the use of invective.[79] That eight of nine justices signed on to Roberts's *Synder* opinion further reveals how much support for this position had grown on the Supreme Court.

A 7–2 majority in *Brown v. Entertainment Merchants Association* (2011) struck down a state law banning sales of violent video games to minors. California had tried to expand the concept of obscenity to include depictions of violence, but Justice Scalia—in the spirit of the Supreme Court's recent trend of contracting what constitutes obscenity—rejected this approach, finding that "the obscenity exception to the First Amendment does not cover whatever a legislature finds shocking."[80] As Scalia confirmed, "Video games qualify for First Amendment protection" because "it is difficult to distinguish politics from entertainment, and dangerous to try."[81] Comparing video games to other media, Scalia explained in the opinion of the Court that, "like the protected books, plays, and movies that preceded them, video games communicate ideas—and even social messages—through many familiar literary devices (such as characters, dialogue, plot, and music)."[82] This reflects Mill's thinking, as he spoke negatively of Puritan efforts "to put down all public, and nearly all private, amusements: especially music, dancing, public games, or other assemblages for purposes of diversion, and the theatre."[83] Several of those types of activities have communicative functions, much in the same way that video games are a communicative form of entertainment.

Although some of the video games in question contained material that was violent, sexist, and racist, Scalia proclaimed for the Supreme Court in *Brown* that "disgust is not a valid basis for restricting expression."[84] Like Mill, Scalia emphasized the difference between expression and harm-causing physical violence, noting how one problem with the California law was "that the *ideas* expressed by speech—whether it be violence, or gore, or racism—and not its objective effects, may be the real reason for governmental proscription."[85] Scalia reiterated that California "acknowledges that it cannot show a direct causal link between violent video games and harm to minors."[86] Recognizing, like Mill, that actual harm (not majoritarian morality) should dictate when expression is protected, Scalia wrote that "under our Constitution, 'esthetic and moral judgments about art and literature . . . are for the individual to make, not for the Government to decree, even with the mandate or approval of a majority.'"[87] Finally, in somewhat of a rejection of *Morse*'s constraints on young people's expressive rights, Scalia wrote in *Brown* that "a State possesses legitimate power to protect children from harm, but that does not include a free-floating power to restrict the ideas to which children may be exposed."[88] This was reminiscent of Mill's idea that children may have their freedoms restricted, but only to the extent that they need protection from themselves or others.[89] One other difference between *Morse* and *Brown* is that in *Morse* the speech involved minors only, while in *Brown* the restrictions were also on adult retailers and creators of video games.[90]

Justices writing the opinion of the Court and in dissent continued using Millian thought on questions about political campaigns, including campaign finance.[91] In *McCutcheon v. FEC* (2014) a 5–4 majority struck down aggregate contribution limits that restricted the total amount that one donor could give to all candidates for federal office. Chief Justice Roberts explained for the Supreme Court that the law was an example of the majority (represented in Congress) constraining the total number of annoying campaign advertisements, with Roberts averring that "many people . . . would be delighted to see fewer television commercials touting a candidate's accomplishments or disparaging an opponent's character."[92] Citing *Texas v. Johnson*, Roberts expounded that numerous forms of expression "may at times seem repugnant to some, but so too does much of what the First Amendment vigorously protects."[93] Roberts explained that if "the First Amendment protects flag burning, funeral protests, and Nazi parades—despite the profound offense such spectacles cause—it surely protects political campaign speech despite popular opposition."[94] Roberts concluded that the law violated the Constitution because "the First Amendment safeguards an individual's right to participate in the public debate through political expression and political association."[95] Still, in recognizing something like Mill's harm principle, Roberts reaffirmed that Congress has the power to prohibit actual bribery, but also that campaign finance "regulation must . . . target what we have called 'quid pro quo' corruption or its appearance."[96]

Justice Breyer dissented in *McCutcheon*, emphasizing that the prevention of corruption potentially caused by excessive campaign spending—not the limiting of annoying campaign advertisements—was the law's primary rationale. Breyer cited Brandeis's *Whitney* concurrence and Hughes's *Stromberg* opinion while discussing a Millian idea introduced into US constitutional law by Holmes: "Political communication seeks to secure government action. A politically oriented 'marketplace of ideas' seeks to form a public opinion that can and will influence elected representatives."[97] According to Breyer, "Where enough money calls the tune, the general public will not be heard. Insofar as corruption cuts the link between political thought and political action, a free marketplace of political ideas loses its point."[98] Thus, as much as Roberts was appealing to a Millian theme of personal autonomy, Breyer's concern about the harms caused by excessive spending in campaigns focused on the Millian search for truth to help facilitate democracy. For our purposes, it is important that by relying on relevant precedent, both the majority and the dissent were appealing to the Millian marketplace of ideas.[99]

The justices on both sides of *Williams-Yulee v. Florida Bar* (2015) applied Millian thinking as well. For a 5–4 majority, Chief Justice Roberts applied strict scrutiny to uphold a state law prohibiting judges and judicial candidates from personally soliciting funds for electoral campaigns. As Roberts explained, the law "restricts a narrow slice of speech" and is designed "to preserve public confidence in the integrity of the judiciary" by ensuring that judges are not personally asking for donations.[100] Roberts saw the Florida prohibition as the equivalent of Mill's idea that one's freedom can be limited if one is performing "some definite duty incumbent on [one] to the public."[101] Just as Mill required that definite damage or risk of it is necessary to restrict the freedom of someone who has taken on public duties, Roberts imposed a high standard for the government to meet when restricting this type of judicial candidate speech: "A State may restrict the speech of a judicial candidate only if the restriction is narrowly tailored to serve a compelling interest."[102] As Roberts explained, the compelling interest (or in Millian terms, the actual harm to be avoided) was "preserving public confidence in the integrity of the judiciary," as "judges, charged with exercising strict neutrality and independence, cannot supplicate campaign donors without diminishing public confidence in judicial integrity."[103] Roberts's opinion reflected the reasoning in campaign finance cases since *Buckley* that applied strict scrutiny to uphold restrictions that cause actual harm.[104] Roberts also made use of numerous other precedents with Millian reasoning in his opinion, including *Stromberg*, *Schneider*, *Holder*, *Brown*, and *R.A.V.*[105]

In response to the *Williams-Yulee* majority, Justice Kennedy, who by the 2010s had already established himself as one of the most libertarian justices on freedom of expression questions, emphasized in dissent the Millian ideas of personal autonomy and the protection of such freedom in service to greater utilitarian purposes.[106] He wrote: "First Amendment protections are both personal and structural. Free speech begins with the right of each person to think and then to express his or her own ideas. Protecting this personal sphere of intellect and conscience, in turn, creates structural safeguards for many of the processes that define a free society. The individual speech here is political speech. The process is a fair election."[107] Directly making the connection between the freedom of expression and democratic self-government, Kennedy maintained that "once the people of a State choose to have [judicial] elections, the First Amendment protects the candidate's right to speak and the public's ensuing right to open and robust debate."[108] Like Mill, Kennedy did not think government should police the civility of campaign expression, and he cited Brandeis's *Whitney* concurrence to make a point: "If there is concern about principled, decent, and thoughtful discourse in election campaigns, the First Amendment provides the answer. That answer is more speech."[109] *Williams-Yulee* is another twenty-first-century case where both the majority opinion and the dissent base their thinking in Mill's political philosophy as ushered into constitutional law by Holmes and Brandeis.

The Supreme Court signaled its continued shift toward Millian free expression theory in *United States v. Alvarez* (2012), where, as explained in the introduction, a 6–3 majority struck down the Stolen Valor Act, which criminalized falsely claiming to have been awarded a US military medal. Alvarez was charged with violating the statute when he falsely introduced himself at a municipal government meeting as having been awarded the Congressional Medal of Honor. Justice Kennedy's reasoning for a plurality of the justices focused on the inescapability of protecting false speech in a free society: "Absent from [the] few categories where the law allows content-based regulation of speech is any general exception to the First Amendment for false statements. This comports with the common understanding that some false statements are inevitable if there is to be an open and vigorous expression of views in public and private conversation, expression the First Amendment seeks to guarantee."[110] As in many other cases, Kennedy connected Mill's theory to justices from the early twentieth century, citing Brandeis's *Whitney* concurrence and Holmes's *Abrams* dissent to explain that the "remedy for speech that is false is speech that is true. This is the ordinary course in a free society."[111] Kennedy harkened back to Mill's argument that if one engages in immoral behavior or expression, then one's "own good, either physical or moral" may be "good reasons for remonstrating with him, or reasoning with, or persuading him, or entreating him, but not for compelling him."[112] Put another way, persuasion in the marketplace of ideas is preferable to punishment.

Kennedy exhibited Millian theory without invoking the philosopher by name, but other opinions in *Alvarez* openly referred to Mill. Justice Breyer in concurrence cited a quote from *On Liberty* that the Supreme Court used in *Sullivan*: "Even a false statement may be deemed to make a valuable contribution to public debate, since it brings about 'the clearer perception and livelier impression of truth, produced by its collision with error.'"[113] Breyer explained that "false factual statements can serve useful human objectives. . . . As the Court has often said, the threat of criminal prosecution for making a false statement can inhibit the speaker from making true statements, thereby 'chilling' a kind of speech that lies at the First Amendment's heart."[114] Breyer explained the practical danger of government overzealousness in criminalizing erroneous statements to shed light on Mill's utilitarian reasoning regarding expression. Breyer, like Mill and Kennedy, understood that "the pervasiveness of false statements, made for better or for worse motives, made thoughtlessly or deliberately, made with or without accompanying harm, provides a weapon to a government broadly empowered to prosecute falsity without more."[115] As explained by Mill, if one is arguing in good faith, there may be some falsity, but the statement "may, and very commonly does, contain a portion of the truth," and it would be a mistake to punish a speaker under such circumstances.[116] For Breyer, even the type of lie being told by Alvarez involved political speech deserving of First Amendment protection.[117]

In his *Alvarez* dissent, Justice Alito requoted the same *On Liberty* passage Breyer used from *Sullivan*, and Alito prefaced it with a statement that also demonstrated Mill's argument: "Even where there is a wide scholarly consensus concerning a particular matter, the truth is served by allowing that consensus to be challenged without fear of reprisal. Today's accepted wisdom sometimes turns out to be mistaken."[118] Nevertheless, Alito disagreed with both the majority and concurrence on how to apply this Millian sentiment in *Alvarez*. There is a question about the appropriateness of extending constitutional protection to factual statements a speaker *knows* are false, especially under a marketplace of ideas theory stemming from Mill, who focused on the discussion of ideas, not factual assertions.[119] As Alito explained, in "stark contrast to hypothetical laws prohibiting false statements about history, science, and similar matters, the Stolen Valor Act presents no risk at all that valuable speech will be suppressed."[120] Instead, averring to something similar to Mill's harm principle, Alito claimed that "the lies proscribed by the Stolen Valor Act inflict substantial harm" because people may lie to obtain financial benefits, and it cheapens the award by making it seem common, thus "[the] diluting effect harms the military by hampering its efforts to foster morale and esprit de corps."[121] However, the majority opinion accounted for the possibility of financial fraud, stating that lies under these circumstances cause harm and are not protected.[122] Likewise, calls to prohibit harms to "morale," as opposed to direct physical and property harms, is like failing to consider the "feelings of others," which Mill thought should be subject to "moral disapprobation," but not formal sanction.[123] Mill himself, a longtime critic of overly burdensome libel laws, personally applied his truth-seeking theory not just to ideas but also to facts.[124] Thus, even though Alito also used Millian reasoning, Kennedy and Breyer applied Mill's philosophy more appropriately to the facts of *Alvarez.*

Given its centrality in modern culture, broadcasting is a curious area of First Amendment jurisprudence where, traditionally, Millian reasoning and outcomes have not been widely adopted by the Supreme Court. However, *FCC v. Fox Television Stations II* (2012) signified some interesting possible developments. The case reviewed *FCC v. Fox Television Stations I* (2009), where the justices ruled that the Administrative Procedures Act permitted the Federal Communications Commission (FCC) to prohibit "fleeting expletives" and "fleeting nudity" on network broadcasts, but the Supreme Court remanded the case to see if such a ban was constitutional.[125] The case arose out of FCC decisions ruling that the commission could fine (although it ultimately chose not to fine) those responsible for several different indecency broadcasts. The first two involved Fox Television Stations' broadcasts of live showings of the Billboard Music Awards. During the 2002 broadcast of the award show, the musical artist Cher stated, "I've also had critics for the last forty years saying that I was on my way out every year. Right. So fuck 'em."[126] During the 2003 airing of the awards program, Nicole Richie, referring to her television show *The Simple Life*, rhetorically asked, "Why do they even call it *The Simple Life*? Have you ever tried to get cow shit out of a Prada purse? It's not so fucking simple."[127] Additionally, an episode of *NYPD Blue*, a program airing on the ABC network, "showed the nude buttocks of an adult female character for approximately seven seconds and for a moment the side of her breast."[128]

In *Fox Television Stations II*, the justices unanimously ruled that the FCC's rule was unconstitutional, with Justice Kennedy's opinion of the Court finding that the rule was too vague: "When speech is involved, rigorous adherence to those requirements is necessary to ensure that ambiguity does not chill protected speech."[129] Kennedy cited multiple decisions that struck down restrictions on expression because of vagueness concerns, most notably *Reno v. ACLU.*[130] Justice Ginsburg in a concurrence would have ruled closer to Mill's thought, as she argued that "the Court's decision in *FCC v. Pacifica Foundation* was wrong when it issued," and she thought the ruling should be reconsidered but found no support from the rest of the justices.[131] The Supreme Court instead rested on an incremental decision that the FCC's action was unconstitutional for not providing proper notice to broadcasters. Mill certainly had concerns about giving a licensing authority too much discretion in restricting expression, building his arguments in *On Liberty* on reasoning from John Milton's antilicensing tract, *Areopagitica*.[132] *Fox Television Stations II*, while maintaining the greater power of the government to restrict expression in broadcasting, limited its scope, with one justice calling its validity into question.

Regarding compelled speech, the Roberts Court of the mid-2010s issued a Millian ruling in *USAID v. Alliance for Open Society International I* (2013), holding that the First Amendment was violated by a federal requirement that US nongovernmental organizations (NGOs) receiving aid establish an antiprostitution policy. As Chief Justice Roberts wrote in a 6–2 decision, it is "a basic First Amendment principle that 'freedom of speech prohibits the government from telling people what they must say.'"[133] As Roberts explained, the "case is not about the Government's ability to enlist the assistance of those with whom it already agrees. It is about compelling a grant recipient to adopt a particular belief as a condition of funding."[134] Citing *Barnette*, Roberts ruled that "the Policy . . . requires [recipients] to pledge allegiance to the Government's policy of eradicating prostitution. . . . In so doing, it violates the First Amendment."[135] Although Mill believed that prostitution is an "evil" and argued in *On Liberty* that pimps could be prosecuted, enforcing a law requiring others to share those policy beliefs runs counter to Mill's philosophy on free expression.[136] *USAID I* provided a stronger protection for the free expression of ideas with those outside of the United States when compared with *Holder v. Humanitarian Law Project*.

Several years later, however, the Supreme Court would return to its longstanding lacunae of First Amendment rights to speech with, or by, foreigners. The majority of justices upheld the same policy as applied to foreign affiliates of US NGOs by a vote of 5–3 in *USAID v. Alliance for Open Society International II* (2020).[137] This is another case showing how some justices fail to apply Millian reasoning in contexts involving foreign speakers, with Chief Justice Roberts and Justice Alito, who voted to strike down the regulations in *USAID I*, changing their votes to uphold those regulations as applied to foreign affiliates in *USAID II*. *USAID II* also reflected how changes in personnel can alter how Millian the Supreme Court's jurisprudence is. Kennedy, who voted to strike down the restriction in *USAID I*, was succeeded by Justice Brett Kavanaugh, who voted to uphold the restriction for foreign affiliates in *USAID II*. Roberts, Alito, and Kavanaugh are each Millian in various contexts, but not with foreign expression with ties to the United States. In his *USAID II* dissent, Justice Breyer emphasized how the policy is detrimental to the marketplace of ideas, expressing not just that Millian-Holmesian analogy but also stressing the importance of protecting expression for all people in all places: "I fear the Court's decision will seriously impede the countless American speakers who communicate overseas. . . . That weakens the marketplace of ideas at a time when the value of that marketplace for Americans, and for others, reaches well beyond our shores."[138]

In *McCullen v. Coakley* (2014) the justices unanimously struck down a thirty-five-foot buffer zone around an abortion facility for not being narrowly tailored. Writing for the Supreme Court, Chief Justice Roberts found that the law unconstitutionally restricted the free speech rights of persons wishing to engage in "sidewalk counseling," which involves "offering information about alternatives to abortion and help pursuing those options," which Roberts contrasted with the tactics of "protestors, who express their moral or religious opposition to abortion through signs and chants or, in some cases, more aggressive methods such as face-to-face confrontation."[139] As Roberts explained, the large buffer zones "compromise petitioners' ability to initiate the close, personal conversations that they view as essential" to express their message, and they "made it substantially more difficult for petitioners to distribute literature to arriving patients."[140] Protecting this expression mirrors the thinking of *On Liberty*, where Mill spoke at length of needing to avoid the "silencing of discussion."[141] Mill contended that "the peculiar evil of silencing the expression of an opinion is that it is robbing the human race . . . of the opportunity of exchanging error for truth."[142] Mill advocated protecting expression even if it is invective and intemperate, which certainly indicates support for protecting the rights of one wishing to engage in the calm, reasoned conversation at issue in *McCullen*.[143] As Roberts explained, "Petitioners wish to converse with their fellow citizens about an important subject on the public streets and sidewalks—sites that have hosted discussions about the issues of the day throughout history."[144] Provided that Roberts's description of "sidewalk counselors" like Eleanor McCullen is accurate, this is a Millian position.[145] *McCullen* represents a break from *Madsen*, *Schenck v. Pro Choice Network*, and *Hill*, as those cases all at least partially upheld similar buffer zones prohibiting expression around abortion clinics.[146] Thus, the Supreme Court in *McCullen* extended its Millian thinking to an area of First Amendment jurisprudence where it had been absent.

The death of Justice Scalia in February 2016 resulted in President Barack Obama nominating a court of appeals judge, Merrick Garland, to the Supreme Court, but the Senate did not act on the nomination before the end of Obama's second term. This resulted in a vacancy that was not filled until President Donald Trump's nominee, Neil Gorsuch, was confirmed in April 2017. In the interim, the eight-member Supreme Court decided several relevant First Amendment cases, all using a Millian approach.[147]

Matal v. Tam (2017) was one of several cases during the second decade of the twenty-first century where the Supreme Court pushed protections for commercial speech closer to protections for political speech.[148] *Matal* unanimously struck down a clause of the Lanham Act that banned registration of a disparaging trademark, a provision known as the disparagement clause. The case arose because the Patent and Trademark Office (PTO) denied an application for a trademark by an Asian American band, the Slants, who use the name to reclaim the derogatory term.[149] Justice Alito, who in the 2010s began to use more Millian reasoning, wrote in the opinion of the Court that this trademark denial was as unconstitutional as government attempts to restrict speech in *Street v. New York* and *Texas v. Johnson*.[150] Borrowing language from *Johnson*, Alito proclaimed that the disparagement clause "offends a bedrock First Amendment principle: Speech may not be banned on the ground that it expresses ideas that offend."[151] Alito quoted Holmes's *Schwimmer* dissent when explaining, "The proudest boast of our free speech jurisprudence is that we protect the freedom to express 'the thought that we hate.'"[152] Alito concluded for the Supreme Court: "The disparagement clause discriminates on the bases of 'viewpoint.' To be sure, the clause evenhandedly prohibits disparagement of all groups. It applies equally to marks that damn Democrats and Republicans, capitalists and socialists, and those arrayed on both sides of every possible issue. It denies registration to any mark that is offensive to a substantial percentage of the members of any group. But in the sense relevant here, that is viewpoint discrimination: Giving offense is a viewpoint."[153]

This passage resembles Mill's arguments that the freedom of speech should extend to the protection of all points of view, and it should go beyond stopping the government from criminally punishing people for the ideas they express: "There needs [to be] protection also . . . against the tendency of society to impose, by other means than civil penalties, its own ideas and practices as rules of conduct on those who dissent from them."[154] Alito's opinion of the Court protecting disparaging speech parallels Mill's notion that we should safeguard expression even if it is "intemperate" and involves "invective."[155] In taking this Millian approach in *Matal*, without overruling *Central Hudson*, the Supreme Court was approaching in practice what Thomas suggested in his concurrence from *44 Liquormart*, by providing elevated protection to commercial speech.[156] If advertisements contain expression of public policy issues, the Millian concern with protecting the free expression of ideas is even more critically important.

In *Packingham v. North Carolina* (2017), the justices unanimously struck down a state law banning registered sex offenders from accessing websites that minors can use. Lester Packingham, a registered sex offender, was convicted of violating the law when he expressed joy on Facebook (which is accessible to minors) about a traffic citation against him being dismissed. There is no evidence that

Packingham communicated with any minors online. In extending the Millian reasoning for online speech that the Supreme Court began with *Reno v. ACLU*, Justice Kennedy's opinion of the Court emphasized that a "fundamental principle of the First Amendment is that all persons have access to places where they can speak and listen, and then, after reflection, speak and listen once more."[157] In the contemporary world, Kennedy explained, the most vital location for such discussion is online: "While in the past there may have been difficulty in identifying the most important places (in a spatial sense) for the exchange of views, today the answer is clear. It is cyberspace—the vast democratic forums of the Internet in general, and social media in particular."[158] Kennedy noted that all ideas are essentially represented on social media: "Social media users employ these websites to engage in a wide array of protected First Amendment activity on topics 'as diverse as human thought.'"[159] Kennedy's Millian approach was on display when he penned that "North Carolina with one broad stroke bars access to what for many are the principal sources for knowing current events, checking ads for employment, speaking and listening in the modern public square, and otherwise exploring the vast realms of human thought and knowledge. These websites can provide perhaps the most powerful mechanisms available to a private citizen to make his or her voice heard."[160] Although we can never know what Mill would have thought about regulating speech online, Kennedy's approach in *Packingham* signals the need to protect both the ability to speak and to have access to the expression of others, which was well within Mill's arguments in *On Liberty*.[161] *Packingham* is another in a series of cases since the late 1980s (including *Sable Communications, Turner Broadcasting, Reno v. ACLU,* and *Free Speech Coalition*) where Mill's arguments were applied by the justices to new media. With the single exception of broadcasting in *Pacifica* in 1978, the Supreme Court consistently used a Millian approach to government power to restrict expression in new media over the last half century.

Furthermore, in *Packingham*, Kennedy affirmed something akin to the harm principle and Mill's indispensable proviso. Kennedy cited *Brandenburg* for the proposition that "this opinion should not be interpreted as barring a State from enacting more specific laws than the one at issue. Specific criminal acts are not protected speech even if speech is the means for their commission."[162] If the law restricting sex offenders' access to minors had been tailored more narrowly, it would be constitutional, as Kennedy explained: "It can be assumed that the First Amendment permits a State to enact specific, narrowly tailored laws that prohibit a sex offender from engaging in conduct that often presages a sexual crime, like contacting a minor or using a website to gather information about a minor. Specific laws of that type must be the State's first resort to ward off the serious harm that sexual crimes inflict."[163] Although this decision did not directly cite Mill, his philosophy is carried through in the case because of earlier Supreme Court opinions writing that philosophy into First Amendment jurisprudence.

Once Neil Gorsuch was seated on the Supreme Court in 2017, the justices continued striking down speech restrictions with a high level of frequency.[164] This is especially true in cases involving compelled expression, where Millian rhetoric is fully displayed. In *National Institute of Family and Life Advocates v. Becerra* (2018), a 5–4 Supreme Court ruled that a state law requiring crisis pregnancy centers to disclose free and low-cost abortion options was likely unconstitutional compelled speech. Writing the opinion of the Court, Justice Thomas, like Mill, emphasized the important place of the freedom of speech in our rights hierarchy when he characterized "regulations of speech" as government action that "so closely touc[h] our most precious freedoms."[165] Reflecting the concept of truth emerging in an open marketplace of ideas, Thomas cited Holmes's *Abrams* dissent and quoted *McCullen*: "When the government polices the content of professional speech, it can fail to 'preserve an uninhibited marketplace of ideas in which truth will ultimately prevail.'"[166] Thomas concluded that the law in question "targets speakers, not speech, and imposes an unduly burdensome disclosure requirement that will chill their protected speech."[167] Even Justice Breyer's dissent in *Becerra* made use of the marketplace of ideas analogy and the need to protect all ideas, explaining how ingrained these propositions have become in the Supreme Court's jurisprudence: "The Court, in justification, refers to widely accepted First Amendment goals, such as the need to protect the Nation from laws that suppress unpopular ideas or information or inhibit the marketplace of ideas in which truth will ultimately prevail."[168] However, Breyer believed that the disclosure requirements served to further a fully functioning marketplace of ideas: "The majority highlights an interest that often underlies our decisions in respect to speech prohibitions—the marketplace of ideas. But that marketplace is fostered, not hindered, by providing information to patients to enable them to make fully informed medical decisions in respect to their pregnancies."[169] Both Thomas and Breyer appealed to Millian themes—even as they emphasized different effects of the law, reached different conclusions about its constitutionality, and did so from two very different places ideologically—which again demonstrated the Supreme Court's acceptance of Mill's thought.

Showing its willingness to overrule outdated precedents that did not use the Supreme Court's current, Millian approach, the justices in *Janus v. AFSCME* (2018) overturned a state law that required nonunion public sector employees to pay union dues; the Supreme Court found this to be a form of compelled expression. Writing for the majority, Justice Alito quoted key language from the Millian *Barnette* decision: "*Stare decisis* applies with perhaps least force of all to decisions that wrongly denied First Amendment rights: 'This Court has not hesitated to overrule decisions offensive to the First Amendment (a fixed star in our constitutional constellation, if there is one).'"[170] Alito identified utilitarian justifications for protecting the freedom of expression: "Free speech serves many ends. It is essential to our democratic form of government, and it furthers the search for truth. Whenever the Federal Government or a State prevents individuals from saying what they think on important matters or compels them to voice ideas with which they disagree, it undermines these ends."[171] As Alito explained, citing *Snyder*, "Unions can also speak out in collective bargaining on controversial subjects such as climate change, the Confederacy, sexual orientation and gender identity, evolution, and minority religions. These are sensitive political topics, and they are undoubtedly matters of profound value and concern to the public."[172] Alito cited several other Millian decisions, including *Wooley*, *Thornhill*, *Keyishian*, *Pickering*, and *Rankin*.[173] Certainly, Mill would support the idea that persons should not be compelled to agree or disagree with opinions expressed on political matters and other controversies.[174] *Janus* represents yet another case where Millian reasoning is applied to stop compelled speech.

Justice Kennedy, one of the most devoted adherents of Millian philosophy since his earliest days on the Supreme Court, retired in 2018. Brett Kavanaugh was appointed to fill the vacancy. The Supreme Court then maintained stable membership for next two terms, and during that time it struck down nearly all restrictions on expression.[175] *Iancu v. Brunetti* (2019) extended the ruling in *Matal* by overturning the Lanham Act's ban on registering trademarks that are "immoral" or "scandalous."[176] The case arose when the PTO denied a trademark to Erik Brunetti for his clothing line named FUCT.[177] Following the *Matal* precedent, Justice Kagan wrote the opinion of the Court in Millian fashion: "The government may not discriminate against speech based on the ideas or opinions it conveys."[178] She expounded on how "the PTO has refused to register marks communicating 'immoral' or 'scandalous' views about (among other things) drug use, religion, and terrorism. But all the while, it has approved registration of marks expressing more accepted views on the same topics."[179] As Kagan explained, the law was unconstitutional because it "distinguishes between two opposed sets of ideas: those aligned with conventional moral standards and those hostile to them; those inducing societal nods of approval and those provoking offense and condemnation. The statute favors the former, and disfavors the latter."[180] Kagan cited examples of the PTO denying trademarks where they were interpreted as expressing what was considered a morally offensive view (such as "AGNUS DEI for safes and MADONNA for wine") while approving trademarks expressing more respectful messages (such as "PRAISE THE LORD for a game and JESUS DIED FOR YOU on clothing").[181]

Kagan's approach in *Iancu* reflects Mill's comment that there should be "absolute freedom of opinion and sentiment on all subjects, practical or speculative, scientific, moral, or theological."[182] As we have explored in this book's preceding chapters, Mill eschewed the restricting of expression deemed immoral.[183] *Iancu* is another in a long line of contemporary cases demonstrating that the Supreme Court is moving commercial speech protections closer to political speech protections; there are only a few additional restrictions remaining on commercial speech, such as when it involves deception or fraud.[184] In this respect, Mill would have generally agreed, as he wanted speech broadly protected but also noted that the government has slightly more regulatory power in situations involving "dealers in promoting intemperance."[185] Mill agreed that government restrictions on expression with political components or involving discussion of matters of public concern should be free from government interference.

Mill's theory was likewise evident in *Barr v. American Association of Political Consultants* (2020), where a 6–3 Supreme Court applied strict scrutiny—the contemporary descendent of the preferred freedoms approach—to strike down a portion of Telephone Consumer Protection Act.[186] The law allowed robocalls to collect government debts, but it prohibited other types of robocalls. Justice Kavanaugh wrote the opinion of the Court, emphasizing the Millian idea that "above all else, the First Amendment means that government generally has no power to restrict expression because of its message, its ideas, its subject matter, or its content. . . . Content-based laws are subject to strict scrutiny."[187] Reflecting the Millian notion that all beliefs are to be debated, Kavanaugh explained that the "First Amendment is a kind of Equal Protection Clause for ideas."[188] Kavanaugh's opinion continued to recognize for the Supreme Court that there is a difference between government regulation of business and government regulation of commercial speech: "Our decision is not intended to . . . affect traditional or ordinary economic regulation of commercial activity."[189] Mill applauded various forms of business regulations and described how "the principle of individual liberty is not involved in the doctrine of free trade."[190] The *Barr* opinion of the Court cited some of the modern opinions containing Millian philosophy, including *Turner Broadcasting* and *Williams-Yulee*, showing how precedent is built on precedent, with contemporary free expression cases continuing to tie back to Holmes's introduction of Mill into First Amendment caselaw in 1919.

In a partial dissent in *Barr*, Justice Breyer emphasized the Millian market-place of ideas analogy that Holmes ushered into First Amendment jurisprudence. Breyer argued that the analogy exists for a particular purpose: "The free marketplace of ideas is not simply a debating society for expressing thought in a vacuum. It is in significant part an instrument for bringing about . . . political and social chang[e]. The representative democracy that 'We the People' have created insists that this be so."[191] With this focus on the analogy as it applies to democratic self-governance, Breyer argued that "it is . . . important that courts not use the First Amendment in a way that would threaten the workings of ordinary regulatory programs posing little threat to the free marketplace of ideas enacted as result of that public discourse."[192] Breyer believed that in *Barr*, the speech restriction should have been upheld: "This case is not about protecting the marketplace of ideas. It is not about the formation of public opinion or the transmission of the people's will to elected representatives. It is fundamentally about a method of regulating debt collection."[193] For Breyer, when considering the government debt collection exception to the ban on robocalls, "it is hard to imagine that such exceptions threaten political speech in the marketplace of ideas, or have any significant impact on the free exchange of ideas."[194] Even though he reached a different conclusion from the majority, Breyer stressed important Millian themes. Breyer cited Millian precedents to reach his conclusions, including *Central Hudson*, *R.A.V.*, *Ward*, and *Alvarez*, providing more proof that justices today are using Mill's philosophy that was introduced into constitutional law by Holmes in 1919.

The death of Ruth Bader Ginsburg and the appointment of Amy Coney Barrett in 2020 did not change the Supreme Court's Millian outlook.[195] Most notably, in *Mahanoy Area School District v. B.L.* (2021), a public high school suspended a fourteen-year-old member of the cheer team for one year for posting on Snapchat a picture of herself and a friend with their middle fingers raised, with the accompanying caption, "Fuck school fuck softball fuck cheer fuck everything."[196] Writing for an 8–1 majority, Justice Breyer overturned the student's suspension. Recognizing, as Mill did, that minors may have additional restrictions on their rights, Breyer acknowledged that schools may need to act in loco parentis under certain circumstances, but reasoned that "a school, in relation to off-campus speech, will rarely stand *in loco parentis*" because "off-campus speech will normally fall within the zone of parental, rather than school-related, responsibility."[197] Acknowledging the growing personal autonomy of high schoolers, Breyer opined that "courts must be more skeptical of a school's efforts to regulate off-campus speech, for doing so may mean the student cannot engage in that kind of speech at all."[198] Finally, Breyer referred to the often used marketplace of ideas analogy in the context of explaining that we protect expression for the utilitarian reason of promoting democracy: "The school itself has an interest in protecting a student's unpopular expression, especially when the expression takes place off campus. America's public schools are the nurseries of democracy. Our representative democracy only works if we protect the 'marketplace of ideas.' This free exchange facilitates an informed public opinion, which, when transmitted to lawmakers, helps produce laws that reflect the People's will. That protection must include the protection of unpopular ideas, for popular ideas have less need for protection."[199] Without citing Mill, Breyer made use of several key components of Mill's theory. Breyer's citations were to Millian cases like *Tinker*, *Cohen*, *Rankin*, and *Snyder*.[200] Unlike in *Bethel*, *Hazelwood*, and *Morse* (which Breyer also cited but distinguished), *Mahanoy* struck down the school district's action. Reflecting the Supreme Court's continued move toward Millian principles, *Mahanoy* reaffirmed *Tinker* and was the first case since *Tinker* in 1969 where the justices found in favor of a public school student's free speech rights.[201] *Mahanoy* was not the last case where the Supreme Court upheld expressive rights in a public school setting.[202]

Mahanoy was also not the last case where Breyer made use of the "marketplace of ideas" analogy before he retired in 2022 and Justice Ketanji Brown Jackson took his seat. Breyer used that analogy four times in a concurrence in *Austin v. Reagan National Advertising* (2022), including once while referencing Holmes's *Abrams* dissent and connecting it to self-government: "The First Amendment helps to safeguard what Justice Holmes described as a marketplace of ideas. . . . The First Amendment, by protecting the 'marketplace' and the 'transmission' of ideas, thereby helps to protect the basic workings of democracy itself."[203]

Mill's indirect influence was evident in a unanimous decision in *Houston Community College System v. Wilson* (2022). The case involved a lawsuit filed by David Wilson, a member of the elected Houston Community College (HCC) Board of Trustees, against the HCC board after they censured him. The censure followed years of animosity, with Wilson often strongly disagreeing with his board colleagues. Wilson's actions extended to bringing lawsuits against his fellow members, arranging robocalls to express his views about his colleagues to their constituents, and hiring a private investigator to conduct surveillance on one member. The resulting censure expressed the view that Wilson's conduct was "not consistent with the best interests of the College" and was "not only inappropriate, but reprehensible."[204] Wilson claimed this censure of him violated the First Amendment.

The Supreme Court unanimously disagreed with Wilson. Writing for his colleagues, Justice Gorsuch cited *Near* for the notion that the First Amendment means "that the government usually may not impose prior restraints on speech. But other implications follow too," including prohibitions generally on government engaging in "retaliatory actions" against someone for engaging in protected speech.[205] However, regarding a purely verbal censure, "we expect elected representatives to shoulder a degree of criticism about their public service from their constituents and their peers—and to continue exercising their free speech rights when the criticism comes."[206] As dozens of prior cases have attested, the normal course of action in our Millian free speech scheme is for critical speech to be answered by more speech, not enforced silence; this is particularly the case for elected officials, who, in the tradition of *Sullivan*, are expected to be subject to an even greater level of expressive scrutiny. As Gorsuch further elaborated in *Wilson*, the "First Amendment surely promises an elected representative like Mr. Wilson the right to speak freely on questions of government policy. But just as surely, it cannot be used as a weapon to silence other representatives seeking to do the same."[207] If Wilson had the right as an individual to express himself, his colleagues on the HCC board equally had the right to join together to express their displeasure of him. This ensures, as Mill advocated, that groups of individuals can collectively exercise an expressive right without interference. Gorsuch's opinion reflected that "when the government interacts with private individuals as sovereign, employer, educator, or licensor, its threat of a censure could raise First Amendment questions. But those cases are not this one."[208] The case also did not involve expulsion, exclusion, or any other type of formal punishment.[209] Thus, it follows Mill in encouraging conversations rather than stifling them through court action—something Mill opposed throughout *On Liberty*. *Wilson* is another demonstration of the Supreme Court indirectly using Mill's philosophy in First Amendment cases over the last century.

Mill's continued sway over the Supreme Court was also evident in *Counterman v. Colorado* (2023). In a 7-2 decision, the justices held that the First Amendment requires that defendants who are criminally prosecuted for making true threats must have had some subjective understanding of the threatening nature of their statements, either by intending them or stating them with recklessness.[210] In the opinion of the Court, Justice Kagan, echoing Mill's harm principle, recognized that "true threats" are outside of First Amendment protection because of "the profound harms, to both individuals and society, that attend true threats of violence."[211] Kagan then continued the Supreme Court's tradition of defining "true threats" narrowly, finding constitutional protection for "jests, 'hyperbole,' or other statements that when taken in context do not convey a real possibility that violence will follow," thus reaffirming the Millian decision *Virginia v. Black*.[212] In requiring prosecutors to show defendants had some subjective understanding that their statements were threatening, Kagan revealed another Millian goal, preventing a chilling effect on expression: "Prohibitions on speech have the potential to chill, or deter, speech outside their boundaries. A speaker may be unsure about the side of a line on which his speech falls. . . . The result is 'self-censorship' of speech that could not be proscribed—a cautious and restrictive exercise of First Amendment freedoms. And an important tool to prevent that outcome—to stop people from steering wide of the unlawful zone—is to condition liability on the State's showing of a culpable mental state."[213] Furthermore, Justice Kagan endorsed for the majority one of the Court's most Millian precedents, *New York Times v. Sullivan*.[214] In addition to *Black* and *Sullivan*, other core Millian decisions relied on by Kagan in *Counterman* included *Stevens, Gertz, Alvarez, Watts, Hess, Brandenburg*, and *Claiborne Hardware*.[215]

Finally, in *303 Creative v. Elenis* (2023), Justice Gorsuch's opinion for a 6-3 majority held that a state could not require a website designer to create expressive designs speaking messages with which the designer disagreed. At issue in the case was a business providing website and graphic design (including for couples seeking websites for their weddings), with the owner of the business refusing to "produce content that 'contradicts biblical truth,'" including her "sincerely held religious conviction" that "marriage is a union between one man and one woman."[216] In his opinion of the Court Gorsuch displayed Mill's concerns with protecting unpopular speech, the ability to join together with likeminded persons to speak, and freedom from compelled ideological expression: "The First Amendment protects an individual's right to speak his mind regardless of whether the government considers his speech sensible and well intentioned or deeply misguided, and likely to cause anguish or incalculable grief. Equally, the First Amendment protects acts of expressive association. Generally, too, the government may not compel a person to speak its own preferred messages."[217] Making use yet again of the famous analogy derived from Holmes and Mill, Gorsuch declared adherence to "the principle that the government may not interfere with an uninhibited marketplace of ideas."[218] Gorsuch concluded his opinion by explaining that "abiding the Constitution's commitment to the freedom of speech means all of us will encounter ideas we consider unattractive, misguided, or even hurtful. But tolerance, not coercion, is our Nation's answer."[219] This bears striking similarities to Mill's admonition that "invective, sarcasm, personality, and the like" must be tolerated in discussion, especially when spoken by those challenging "prevailing opinion," with the proper response to offensive expression being "censure" of that speaker through discussion rather than legal sanction.[220] Gorsuch's opinion in

303 Creative was saturated with Millian philosophy, and Gorsuch cited a host of precedents reflecting Mill's thinking, including *Barnette*, *McCullen*, *Snyder*, *Tinker*, *Becerra*, *Reno v. ACLU*, *Brown*, and Brandeis's *Whitney* concurrence.[221]

Justice Sotomayor, dissenting in *303 Creative*, argued that the crux of the case was not expression but discriminatory business conduct, exhibiting Mill's notion that "trade is a social act" subject to more government regulation than the freedoms he delineated in *On Liberty*.[222] According to Sotomayor, the majority in the case ruled that "because the business offers services that are customized and expressive, the Free Speech Clause of the First Amendment shields the business from a generally applicable law that prohibits discrimination in the sale of publicly available goods and services. That is wrong. Profoundly wrong. . . . the law in question targets conduct, not speech, for regulation, and the *act* of discrimination has never constituted protected expression under the First Amendment. Our Constitution contains no right to refuse service to a disfavored group."[223] Rather than being a case about the "marketplace of ideas," Sotomayor alleged the state anti-discrimination law at issue prohibited conduct that was outside of Millian concerns about individual liberties because it dealt with "the harm from status-based discrimination in the public marketplace."[224] *303 Creative* is one more modern free speech case revealing how Mill's influence on the Court is so strong that his philosophy appears in both the opinion of the Court and the dissent.

The Roberts Court, like other Supreme Courts before it, has not always reached Millian outcomes, but the justices during John Roberts's tenure as chief justice are almost always arguing over the use of Millian themes—from the harm principle to the tyranny of the majority to the marketplace of ideas—whether they are conscious of Mill's influence or not. They do this by following the power of precedent, with Holmes remaining the catalyst that brought Mill to life in US constitutional law. Since questions raised by the freedom of expression are enduring, even if they take different forms with changes in technology and culture, Mill's theory continues to thrive in our jurisprudence. As we will explain in our conclusion, however, as strong, and even dominant, as this jurisprudential trend has become, it could come to a crashing halt without the Supreme Court's continuing commitment that the freedom of speech is necessary to promote the search for truth, democratic self-government, and personal autonomy.

Conclusion

The Future of Mill, the Supreme Court, and Free Speech

John Stuart Mill's *On Liberty* remains one of the strongest defenses of the freedom of expression more than a century and a half after it was written. Mill is mostly and most famously known for the truth-seeking rationale to protect the freedom of speech, but democracy and autonomy were important reasons to safeguard free expression for him as well. Mill's theories remain relevant today because the freedom of expression raises enduring questions. Those questions have been with society since at least the time of Socrates. They were present in the decision regarding Xavier Alvarez's false claims about winning the Congressional Medal of Honor. They continue to be at the heart of the controversies surrounding then-President Trump's now notorious speech at the Ellipse on January 6, 2021, and Elon Musk's purchase of Twitter in 2022. In those cases and many others, discussions about politics, communication, and freedom generate strong feelings among partisans on all sides. Those questions remain so important because the freedom of expression has become such an integral part of our political culture, and this cultural imperative has been driven, in part, by Holmes and his fellow Millian justices. As the preceding chapters have shown, there is a greater embrace of Mill today on the Supreme Court than ever before, even if the justices do not always apply his theory in a consistent manner or cite him by name. The Supreme Court's rhetoric in these cases has become what lawyers, politicians, journalists, and others quote when discussing what the freedom of speech means in the United States.

For example, in *Alvarez*, Justice Kennedy explained how relying on the marketplace of ideas ultimately resolved the problems raised by Alvarez's lies without needing to resort to criminal action via the Stolen Valor Act: "The facts of this case indicate that the dynamics of free speech, of counterspeech, of refutation, can overcome the lie. [Alvarez] lied at a public meeting. Even before the FBI began investigating him for his false statements 'Alvarez was perceived as a phony.' Once the lie was made public, he was ridiculed online, his actions were reported in the press, and a fellow board member called for his resignation. There is good reason to believe that a similar fate would befall other false claimants."[1]

The *Alvarez* case is proof that Mill's vision, particularly as adopted by the Supreme Court through Holmes, can work, and has worked. When the 2005 version of the Stolen Valor Act, which criminalized any lies about winning service medals, was struck down in *Alvarez*, Congress responded by passing a new version of the law in 2013 making it a crime to lie about having won a service medal to engage in fraud to obtain "money, property, or other tangible benefit."[2] The Supreme Court's decision sparked meaningful change by Congress, with the law now reflecting Mill's harm principle, as the marketplace of ideas is protected short of direct financial harm being inflicted. Mill's influence is evident in this and many other decisions.

Although there remain a few areas of First Amendment freedom of expression jurisprudence where the Supreme Court has not fully adopted Mill's philosophy, it is present in many areas, including in the adoption of *Brandenburg's* imminent lawless action test, the embrace of the marketplace of ideas analogy, and in adherence to the idea that the government is generally banned from engaging in viewpoint discrimination. Mill's arguments about protecting the freedom of expression for utilitarian reasons—to promote democracy, to seek truth, and to ensure we have a fully functioning society of autonomous individuals—run throughout many justices' opinions. Even in areas of jurisprudence where the Supreme Court still formally maintains a less than Millian standard—such as with fighting words or obscenity—the doctrines are often on life support. Only in a select few types of cases—such as those involving broadcasting and the First Amendment rights of prisoners and foreigners—does the Supreme Court continue to take an approach that is significantly different from Mill.

Thus, Mill's impact on the justices' free expression jurisprudence over the last century has been undeniable. The Supreme Court's adoption of Millian philosophy is the result of the inertia of stare decisis and the appointment of justices who have, or have adopted, a Millian philosophy. In the preceding chapters, we have demonstrated the power of precedent, which has been a major driving force behind this trend. It also matters who gets appointed to the Supreme Court, as justices who are less supportive of Mill's liberalism or adherence to precedent may be less likely to continue protecting the freedom of expression to the degree that it is safeguarded now.

Sometimes justices do not use Millian thinking in a case, even if they usually do, because they refer to a non-Millian precedent. This is sometimes also due to ideological factors. Studies have shown that conservative justices are more likely to strike down restrictions on conservative speakers, and liberal justices are more likely to strike down restrictions on liberal speakers.[3] Of course, as the preceding chapters have shown, both liberal and conservative justices are increasingly likely to strike down speech restrictions on all speakers. But if there is an ideological component that explains at least some of the Supreme Court's free expression decisions, justices may be more likely to appeal to Millian rhetoric in cases where they want to strike down restrictions applied to speakers similar to them ideologically.

Mill has not been the only philosophical or scholarly influence over the justices in freedom of expression cases. Some justices have emphasized originalist jurisprudence in First Amendment cases.[4] James Madison, the primary draftsperson of the First Amendment, has been frequently cited by the justices as an authority on the freedom of expression.[5] Thomas Jefferson, another towering figure of the founding generation, has been cited often in free speech cases.[6] William Blackstone's position on prior restraints and on blasphemous speech was once the controlling authority among the justices (before Mill's philosophy gained more favor) and was cited repeatedly in their opinions.[7] Another English philosopher, John Locke, has been referenced in multiple free expression dissents.[8] Alexis de Tocqueville's writings have made several appearances in the Supreme Court's First Amendment cases.[9] The justices have cited numerous scholars to help elucidate the meaning of the freedom of expression, including Zechariah Chafee, Alexander Meiklejohn, Thomas Emerson, and Burt Neuborne.[10] That having been said, the connections to Mill outlined in this book dwarf the appeals to any other person in free expression caselaw, with only the First Amendment's primary author, Madison, coming close.[11]

As for Mill, perhaps he would not be surprised at how much his philosophy has captured the Supreme Court. Writing in his *Autobiography* near the end of his life, Mill spoke of *On Liberty* as his greatest work, remarking that "it far surpasses, as a mere specimen of composition, anything which has proceeded from me either before or since."[12] The work impressed Holmes enough for him to usher it into First Amendment jurisprudence, where it has flourished. On the Supreme Court, Mill's premonition about *On Liberty* has come true, as he further noted in his *Autobiography* that *On Liberty* "is likely to survive longer than anything else that I have written."[13] Nevertheless, Mill, humbly aware of his own station in the long line of philosophy, said of *On Liberty* that "the book which bears my name claimed no originality for any of its doctrines, and was not intended to write their history."[14] Instead, Mill viewed himself as but one philosopher penning ideas on freedom, and he listed Johann Fichte, William Maccall, and Josiah Warren as contemporaries who were advancing some of the same ideas.[15] Others have argued that Mill's ideas reflected the intellectual work of Demosthenes and Elie Luzac.[16] As explored in earlier chapters, Mill's ideas were also built on those of Milton and Tocqueville. Mill was one link (albeit a very important one) in a larger free expression chain.

Justice Holmes, who earlier in his life had met Mill, likely viewed himself in a similar way: he did not originate this theory, but he was thinking about it, refining it, and promoting it to the world. Holmes's introduction of this philosophy into US constitutional law more than one hundred years ago has resulted in a jurisprudence promoting an approach to the freedom of speech that reflects what Mill wrote in the middle of the nineteenth century. As Mill noted, "History is teeming with instances of truth put down."[17] Movement toward freedom is not inevitable, and our analysis has shown the precarity of freedom of expression as it has developed in the United States. Holmes might not have made use of Mill's theory, first narrowly in *Schenck* and then more broadly in *Abrams*. Brandeis might not have joined Holmes in advancing it in the 1920s. The Hughes Court might not have adopted it and moved toward a preferred freedoms understanding of expression that was embraced by the Stone Court. And all of those earlier Hughes and Stone Court decisions nearly died during the Vinson and early Warren Courts, only to be resurrected and advanced deep into US constitutional law by Black, Douglas, Warren, Brennan, Marshall, Kennedy, Roberts, Breyer, and other jurists. These justices not only have helped to promote a jurisprudential theory of the freedom of expression but alo have fostered the growth of an US free speech culture.

That experience during the early days of the Cold War is instructive. The Millian approach that has protected so many speakers from government overreach nearly ended permanently. That means that it could end again. There have been several opinions by justices (Thomas and Gorsuch) since 2019 questioning one of the most Millian precedents, *Sullivan*, and that case's adoption of the actual malice standard for defamation of public figures.[18] An abandonment of long-standing First Amendment precedent might seem unlikely, given the mountain of caselaw now supporting it. But one should not ignore that as much as Millian themes have become the lingua franca of First Amendment jurisprudence, Millian ideas have been used in both majority opinions and dissents. Mill's ideas can (and have been) marshalled by jurists in ways that lead away from a robust climate of expression. With a change of opinion by a few justices—or the appointment of a few new justices—precedents like *Sullivan* could be overruled. The Supreme Court did that, for a time, with free speech during the Cold War. A majority of justices recently overturned nearly a half century of precedents protecting another liberal right of personal autonomy—abortion—in *Dobbs v. Jackson Women's Health Organization* (2022), and a concurring opinion in that case advocated reconsidering several other core precedents safeguarding personal autonomy, including *Griswold v. Connecticut* (1965) (protecting married couples' access to contraceptives and, more broadly, protecting a right to privacy), *Lawrence v. Texas* (2003) (protecting the rights of consenting adults to privately engage in acts of sexual intimacy), and *Obergefell v. Hodges* (2015) (protecting the right to same-sex marriage).[19] Vigilance is necessary—on the Supreme Court, during the nomination and confirmation process, and within our culture generally—to ensure that these rights do not slip away, and that the freedom of expression does not join any lists of endangered rights.

Even if the mountain of relevant First Amendment precedents continues to be upheld, Mill himself would advocate that we engage in active discussion of them, so we can ensure that they still deserve our adherence: "However unwillingly a person who has a strong opinion may admit the possibility that his opinion may be false, he ought to be moved by the consideration that, however true it may be, if it is not fully, frequently, and fearlessly discussed, it will be held as a dead dogma, not a living truth."[20] Holmes agreed, writing in 1897 of precedent that "it is revolting to have no better reason for a rule of law than that so it was laid down in the time of Henry IV. It is still more revolting if the grounds upon which it was laid down have vanished long since, and the rule simply persists from blind imitation of the past."[21] If we enjoy the Millian precedents brought to us over the years—with their constitutional genesis in the opinions of Holmes—then we honor the legacy of Mill, Holmes, and all of the subsequent justices who have embraced *On Liberty*'s arguments by enthusiastically discussing what is, and what should be, protected by the First Amendment.

Notes

Introduction

1. See I. F. Stone, *The Trial of Socrates* (Boston: Little, Brown, 1988), 197.

2. Keith Werhan, *Freedom of Speech: A Reference Guide to the United States Constitution* (Westport, CT: Praeger, 2004), 2.

3. Nigel Warburton, *Free Speech: A Very Short Introduction* (Oxford: Oxford University Press, 2009), 103.

4. Werhan, *Freedom of Speech*, 6–7.

5. Robert Corn-Revere, *The Mind of the Censor and the Eye of the Beholder* (New York: Cambridge University Press, 2021), 19.

6. Eric Berkowitz, *Dangerous Ideas: A Brief History of Censorship in the West, from the Ancients to Fake News* (Boston: Beacon Press, 2021), 178–83, 209–10.

7. Corn-Revere, *Mind of the Censor*, 205.

8. Donald Alexander Downs, *Free Speech and Liberal Education* (Washington, DC: Cato Institute, 2020), 81.

9. Berkowitz, *Dangerous Ideas*, 226.

10. Rose Horowitch, "Florida's 'Stop WOKE' Law to Remain Blocked in Colleges, Appeals Court Rules," *NBC News*, March 17, 2023, https://www.nbcnews.com/politics/politics-news/floridas-stop-woke-law-remain-blocked-colleges-appeals-court-rules-rcna75455.

11. See G. Edward White, "The First Amendment Comes of Age: The Emergence of Free Speech in Twentieth-Century America," *Michigan Law Review* 95, no. 2 (1996): 299–392.

12. United States v. Carolene Products Co., 304 U.S. 144, 153 n.4 (1938).

13. Gitlow v. New York, 268 U.S. 562, 666 (1925).

14. *Carolene Products*, 304 U.S. at 153 n.4.

15. Robert W. Hoag, "Happiness and Freedom: Recent Work on John Stuart Mill," *Philosophy & Public Affairs* 15, no. 2 (1986): 188–99, 192.

16. John Stuart Mill, *On Liberty*, ed. Elizabeth Rapaport (Indianapolis, IN: Hackett, 1978), 15–52.

17. Terence H. Qualter, "John Stuart Mill, Disciple of de Tocqueville," *Western Political Quarterly* 13, no. 4 (1960): 880–89, 882–84.

18. Mill, *On Liberty*, 9.

19. Mill, 9.

20. United States v. Alvarez, 567 U.S. 709, 713 (2012).

21. *Alvarez*, 567 U.S. at 714.

22. *Alvarez*, 567 U.S. at 713–16; United States v. Alvarez, 617 F.3d 1198, 1201 (9th Cir. 2010).

23. *Alvarez*, 567 U.S. at 719.

24. *Alvarez*, 567 U.S. at 727.

25. *Alvarez*, 567 U.S. at 732, 733 (Breyer, J., concurring) (emphasis added).

26. *Alvarez*, 567 U.S. at 732, 733.

27. *Alvarez*, 567 U.S. at 732, 733 (quoting New York Times v. Sullivan, 376 U.S. 254, 279, n.19 (1964)).

28. *Alvarez*, 567 U.S. at 752 (Alito, J., dissenting).

29. *Alvarez*, 567 U.S. at 752.

30. *Alvarez*, 567 U.S. at 752.

31. These caveats include restrictions on freedom that government may impose on children, on persons in "backward states of society," and on those who must "perform certain acts of individual beneficence." Mill, *On Liberty*, 9–12.

32. Mill, 11.

33. Abrams v. United States, 250 U.S. 616, 630 (1919) (Holmes, J., dissenting). There is no recorded use of Holmes using the exact phrase "marketplace of ideas," but he did refer to the "competition of the market." Vince Blasi, "Holmes and the Market-place of Ideas," *Supreme Court Review* 2004 (2004): 1–46, 24.

34. *Abrams*, 250 U.S. at 630 (Holmes, J., dissenting).

35. Thomas v. Collins, 323 U.S. 516, 530 (1945).

36. Dennis v. United States, 341 U.S. 494, 503 (1951).

37. Texas v. Johnson, 491 U.S. 397, 414 (1989).

38. See James M. Boland, "Is Free Speech Compatible with Human Dignity, Equality, and Democratic Government: America, a Free Speech Island in a Sea of Censorship?," *Drexel Law Review* 6, no. 1 (2013): 1–46.

39. See William Blackstone, *Commentaries on the Laws of England*, vol. 4 (Chicago: University of Chicago Press, 1979), 151; New York State Rifle & Pistol Association v. Bruen, 142 S. Ct. 2111, 2137 (2022).

40. See Alexander Meiklejohn, *Free Speech and Its Relation to Self-Government* (New York: Harper and Brothers, 1948), 26–27.

41. See Patrick Devlin, *The Enforcement of Morals* (Oxford: Oxford University Press, 1965); Robert H. Bork, *The Tempting of America: The Political Seduction of the Law* (New York: Touchstone, 1990); Catharine A. MacKinnon, *Feminism Unmodified: Discourses on Life and Law* (Cambridge, MA: Harvard University Press, 1988); Abigail Levin, *The Cost of Free Speech: Pornography, Hate Speech, and Their Challenge to Liberalism* (New York: Palgrave Macmillan, 2010).

42. See Paul L. Murphy, *The Meaning of the Freedom of Speech: First Amendment Freedoms from Wilson to FDR* (Westport, CT: Greenwood, 1972).

43. See, e.g., Marc A. Greendorfer, "The BDS Movement: That Which We Call a Foreign Boycott, by Any Other Name, Is Still Illegal," *Roger Williams University Law Review* 22, no. 1 (2017): 1–146; Chris Demaske, "Social Justice, Recognition Theory and the First Amendment: A New Approach to Hate Speech Restriction," *Communication Law and Policy* 24, no. 3 (2019): 347–401; Joseph F. Morrissey, "A Contractarian Critique of Citizens United," *University of Pennsylvania Journal of Constitutional Law* 15, no. 3 (2013): 765–830.

1. Absolute Freedom

1. John Stuart Mill, *On Liberty*, ed. Elizabeth Rapaport (Indianapolis, IN: Hackett, 1978), 1.

2. Mark Tunick, "Tolerant Imperialism: John Stuart Mill's Defense of British Rule in India," *Review of Politics* 68, no. 4 (2006): 586–611, 598–99.

3. Mill, *On Liberty*, 5.

4. Mill, 3.

5. Mill, 1.

6. Richard W. Krouse, "Two Concepts of Democratic Representation: James and John Stuart Mill," *Journal of Politics* 44, no. 2 (1982): 509–37, 529.

7. Mill, *On Liberty*, 3–4.

8. Mill, 4 (emphasis in original).

9. Mill, 4.

10. David P. Currie, "The Distribution of Powers after *Bowsher*," *Supreme Court Review* 1986 (1986): 19–40, 21.

11. Mill, *On Liberty*, 4.

12. Mill, 4.

13. Mill, 5.

14. Alex Rajczi, "A Populist Argument for Legalizing Same-Sex Marriage," *The Monist* 91, no. 3/4 (2008): 475–505, 487.

15. Mill, *On Liberty*, 6.

16. Mill, 6–8.

17. Laurence D. Houlgate, *Understanding John Stuart Mill: The Smart Student's Guide to "Utilitarianism" and "On Liberty"* (San Luis Obispo, CA: Houlgate Books, 2018), 67–68; Cassie Miller, "SPLC Poll Finds Substantial Support for 'Great Replacement' Theory and Other Hard-Right Ideas," Southern Poverty Law Center, June 1, 2022, https://www.splcenter.org/news/2022/06/01/poll-finds-support-great-replace ment-hard-right-ideas.

18. Rachel Janik and Keegan Hankes, "The Year in Hate and Extremism Report 2021," Southern Poverty Law Center, March 9, 2022, https://www.splcenter.org /20220309/year-hate-extremism-report-2021.

19. Aidan Connaughton, "In Both Parties, Fewer Now Say Being Christian or Being Born in U.S. Is Important to Being 'Truly American,'" Pew Research Center, May 25, 2021, https://www.pewresearch.org/fact-tank/2021/05/25/in-both-parties-fewer-now -say-being-christian-or-being-born-in-u-s-is-important-to-being-truly-american/.

20. Michael Lipka, "Half of Americans Say Bible Should Influence U.S. Laws, Including 28% Who Favor It over the Will of the People," Pew Research Center, April 13, 2020, https://www.pewresearch.org/fact-tank/2020/04/13/half-of-americans-say -bible-should-influence-u-s-laws-including-28-who-favor-it-over-the-will-of-the -people/.

21. "What Americans Know about Religion," Pew Research Center, July 23, 2019, https://www.pewforum.org/2019/07/23/feelings-toward-religious-groups/.

22. Mill, *On Liberty*, 5.

23. J. Thomas Wren, *Inventing Leadership: The Challenge of Democracy* (Northampton, MA: Edward Elgar, 2007), 254.

24. Mill, *On Liberty*, 8.

25. Mill, 9.

26. Mill, 9.

27. Mill, 9.

28. G. W. Smith, "Social Liberty and Free Agency: Some Ambiguities in Mill's Conception of Freedom," in *J. S. Mill's "On Liberty": In Focus*, ed. John Gray and G. W. Smith (New York: Routledge, 1991), 239–59, 252.

29. Mill, *On Liberty*, 9.

30. Daniel Jacobson, "Utilitarianism without Consequentialism: The Case of John Stuart Mill," *Philosophical Review* 117, no. 2 (2008): 159–91, 189.

31. Mill, *On Liberty*, 9.

32. Mill, 1.

33. John Stuart Mill, *Utilitarianism and the 1868 Speech on Capital Punishment*, 2nd ed., ed. George Sher (Indianapolis, IN: Hackett, 2001), 59.

34. Mill, *Utilitarianism*, 54.

35. Mill, *Utilitarianism*, 59.

36. Mill, *Utilitarianism*, 7.

37. Mill, *On Liberty*, 10.

38. K. C. O'Rourke, *John Stuart Mill and Freedom of Expression: The Genesis of a Theory* (New York: Routledge, 2001), 76.

39. Mill, *On Liberty*, 9.

40. Henry M. Magid, "Mill and the Problem of Freedom of Thought," *Social Research* 21, no. 1 (1954): 43–61, 52.

41. Mill, *On Liberty*, 80.

42. Harry M. Clor, "Mill and Millians on Liberty and Moral Character," *Review of Politics* 47, no. 1 (1985): 3–26, 15.

43. Mill, *On Liberty*, 10.

44. Ajume H. Wingo, "The Immortals in Our Midst: Why Democracies in Africa Need Them," *Journal of Ethics* 19, no. 3-4 (2015): 237–55, 244.

45. Wingo, 10.

46. Bruce Baum, *Rereading Power and Freedom in J. S. Mill* (Toronto: University of Toronto Press, 2000), 149.

47. Nell Irvin Painter, *The History of White People* (New York: W. W. Norton, 2010), 212–27.

48. Mill, *On Liberty*, 10.

49. Gregory Claeys, *Mill and Paternalism* (New York: Cambridge University Press, 2013), 96.

50. Mill, *On Liberty*, 67.

51. Mill, 67.

52. Jacob Mchangama, *Free Speech: A History from Socrates to Social Media* (New York: Basic Books, 2022), 211, 250–51.

53. Ian Cook, *Reading Mill: Studies in Political Theory* (New York: St. Martin's Press, 1998), 49.

54. Mill, *On Liberty*, 10.

55. Mill, 67.

56. Mill, 5.

57. Victor Tadros, "Between Governance and Discipline: The Law and Michel Foucault," *Oxford Journal of Legal Studies* 18, no. 1 (1998): 75–103, 83.

58. Mill, *On Liberty*, 5.

59. David Lyons, "Benevolence and Justice in Mill," in *The Limits of Utilitarianism*, ed. Harlan B. Miller and William H. Williams (Minneapolis: University of Minnesota Press, 1982), 42–70, 49–51.

60. Mill, *On Liberty*, 79.

61. Mill, 104.

62. On his criticism of standardized education, see Mill, 104.

63. Andrew Valls, "Self-Development and the Liberal State: The Cases of John Stuart Mill and Wilhelm von Humboldt," *Review of Politics* 61, no. 2 (1999): 251–74, 269–70.

64. D. G. Brown, "Mill on Liberty and Morality," in *John Stuart Mill's Social and Political Thought: Critical Assessments*, vol. 2, *Freedom*, ed. G. W. Smith (New York: Routledge, 1998), 102–22, 110.

65. Mill, *On Liberty*, 11.

66. Mill, 79.

67. Mill, 79–80.

68. Clarence Morris, "On Liberation and Liberty: Marcuse's and Mill's Essays Compared," *University of Pennsylvania Law Review* 118, no. 5 (1970): 735–45, 740.

69. Mill, *On Liberty*, 80.

70. Mill, 73.

71. David Dyzenhaus, "John Stuart Mill and the Harm of Pornography," *Ethics* 102, no. 3 (April 1992): 545.

72. Mill, *On Liberty*, 73.

73. See Mill, *Autobiography*, 5–44; O'Rourke, *Mill and Freedom of Expression*, 9–10.

74. O'Rourke, 10; Mchangama, *Free Speech*, 211.

75. Mchangama, *Free Speech*, 211.

76. Mill, *Autobiography*, 32.

77. Mill, 27.

78. Mill, 64.

79. Raphael Cohen-Almagor, "J. S. Mill's Boundaries of Freedom of Expression: A Critique," *Philosophy* 92, no. 362 (2017): 565–96, 569.

80. Cohen-Almagor, 569–70.

81. O'Rourke, *Mill and Freedom of Expression*, 16.

82. O'Rourke, 40.

83. O'Rourke, 70.

84. Mill, *On Liberty*, 11.

85. Mill, 11–12.

86. Mill, 15.

87. Mill, 16.

88. Mill, 16.

89. Richard Lichtman, "The Surface and Substance of Mill's Defense of Freedom," *Social Research* 30, no. 4 (1963): 469–94, 477.

90. Mill, *On Liberty*, 16.

91. John Milton, *Areopagitica*, in *Areopagitica and Other Prose Works*, intro. C. E. Vaughan (Mineola, NY: Dover, 2016), 1–40, 35.

92. Stewart Justman, *The Hidden Text of Mill's "Liberty"* (Savage, MD: Rowman & Littlefield, 1991), 75–110. These arguments by Mill also reflect the sentiments of the ancient Greek orator Demosthenes. Mchangama, *Free Speech*, 214.

93. Justman, *Hidden Text*, 78 (e.g., Justman explains how Milton's description of printing press licensing as "hindring and cropping" the search for truth is similar to Mill's belief that censorship of ideas would make us "cramped and dwarfed").

94. Mill, *On Liberty*, 27.

95. Mill, 49–50.

96. Philip Kitcher, "Varieties of Freedom and Their Distribution," *Social Research* 77, no. 3 (2010): 857–72, 858–59.

97. Mill, *On Liberty*, 16.

98. Mill, 16.

99. Mill, 17 (emphasis in original).

100. Elisabeth A. Lloyd, "Feyerabend, Mill, and Pluralism," *Philosophy of Science* 64, supplement (1997): S396–S407, S399.

101. Mill, *On Liberty*, 19.

102. Kimberly A. Gross and Donald R. Kinder, "A Collision of Principles? Free Expression, Racial Equality and the Prohibition of Racist Speech," *British Journal of Political Science* 28, no. 3 (1998): 445–71, 445.

103. Robert C. Binkley, "Mill's Liberty Today," *Foreign Affairs* 16, no. 4 (1938): 563–73, 567.

104. Mill, *On Liberty*, 23.

105. Mill, 26.

106. Mill, 28.

107. Murray Dry, *Civil Peace and the Quest for Truth: The First Amendment Freedoms in American Constitutionalism* (Lanham, MD: Lexington Books, 2004), 136.

108. Mill, *On Liberty*, 21.

109. Mill, 44.

110. Mill, 44.

111. Mill, 46.

112. Mill, 46.

113. Mill, 50.

114. Struan Jacobs, "From Logic to Liberty: Theories of Knowledge in Two Works of John Stuart Mill," *Canadian Journal of Philosophy* 16, no. 4 (1986): 751–67, 764.

115. Mill, *On Liberty*, 45.

116. Mill, 45.

117. Frederick Rosen, "J. S. Mill on Truth, Liberty, and Democracy," in *Truth and Democracy*, ed. Jeremy Elkins and Andrew Norris (Philadelphia: University of Pennsylvania Press, 2012), 181–96, 192–93.

118. Mill, *On Liberty*, 50.

119. Mill, 50.

120. Mill, 34.

121. Mill, 35.

122. Mill, 41.

123. Keith E. Whittington, *Speak Freely: Why Universities Must Defend Free Speech* (Princeton, NJ: Princeton University Press, 2018), 44.

124. Mill, *On Liberty*, 50.

125. Mill, 54.

126. Christopher Clausen, "John Stuart Mill's 'Very Simple Principle,'" *Wilson Quarterly* 33, no. 2 (Spring 2009): 40–46, 44.

127. Mill, *On Liberty*, 37.

128. Mill, 20.

129. Mill, 50.

130. Mill, 50–51.

131. Mill, 51.

132. Jeremy Waldron, "Homelessness and Community," *University of Toronto Law Journal* 50, no. 4 (2000): 371–406, 381.

133. Mill, *On Liberty*, 51.

134. Mill, 51.

135. Mill, 52.

136. Alan Charles Kors and Harvey A. Silverglate, *The Shadow University: The Betrayal of Liberty on America's Campuses* (New York: Free Press, 1998), 110.

137. Mill, *On Liberty*, 53.

138. Nick Cowen, "Millian Liberalism and Extreme Pornography," *American Journal of Political Science* 60, no. 2 (2016): 509–20, 516.

139. Mill, *On Liberty*, 53.

140. Marvin Glass, "Anti-racism and Unlimited Freedom of Speech: An Untenable Dualism," *Canadian Journal of Philosophy* 8, no. 3 (1978): 559–75, 562.

141. Mark Strasser, "Mill, Holmes, Brandeis, and a True Threat to Brandenburg," *BYU Journal of Public Law* 26, no. 1 (2011): 37–72, 42.

142. Mill, *On Liberty*, 97.

143. Mill, 53.

144. Kitcher, "Varieties of Freedom," 858–59.

145. Mill, *On Liberty*, 79.

146. Mill, 55.

147. Mill, 12.

148. Mill, 97.

149. Mill, 84.

150. Mill, 108.

151. Sheldon Leader, *Freedom of Association: A Study in Labor Law and Political Theory* (New Haven, CT: Yale University Press, 1992), 4.

152. Mill, *On Liberty*, 12.

153. O'Rourke, *Mill and Freedom of Expression*, 142.

154. Mill, *On Liberty*, 113.

2. Preventing Substantive Evils

1. See Michael Kent Curtis, *Free Speech, "The People's Darling Privilege": Struggles for Freedom of Expression in American History* (Durham, NC: Duke University Press, 2000), 3; Michael T. Gibson, "The Supreme Court and Freedom of Expression from 1791 to 1917," *Fordham Law Review* 55, no. 3 (1986): 270–71.

2. Curtis, *Free Speech*, 3; David M. Rabban, *Free Speech in Its Forgotten Years, 1870–1920* (New York: Cambridge University Press, 1997), 30; David M. Rabban, "The First Amendment in Its Forgotten Years," *Yale Law Journal* 90, no. 3 (1981): 514–95, 553–55.

3. Representative James Madison, speaking on the Bill of Rights, June 8, 1789, 1st Cong., 1st Sess., 1 Annals of Cong. 457 (1789).

4. Gitlow v. New York, 268 U.S. 652 (1925).

5. Gibson, "Supreme Court and Freedom of Expression," 268.

6. Gibson, 271.

7. Rabban, "First Amendment Forgotten Years," 523.

8. Richard H. Eliel, "Freedom of Speech," *American Political Science Review* 18, no. 4 (1924): 712–36, 723.

9. William Blackstone, *Commentaries on the Laws of England*, vol. 4 (Chicago: University of Chicago Press, 1979), 151 (emphasis in original).

10. Blackstone, 4:151.

11. See Leonard W. Levy, *Origins of the Bill of Rights* (New Haven, CT: Yale University Press, 1999), 126.

12. Genevieve Lakier, "The Invention of Low-Value Speech," *Harvard Law Review* 128, no. 8 (2015): 2166–233, 2182.

13. *Ex Parte Jackson*, 96 U.S. 727, 733 (1877).

14. *Ex Parte Jackson*, 96 U.S. at 736 (emphasis added).

15. *Ex Parte Jackson*, 96 U.S. at 736, 737.

16. *In re Rapier*, 143 U.S. 110, 134 (1892).

17. *In re Rapier*, 143 U.S. at 133 (emphasis added).

18. Lakier, "Invention of Low-Value Speech," 2183.

19. John Stuart Mill, *On Liberty*, ed. Elizabeth Rapaport (Indianapolis, IN: Hackett, 1978), 11.

20. Rosen v. United States, 161 U.S. 29, 42 (1896).

21. *Rosen*, 161 U.S. at 43.

22. Regina v. Hicklin, 3 Q.B. 360 (1868).

23. Carlos A. Ball, "Obscenity, Morality, and the First Amendment: The First LGBT Rights Cases before the Supreme Court," *Columbia Journal of Gender and Law* 28, no. 2 (2015): 229–314, 235–36.

24. Mill, *On Liberty*, 103.

25. *Rosen*, 161 U.S. at 38.

26. See *Rosen*, 161 U.S. at 44–46 (White, J., dissenting).

27. Gibson, "Supreme Court and Freedom of Expression," 308.

28. James Gray Pope, "The Thirteenth Amendment at the Intersection of Class and Gender: *Robertson v. Baldwin*'s Exclusion of Infants, Lunatics, Women, and Seamen," *Seattle University Law Review* 39, no. 3 (2016): 901–26, 906.

29. Robertson v. Baldwin, 165 U.S. 275, 281 (1897).

30. Howard Owen Hunter, "Problems in Search of Principles: The First Amendment in the Supreme Court from 1791–1930," *Emory Law Journal* 35, no. 1 (1986): 59–137, 84.

31. Joel Feinberg, *Offense to Others*, vol. 2 of *The Moral Limits of the Criminal Law* (New York: Oxford University Press, 1985), 94.

32. Davis v. Massachusetts, 167 U.S. 43 (1897).

33. *Davis*, 167 U.S. at 47–48 (internal citations omitted).

34. *Davis*, 167 U.S. at 47 (quoting Commonwealth v. Davis, 162 Mass. 510, 511 (1895)).

35. William E. Lee, "Modernizing the Law of Open-Air Speech: The Hughes Court and the Birth of Content-Neutral Balancing, *William & Mary Bill of Rights Journal* 13, no. 4 (2005): 1219–65, 1231.

36. Mill, *On Liberty*, 28.

37. See Hague v. CIO, 307 U.S. 496 (1939).

38. Gibson, "Supreme Court and Freedom of Expression," 298.

39. Gibson, 298.

40. American School of Magnetic Healing v. McAnnulty, 187 U.S. 94, 104 (1902).

41. *Magnetic Healing*, 187 U.S. at 104.

42. *Magnetic Healing*, 187 U.S. at 106.

43. See Mill, *On Liberty*, 94.

44. Gibson, "Supreme Court and Freedom of Expression," 299.

45. United States ex rel. Turner v. Williams, 194 U.S. 279 (1904).

46. Heather R. Henthorne, "Resident Aliens and the First Amendment: The Need for Judicial Recognition of Full Free Speech and Association Rights," *Catholic University Law Review* 39, no. 2 (1990): 595–637, 602

47. Rabban, "First Amendment Forgotten Years," 537.

48. *Turner*, 194 U.S. at 292.

49. *Turner*, 194 U.S. at 292.

50. *Turner*, 194 U.S. at 294.

51. *Turner*, 194 U.S. at 294.

52. Susan Dente Ross, "In the Shadow of Terror: The Illusive First Amendment Rights of Aliens," *Communication Law and Policy* 6, no. 1 (2001): 75–122, 116–17.

53. Mill, *On Liberty*, 67, 69.

54. People ex rel. Attorney General v. News-Times Pub. Co., 35 Colo. 253, 256–77 (1906).

55. Curtis, *Free Speech*, 386–87.

56. Patterson v. Colorado, 205 U.S. 454, 461 (1907).

57. *Patterson*, 205 U.S. at 462. Justice Harlan argued in dissent that the freedom of speech should apply against state governments (465).

58. *Patterson*, 205 U.S. at 462.

59. *Patterson*, 205 U.S. at 462.

60. *Patterson*, 205 U.S. at 462.

61. *Patterson*, 205 U.S. at 465 (Harlan, J., dissenting).

62. Eliel, "Freedom of Speech," 720.

63. Thomas I. Emerson, "Toward a General Theory of the First Amendment," *Yale Law Review* 72, no. 5 (1963): 877–956, 909. The roots of the bad tendency test extend back to at least *Rosen*, as applied to obscenity ("The test of obscenity is whether the *tendency* of the matter is to deprave and corrupt the morals of those whose minds are open to such influence and into whose hands a publication of this sort may fall"). *Rosen*, 161 U.S. at 43 (emphasis added).

64. *Patterson*, 205 U.S. at 462.

65. *Patterson*, 205 U.S. at 462.

66. Rabban, "First Amendment Forgotten Years," 534.

67. Blackstone, *Commentaries on the Laws of England*, 4:150.

68. Blackstone, 4:151.

69. Mill, *On Liberty*, 56.

70. Halter v. Nebraska, 205 U.S. 34, 40–41 (1907).

71. Falguni A. Sheth, "John Stuart Mill on Race, Liberty, and Markets," in *Race, Liberalism, and Economics*, ed. David Colander, Robert E. Prasch, and Falguni A. Sheth (Ann Arbor: University of Michigan Press, 2004), 100–120, 116.

72. *Halter*, 205 U.S. at 41.

73. Mill, *On Liberty*, 81.

74. *Halter*, 205 U.S. at 42.

75. *Halter*, 205 U.S. at 43.

76. Mill, *On Liberty*, 24.

77. See Loewe v. Lawlor, 208 U.S. 274 (1908) (upholding an injunction that prohibited a union from publicly disseminating information about a planned boycott of a hat manufacturer), and Gompers v. Bucks Stove & Range Co., 221 U.S. 418 (1911) (upholding an injunction that stopped publication of a "do not patronize" list by the American Federation of Labor).

78. Mutual Film Corp. v. Industrial Commission of Ohio, 236 U.S. 230, 241 (1915).

79. *Mutual Film Corp.*, 236 U.S. at 241–42.

80. *Mutual Film Corp.*, 236 U.S. at 242.

81. *Mutual Film Corp.*, 236 U.S. at 243.

82. *Mutual Film Corp.*, 236 U.S. at 243.

83. *Mutual Film Corp.*, 236 U.S. at 244.

84. Alexandra Gil, "Great Expectations: Content Regulation in Film, Radio, and Television," *Denver University Sports and Entertainment Law Journal* 6 no. 2 (2009): 31–64, 43–44.

85. Samantha Barbas, "How the Movies Became Speech," *Rutgers Law Review* 64, no. 3 (2012): 665–740, 665–66; Joseph Burstyn v. Wilson, 343 U.S. 495 (1952).

86. Jay Douglas Steinmetz, *Beyond Free Speech and Propaganda: The Political Development of Hollywood, 1907–1927* (Lanham, MD: Lexington Books, 2018), 60.

87. See Mill, *On Liberty*, 84.

88. Fox v. Washington, 236 U.S. 273, 275–77 (1915).

89. *Fox*, 236 U.S. at 277.

90. G. Edward White, "Justice Holmes and the Modernization of Free Speech Jurisprudence: The Human Dimension," *California Law Review* 80, no. 2 (1992): 391–467, 402.

91. *Fox*, 236 U.S. at 277, 278.

92. White, "Justice Holmes and Modernization," 401–2.

93. *Fox*, 236 U.S. at 277.

94. See Hitchman Coal & Coke Co. v. Mitchell, 245 U.S. 229 (1917) (upholding a federal injunction barring union organizers from speaking with employees who signed yellow-dog contracts).

95. Toledo Newspaper Co. v. United States, 247 U.S. 402, 420, 421 (1918).

96. *Toledo Newspaper Co.*, 247 U.S. at 419.

97. *Toledo Newspaper Co.*, 247 U.S. at 420.

98. Stephen M. Feldman, "Free Speech, World War I, and Republican Democracy: The Internal and External Holmes," *First Amendment Law Review* 6, no. 2 (2008): 192–251, 234 n.205.

99. *Toledo Newspaper Co.*, 247 U.S. at 423 (Holmes, J., dissenting).

100. *Toledo Newspaper Co.*, 247 U.S. at 423.

101. David M. Rabban, "The Emergence of Modern First Amendment Doctrine," *University of Chicago Law Review* 50, no. 4 (1983): 1207–1355, 1257.

102. *Toledo Newspaper Co.*, 247 U.S. at 424 (Holmes, J., dissenting) (emphasis added).

103. Schenck v. United States, 249 U.S. 47, 48–49 (1919); Sarah Sorial, *Sedition and the Advocacy of Violence: Free Speech and Counter-Terrorism* (New York: Routledge, 2012), 17.

104. *Schenck*, 249 U.S. at 49–51.

105. *Schenck*, 249 U.S. at 52.

106. *Schenck*, 249 U.S. at 52.

107. *Schenck*, 249 U.S. at 52.

108. *Schenck*, 249 U.S. at 52–53.

109. *Schenck*, 249 U.S. at 51.

110. See Mill, *On Liberty*, at 53.

111. *Schenck*, 249 U.S. at 51–52.

112. Feldman, "Free Speech, World War I," 208–9.

113. *Schenck*, 249 U.S. at 49–50.

114. *Schenck*, 249 U.S. at 50–51.

115. Mark Strasser, "Mill, Holmes, Brandeis, and a True Threat to *Brandenburg*," *BYU Journal of Public Law* 26, no. 1 (2011): 37–72, 45.

116. Strasser, 44.

117. *Schenck*, 249 U.S. at 52.

118. Christina E. Wells, "Fear and Loathing in Constitutional Decision-Making," *Wisconsin Law Review* 2005, no. 1 (2005): 115–223, 152 n.218

119. Louis Menand, *The Metaphysical Club: A Story of Ideas in America* (New York: Farrar, Straus and Giroux, 2001), 25–26; Catherine Drinker Bowen, *Yankee from Olympus: Justice Holmes and His Family* (Boston: Little, Brown, 1945), 187, 225, 228; Gary J. Aichele, *Oliver Wendell Holmes, Jr.: Soldier, Scholar, Judge* (Boston: Twayne, 1989), 77–81.

120. Thomas Healy, *The Great Dissent: How Oliver Wendell Holmes Changed His Mind—and Changed the History of Free Speech in America* (New York: Metropolitan Books, 2013), 30, 36, 98.

121. Oliver Wendell Holmes Jr. to Harold Laski, February 28, 1919, in *The Essential Holmes*, ed. Richard A. Posner (Chicago: University of Chicago Press, 1992), 143.

122. See *Schenck*, 249 U.S. at 47.

123. Menand, *Metaphysical Club*, 62–63.

124. Sugarman v. United States, 249 U.S. 182 (1919).

125. Frohwerk v. United States, 249 U.S. 204, 206 (1919).

126. *Frohwerk*, 249 U.S. at 208, 209.

127. Debs v. United States, 249 U.S. 211, 214–15 (1919).

128. White, "Justice Holmes and Modernization," 418.

3. The Marketplace of Ideas

1. See Zechariah Chafee Jr., "Freedom of Speech in War Time," *Harvard Law Review* 32, no. 8 (1919): 932–73, 967–69.

2. Thomas Healy, *The Great Dissent: How Oliver Wendell Holmes Changed His Mind—and Changed the History of Free Speech in America* (New York: Metropolitan Books, 2013), 98.

3. Harold Laski to Oliver Wendell Holmes Jr., March 16, 1919, in *The Essential Holmes*, ed. Richard A. Posner (Chicago: University of Chicago Press, 1992), 316.

4. Healy, *Great Dissent*, 57, 109, 154, 158; Philippa Strum, "Brandeis: The Public Activist and Freedom of Speech," *Brandeis Law Journal* 45, no. 4 (2007): 659–709, 675–76; David M. Rabban, "The First Amendment in Its Forgotten Years," *Yale Law Journal* 90, no. 3 (1981): 594; Louis Menand, *The Metaphysical Club: A Story of Ideas in America* (New York: Farrar, Straus and Giroux, 2001), 424–28.

5. Chafee, "Freedom of Speech in War Time," 938 (emphasis in original).

6. Chafee, 939.

7. Chafee, 938.

8. *Schenck*, 249 U.S. at 52; Chafee, "Freedom of Speech in War Time," 944.

9. Chafee, "Freedom of Speech in War Time," 945.

10. Chafee, 967.

11. Chafee, 967–68.

12. Chafee, 938, 943, 945, 955, 959, 963, 967–69.

13. Chafee, 933.

14. Chafee, 955.

15. Chafee, 956.

16. Oliver Wendell Holmes Jr. to Harold Laski (October 26, 1919), in *Essential Holmes*, 321.

17. Abrams v. United States, 250 U.S. 616, 621–22 (1919); Steven J. Heyman, "The Dark Side of the Force: The Legacy of Justice Holmes for First Amendment Jurisprudence," *William & Mary Bill of Rights Journal* 19, no. 3 (2011): 661–723, 679.

18. *Abrams*, 250 U.S. at 620.

19. *Abrams*, 250 U.S. at 617.

20. *Abrams*, 250 U.S. at 622.

21. *Abrams*, 250 U.S. at 624.

22. John Stuart Mill, *On Liberty*, ed. Elizabeth Rapaport (Indianapolis, IN: Hackett, 1978), 15–16.

23. Joseph Russomanno, "Cause and Effect: The Free Speech Transformation as Scientific Revolution," *Communication Law and Policy* 20, no. 3 (2015): 213–59, 244.

24. *Abrams*, 250 U.S. at 628 (Holmes, J., dissenting).

25. *Abrams*, 250 U.S. at 628.

26. Mill, *On Liberty*, 9.

27. *Abrams*, 250 U.S. at 628–29 (Holmes, J., dissenting).

28. *Abrams*, 250 U.S. at 630 (Holmes, J., dissenting).

29. Mill, *On Liberty*, 20 (emphasis in original).

30. *Abrams*, 250 U.S. at 630 (Holmes, J., dissenting).

31. Mill, *On Liberty*, 17.

32. *Abrams*, 250 U.S. at 630 (Holmes, J., dissenting).

33. Mill, *On Liberty*, 18.

34. Mill, 34.

35. See Vincent Blasi, "Holmes and the Marketplace of Ideas," *Supreme Court Review* 2004 (2004): 2, 24.

36. Rodney A. Smolla, *The Constitution Goes to College: Five Constitutional Ideas that Have Shaped the American University* (New York: New York University Press, 2011), 102–3.

37. Mill, *On Liberty*, 28.

38. Mill, 19.

39. Mill, 28.

40. Jill Gordon, "John Stuart Mill and the 'Marketplace of Ideas,'" *Social Theory and Practice* 23, no. 2 (1997): 235–49, 241–42.

41. Stephen M. Feldman, "Free Speech, World War I, and Republican Democracy: The Internal and External Holmes," *First Amendment Law Review* 6, no. 2 (2008): 192–251, 236.

42. *Abrams*, 250 U.S. at 630 (Holmes, J., dissenting).

43. Mill, *On Liberty*, 18, 54.

44. *Abrams*, 250 U.S. at 630 (Holmes, J., dissenting).

45. Mill, *On Liberty*, 34.

46. Healy, *Great Dissent*, 202; Mill, *On Liberty*, 53.

47. Feldman, "Free Speech, World War I," 236.

48. David S. Bogen, "The Free Speech Metamorphosis of Mr. Justice Holmes," *Hofstra Law Review* 11, no. 1 (1982): 97–189, 188.

49. Healy, *Great Dissent*, 220–21.

50. Healy, 213.

51. Richard Polenberg, *Fighting Faiths: The Abrams Case, the Supreme Court, and Free Speech* (New York: Penguin Books, 1987), 241; Rabban, "First Amendment Forgotten Years," 591.

52. Schaefer v. United States, 251 U.S. 466, 480 (1920); Stewart Jay, "The Creation of the First Amendment Right to Free Expression: From the Eighteenth Century to the Mid-Twentieth Century," *William Mitchell Law Review* 34, no. 3 (2008): 773–1020, 854–55.

53. *Schaefer*, 251 U.S. at 479.

54. *Schaefer*, 251 U.S. at 481.

55. Feldman, "Free Speech, World War I," 243.

56. *Schaefer*, 251 U.S. at 482 (Brandeis, J., dissenting).

57. *Schaefer*, 251 U.S. at 483.

58. *Schaefer*, 251 U.S. at 494–95.

59. Mill, *On Liberty*, 4.

60. Mill, 16.

61. *Schaefer*, 251 U.S. at 486 (Brandeis, J., dissenting).

62. Jay, "First Amendment Right to Free Expression," 856.

63. Pierce v. United States, 252 U.S. 239, 249 (1920).

64. *Pierce*, 252 U.S. at 250.

65. *Pierce*, 252 U.S. at 266 (Brandeis, J., dissenting).

66. *Pierce*, 252 U.S. at 267.

67. Mill, *On Liberty*, 35.

68. *Pierce*, 252 U.S. at 269 (Brandeis, J., dissenting).

69. *Pierce*, 252 U.S. at 273.

70. Jay, "First Amendment Right to Free Expression," 859.

71. Kent Greenawalt, *Speech, Crime, and the Uses of Language* (New York: Oxford University Press, 1992), 16.

72. C. Edwin Baker, *Human Liberty and Freedom of Speech* (New York: Oxford University Press, 1989), 7–8.

73. Gilbert v. Minnesota, 254 U.S. 325, 326 (1920).

74. *Gilbert*, 254 U.S. at 327.

75. *Gilbert*, 254 U.S. at 332.

76. Quentin Taylor, "John Stuart Mill, Political Economist: A Reassessment," *Independent Review* 21, no. 1 (2016): 73–94, 78.

77. *Gilbert*, 254 U.S. at 333.

78. *Gilbert*, 254 U.S. at 334 (Brandeis, J., dissenting).

79. *Gilbert*, 254 U.S. at 335.

80. *Gilbert*, 254 U.S. at 338.

81. *Gilbert*, 254 U.S. at 338.

82. Howard Owen Hunter, "Problems in Search of Principles: The First Amendment in the Supreme Court from 1791–1930," *Emory Law Journal* 35, no. 1 (1986): 59–137, 112–13.

83. Feldman, "Free Speech, World War I," 246–47; see United States ex rel. Milwaukee Social Democratic Publishing v. Burleson, 255 U.S. 407 (1921) (upholding the postmaster general's decision to reject second-class mailing status to the *Milwaukee Leader*, a socialist newspaper; Brandeis and Holmes each wrote a dissent, with Holmes arguing that "the use of the mails is almost as much a part of free speech as the right to use our tongues"); Leach v. Carlile, 258 U.S. 138 (1922) (upholding the postmaster general's order to refuse to deliver advertisements for what were deemed fraudulent claims of the medical benefits of "Organo Tablets," and Holmes (joined by Brandeis) dissented, remarking, "I do not suppose that anyone would say that the freedom of written speech is less protected by the First Amendment than the freedom of spoken words. Therefore I cannot understand by what authority Congress undertakes to authorize anyone to determine in advance, on the grounds before us, that certain words shall not be uttered").

84. Gitlow v. New York, 268 U.S. 652, 655 (1925).

85. *Gitlow*, 268 U.S. at 655–59.

86. *Gitlow*, 268 U.S. at 666.

87. Hunter, "Problems in Search of Principles," 112–13, 117.

88. *Gitlow*, 268 U.S. at 667.

89. *Gitlow*, 268 U.S. at 671.

90. *Gitlow*, 268 U.S. at 669.

91. Terry Heinrichs, "Gitlow Redux: 'Bad Tendencies' in the Great White North," *Wayne Law Review* 48, no. 3 (2002): 1101–56, 1105.

92. *Gitlow*, 268 U.S. at 673 (Holmes, J., dissenting).

93. *Gitlow*, 268 U.S. at 673.

94. Philippa Strum, *Speaking Freely:* Whitney v. California *and American Speech Law* (Lawrence: University Press of Kansas, 2015), 104.

95. *Gitlow*, 268 U.S. at 673 (Holmes, J., dissenting).

96. Mill, *On Liberty*, 53.

97. Spencer Bradley, "Whose Market Is It Anyway? A Philosophy and Law Critique of the Supreme Court's Free-Speech Absolutism," *Dickinson Law Review* 123, no. 2 (2019): 517–49, 524.

98. Mill, *On Liberty*,17.

99. Strum, *Speaking Freely*, 74.

100. Strum, 75.

101. Whitney v. California, 274 U.S. 357, 371 (1927).

102. *Whitney*, 274 U.S. at 371.

103. Strum, *Speaking Freely*, 125.

104. Strum, 108–9.

105. Strum, 112; David M. Rabban, "The Emergence of Modern First Amendment Doctrine," *University of Chicago Law Review* 50, no. 4 (1983): 1207–355, 1320–21, 1336–38.

106. *Whitney*, 274 U.S. at 373 (Brandeis, J., concurring).

107. *Whitney*, 274 U.S. at 373.

108. *Whitney*, 274 U.S. at 375–76.

109. Baker, *Human Liberty and Freedom of Speech*, 8; Christoph Bezemek, "The Epistemic Neutrality of the 'Marketplace of Ideas': Milton, Mill, Brandeis, and Holmes on Falsehood and Freedom of Speech," *First Amendment Law Review* 14, no. 1 (2015): 159–81, 170.

110. Mill, *On Liberty*, 61.

111. Mill, 16.

112. Mill, 41.

113. Mill, 4.

114. Mill, 6.

115. Mill, 22.

116. Baker, *Human Liberty and Freedom of Speech*, 8

117. Mill, *On Liberty*, 20.

118. *Whitney*, 274 U.S. 357, 377 (Brandeis, J., concurring).

119. Mill, *On Liberty*, 19.

120. Fiske v. Kansas, 274 U.S. 380 (1927).

121. United States v. Schwimmer, 279 U.S. 644, 646–47 (1929).

122. *Schwimmer*, 279 U.S. at 654–55 (Holmes, J., dissenting).

123. Robert Post, "Reconciling Theory and Doctrine in First Amendment Jurisprudence," in *Eternally Vigilant: Free Speech in the Modern Era*, ed. Lee C. Bollinger and Geoffrey R. Stone (Chicago: University of Chicago Press, 2002), 152–73, 158; Mill, *On Liberty*, 37.

124. *Schwimmer*, 279 U.S. at 654 (Holmes, J., dissenting).

125. Mill, *On Liberty*, 69.

4. Preferred Freedoms

1. Andrew P. Napolitano, "A Legal History of National Security Law and Individual Rights in the United States," *New York University Journal of Law and Liberty* 8, no. 2 (2014): 396–555, 481.

2. David M. Rabban, "The First Amendment in Its Forgotten Years," *Yale Law Journal* 90, no. 3 (1981): 521.

3. Paul L. Murphy, *The Meaning of the Freedom of Speech: First Amendment Freedoms from Wilson to FDR* (Westport, CT: Greenwood, 1972), 5; Peter Linzer, "The *Carolene Products* Footnote and the Preferred Position of Individual Rights: Louis Lusky and John Hart Ely vs. Harlan Fiske Stone," *Constitutional Commentary* 12, no. 2 (1995): 277–303, 300.

4. Stromberg v. California, 283 U.S. 359, 361–62 (1931); Stewart Jay, "The Creation of the First Amendment Right to Free Expression: From the Eighteenth Century to the Mid-Twentieth Century," *William Mitchell Law Review* 34, no. 3 (2008): 879.

5. *Stromberg*, 283 U.S. at 369.

6. William E. Lee, "Modernizing the Law of Open-Air Speech: The Hughes Court and the Birth of Content-Neutral Balancing," *William & Mary Bill of Rights Journal* 13, no. 4 (2005): 1219–65, 1237.

7. John Stuart Mill, *On Liberty*, ed. Elizabeth Rapaport (Indianapolis, IN: Hackett, 1978), 46.

8. See Jay, "Creation of the First Amendment Right," 863–78.

9. Mill, *On Liberty*, 18.

10. Near v. Minnesota, 283 U.S. 697, 704 (1931).

11. *Near*, 283 U.S. at 702–3.

12. *Near*, 283 U.S. at 713–14.

13. *Near*, 283 U.S. at 723 (Butler, J., dissenting).

14. *Near*, 283 U.S. at 713.

15. *Near*, 283 U.S. at 713.

16. Mill, *On Liberty*, 3.

17. *Near*, 283 U.S. at 713, 721.

18. *Near*, 283 U.S. at 714–15.

19. *Near*, 283 U.S. at 722.

20. Justin Kirk Houser, "Is Hate Speech Becoming the New Blasphemy? Lessons from an American Constitutional Dialectic," *Penn State Law Review* 114, no. 2 (2009): 571–609, 585.

21. Mill, *On Liberty*, 51–52.

22. *Near*, 283 U.S. at 707.

23. Mill, *On Liberty*, 11–12.

24. James A. Henretta, "Charles Evans Hughes and the Strange Death of Liberal America," *Law and History Review* 24, no. 1 (2006): 115–71, 171.

25. Henretta, 138; William G. Ross, *The Chief Justiceship of Charles Evans Hughes, 1930–1941* (Columbia: University of South Carolina Press, 2007), 227.

26. Ross, *Chief Justiceship*, 227.

27. See also Grosjean v. American Press, 297 U.S. 233 (1936) (overturning a licensing tax on newspapers).

28. DeJonge v. Oregon, 299 U.S. 353, 364 (1937).

29. Mill, *On Liberty*, 11–12, 53.

30. Mill, 53.

31. *DeJonge*, 299 U.S. at 364–65.

32. *DeJonge*, 299 U.S. at 365.

33. Lovell v. Griffin, 303 U.S. 444, 452 (1938).

34. Mill, *On Liberty*, 53.

35. Mill, 53.

36. Robert Young, "The Value of Autonomy," *Philosophical Quarterly* 32, no. 126 (1982): 35–44, 36.

37. See also Herndon v. Lowry, 301 U.S. 242 (1937) (Roberts wrote for the Supreme Court in overturning a criminal conviction for syndicalism against a Communist Party recruiter where there was no clear and present danger proven).

38. Schneider v. State, 308 U.S. 147, 160 (1939).

39. *Schneider*, 308 U.S. at 161.

40. See Frederick Rosen, "J. S. Mill on Truth, Liberty, and Democracy," in *Truth and Democracy*, ed. Jeremy Elkins and Andrew Norris (Philadelphia: University of Pennsylvania Press, 2012), 192–93, on arguments from Mill's *On Liberty*.

41. *Schneider*, 308 U.S. at 163.

42. Hague v. CIO, 307 U.S. 496, 513 (1939).

43. *Hague*, 307 U.S. at 515.

44. Marc Jonathan Blitz, "Constitutional Safeguards for Silent Experiments in Living: Libraries, the Right to Read, and a First Amendment Theory for an Unaccompanied Right to Receive Information," *UMKC Law Review* 74, no. 4 (2006): 799–882, 804.

45. Lee, "Modernizing the Law," 1256.

46. Lee, "Modernizing the Law," 1256.

47. Palko v. Connecticut, 302 U.S. 319, 326–27 (1937).

48. Mill, *On Liberty*, 53, 97.

49. United States v. Carolene Products Co., 304 U.S. 144, 152 n4 (1938).

50. *Carolene Products*, 304 U.S. 144, at 152 n4.

51. *Carolene Products*, 304 U.S. 144, at 152 n4.

52. *Carolene Products*, 304 U.S. 144, at 152 n4.

53. *Carolene Products*, 304 U.S. 144, at 152 n4; Douglas Laycock, "Constitutional Theory Matters," *Texas Law Review* 65, no. 4 (1987): 767–75, 770 n.15.

54. Henretta, "Charles Evans Hughes," 115–71, 152.

55. Mill, *On Liberty*, 15.

56. Thornhill v. Alabama, 310 U.S. 88, 95 (1940).

57. *Thornhill*, 310 U.S. at 95.

58. Mill, *On Liberty*, 41.

59. *Thornhill*, 310 U.S. at 104.

60. *Thornhill*, 310 U.S. at 104.

61. *Thornhill*, 310 U.S. at 95–98.

62. *Thornhill*, 310 U.S. at 105.

63. See Carlson v. California, 310 U.S. 106 (1940) (ruling that a law prohibiting labor picketing was unconstitutional in the absence of a clear and present danger); American Federation of Labor v. Swing, 312 U.S. 321 (1941) (ruling unconstitutional a state prohibition on labor picketing); Bakery and Pastry Drivers and Helpers Local v. Wohl, 315 U.S. 769 (1942) (overturning an injunction on labor pickets of independent bakery peddlers). But see also Milk Wagon Drivers Union v. Meadowmoor, 312 U.S. 287 (1941) (upholding an injunction on labor union picketing because of past violence in Chicago over labor relations in milk distribution, with Justice Black dissenting because he found no "imminent, clear and present danger as to justify an abridgment of the rights of freedom of speech and the press").

64. Bridges v. California, 314 U.S. 252, 263 (1941) (emphasis added).

65. *Bridges*, 314 U.S. at 262 (quoting *Thornhill*, 310 U.S. at 105).

66. *Bridges*, 314 U.S. at 261 (internal quotation omitted).

67. *Bridges*, 314 U.S. at 263.

68. Mill, *On Liberty*, 51; *Bridges*, 314 U.S. at 270.

69. *Bridges*, 314 U.S. at 262, n5.

70. *Bridges*, 314 U.S. at 279 (Frankfurter, J., dissenting).

71. *Bridges*, 314 U.S. at 290.

72. *Bridges*, 314 U.S. at 296; David M. Rabban, "The Emergence of Modern First Amendment Doctrine," *University of Chicago Law Review* 50, no. 4 (1983): 1261.

73. *Bridges*, 314 U.S. at 296 (Frankfurter, J., dissenting); Rabban, "Emergence of Modern First Amendment Doctrine," 1261 n.331.

74. Valentine v. Chrestensen, 316 U.S. 52, 54 (1942).

75. *Valentine*, 316 U.S. at 54.

76. Mill, *On Liberty*, 94.

77. Mill, 94.

78. Mill, 94. Mill personally disliked restraints on free trade but found them permissible as a matter of public policy if adopted by the government. D. A. Lloyd Thomas, "Liberalism and Utilitarianism," *Ethics* 90, no. 3 (1980): 319–34, 332.

79. Mill, *On Liberty*, 98, 99.

80. Soontae An, "From a Business Pursuit to a Means of Expression: The Supreme Court's Disputes over Commercial Speech from 1942 to 1976," *Communication Law and Policy* 8, no. 2 (2003): 201–25, 211.

81. Lee, "Modernizing the Law," 1256–57.

82. See G. Richard Shell, "Contracts in the Modern Supreme Court," *California Law Review* 81, no. 2 (1993): 433–529, 489–91.

83. Chaplinsky v. New Hampshire, 315 U.S. 568, 573 (1942).

84. *Chaplinsky*, 315 U.S. at 572.

85. See Mill, *On Liberty*, 22, 51.

86. *Chaplinsky*, 315 U.S. at 572; Mill, *On Liberty*, 11 (emphasis added).

87. Keith N. Hylton, "Implications of Mill's Theory of Liberty for the Regulation of Hate Speech and Hate Crimes," *University of Chicago Law School Roundtable* 3, no. 1 (1996): 35–57, 52.

88. Burton Caine, "The Trouble with 'Fighting Words': *Chaplinsky v. New Hampshire* Is a Threat to First Amendment Values and Should Be Overruled," *Marquette Law Review* 88, no. 3 (2004): 441–562, 446.

89. National Broadcasting Co. v. United States, 319 U.S. 190, 195 (1943).

90. *National Broadcasting Co.*, 319 U.S. at 226.

91. See Matthew L. Spitzer, "Controlling the Content of Print and Broadcast," *Southern California Law Review* 58 (1985): 1349–405, 1358–64.

92. See Justman, *The Hidden Text of Mill's "Liberty,"* 75–110.

93. *National Broadcasting Co.*, 319 U.S. at 227.

94. Cantwell v. Connecticut, 310 U.S. 296, 306 (1940).

95. *Cantwell*, 310 U.S. at 305.

96. Mill, *On Liberty*, 23–24.

97. Shawn Francis Peters, *Judging Jehovah's Witnesses: Religious Persecution and the Dawn of the Rights Revolution* (Lawrence: University Press of Kansas, 2000), 10–11. See Cox v. New Hampshire, 312 U.S. 569 (1941) (upholding the convictions of Jehovah's Witnesses for peacefully parading on sidewalks and handing out leaflets without a permit); Minersville School District v. Gobitis, 310 U.S. 586 (1940) (upholding public school expulsions of Jehovah's Witness children who refused to salute the US flag).

98. Jones v. Opelika, 316 U.S. 584, 593 (1942).

99. *Jones*, 316 U.S. at 595–96.

100. *Jones*, 316 U.S. at 608 (Stone, C. J., dissenting).

101. *Jones*, 316 U.S. at 608.

102. *Jones*, 316 U.S. at 611 (Murphy, J., dissenting).

103. *Jones*, 316 U.S. at 611–12.

104. *Jones*, 316 U.S. at 618.

105. Mill, *On Liberty*, 53.

106. Jeremy K. Kessler, "The Early Years of First Amendment Lochnerism," *Columbia Law Review* 116, no. 8 (2016): 1915–2004, 1964–65.

107. See Stephen M. Feldman, "Unenumerated Rights in Different Democratic Regimes," *University of Pennsylvania Journal of Constitutional Law* 9, no. 1 (2006): 47–105, 84–85.

108. See Jamison v. Texas, 318 U.S. 413 (1943) (overturning Jehovah's Witnesses' convictions for distributing religious handbills); Largent v. Texas, 318 U.S. 418 (1943) (overturning a conviction for soliciting book orders without a permit); Martin v. Struthers, 319 U.S. 141 (1943) (overturning conviction for going door-to-door in residential neighborhoods to distribute handbills).

109. Jones v. Opelika II, 319 U.S. 103 (1943); Murdock v. Pennsylvania, 319 U.S. 105, 113, 115 (1943).

110. *Gobitis*, 310 U.S. at 598.

111. West Virginia v. Barnette, 319 U.S. 624, 633 (1943).

112. *Barnette*, 319 U.S. at 633.

113. *Barnette*, 319 U.S. at 633–34.

114. *Barnette*, 319 U.S. at 638.

115. *Barnette*, 319 U.S. at 639.

116. *Barnette*, 319 U.S. at 640; Mill, *On Liberty*, 24.

117. Mill, 23; *Barnette*, 319 U.S. at 641.

118. *Barnette*, 319 U.S. at 642.

119. *Barnette*, 319 U.S. at 641–42.

120. See also *Barnette*'s companion case, Taylor v. Mississippi, 319 U.S. 583 (1943) (overturning prison sentences for adult Jehovah's Witnesses who were convicted of distributing literature that claimed the flag salute constitutes a form of idol worship).

121. Eric Michael Prock, "Religion and the Three Wisemen: A Philosophical Inquiry into Selected First Amendment Jurisprudence," *Penn State Law Review* 112, no. 4 (2008): 1071–1123, 1097.

122. See Cafeteria Employees Union v. Angelos, 320 U.S. 293 (1943) (overturning an injunction of a labor union picket); Follett v. McCormick, 321 U.S. 573 (1944) (overturning a licensing tax on the door-to-door selling of religious publications).

123. Hartzel v. United States, 322 U.S. 680, 686 (1944) (quoting Abrams v. United States, 250 U.S. 616, 627 (1919) (Holmes, J., dissenting)).

124. *Hartzel*, 322 U.S. at 689.

125. See Mill, *On Liberty*, 51.

126. Geoffrey R. Stone, *Perilous Times: Free Speech in Wartime* (New York: Norton, 2004), 282.

127. Baumgardner v. United States, 322 U.S. 665, 673 (1944) (quoting Luria v. United States, 231 U.S. 9, 22 (1913)).

128. *Baumgardner,* 322 U.S. at 674. See G. Edward White, "The First Amendment Comes of Age: The Emergence of Free Speech in Twentieth-Century America," *Michigan Law Review* 95, no. 2 (1996): 299–392, 334 (explaining Frankfurter's support for majoritarian restrictions on expression in cases like *Gobitis*).

129. *Baumgardner,* 322 U.S. at 674.

130. See Schneiderman v. United States, 320 U.S. 118, 138 (1943) (overturning a cancellation of citizenship due to membership in the Workers (Communist) Party because "criticism of, and the sincerity of desires to improve, the Constitution should not be judged by conformity to prevailing thought"); Bridges v. Wixon, 326 U.S. 135 (1945) (overturning a decision to deport an alien from Australia based on his past affiliation with the Communist Party).

131. Mill, *On Liberty,* 16.

132. Thomas v. Collins, 323 U.S. 516, 530 (1945).

133. *Thomas,* 323 U.S. at 530.

134. *Thomas,* 323 U.S. at 530.

135. *Thomas,* 323 U.S. at 537 (emphasis added).

136. *Thomas,* 323 U.S. at 537.

137. *Thomas,* 323 U.S. at 531; Mill, *On Liberty,* 11.

138. *Thomas,* 323 U.S. at 531; An, "From a Business Pursuit," 211.

139. Alan Story, "Employer Speech, Union Representation Elections, and the First Amendment," *Berkeley Journal of Employment and Labor Law* 16, no. 2 (1995): 356–457, 378, n.107.

140. See Pennekamp v. Florida, 328 U.S. 331 (1946) (overturning a contempt citation against the editor of the *Miami Herald* for publishing a cartoon and two editorials that were critical of a trial court judge's handling of a criminal case); Tucker v. Texas, 326 U.S. 517 (1946) (reversing the conviction of a Jehovah's Witness who had been arrested for going door-to-door); Hannegan v. Esquire, 327 U.S. 146, 149 (1946) (overturning the suspension of a second-class mailing permit for *Esquire* magazine after the postmaster general found that it contained writings and pictures deemed "indecent, vulgar, and risqué"); Craig v. Harney, 331 U.S. 367, 377 (1947) (using the clear and present danger test when overturning contempt convictions of newspaper employees for writing articles critical of a judge).

141. Elizabeth J. Wallmeyer, "Filled Milk, Footnote Four and the First Amendment: An Analysis of the Preferred Position of Speech after the *Carolene Products* Decision," *Fordham Intellectual Property, Media, and Entertainment Law Journal* 13, no. 4 (2003): 1019–52, 1020.

142. Wallmeyer, 1021–23.

143. Wallmeyer, 1026.

144. Mill, *On Liberty,* 11.

145. See also Giboney v. Empire Storage and Ice, 336 U.S. 490, 503 (1949) (applying the clear and present danger test to uphold an injunction against a labor union that had attempted to induce wholesale distributors to agree not to sell ice to nonunion merchants).

146. United Public Workers of America v. Mitchell, 330 U.S. 75, 78 (1947).

147. *United Public Workers of America,* 330 U.S. at 103.

148. Mill, *On Liberty,* 80.

149. *United Public Workers of America*, 330 U.S. at 100.

150. Mill, *On Liberty*, 80 (emphasis added).

151. Elliott Hughes, "Political Speech in the Armed Forces: Shouting Fire in a Crowded Cyberspace?," *Washington University Jurisprudence Review* 11, no. 1 (2019): 139–64, 156.

152. *United Public Workers of America*, 330 U.S. at 107, 110 (Black, J., dissenting).

153. See *Saia v. New York*, 334 U.S. 558, 562 (1948) (finding unconstitutional a police chief's refusal to issue a permit to Jehovah's Witnesses to use sound amplification equipment, because "the freedoms of the First Amendment [are] in a preferred position"); *Winters v. New York*, 333 U.S. 507, 510 (1948) (overturning a law that prohibited as "obscene" any publication "principally made up of criminal news, police reports, or accounts of criminal deeds, or pictures, or stories of deeds of bloodshed, lust or crime," because "though we can see nothing of any possible value to society in these magazines, they are as much entitled to the protection of free speech as the best of literature").

154. *Terminiello v. Chicago*, 337 U.S. 1, 26 (1949) (Jackson, J., dissenting).

155. *Terminiello*, 337 U.S. at 4 (internal citation omitted).

156. *Terminiello*, 337 U.S. at 4.

157. Christina E. Wells, "Fear and Loathing in Constitutional Decision-Making," *Wisconsin Law Review* 2005, no. 1 (2005): 152 n.218.

158. Caine, "Trouble with 'Fighting Words,'" 504–5; *Terminiello*, 337 U.S. at 4.

159. *Terminiello*, 337 U.S. at 4–5.

160. See *Saia*, 334 U.S. at 564 (Frankfurter, J., dissenting) ("That people complained about an *annoyance* would seem to be a pretty solid basis in experience for not sanctioning its continuance" (emphasis added)); *Winters*, 333 U.S. at 527 (Frankfurter, J., dissenting) ("incitement *may* be caused by the written word no less than by the spoken" (emphasis added)).

161. *Terminiello*, 337 U.S. at 37 (Jackson, J., dissenting).

162. See David P. Currie, "The Constitution in the Supreme Court: 1946–1953," *Emory Law Journal* 37, no. 2 (1988): 249–94, 256–76.

163. Noah Feldman, *Scorpions: The Battles and Triumphs of FDR's Great Supreme Court Justices* (New York: Twelve, 2010), 349–50.

164. *Terminiello*, 337 U.S. at 24 (Jackson, J., dissenting).

165. *Terminiello*, 337 U.S. at 24.

166. *Terminiello*, 337 U.S. at 25.

167. *Kovacs v. Cooper*, 336 U.S. 77, 78 (1949).

168. *Kovacs*, 336 U.S. at 83.

169. Falguni A. Sheth, "John Stuart Mill on Race, Liberty, and Markets," in *Race, Liberalism, and Economics*, ed. David Colander et al. (Ann Arbor: University of Michigan Press, 2004), 100–120, 116.

170. *Kovacs*, 336 U.S. at 87.

171. *Kovacs*, 336 U.S. at 88, 89.

172. *Kovacs*, 336 U.S. at 90 (Frankfurter, J., concurring).

173. *Kovacs*, 336 U.S. at 90–94.

174. *Kovacs*, 336 U.S. at 90–94.

175. *Kovacs*, 336 U.S. at 89.

176. *Kovacs*, 336 U.S. at 95.
177. *Kovacs*, 336 U.S. at 97.
178. *Kovacs*, 336 U.S. at 101 (Black, J., dissenting).
179. *Kovacs*, 336 U.S. at 102.
180. *Kovacs*, 336 U.S. at 103.
181. *Kovacs*, 336 U.S. at 104.

5. No Law Means No Law

1. Justice Murphy also authored a more libertarian decision for the Supreme Court in *Carlson v. California* (1940).

2. David Alistair Yalof, *Pursuit of Justices: Presidential Politics and the Selection of Supreme Court Nominees* (Chicago: University of Chicago Press, 1999), 35.

3. Linda C. Gugin, *Sherman Minton: New Deal Senator, Cold War Justice* (Indianapolis: Indiana Historical Society Press, 1997), 223.

4. See Ring Lardner Jr. and Frances Chaney Lardner, "The Beginning: The Hollywood Ten," in *It Did Happen Here: Recollections of Political Repression in America*, ed. Bud Schultz and Ruth Schultz (Berkeley: University of California Press, 1989), 101–16, 106.

5. American Communications Association v. Douds, 339 U.S. 382, 395 (1950).

6. *Douds*, 339 U.S. at 396.

7. *Douds*, 339 U.S. at 397.

8. *Douds*, 339 U.S. at 398.

9. *Douds*, 339 U.S. at 399.

10. Alan I. Bigel, "The First Amendment and National Security: The Court Responds to Governmental Harassment of Alleged Communist Sympathizers," *Ohio Northern University Law Review* 19 (1993): 885–926, 911–12.

11. *Douds*, 339 U.S. at 422–23 (Jackson., J, concurring in part and dissenting in part).

12. *Douds*, 339 U.S. at 434–35.

13. Gregory S. Chernack, "The Clash of Two Worlds: Justice Robert H. Jackson, Institutional Pragmatism, and *Brown*," *Temple Law Review* 72, no. 1 (1999): 51–109, 77–78.

14. John Stuart Mill, *On Liberty*, ed. Elizabeth Rapaport (Indianapolis, IN: Hackett, 1978), 11; *Douds*, 339 U.S. at 445–46 (Black, J., dissenting) (quoting Jones v. Opelika, 316 U.S. 584, 618 (1942) (Murphy, J., dissenting)).

15. *Douds*, 339 U.S. at 448.

16. *Douds*, 339 U.S. at 447.

17. Joseph Hamburger, *John Stuart Mill on Liberty and Control* (Princeton, NJ: Princeton University Press, 1999), 87–88.

18. *Douds*, 339 U.S. at 446–47 (Black, J., dissenting).

19. *Douds*, 339 U.S. at 452.

20. *Douds*, 339 U.S. at 453.

21. Virginia Van der Veer Hamilton, *Hugo Black: The Alabama Years* (Tuscaloosa: University of Alabama Press, 1972), 171; Arthur John Keeffe, "Mr. Justice Black and His Books," *American Bar Association Journal* 60, no. 11 (1974): 1458–60, 1458.

22. Michael Paris and Kevin J. McMahon, "Absolutism and Democracy: Hugo Black's Free Speech Jurisprudence," in *Judging Free Speech: First Amendment Jurispru-*

dence of US Supreme Court Justices, ed. Helen J. Knowles and Steven B. Lichtman (New York: Palgrave Macmillan, 2015), 75–97, 88.

23. Paris and McMahon, 87; Garner v. Board of Public Works, 341 U.S. 716 (1951) (upholding city employee-mandated loyalty oaths affirming that they did not advise, advocate, or teach the overthrow of the government by force); Breard v. Alexandria, 341 U.S. 622, 642 (1951) (upholding a law prohibiting unsolicited door-to-door commercial speech).

24. Hughes v. Superior Court of California, 339 U.S. 460 (1950); International Brotherhood of Teamsters v. Hanke, 339 U.S. 470 (1950); Building Service Employees International Union v. Gazzam, 339 U.S. 532 (1950); International Brotherhood of Electrical Workers v. NLRB, 341 U.S. 694 (1951); United Association of Journeymen Plumbers and Steamfitters v. Graham, 345 U.S. 192 (1953); Catherine Fisk and Jessica Rutter, "Labor Protest under the New First Amendment," *Berkeley Journal of Employment and Labor Law* 36, no. 2 (2015): 277–329, 298.

25. Dennis v. United States, 341 U.S. 494, 496 (1951).

26. *Dennis*, 341 U.S. at 503.

27. *Dennis*, 341 U.S. at 510 (emphasis added) (internal quotation marks omitted); Michael P. Downey, "The Jeffersonian Myth in Supreme Court Sedition Jurisprudence," *Washington University Law Quarterly* 76, no. 2 (1998): 683–720, 708–9.

28. *Dennis*, 341 U.S. at 510.

29. Christina E. Wells, "Fear and Loathing in Constitutional Decision-Making," *Wisconsin Law Review* 2005 (2005): 152 n.218.

30. Ashutosh Bhagwat, *Our Democratic First Amendment* (New York: Cambridge University Press, 2020), 35.

31. Abrams v. United States, 250 U.S. 616, 627–28 (1919).

32. *Whitney*, 274 U.S. at 373 (Brandeis, J., concurring).

33. Bhagwat, *Our Democratic First Amendment*, 41.

34. *Dennis*, 341 U.S. at 524–25 (Frankfurter, J., concurring).

35. *Dennis*, 341 U.S. at 553 (quoting Sir William Haley, "What Standards for Broadcasting?," *Measure* 1, no. 3 (Summer 1950): 211–12).

36. Noah Feldman, *Scorpions: The Battles and Triumphs of FDR's Great Supreme Court Justices* (New York: Twelve, 2010), 118; *Dennis*, 341 U.S. at 556 (Frankfurter, J., concurring).

37. Mill, *On Liberty*, 4.

38. Mill, 4.

39. *Dennis*, 341 U.S. at 524, n.5 (Frankfurter, J., concurring).

40. *Dennis*, 341 U.S. at 524, n.5 (quoting Alexander Meiklejohn, *Free Speech and Its Relation to Self-Government* (New York: Harper and Brothers, 1948), 39, 99–100, 104).

41. *Dennis*, 341 U.S. at 567 (Jackson, J., concurring).

42. *Dennis*, 341 U.S. at 367 n.9 (quoting Meiklejohn, *Free Speech*, 29).

43. *Dennis*, 341 U.S. at 570.

44. *Dennis*, 341 U.S. at 579 (Black, J., dissenting).

45. *Dennis*, 341 U.S. at 579.

46. *Dennis*, 341 U.S. at 580.

47. *Dennis*, 341 U.S. at 580.

48. Mill, *On Liberty*, 53.

49. *Dennis*, 341 U.S. at 584–85 (Douglas, J., dissenting).

50. *Dennis*, 341 U.S. at 585.

51. *Dennis*, 341 U.S. at 585–88.

52. *Dennis*, 341 U.S. at 591.

53. *Dennis*, 341 U.S. at 585.

54. William O. Douglas, "The Need for Fundamental Education in the U.S. Constitutional System," *Phi Delta Kappan* 47, no. 9 (1966): 472–475, 475.

55. See, e.g., Harisiades v. Shaughnessy, 342 U.S. 580 (1952) (upholding deportations of resident aliens due to their former Communist Party membership).

56. Feiner v. New York, 340 U.S. 315, 317 (1951).

57. *Feiner*, 340 U.S. at 316–19.

58. *Feiner*, 340 U.S. at 321.

59. Brett G. Johnson, "The Heckler's Veto: Using First Amendment Theory and Jurisprudence to Understand Current Audience Reactions against Controversial Speech," *Communication Law and Policy* 21, no. 2 (2016): 175–220, 186.

60. R. George Wright, "The Heckler's Veto Today," *Case Western Reserve Law Review* 68, no. 1 (2017): 159–88, 166.

61. *Feiner*, 340 U.S. at 326 (Black, J., dissenting).

62. *Feiner*, 340 U.S. at 328.

63. *Feiner*, 340 U.S. at 330–31 (Douglas, J., dissenting).

64. Mill, *On Liberty* 51.

65. Mill, 5.

66. *Feiner*, 340 U.S. at 331 (Douglas, J., dissenting).

67. Beauharnais v. Illinois, 343 U.S. 250, 251 (1952).

68. *Beauharnais*, 343 U.S. at 252.

69. *Beauharnais*, 343 U.S. at 266.

70. *Beauharnais*, 343 U.S. at 262.

71. *Beauharnais*, 343 U.S. at 270 (Black, J., dissenting).

72. *Beauharnais*, 343 U.S. at 270.

73. *Beauharnais*, 343 U.S. at 274–75.

74. *Beauharnais*, 343 U.S. at 275.

75. *Beauharnais*, 343 U.S. at 290 (Jackson, J., dissenting) (internal citation omitted).

76. *Beauharnais*, 343 U.S. at 291–92.

77. David P. Currie, "The Constitution in the Supreme Court: 1946–1953," *Emory Law Journal* 37, no. 2 (1988): 269.

78. See, e.g., Kunz v. New York, 340 U.S. 290 (1951) (overturning a conviction for a street preacher speaking without a permit); Niemotko v. Maryland, 340 U.S. 268 (1951) (reversing disorderly conduct convictions for members of a religious group who held a Bible study in a public park without a permit); Wieman v. Updegraff, 344 U.S. 183 (1952) (striking down a loyalty oath for state employees to affirm that they were not members of a communist or subversive organization); Fowler v. Rhode Island, 345 U.S. 67 (1953) (overturning the conviction of a Jehovah's Witness minister for giving a religious address in a public park when services had been allowed in that park for other religious groups).

79. Joseph Burstyn, Inc. v. Wilson, 343 U.S. 495, 501 (1952).

80. Samantha Barbas, "How the Movies Became Speech," *Rutgers Law Review* 64, no. 3 (2012): 665–745, 667–70.

81. Mill, *On Liberty*, 64–65.

82. Mill, 70.

83. Greg Lastowka, *Virtual Justice: The New Laws of Online Worlds* (New Haven, CT: Yale University Press, 2011), 116; *Burstyn*, 343 U.S. at 501.

84. *Burstyn*, 343 U.S. at 501.

85. *Burstyn*, 343 U.S. at 502. See also Gelling v. Texas, 343 U.S. 960, 961 (1952) (striking down a conviction for "exhibiting a picture after being denied permission to do so by the local Board of Censors"); Superior Films v. Department of Education, 346 U.S. 587 (1954) (overturning laws permitting state agencies to refuse to issue licenses to show certain films).

86. Harry Kalven Jr., "Upon Rereading Mr. Justice Black on the First Amendment," *UCLA Law Review* 14, no. 2 (1967): 428–53, 437–38.

87. Poulos v. New Hampshire, 345 U.S. 395 (1953).

88. *Poulos*, 345 U.S. at 423 (Douglas, J., dissenting).

89. *Poulos*, 345 U.S. at 423 (emphasis in original).

90. *Poulos*, 345 U.S. at 423 (internal citation omitted).

91. *Poulos*, 345 U.S. at 423.

92. United States v. Rumely, 345 U.S. 41, 56 (1953) (Douglas, J., concurring).

93. See Yates v. United States, 354 U.S. 298, 319–20 (1957) (overturning convictions or ordering new trials of Communist Party members for violating the Smith Act, the same law upheld by the Supreme Court in *Dennis*, but not applying the clear and present danger test). In a partial concurrence, Justice Black argued, "I believe that the First Amendment forbids Congress to punish people for talking about public affairs, whether or not such discussion incites to action, legal or illegal" (340).

94. See also Sweezy v. New Hampshire, 354 U.S. 234, 245 (1957) (Chief Justice Warren's plurality opinion overturned a contempt conviction against a university professor who refused to answer questions about his Progressive Party affiliation, advocacy of socialism, and a lecture he delivered, with Warren emphasizing the importance of the "freedom of speech or press, freedom of political association, and freedom of communication of ideas, particularly in the academic community").

95. Roth v. United States, 354 U.S. 476, 488–89 (1957) (internal citation omitted).

96. *Roth*, 354 U.S. at 484.

97. *Roth*, 354 U.S. at 488.

98. *Roth*, 354 U.S. at 487.

99. Mill, *On Liberty*, 84.

100. *Roth*, 354 U.S. at 484.

101. Bret Boyce, "Obscenity and Community Standards," *Yale Journal of International Law* 33, no. 2 (2008): 299–368, 316.

102. See Alberts v. California, 354 U.S. 476 (1957); Kingsley Books, Inc. v. Brown, 354 U.S. 436 (1957). See Butler v. Michigan, 352 U.S. 380, 383 (1957) (overturning a Michigan law that made it a crime to sell printed materials "tending to the corruption of the morals of youth," because, according to the Supreme Court, "the incidence of this enactment is to reduce the adult population of Michigan to reading only what is fit for children"); Smith v. California, 361 U.S. 147 (1959) (invalidating a state strict liability obscenity law for reasons of vagueness); Manual Enterprises v. Day, 370 U.S. 478 (1962) (applying *Roth* to find that homoerotic magazines were not patently offensive, and hence not obscene).

103. *Roth*, 354 U.S. at 512 (Douglas, J., dissenting).

104. *Roth*, 354 U.S. at 512.

105. *Roth*, 354 U.S. at 513.

106. *Roth*, 354 U.S. at 514.

107. *Roth*, 354 U.S. at 514.

108. Mill, *On Liberty*, 32.

109. On unions, see International Brotherhood of Teamsters Union v. Vogt, 354 U.S. 284 (1957) (upholding an injunction that halted a union's peaceful picketing of a gravel pit) compared to Staub v. Baxley, 355 U.S. 313, 322 (1958) (overturning an ordinance requiring persons soliciting membership in a union to first obtain a permit). On movies, compare Kingsley International Pictures v. Board of Regents, 360 U.S. 684, 688 (1959) (finding unconstitutional New York's state film licensing system as applied to deny a showing of *Lady Chatterley's Lover*, which had been deemed immoral by the state, with the Supreme Court describing that "what New York has done . . . is to prevent the exhibition of a motion picture because that picture advocates an idea—that adultery under certain circumstances may be proper behavior") with Times Film Corp. v. Chicago, 365 U.S. 43 (1961) (finding that an ordinance requiring licenses to exhibit films was constitutional on its face). See Robert L. Anderson, "Free Speech and Obscenity: A Search for Constitutional Procedures and Standards," *UCLA Law Review* 12 (1965): 532–60.

110. See In re Sawyer, 360 U.S. 622 (1959) (overturning an attorney's suspension for criticizing her client's trial proceedings); Talley v. California, 362 U.S. 60, 64 (1960) (striking down an ordinance requiring handbills to identify the person who printed and distributed them); Garner v. Louisiana, 368 U.S. 157 (1961) (holding that the use of a state breach of the peace statute to convict peaceful sit-in civil rights protestors was unconstitutional); Wood v. Georgia, 370 U.S. 375, 384 (1962) (overturning a contempt of court conviction of a sheriff for issuing press releases where he alleged judges engaged in race baiting).

111. Jerome A. Barron, "The Electronic Media and the Flight from First Amendment Doctrine: Justice Breyer's New Balancing Approach," *University of Michigan Journal of Law Reform* 31, no. 4 (1998): 817–85, 822, n.22.

112. Barenblatt v. United States, 360 U.S. 109, 126 (1959).

113. *Barenblatt*, 360 U.S. at 128.

114. *Barenblatt*, 360 U.S. at 129.

115. *Barenblatt*, 360 U.S. at 134.

116. *Barenblatt*, 360 U.S. at 138, 141 (Black, J., dissenting).

117. *Barenblatt*, 360 U.S. at 145.

118. *Barenblatt*, 360 U.S. at 145–46.

119. Mill, *On Liberty*, 10.

120. Graham Badley, "A Place from Where to Speak: The University and Academic Freedom," *British Journal of Educational Studies* 57, no. 2 (2009): 146–63, 150.

121. *Barenblatt*, 360 U.S. at 146 (Black, J., dissenting).

122. *Barenblatt*, 360 U.S. at 150–51.

123. *Barenblatt*, 360 U.S. at 151.

124. Mill, *On Liberty*, 15–16.

125. *Barenblatt*, 360 U.S. at 159 n.38 (Black, J., dissenting).

126. Mill, *On Liberty*, 24.

127. See Uphaus v. Wyman I, 360 U.S. 72 (1959) (a 5–4 majority used a rational basis review to uphold the contempt conviction of a Methodist minister who refused to produce records of attendees at a summer camp to a state attorney general investigating communism); Communist Party of United States v. Subversive Activities Control Bd., 367 U.S. 1 (1961) (a 5–4 majority upheld a law requiring the Communist Party to register with the federal government); Wilkinson v. United States, 365 U.S. 399 (1961) (a 5–4 Supreme Court upheld a conviction for refusing to answer HUAC questions about communist involvement); Braden v. United States, 365 U.S. 431 (1961) (a 5–4 Supreme Court upheld a conviction for refusing to answer HUAC questions about expression of communist ideas); In re Anastaplo, 366 U.S. 82 (1961) (upholding by a 5–4 vote the exclusion from the Illinois bar of an attorney who refused to answer questions about Communist Party membership).

128. Konigsberg v. State Bar of California, 366 U.S. 36, 49 (1961) (internal citation omitted).

129. *Konigsberg*, 366 U.S. at 51.

130. *Konigsberg*, 366 U.S. at 61, 62–63 (Black, J., dissenting).

131. *Konigsberg*, 366 U.S. at 63.

132. *Konigsberg*, 366 U.S. at 63.

133. Jeff Sanders, "Extraterritorial Application of the First Amendment to Defamation Claims against American Media," *North Carolina Journal of International Law and Commercial Regulation* 19, no. 3 (1994): 515–52, 541 n.201.

134. Scales v. United States, 367 U.S. 203, 228 (1961).

135. *Scales*, 367 U.S. at 262 (Black, J., dissenting).

136. *Scales*, 367 U.S. at 261.

137. *Scales*, 367 U.S. at 263 (Douglas, J., dissenting).

138. Mill, *On Liberty*, 108.

139. *Scales*, 367 U.S. at 270–71 (Douglas, J., dissenting).

140. Mill, *On Liberty*, 53.

141. See, e.g., Noto v. United States, 367 U.S. 290 (1961) (avoiding the First Amendment question of clear and present danger by interpreting the Smith Act to not prohibit abstract teaching of the use of violence); Cramp v. Board of Public Instruction, 368 U.S. 278 (1961) (overturning a statute requiring public employees to swear a loyalty oath on vagueness grounds).

142. Harry H. Wellington, "On Freedom of Expression," *Yale Law Journal* 88, no. 6 (1979): 1105–42, 1107 (quoting Edmund Cahn, "Justice Black and First Amendment 'Absolutes': A Public Interview," *New York University Law Review* 37, no. 4 (1962): 553) (emphasis in original).

143. Paris and McMahon, "Absolutism and Democracy," 75; Mill, *On Liberty*, 11.

6. Imminent Lawless Action

1. See Kovacs v. Cooper, 336 U.S. 77, 90 (1949) (Frankfurter, J., concurring).

2. See Edwards v. South Carolina, 372 U.S. 229, 237 (1963) (overturning breach-of-the-peace convictions for African American students protesting segregation on the grounds of the state capitol, with the Supreme Court ruling the Constitution "does not permit a State to make criminal the peaceful expression of unpopular views"); Gibson v. Florida

Legislative Investigation Committee, 372 U.S. 539, 544 (1963) (a legislative committee could not constitutionally demand the NAACP produce its membership list because "rights of free speech and free association are fundamental and highly prized, and need breathing space to survive"); Cox v. Louisiana, 379 U.S. 536 (1965) (barring states from using breach-of-the-peace statutes against peaceful civil rights protest that included speeches, songs, and prayers outside of a courthouse); Dombrowski v. Pfister, 380 U.S. 479 (1965) (overturning enforcement of a Louisiana law that had been used to declare that the Southern Conference Education Fund, which advocated for racial desegregation, was a subversive organization); Brown v. Louisiana, 383 U.S. 131 (1966) (ruling that a silent sit-in demonstration to protest segregation at a public library is protected by the First Amendment).

3. NAACP v. Button, 371 U.S. 415, 444–45 (1963).

4. *Button*, 371 U.S. at 429.

5. Philip Kitcher, "Varieties of Freedom and Their Distribution," *Social Research* 77, no. 3 (2010): 857–72, 858–59.

6. Kitcher, 858–59.

7. See John Stuart Mill, *On Liberty*, ed. Elizabeth Rapaport (Indianapolis, IN: Hackett, 1978), 53.

8. See James C. Foster, "Justice Civility: William J. Brennan Jr.'s Free Speech Jurisprudence," in *Judging Free Speech: First Amendment Jurisprudence of US Supreme Court Justices*, ed. Helen J. Knowles and Steven B. Lichtman (New York: Palgrave Macmillan, 2015), 123–46, 123–24.

9. *Button*, 371 U.S. at 437.

10. *Button*, 371 U.S. at 438.

11. Alexander Meiklejohn, *Free Speech and Its Relation to Self-Government* (New York: Harper and Brothers, 1948), 39.

12. New York Times Co. v. Sullivan, 376 U.S. 254, 270 (1964).

13. *Sullivan*, 376 U.S. at 271.

14. *Sullivan*, 376 U.S. at 271–72 (quoting *Button*, 371 U.S. at 433).

15. See Mill, *On Liberty*, 44; *Sullivan*, 376 U.S. at 273.

16. *Sullivan*, 376 U.S. at 279.

17. *Sullivan*, 376 U.S. at 272 n.13 (quoting Mill, *On Liberty* (Oxford: Blackwell, 1947), at 47).

18. *Sullivan*, 376 U.S. at 279 n.19 (quoting Mill, *On Liberty*, at 15).

19. Mark Tushnet, "*New York Times v. Sullivan* around the World," *Alabama Law Review* 66, no. 2 (2014): 337–56, 343.

20. *Sullivan*, 376 U.S. at 279–80.

21. See Mill, *On Liberty*, 3.

22. K. C. O'Rourke, *John Stuart Mill and Freedom of Expression: The Genesis of a Theory* (New York: Routledge, 2001), 10–11, 19–20, 68.

23. William J. Brennan Jr., "The Supreme Court and the Meiklejohn Interpretation of the First Amendment," *Harvard Law Review* 79, no. 1 (1965): 1–20, 14.

24. Brennan, 19.

25. Brennan, 1.

26. "Meiklejohn, Alexander (1872–1964)," Office of the University Curator, Brown University, accessed May 10, 2023, https://library.brown.edu/cds/portraits/display.php?idno=168.

27. Brennan, "Supreme Court and the Meiklejohn Interpretation," 19 (emphasis added).

28. See Brennan, 19.

29. Tamara R. Piety, *Brandishing the First Amendment: Commercial Expression in America* (Ann Arbor: University of Michigan Press, 2015), 63.

30. Foster, "Justice Civility," 124

31. Lamont v. Postmaster General, 381 U.S. 301, 308 (1965) (Brennan, J., concurring); Vincent Blasi, "Holmes and the Marketplace of Ideas," *Supreme Court Review* 2004 (2004): 24 n.80.

32. Abrams v. United States, 250 U.S. 616, 630 (1919) (Holmes, J., dissenting).

33. *Sullivan*, 376 U.S. at 293 (Black, J., concurring).

34. *Sullivan*, 376 U.S. at 294–95.

35. *Sullivan*, 376 U.S. at 295.

36. *Sullivan*, 376 U.S. at 298 (Goldberg, J., concurring).

37. See *Sullivan*, 376 U.S. at 304, 305.

38. See O'Rourke, *Mill and Freedom of Expression*, 19–20.

39. Mill, *On Liberty*, 11.

40. Michael Kent Curtis, "Monkey Trials: Science, Defamation, and the Suppression of Dissent," *William & Mary Bill of Rights Journal* 4, no. 2 (1995): 507–93, 551.

41. See Garrison v. Louisiana, 379 U.S. 64 (1964) (overturning the criminal libel conviction of a district attorney for criticizing judges, finding that the statute had to meet the same actual malice standard that the Supreme Court had announced in civil cases); Time v. Hill, 385 U.S. 374, 389 (1967) (the actual malice standard applies to false light claims on matters of public interest, whether they involve public officials or private persons).

42. See *Garrison*, 379 U.S. at 72–73 ("Where the criticism is of public officials and their conduct of public business, the interest in private reputation is overborne by the larger public interest, secured by the Constitution, in the dissemination of truth"); Curtis Publishing v. Butts, 388 U.S. 130 (Chief Justice Warren wrote an opinion on behalf of five justices extending the actual malice standard to libel cases involving public figures). See also Henry v. Collins, 380 U.S. 356 (1965); Ashton v. Kentucky, 384 U.S. 195 (1966); Rosenblatt v. Baer, 383 U.S. 75 (1966); and St. Amant v. Thompson, 390 U.S. 727 (1968).

43. See Mill, *On Liberty*, 10 ("Utility [is] the ultimate appeal on all ethical questions").

44. Jacobellis v. Ohio, 378 U.S. 184, 187 (1964).

45. See J. Todd Metcalf, "Obscenity Prosecutions in Cyberspace: The *Miller* Test Cannot 'Go Where No [Porn] Has Gone Before,'" *Washington University Law Quarterly* 74, no. 2 (1996): 481–523, 506–7.

46. *Jacobellis*, 378 U.S. at 195.

47. *Jacobellis*, 378 U.S. at 193–94.

48. Mill, *On Liberty*, 67.

49. *Jacobellis*, 378 U.S. at 191.

50. Peter C. Bronson, "New Prosecutorial Techniques and Continued Judicial Vagueness: An Argument for Abandoning Obscenity as a Legal Concept," *UCLA Law Review* 21, no. 1 (1973): 181–241, 190.

51. This included Justice Potter Stewart, who famously quipped about "hard-core pornography": "I know it when I see it, and the motion picture involved in this case is not that." *Jacobellis*, 378 U.S. at 197 (Stewart, J., concurring).

52. See Grove Press v. Gerstein, 378 U.S. 577 (1964) (overturning a Dade County, Florida, ban on Henry Miller's book, *Tropic of Cancer*); Memoirs v. Massachusetts, 383 U.S. 413 (1966) (overturning a state determination that John Cleland's novel, *Memoirs of a Woman of Pleasure* (also known as *Fanny Hill*), was obscene).

53. *Memoirs*, 383 U.S. at 419 (emphasis in original); see Eric Hoffman, "Feminism, Pornography, and Law," *University of Pennsylvania Law Review* 133, no. 2 (1985): 497–534, 507–8.

54. Donald A. Downs, "Skokie Revisited: Hate Group Speech and the First Amendment," *Notre Dame Law Review* 60, no. 4 (1985): 629–85, 671 n.174.

55. *Memoirs*, 383 U.S. at 431 (Douglas, J., concurring).

56. For decisions of this era that were non-Millian, see Ginzburg v. United States, 383 U.S. 463, 474 (1966) (upholding an obscenity conviction for mail-marketing publications—including *EROS*, *Liaison*, and *The Housewife's Handbook on Selective Promiscuity*—in what the Supreme Court determined was a "pandering" fashion); Mishkin v. New York, 383 U.S. 502, 508 (1966) (holding that for material depicting what the Supreme Court defined as "various deviant sexual practices, such as flagellation, fetishism, and lesbianism," *Roth*'s prurient-appeal prong is met "if the dominant theme of the material taken as a whole appeals to the prurient interest in sex of the members of that group").

57. Redrup v. New York, 386 U.S. 767, 768 (1967).

58. *Redrup*, 386 U.S. at 770.

59. *Redrup*, 386 U.S. at 769.

60. O. John Rogge, "The Obscenity Terms of the Court," *Villanova Law Review* 17, no. 3 (1972): 393–462, 448–51.

61. Ginsberg v. New York, 390 U.S. 629, 641 (1968).

62. *Ginsberg*, 390 U.S. at 639, 640–41 (internal quotations omitted).

63. See Richard Vernon, "John Stuart Mill and Pornography: Beyond the Harm Principle," *Ethics* 106, no. 3 (1996): 621–32, 630.

64. See Freedman v. Maryland, 380 U.S. 51 (1965) (declaring that a law requiring all movies to be submitted to a state board of censors for approval was an unconstitutional prior restraint).

65. Interstate Circuit v. Dallas, 390 U.S. 676, 678 (1968).

66. *Interstate Circuit*, 390 U.S. at 682.

67. *Interstate Circuit*, 390 U.S. at 690.

68. *Interstate Circuit*, 390 U.S. at 689 (quoting People v. Kahan, 15 N.Y. 2d 311, 313 (1965) (Fuld, J., concurring)).

69. Mill, *On Liberty*, 9.

70. Don A. Habibi, *John Stuart Mill and the Ethic of Human Growth* (Boston: Kluwer, 2001), 712; see Amy Gutmann, "Children, Paternalism, and Education: A Liberal Argument," *Philosophy and Public Affairs* 9, no. 4 (1980): 338–58.

71. D. S. Greenberg, "Cold War Thaw? Several Signs in Recent Months Suggest that East-West Relations Are Improving," *Science*, July 19, 1963, 251–53.

72. See Baggett v. Bullitt, 377 U.S. 360 (1964) (invalidating as too vague a law requiring state employees to take loyalty oaths that they were not members of "subversive" organizations); Elfbrandt v. Russell, 384 U.S. 11 (1966) (striking down as overbroad a law requiring teachers to sign a loyalty oath); DeGregory v. Attorney Gen. of New

Hampshire, 383 U.S. 825 (1966) (overturning a conviction for failing to testify before a state attorney general about Communist Party activities); United States v. Robel, 389 U.S. 258 (1967) (holding unconstitutional as overbroad a law that banned Communist Party members from working in defense facilities); Whitehill v. Elkins, 389 U.S. 54, 60 (1967) (striking down a loyalty oath at the University of Maryland requiring one to affirm that they would not engage in the alteration of the government).

73. Keyishian v. Board of Regents, 385 U.S. 589, 603 (1967).

74. *Keyishian*, 385 U.S. at 603 (internal citations omitted).

75. *Keyishian*, 385 U.S. at 607.

76. Mill, *On Liberty*, 32.

77. Mill, 90.

78. Mill, 37.

79. Mill, 79–80.

80. Gabriel J. Chin and Saira Rao, "Pledging Allegiance to the Constitution: The First Amendment and Loyalty Oaths for Faculty at Private Universities," *University of Pittsburgh Law Review* 64, no. 3 (2003): 431–82, 469.

81. Pickering v. Board of Education, 391 U.S. 563, 568 (1968).

82. *Pickering*, 391 U.S. at 573.

83. *Pickering*, 391 U.S. at 572, 571.

84. *Pickering*, 391 U.S. at 574.

85. Mill, *On Liberty*, 80.

86. Mill, 80.

87. See also Bond v. Floyd, 385 U.S. 116, 136 (1966) (declaring that the Georgia House of Representatives violated the First Amendment by excluding duly elected state representative Julian Bond for his statements critical of the Vietnam War, because "statements criticizing public policy and the implementation of it must be . . . protected"); Mills v. Alabama, 384 U.S. 214, 219 (1966) (ruling that a law criminalizing Election Day newspaper editorials violated the First Amendment, because "the press serves and was designed to serve as a powerful antidote to any abuses of power by governmental officials"); Carroll v. President and Commissioners of Princess Anne, 393 U.S. 175 (1968) (overturning a ten-day injunction that barred a white supremacist group from holding rallies, with the Supreme Court finding that the injunction was an unconstitutional prior restraint).

88. See also Walker v. Birmingham, 388 U.S. 307 (1967) (upholding a contempt conviction for civil rights protestors who violated a court order prohibiting them from marching).

89. Adderley v. Florida, 385 U.S. 39, 47 (1966).

90. Davis v. Massachusetts, 167 U.S. 43, 47 (1897).

91. *Adderley*, 385 U.S. at 56 (Douglas, J., dissenting).

92. *Adderley*, 385 U.S. at 49–50.

93. Karen Zivi, "Cultivating Character: John Stuart Mill and the Subject of Rights," *American Journal of Political Science* 50, no. 1 (2006): 49–61, 58; Mill, *On Liberty*, 53; *Adderley*, 385 U.S. at 50–51 (Douglas, J., dissenting).

94. James M. McGoldrick Jr., "*United States v. O'Brien* Revisited: Of Burning Things, Waving Things, and G-Strings," *University of Memphis Law Review* 36, no. 4 (2006): 903–49, 916 n.65.

95. United States v. O'Brien, 391 U.S. 367, 377 (1968).

96. *O'Brien*, 391 U.S. at 376.

97. *O'Brien*, 391 U.S. at 389–90 (Douglas, J., dissenting).

98. See Eric T. Kasper and Troy A. Kozma, "Absolute Freedom of Opinion and Sentiment on All Subjects: John Stuart Mill's Enduring (and Ever-Growing) Influence on the Supreme Court's First Amendment Free Speech Jurisprudence," *University of Massachusetts Law Review* 15, no. 1 (2020): 2–53, 27–28.

99. See also Shuttlesworth v. Birmingham, 394 U.S. 147 (1969) (overturning the conviction of a minister leading a civil rights protest on the sidewalk, for marching without a permit); Gregory v. Chicago, 394 U.S. 111 (1969) (overturning the convictions of peaceful civil rights demonstrators who failed to disperse when police ordered them to do so after police expressed concern over "unruly" onlookers).

100. Brandenburg v. Ohio, 395 U.S. 444, 447 (1969).

101. Mill, *On Liberty*, 53.

102. *Brandenburg*, 395 U.S. at 449.

103. *Brandenburg*, 395 U.S. at 448.

104. See Bernard Schwartz, "Holmes versus Hand: Clear and Present Danger or Advocacy of Unlawful Action?," *Supreme Court Review* 1994 (1994): 209–245, 239.

105. Schwartz, 240.

106. *Brandenburg*, 395 U.S. at 450–54 (Douglas, J., concurring).

107. *Brandenburg*, 395 U.S. at 454.

108. *Brandenburg*, 395 U.S. at 455–56.

109. *Brandenburg*, 395 U.S. at 457.

110. Watts v. United States, 394 U.S. 705, 706 (1969).

111. *Watts*, 394 U.S. at 708.

112. *Watts*, 394 U.S. at 708.

113. Mill, *On Liberty*, 51.

114. *Watts*, 394 U.S. at 709 (Douglas, J., concurring).

115. *Watts*, 394 U.S. at 709–12.

116. *Watts*, 394 U.S. at 712.

117. Mill, *On Liberty*, 15–16.

118. Street v. New York, 394 U.S. 576, 578–79 (1969).

119. *Street*, 394 U.S. at 590.

120. *Street*, 394 U.S. at 592.

121. *Street*, 394 U.S. at 593 (quoting West Virginia v. Barnette, 319 U.S. 624, 641–42 (1943)).

122. *Street*, 394 U.S. at 594.

123. Mill, *On Liberty*, 24.

124. Tinker v. Des Moines, 393 U.S. 503, 506 (1969).

125. *Tinker*, 393 U.S. at 513.

126. *Tinker*, 393 U.S. at 508.

127. *Tinker*, 393 U.S. at 508.

128. *Tinker*, 393 U.S. at 509.

129. Lackland H. Bloom Jr., "The Rise of the Viewpoint-Discrimination Principle," *SMU Law Review Forum* 72 (2019): 20–40, 36–37.

130. *Tinker*, 393 U.S. at 510–11.

131. Michael A. Henderson, "Today's Symbolic Speech Dilemma: Flag Desecration and the Proposed Constitutional Amendment," *South Dakota Law Review* 41, no. 3 (1996): 533–73, 553.

132. *Tinker*, 393 U.S. at 517 (Black, J., dissenting).

133. *Tinker*, 393 U.S. at 522.

134. *Tinker*, 393 U.S. at 522.

135. Mill, *On Liberty*, 9.

136. See Kasper and Kozma, "Absolute Freedom," 47–48.

137. Mill, *On Liberty*, 80.

138. Kasper and Kozma, "Absolute Freedom," 47–48.

139. Red Lion Broadcasting Co. v. FCC, 395 U.S. 367, 390 (1969).

140. *Red Lion*, 395 U.S. at 390.

141. Mill, *On Liberty*, 4; Jill Gordon, "John Stuart Mill and the 'Marketplace of Ideas,'" *Social Theory and Practice* 23, no. 2 (1997): 235–49, 237–38.

142. *Red Lion*, 395 U.S. at 392.

143. *Red Lion*, 395 U.S. at 392 n.18.

144. Mill, *On Liberty*, 49–50.

7. No Such Thing as a False Idea

1. For Burger's rejection of Millian theory, see Larry Arnhart, *Political Questions: Political Philosophy from Plato to Pinker* (Long Grove, IL: Waveland Press, 2015), 106.

2. See Schacht v. United States, 398 U.S. 58 (1970) (voiding a conviction for a Vietnam War protestor wearing a US military uniform during an outdoor theatrical skit); Bachellar v. Maryland, 397 U.S. 564 (1970) (overturning disorderly conduct convictions of anti–Vietnam War protestors who demonstrated in front of a US Army recruiting office); Greenbelt Cooperative Publishing Association v. Bresler, 398 U.S. 6, 14 (1970) (holding that a newspaper's use of the word "blackmail" was not defamatory when describing the bargaining position of a real estate developer who was also a state legislator); Cain v. Kentucky, 397 U.S. 319 (1970) (reversing a lower court that had declared the pornographic film *I, a Woman* was obscene).

3. See William Stacy Johnson, *A Time to Embrace: Same-Sex Relationships in Religion, Law, and Politics* (Grand Rapids, MI: Eerdmans, 2012), 329.

4. See Coates v. Cincinnati, 402 U.S. 611, 611 (1971) (striking down an ordinance that made it illegal for "three or more persons to assemble . . . on any of the sidewalks . . . and there conduct themselves in a manner annoying to persons passing by"); United Transportation Union v. State Bar of Michigan, 401 U.S. 576 (1971) (finding unconstitutionally vague a law that prohibited a union from giving legal advice to its members).

5. Cohen v. California, 403 U.S. 15, 21 (1971).

6. *Cohen*, 403 U.S. at 23.

7. *Cohen*, 403 U.S. at 24, 24–25, 25, 26.

8. For connections between *Cohen*'s jurisprudence and Mill's *On Liberty*, see Joseph Russomanno, "'Freedom for the Thought that We Hate': Why Westboro Had to Win," *Communication Law and Policy* 17, no. 2 (2012): 133–73, 149.

9. John Lawrence Hill, "The Father of Modern Constitutional Liberalism," *William & Mary Bill of Rights Journal* 27, no. 2 (2018): 431–99, 491.

10. John Stuart Mill, *On Liberty*, ed. Elizabeth Rapaport (Indianapolis, IN: Hackett, 1978), 19.

11. Douglas E. Edlin, "'Another's Lyric': John Marshall Harlan II, Judicial Conservatism, and Free Speech, in *Judging Free Speech: First Amendment Jurisprudence of US Supreme Court Justices*, ed. Helen J. Knowles and Steven B. Lichtman (New York: Palgrave Macmillan, 2015), 99–122, 113.

12. Hill, "Father of Modern Constitutional Liberalism," 483–84.

13. Hill, 491.

14. *Cohen*, 403 U.S. at 27 (Blackmun, J., dissenting).

15. Gooding v. Wilson, 405 U.S. 518, 519 (1972).

16. Rosenfeld v. New Jersey, 408 U.S. 901 (1972).

17. The justices struck down prior restraints consistently throughout the Burger Court. See, e.g., Nebraska Press Association v. Stuart, 427 U.S. 539, 559 (1976); Oklahoma Publishing v. Oklahoma County District Court, 430 U.S. 308 (1977); National Socialist Party of America v. Skokie, 432 U.S. 43 (1977); Landmark Communications v. Virginia, 435 U.S. 829 (1978); Smith v. Daily Mail Publishing, 443 U.S. 97 (1979); Vance v. Universal Amusement Co., 445 U.S. 308 (1980); Richmond Newspapers Inc. v. Virginia, 448 U.S. 555 (1980); Globe Newspaper Co. v. Superior Court, 457 U.S. 596 (1982).

18. New York Times Co. v. United States, 403 U.S. 713, 714 (1971) (quoting Bantam Books v. Sullivan, 372 U.S. 58, 70 (1963) and Organization for a Better Austin v. Keefe, 402 U.S. 415, 419 (1971)).

19. Leonard W. Levy, *Origins of the Bill of Rights* (New Haven, CT: Yale University Press, 1999), 126.

20. *New York Times Co.*, 403 U.S. at 714–15 (Black, J., concurring).

21. *New York Times Co.*, 403 U.S. at 717.

22. *New York Times Co.*, 403 U.S. at 724 (Douglas, J., concurring).

23. *New York Times Co.*, 403 U.S. at 725 (Brennan, J., concurring).

24. *New York Times Co.*, 403 U.S. at 726–27.

25. See Monitor Patriot v. Roy, 401 U.S. 265 (1971) (confirming that the *Sullivan* actual malice standard in libel cases applies to candidates for public office, not just public officials already elected); Ocala Star-Banner v. Damron, 401 U.S. 295 (1971) (overturning a libel judgment for a losing mayoral candidate); Time v. Pape, 401 U.S. 279 (1971) (applying the *Sullivan* standard).

26. Rosenbloom v. Metromedia, 403 U.S. 29, 36 (1971).

27. *Rosenbloom*, 403 U.S. at 41.

28. Mill, *On Liberty*, 11; *Rosenbloom*, 403 U.S. at 43.

29. *Rosenbloom*, 403 U.S. at 51.

30. Jeremy J. Ofseyer, "Taking Liberties with John Stuart Mill," *Annual Survey of American Law* 1999, no. 4 (1999): 395–433, 396–97.

31. See Law Students Civil Rights Research Council v. Wadmond, 401 U.S. 154 (1971) (upholding a state bar requirement that lawyers had to provide proof of loyalty to the US government); Cole v. Richardson, 405 U.S. 676 (1972) (upholding a state loyalty oath). But see also Baird v. State Bar of Arizona, 401 U.S. 1 (1971) (striking down a denial of bar admission for refusing to answer questions about organizational involvement and beliefs); Connell v. Higginbotham, 403 U.S. 207 (1971) (striking down loyalty oaths for Florida state employees, including substitute teachers).

32. See Ailsa W. Chang, "Resuscitating the Constitutional 'Theory' of Academic Freedom: A Search for a Standard Beyond *Pickering* and *Connick*," *Stanford Law Review* 53, no. 3 (2001): 915–66, 917–20.

33. See Grove Press v. Maryland State Board of Censors, 401 U.S. 480 (1971) (an equally divided Supreme Court let stand a lower court decision upholding a statewide ban of the film *I Am Curious (Yellow)*); United States v. Reidel, 402 U.S. 351 (1971) (upholding a federal law prohibiting distribution of obscene materials, limiting the reach of *Stanley v. Georgia*, 394 U.S. 557 (1969)).

34. See California v. LaRue, 409 U.S. 109, 118 (1972) (upholding a state prohibition of certain types of nude entertainment on premises where liquor is sold, because such "'performances' . . . partake more of gross sexuality than of communication").

35. Miller v. California, 413 U.S. 15, 18 (1973).

36. *Miller*, 413 U.S. at 24 (internal quotations and citations omitted).

37. Jason Kipness, "Revisiting *Miller* after the Striking of the Communications Decency Act: A Proposed Set of Internet Specific Regulations for Pornography on the Information Superhighway," *Santa Clara Computer and High Technology Law Journal* 14, no. 2 (1998): 391–434, 420–27.

38. Mill, *On Liberty*, 98, 89–90.

39. Mill, 5.

40. Mill, 6.

41. *Miller*, 413 U.S. at 44 (Douglas, J., dissenting).

42. Mill, *On Liberty*, 12; *Miller*, 413 U.S. at 40–41 (Douglas, J., dissenting).

43. *Miller*, 413 U.S. at 41.

44. *Miller*, 413 U.S. at 45.

45. See Patrick T. Egan, "Virtual Community Standards: Should Obscenity Law Recognize the Contemporary Community Standard of Cyberspace?," *Suffolk University Law Review* 30, no. 1 (1996): 117–52.

46. Paris Adult Theatre I v. Slaton, 413 U.S. 49, 68, n.14 (1973).

47. Arnhart, *Political Questions*, 106

48. *Paris Adult Theatre I*, 413 U.S. at 73–74 (Brennan, J., dissenting).

49. *Paris Adult Theatre I*, 413 U.S. at 91–93.

50. *Paris Adult Theatre I*, 413 U.S. at 108 (internal citation omitted).

51. *Paris Adult Theatre I*, 413 U.S. at 112.

52. *Paris Adult Theatre I*, 413 U.S. at 113.

53. James C. Foster, "Justice Civility: William J. Brennan Jr.'s Free Speech Jurisprudence," in Knowles and Lichtman, *Judging Free Speech*, 123–46, 129.

54. Kaplan v. California, 413 U.S. 115 (1973) (holding books without pictures or drawings may be deemed obscene); United States v. Orito, 413 U.S. 139 (1973) (ruling that any right to possess obscene materials at home does not extend to transporting it); United States v. 12 200-Ft. Reels of Super 8MM Film, 413 U.S. 123 (1973) (holding the government may constitutionally ban the importation of obscene materials for personal use); Hamling v. United States, 418 U.S. 87 (1974) (upholding obscenity convictions for advertising *The Illustrated Presidential Report of the Commission on Obscenity and Pornography*, which modified an official government report by adding sexually explicit photographs similar to the evidence considered by the President's Commission on Obscenity and Pornography).

55. Jenkins v. Georgia, 418 U.S. 153, 161 (1974).

56. *Jenkins*, 418 U.S. at 160.

57. *Jenkins*, 418 U.S. at 162 (Douglas, J., concurring); *Jenkins*, 418 U.S. at 163 (Brennan, J., concurring); Leslie Kendrick, "Speech, Intent, and the Chilling Effect," *William & Mary Law Review* 54, no. 5 (2013): 1633–91, 1663–64.

58. See also Erznoznik v. Jacksonville, 422 U.S. 205 (1975) (holding unconstitutional an ordinance prohibiting drive-in theaters from showing films containing nudity if the screen is visible from a public place, including as it involved a film titled "'Class of '74,' [which] had been rated 'R' by the Motion Picture Association of America. . . . It includes pictures of uncovered female breasts and buttocks" (206)) and Southeastern Promotions v. Conrad, 420 U.S. 546 (1975) (finding a First Amendment violation for a city denying a request to use a theater to present the musical *Hair*, which contains a nude scene).

59. Gertz v. Robert Welch, Inc., 418 U.S. 323, 339–40 (1974).

60. *Gertz*, 418 U.S. at 340.

61. *Gertz*, 418 U.S. at 340–41.

62. Jeffrey Omar Usman, "Finding the Lost Involuntary Public Figure," *Utah Law Review* 2014, no. 5 (2014): 951–1012, 967–72.

63. Usman, 351–52. The Supreme Court followed *Gertz* with Cantrell v. Forest City Publishing, 419 U.S. 245, 253 (1974) (holding that "calculated falsehoods" are not protected by the First Amendment).

64. *Gertz*, 418 U.S. at 361 (Brennan, J., dissenting).

65. K. C. O'Rourke, *John Stuart Mill and Freedom of Expression: The Genesis of a Theory* (New York: Routledge, 2001), 19–20.

66. Old Dominion Branch No. 496 v. Austin, 418 U.S. 264, 283, 286 (1974).

67. Mill, *On Liberty*, 51.

68. See Herbert v. Lando, 441 U.S. 153 (1979) (holding that the editorial process was not shielded from discovery in libel lawsuits). Conflicting rulings also existed in the Supreme Court's jurisprudence regarding picketing in public forums. See Police Department of Chicago v. Mosley, 408 U.S. 92 (1972) (overturning a disorderly conduction conviction for a man protesting within 150 feet of a school when the school was in session); Grayned v. City of Rockford, 408 U.S. 104 (1972) (striking down a similar ordinance as overbroad); American Radio Association v. Mobile Steamship Association, 419 U.S. 215, 229 (1974) (upholding an injunction against picketing foreign vessels).

69. Kleindienst v. Mandel, 408 U.S. 753, 765 (1972) (internal quotation omitted).

70. *Kleindienst*, 408 U.S. at 772 (Douglas, J., dissenting).

71. *Kleindienst*, 408 U.S. at 776 (Marshall, J., dissenting).

72. *Kleindienst*, 408 U.S. at 780.

73. Detlev F. Vagts, "Repealing the Cold War," *American Journal of International Law* 88, no. 3 (1994): 506–11, 510. Congress later restricted the attorney general's power under the law used to exclude Mandel (510).

74. Communist Party of Indiana v. Whitcomb, 414 U.S. 441 (1974).

75. See Mill, *On Liberty*, 28.

76. Procunier v. Martinez, 416 U.S. 396 (1974).

77. Pell v. Procunier, 417 U.S. 817, 834 (1974).

78. Saxbe v. Washington Post, 417 U.S. 843, 849–50 (1974).

79. *Pell*, 417 U.S. at 839 (Douglas, J., dissenting).

80. *Pell*, 417 U.S. at 839–40.

81. Alana M. Sitterly, "Silencing Death Row Inmates: How *Hammer v. Ashcroft* Needs a Rational Basis for Its Rational Basis," *George Mason University Civil Rights Law Journal* 21, no. 2 (2011): 323–47, 328–29.

82. See CBS v. Democratic National Committee, 412 U.S. 94 (1973) (holding that a broadcaster was entitled under the First Amendment to refuse to run a paid editorial advertisement); Miami Herald v. Tornillo, 418 U.S. 241 (1974) (overturning a government-mandated right of reply law for newspapers); Cox Broadcasting v. Cohn, 420 U.S. 469 (1975) (facts in criminal prosecutions are matters of public concern protected by the Free Press Clause if obtained from public documents); Nebraska Press Association, 427 U.S. at 559 (ruling that a gag order on the press to prohibit reporting on a crime before a trial jury was impaneled constituted an unconstitutional prior restraint, because "if it can be said that a threat of criminal or civil sanctions after publication 'chills' speech, prior restraint 'freezes' it at least for the time").

83. Steven J. Heyman, "Spheres of Autonomy: Reforming the Content Neutrality Doctrine in First Amendment Jurisprudence," *William & Mary Bill of Rights Journal* 10, no. 3 (2002): 647–717, 650. See also Flower v. United States, 407 U.S. 197 (1972) (upholding a right to distribute leaflets at military bases).

84. Hess v. Indiana, 414 U.S. 105, 106–7 (1973).

85. Lewis v. New Orleans, 415 U.S. 130, 132 (1974); see also *Lewis*, 415 U.S. at 138 (Blackmun, J., dissenting).

86. *Lewis*, 415 U.S. at 134.

87. Mill, *On Liberty*, 51–52.

88. Smith v. Goguen, 415 U.S. 566 (1974); Spence v. Washington, 418 U.S. 405 (1974).

89. Healy v. James, 408 U.S. 169, 180 (1972).

90. *Healy*, 408 U.S. at 180.

91. Christina E. Wells, "Mandatory Student Fees: First Amendment Concerns and University Discretion," *University of Chicago Law Review* 55, no. 1 (1988): 363–95, 370.

92. John Stuart Mill, "Civilization," in *Dissertations and Discussions: Political, Philosophical, and Historical* (London: Parker, 1859), 1:196.

93. Papish v. Board of Curators of the University of Missouri, 410 U.S. 667, 670 (1973).

94. *Papish*, 410 U.S. at 671.

95. Mill, *On Liberty*, 9, 43.

96. Bigelow v. Virginia, 421 U.S. 809, 821, 822 (1975).

97. *Bigelow*, 421 U.S. at 826.

98. See Mill, *On Liberty*, 94 (characterizing trade as a social act) and 98 (questioning how much vices, and promoting them, can be prohibited by law).

99. Charles Fischette, "A New Architecture of Commercial Speech Law," *Harvard Journal of Law and Public Policy* 31, no. 2 (2008): 663–715, 666.

100. This more liberal view of commercial speech rights continued in Virginia State Board of Pharmacy v. Virginia Citizens Consumer Council, 425 U.S. 748 (1976) (overturning a ban on advertising prescription drug prices).

101. Allen Rostron, "Pragmatism, Paternalism, and the Constitutional Protection of Commercial Speech," *Vermont Law Review* 37, no. 3 (2013): 527–89, 534.

102. M. Charles Wallfisch, "Justice Douglas: Advocate of Free Expression in Schools," *High School Journal* 63, no. 7 (April 1980): 303–7, 303.

103. Stephanie A. Sprague, "The Restriction of Political Associational Rights under Current Campaign Finance Reform First Amendment Jurisprudence," *New England Law Review* 40 (2006): 947–86, 983.

104. Buckley v. Valeo, 424 U.S. 1, 15 (1976) (internal quotations omitted).

105. *Buckley*, 424 U.S. at 57.

106. *Buckley*, 424 U.S. at 58.

107. See First National Bank of Boston v. Bellotti, 435 U.S. 765 (1978); Brown v. Hartlage, 456 U.S. 45, 53 (1982); FEC v. National Conservative PAC, 470 U.S. 480 (1985).

108. For a more Millian decision, see Elrod v. Burns, 427 U.S. 347 (1976) (ruling unconstitutional the firing of non-policy-making public employees based on political party affiliation). For less Millian decisions, see Kelley v. Johnson, 425 U.S. 238 (1976) (upholding a restriction on the length of male police officers' hair); Greer v. Spock, 424 U.S. 828 (1976) (upholding restrictions on free speech rights by civilians on military bases); Time v. Firestone, 424 U.S. 448 (1976) (offering an expansive definition of "private person" in libel cases).

109. Young v. American Mini Theatres, 427 U.S. 50, 69 (1976).

110. *Young*, 427 U.S. at 70.

111. *Young*, 427 U.S. at 71 n.34, 85 (Stewart, J., dissenting)

112. *Young*, 427 U.S. at 87 (internal citation omitted).

113. See David Dyzenhaus, "John Stuart Mill and the Harm of Pornography," *Ethics* 102, no. 3 (1992): 534–51; Robert Skipper, "Mill and Pornography," *Ethics* 103, no. 4 (1993): 726–30.

114. Mill, *On Liberty*, 98.

115. Mill, 99.

116. Mill, 99.

117. Smith v. United States, 431 U.S. 291 (1977) (affirming that local juries, not state legislatures, define community standards under the *Miller* test); Pinkus v. United States, 436 U.S. 293 (1978); New York State Liquor Authority v. Bellanca, 452 U.S. 714 (1981) (upholding a ban on nude dancing in places where alcohol is served). But see Schad v. Mt. Ephraim, 452 U.S. 61, 65–66 (1981) (striking down a ban on all nude dancing).

118. Wolston v. Reader's Digest Association, 443 U.S. 157 (1979); Jones v. North Carolina Prisoners' Union, 433 U.S. 119 (1977) (prohibiting prisoners from soliciting other inmates to join a prisoner labor union); Houchins v. KQED, 438 U.S. 1 (1978) (holding that the news media does not have a First Amendment right to interview prisoners beyond the general public's right of access to a county jail).

119. FCC v. Pacifica Foundation, 438 U.S. 726, 745 (1978). The words discussed in the broadcast were "shit, piss, fuck, cunt, cocksucker, motherfucker, and tits" (751).

120. *Pacifica*, 438 U.S. at 747.

121. *Pacifica*, 438 U.S. at 748.

122. *Pacifica*, 438 U.S. at 766 (Brennan, J., dissenting).

123. *Pacifica*, 438 U.S. at 772.

124. *Pacifica*, 438 U.S. at 777.

125. Mill, *On Liberty*, 16.

126. Bates v. State Bar of Arizona, 433 U.S. 350, 365 (1977).

127. *Bates*, 433 U.S. at 364.

128. *Bates*, 433 U.S. at 374–75.

129. *Bates*, 433 U.S. at 383.

130. Kathleen M. Sullivan, "Cheap Spirits, Cigarettes, and Free Speech: The Implications of *44 Liquormart*," *Supreme Court Review* 1996 (1996): 123–61, 133–34.

131. See Carey v. Population Services International, 431 U.S. 678 (1977) (striking down a law prohibiting the advertising of contraceptives); Linmark Associates v. Willingboro, 431 U.S. 85 (1977) (overturning an ordinance prohibiting the posting of "for sale" and "sold" real estate signs). But also see Ohralik v. Ohio State Bar Association, 436 U.S. 447 (1978) (upholding a state bar ban on face-to-face solicitation by attorneys); Friedman v. Rogers, 440 U.S. 1 (1979) (ruling that states may ban optometrists from advertising under a trade name).

132. Mill, *On Liberty*, 98–99.

133. Central Hudson Gas and Electric v. Public Service Commission, 447 U.S. 557, 561–62 (1980).

134. Mill, *On Liberty*, 50; *Central Hudson*, 447 U.S. at 562.

135. *Central Hudson*, 447 U.S. at 563.

136. *Central Hudson*, 447 U.S. at 566.

137. Sullivan, "Cheap Spirits," 133–34.

138. *Central Hudson*, 447 U.S. at 584 (Rehnquist, J., dissenting)

139. *Central Hudson*, 447 U.S. at 592 (internal citation omitted).

140. Wooley v. Maynard, 430 U.S. 705, 714 (1977) (internal quotations omitted); Mill, *On Liberty*, 32.

141. *Wooley*, 430 U.S. at 715.

142. See, e.g., cases striking down content-based restrictions on speech, including Carey v. Brown, 447 U.S. 455 (1980); Metromedia v. San Diego, 453 U.S. 490 (1981); Widmar v. Vincent, 454 U.S. 263 (1981).

143. For cases broadly interpreting the protections of *Pickering*, see Madison v. Wisconsin Employment Relations Commission, 429 U.S. 167 (1976); Givhan v. Western Line Consolidated School District, 439 U.S. 410 (1979); Branti v. Finkel, 445 U.S. 507 (1980). For cases narrowing the protections of *Pickering*, Parker v. Levy, 417 U.S. 733, 758 (1974) (upholding punishment of members of the military for expression critical of the military's handling of matters related to the Vietnam War); U.S. Civil Service Commission v. National Association of Letter Carriers, 413 U.S. 548 (1973) and Broadrick v. Oklahoma, 413 U.S. 601 (1973) (upholding federal and state laws that restricted public employees from active involvement in political campaigns for public office). See also Jonathan Alen Marks, "*Connick v. Myers*: Narrowing the Scope of Protected Speech for Public Employees," *University of Bridgeport Law Review* 5 (1984): 337–62.

144. Connick v. Myers, 461 U.S. 138, 151 (1983) (internal quotations omitted).

145. *Connick*, 461 U.S. at 156 (Brennan, J., dissenting).

146. *Connick*, 461 U.S. at 170.

147. Toni M. Massaro, "Significant Silences: Freedom of Speech in the Public Sector Workplace," *Southern California Law Review* 61, no. 1 (1987): 3–77, 31; Mill, *On Liberty*, 80; Glyn Morgan, "The Mode and Limits of John Stuart Mill's Toleration," *Nomos* 48 (2008): 139–67, 149.

148. Massaro, "Significant Silences," 31, n.126.

149. Bethel School District v. Fraser, 478 U.S. 675, 682 (1986).

150. *Bethel*, 478 U.S. at 683.

151. *Bethel*, 478 U.S. at 690 (Marshall, J., dissenting).

152. *Bethel*, 478 U.S. at 690.

153. *Bethel*, 478 U.S. at 696 (Stevens, J., dissenting).

154. Mill, *On Liberty*, 9, 80.

155. Eric T. Kasper and Troy A. Kozma, "Absolute Freedom of Opinion and Sentiment on All Subjects: John Stuart Mill's Enduring (and Ever-Growing) Influence on the Supreme Court's First Amendment Free Speech Jurisprudence," *University of Massachusetts Law Review* 15, no. 1 (2020): 2–53, 47–48.

156. See Board of Education v. Pico, 457 U.S. 853 (1982) (finding that the First Amendment limits school boards from removing books from middle and high school libraries if doing so would suppress ideas).

157. New York v. Ferber, 458 U.S. 747, 758 (1982).

158. *Ferber*, 458 U.S. at 764.

159. Mill, *On Liberty*, 9.

160. Mill, 9.

161. Alyssa N. Sheets, "Paternalism as a Justification for Federally Regulating Advertising E-Cigarettes to Children," *Washington University Jurisprudence Review* 12, no. 2 (2020): 321–52, 337–38.

162. See Brockett v. Spokane Arcades, 472 U.S. 491 (1985) (upholding a law that prohibited a "moral nuisance," defined as "any place where lewd films are publicly exhibited as a regular course of business"); Arcara v. Cloud Books, 478 U.S. 697 (1986) (upholding the closure of an adult bookstore by applying the deferential *O'Brien* test).

163. Renton v. Playtime Theatres, 475 U.S. 41, 43 (1986).

164. *Renton*, 475 U.S. at 48.

165. *Renton*, 475 U.S. at 47.

166. Santiago Legarre and Gregory J. Mitchell, "Secondary Effects and Public Morality," *Harvard Journal of Law and Public Policy* 40, no. 2 (2017): 321–59, 354.

167. *Renton*, 475 U.S. at 57 (Brennan, J., dissenting).

168. *Renton*, 475 U.S. at 63.

169. For cases involving symbolic speech or expressive conduct, see Clark v. Community for Creative Non-Violence, 468 U.S. 288 (1984); Wayte v. United States, 470 U.S. 598 (1985). In defamation cases, contrast Bose v. Consumers Union, 466 U.S. 485 (1984) (holding that the *Sullivan* actual malice standard applies to product disparagement claims) with Dun & Bradstreet v. Greenmoss Builders, 472 U.S. 749 (1985) (interpreting the concept of "public interest" narrowly to make it easier to win a libel suit).

170. NAACP v. Claiborne Hardware, 458 U.S. 886, 910 (1982).

171. *Claiborne Hardware*, 458 U.S. at 928.

172. *Claiborne Hardware*, 458 U.S. at 928.

173. Michael J. Sherman, "*Brandenburg* v. Twitter," *George Mason University Civil Rights Law Journal* 28, no. 2 (2018): 127–72, 131.

174. Mill, *On Liberty*, 22.

175. United States v. Grace, 461 U.S. 171 (1983) (declaring that sidewalks outside the US Supreme Court building are a public forum and peaceful picketing there is protected); Perry Education Association v. Perry Local Educators' Association, 460 U.S.

37, 45 (1983) (holding that in "places which by long tradition or by government fiat have been devoted to assembly and debate, the rights of the State to limit expressive activity are sharply circumscribed").

176. In re R.M.J., 455 U.S. 191 (1982) (overturning categorical restrictions on attorney advertising); Bolger v. Youngs Drug Products, 463 U.S. 60 (1983) (finding that a federal rule prohibiting the mailing of unsolicited contraceptive advertisements violated the First Amendment); Zauderer v. Office of Disciplinary Counsel, 471 U.S. 626, 648 (1985) (holding protected, over bar association rules to the contrary, an attorney's newspaper advertisement that included an illustration).

177. Posadas de Puerto Rico Associates v. Tourism Co., 478 U.S. 328, 340 (1986) (internal quotations omitted).

178. *Posadas*, 478 U.S. at 340–41.

179. Mill, *On Liberty*, 99.

180. Ibid.Mill, 98, 99.

181. *Posadas*, 478 U.S. at 350 (Brennan, J., dissenting).

182. *Posadas*, 478 U.S. at 351.

183. Dale Carpenter, "The Antipaternalism Principle in the First Amendment," *Creighton Law Review* 37, no. 3 (2004): 579–651, 579–80, 603, n.111.

8. A Bedrock Principle

1. See Newport v. Iacobucci, 479 U.S. 92 (1986) (upholding an ordinance banning nude or nearly nude dancing in businesses with alcohol licenses), where Justice Stevens wrote in dissent that "forms of expressive conduct or attire that might be offensive to the majority, or perhaps likely to stimulate violent reactions," are still "entitled to First Amendment protection" (102–3). See also San Francisco Arts and Athletics v. U.S. Olympic Committee, 483 U.S. 522 (1987) (sustaining the US Olympic Committee's legal objection to the San Francisco Arts and Athletics' use of the name "Gay Olympic Games"), where Justice Brennan dissented, arguing that the law at issue "unconstitutionally infringes on the SFAA's right to freedom of expression" (561).

2. Turner v. Safley, 482 U.S. 78, 89 (1987); see Procunier v. Martinez, 416 U.S. 396 (1974).

3. *Turner*, 482 U.S. at 84–85.

4. *Turner*, 482 U.S. at 92 (emphasis added).

5. *Turner*, 482 U.S. at 101 (Stevens, J., dissenting).

6. *Turner*, 482 U.S. at 116.

7. See Beth E. Warner, "John Stuart Mill's Theory of Bureaucracy within Representative Government: Balancing Competence and Participation," *Public Administration Review* 61, no. 4 (2001): 403–13, 405.

8. Pope v. Illinois, 481 U.S. 497, 500–1 (1987).

9. *Pope*, 481 U.S. at 501 n.3.

10. Steven G. Gey, "The Apologetics of Suppression: The Regulation of Pornography as Act and Idea," *Michigan Law Review* 86, no. 7 (1988): 1564–634, 1580.

11. Gey, 1581.

12. *Pope*, 481 U.S. at 513 (Stevens, J., dissenting).

13. *Pope*, 481 U.S. at 507 (Brennan, J., dissenting) (emphasis in original) (internal quotations omitted).

14. See FEC v. Massachusetts Citizens for Life, 479 U.S. 238 (1986) (overturning a campaign finance law that prohibited a nonprofit organization from using general treasury funds on campaign-related expenditures, including to produce flyers that described candidates' voting positions, with Justice Brennan writing for the Supreme Court and citing the marketplace of ideas analogy from Holmes's *Abrams* dissent); Board of Airport Commissioners v. Jews for Jesus, 482 U.S. 569 (1987) (striking down a ban on all "First Amendment activities" at the Los Angeles International Airport).

15. Rankin v. McPherson, 483 U.S. 378, 380 (1987).

16. *Rankin*, 483 U.S. at 384.

17. Beth Anne Roesler, *"Garcetti v. Ceballos*: Judicially Muzzling the Voices of Public Sector Employees," *South Dakota Law Review* 53, no. 2 (2008): 397–424, 420, n.217.

18. *Rankin*, 483 U.S. at 388.

19. John Stuart Mill, *On Liberty*, ed. Elizabeth Rapaport (Indianapolis, IN: Hackett, 1978), 80; *Rankin*, 483 U.S. at 389.

20. See United States v. National Treasury Employees Union, 513 U.S. 454 (1995) (overturning a ban on public employees receiving honoraria for speeches); San Diego v. Roe, 543 U.S. 77 (2004) (ruling constitutional the firing of a police officer for making and selling a video of himself stripping off a police uniform and engaging in sexual activity because the expression did not involve speech on matters of public concern).

21. Houston v. Hill, 482 U.S. 451, 455 (1987).

22. *Hill*, 482 U.S. at 454.

23. *Hill*, 482 U.S. at 461; Mill, *On Liberty*, 51.

24. *Hill*, 482 U.S. at 462–63.

25. *Hill*, 482 U.S. at 471–72.

26. Burton Caine, "The Trouble with 'Fighting Words': *Chaplinsky v. New Hampshire* Is a Threat to First Amendment Values and Should Be Overruled," *Marquette Law Review* 88, no. 3 (2004): 441–562, 543.

27. Henry J. Abraham, *Justices, Presidents, and Senators: A History of U.S. Supreme Court Appointments from Washington to Bush II* (Lanham, MD: Rowman & Littlefield, 2008), 281–85.

28. Hazelwood School District v. Kuhlmeier, 484 U.S. 260, 271 (1988).

29. *Hazelwood*, 484 U.S. at 271.

30. *Hazelwood*, 484 U.S. at 287 (Brennan, J., dissenting).

31. Jonathan David Shaub, "Children's Freedom of Speech and Expressive Maturity," *Law and Psychology Review* 36 (2012) 191–242, 198.

32. Kimberly A. Gross and Donald R. Kinder, "A Collision of Principles? Free Expression, Racial Equality and the Prohibition of Racist Speech," *British Journal of Political Science* 28, no. 3 (1998): 445–71, 445.

33. *Hazelwood*, 484 U.S. at 278 (Brennan, J., dissenting) (internal citation omitted).

34. See Boos v. Barry, 485 U.S. 312, 315 (1988) (striking down a Washington, DC, ban on signs displayed within five hundred feet of a foreign embassy that would tend to bring that embassy's government into "public odium" or "public disrepute"); Lakewood v. Plain Dealer Publishing, 486 U.S. 750 (1988) (overturning a law requiring the

licensing of news racks on city property that provided the mayor discretionary power over the issuance of the license).

35. Hustler Magazine v. Falwell, 485 U.S. 46, 50 (1988).

36. *Falwell*, 485 U.S. at 52 (1988) (internal quotation and citation omitted).

37. Jill Gordon, "John Stuart Mill and the 'Marketplace of Ideas,'" *Social Theory and Practice* 23, no. 2 (1997): 235–49, 241.

38. *Falwell*, 485 U.S. at 55.

39. *Falwell*, 485 U.S. at 56.

40. Texas v. Johnson, 491 U.S. 397, 413 (1989).

41. *Johnson*, 491 U.S. at 414.

42. *Johnson*, 491 U.S. at 418 (internal citation omitted).

43. James C. Foster, "Justice Civility: William J. Brennan Jr.'s Free Speech Jurisprudence," in *Judging Free Speech: First Amendment Jurisprudence of US Supreme Court Justices*, ed. Helen J. Knowles and Steven B. Lichtman (New York: Palgrave Macmillan, 2015), 123–46, 139.

44. Foster, 127.

45. *Johnson*, 491 U.S. at 412 (internal quotations omitted).

46. *Johnson*, 491 U.S. at 419.

47. *Johnson*, 491 U.S. at 410; James M. McGoldrick Jr., "Symbolic Speech: A Message from Mind to Mind," *Oklahoma Law Review* 61, no. 1 (2008): 1–82, 28–29, n.124.

48. *Johnson*, 491 U.S. at 418–19.

49. Foster, "Justice Civility," 136. In United States v. Eichman, 496 U.S. 310 (1990), Brennan wrote for the same 5–4 majority that a federal flag desecration statute violated the First Amendment.

50. See Florida Star v. B.J.F., 491 U.S. 524 (1989) (the First Amendment protects a newspaper publishing legally obtained truthful information); Butterworth v. Smith, 494 U.S. 624 (1990) (overturning a state law prohibiting grand jury witnesses from discussing their testimony after the end of the grand jury term); Keller v. State Bar of California, 496 U.S. 1 (1990) (holding that attorneys' required bar dues may not be used to promote political causes with which an attorney disagrees); Rutan v. Republican Party of Illinois, 497 U.S. 62 (1990) (striking down a governor's practice of hiring and firing low-level public employees based on political party affiliation).

51. See Fort Wayne Books v. Indiana, 489 U.S. 46 (1989) (declaring the seizure of allegedly obscene materials before trial to be an unconstitutional prior restraint); Osborne v. Ohio, 495 U.S. 103 (1990) (holding that states may ban private possession of child pornography due to the harms to children involved).

52. Sable Communications of California v. FCC, 492 U.S. 115, 126 (1989).

53. *Sable*, 492 U.S. at 126, 131.

54. *Sable*, 492 U.S. at 133 (Brennan, J., dissenting).

55. *Sable*, 492 U.S. at 135.

56. Mill, *On Liberty*, 9.

57. David F. McGowan, "A Critical Analysis of Commercial Speech," *California Law Review* 78, no. 2 (1990): 359–448, 375.

58. See Shapero v. Kentucky Bar Association, 486 U.S. 466 (1988) (ruling that a complete ban on direct mail solicitation by lawyers is unconstitutional); Peel v. Attorney Disciplinary Commission, 496 U.S. 91 (1990) (ruling that a state unconstitutionally punished

an attorney for placing on his letterhead truthful information that he held a "Certificate in Civil Trial Advocacy" from the National Board of Trial Advocacy).

59. Board of Trustees v. Fox, 492 U.S. 469, 475 (1989) (internal quotation omitted).

60. Victor Brudney, "The First Amendment and Commercial Speech," *Boston College Law Review* 53, no. 4 (2012): 1153–223, 1193 n.132.

61. *Fox*, 492 U.S. at 480.

62. *Fox*, 492 U.S. at 488 (Blackmun, J., dissenting).

63. *Fox*, 492 U.S. at 487.

64. *Fox*, 492 U.S. at 488. For other decisions by the Rehnquist Court on the freedom of expression at public universities, see Rosenberger v. University of Virginia, 515 U.S. 819 (1995) (holding that a public university may not deny funding to a registered student organization based on viewpoint); Board of Regents v. Southworth, 529 U.S. 217 (2000) (upholding mandatory student fees used to fund registered student organizations at public universities).

65. Brudney, "First Amendment and Commercial Speech," 1209–10, nn.187–90.

66. For a case where the Supreme Court struck down one of these speech restrictions, see Riley v. National Federation of the Blind, 487 U.S. 781 (1988) (overturning restrictions on charitable solicitors). For a case upholding such a restriction, see Frisby v. Schultz, 487 U.S. 474 (1988) (finding that a city ordinance prohibiting picketing in residential neighborhoods was constitutional).

67. Ward v. Rock Against Racism, 491 U.S. 781, 796 (1989).

68. *Ward*, 491 U.S. at 808 (Marshall, J., dissenting).

69. *Ward*, 491 U.S. at 806.

70. *Ward*, 491 U.S. at 791.

71. *Ward*, 491 U.S. at 790.

72. Mill, *On Liberty*, 65.

73. For a Millian decision, see Eu v. San Francisco County Democratic Central Committee, 489 U.S. 214 (1989) (striking down a state law that banned political parties from endorsing candidates in party primaries).

74. Austin v. Michigan Chamber of Commerce, 494 U.S. 652, 657 (1990) (internal quotations omitted).

75. *Austin*, 494 U.S. at 660.

76. *Austin*, 494 U.S. at 713 (Kennedy, J., dissenting).

77. *Austin*, 494 U.S. at 679–80 (Scalia, J., dissenting).

78. On libel, see Harte-Hanks Communications v. Connaughton, 491 U.S. 657 (1989) (holding that actual malice can be shown by a publisher ignoring obvious sources and reporting with reckless disregard for the truth); Milkovich v. Lorain Journal, 497 U.S. 1 (1990) (holding that opinions can be defamatory and subject to lawsuit, although "imaginative expression" and "rhetorical hyperbole" are protected). On inmates, see Thornburgh v. Abbott, 490 U.S. 401 (1989) (upholding restrictions on incoming letters and publications to prisoners under a deferential reasonableness standard).

79. Kim Isaac Eisler, *A Justice for All: William J. Brennan, Jr., and the Decisions that Transformed America* (New York: Simon & Schuster, 1993), 281.

80. Eisler, 281.

81. See Gentile v. State Bar of Nevada, 501 U.S. 1030 (1991) (overturning an attorney's reprimand for a statement he made accusing police of corruption); Simon &

Schuster v. Members of the New York State Crime Victims Board, 502 U.S. 105 (1991) (finding unconstitutional a "Son of Sam" law requiring profits from criminals' books or movies to be given to crime victims).

82. Barnes v. Glen Theatre, 501 U.S. 560, 569 (1991) (emphasis added).

83. *Barnes*, 501 U.S. at 566.

84. *Barnes*, 501 U.S. at 583–84 (Souter, J., concurring).

85. *Barnes*, 501 U.S. at 583.

86. Stephen E. Gottlieb, "The Philosophical Gulf on the Rehnquist Court," *Rutgers Law Journal* 29, no. 1 (1997): 1–42, 13–15.

87. Mill, *On Liberty*, 98–99.

88. John Stuart Mill to Lord Amberley, February 2, 1870, in *The Letters of John Stuart Mill*, ed. Hugh Elliot (New York: Longmans and Green, 1910), 2:241.

89. Clare McGlynn, "John Stuart Mill on Prostitution: Radical Sentiments, Liberal Proscriptions," *Nineteenth-Century Gender Studies* 8, no. 2 (Summer 2012), http://www.ncgsjournal.com/issue82/PDFs/mcglynn.pdf.

90. *Barnes*, 501 U.S. at 594 (White, J., dissenting).

91. *Barnes*, 501 U.S. at 593–94.

92. Masson v. New Yorker Magazine, 501 U.S. 496, 517 (1991).

93. *Masson*, 501 U.S. at 511.

94. *Masson*, 501 U.S. at 512–14.

95. *Masson*, 501 U.S. at 514–15.

96. *Masson*, 501 U.S. at 516.

97. *Masson*, 501 U.S. at 517 (internal quotation omitted).

98. Meiring de Villiers, "Substantial Truth in Defamation Law," *American Journal of Trial Advocacy* 32, no. 1 (2008): 91–123, 121–22. See also Leathers v. Medlock, 499 U.S. 439 (1991) (finding that the First Amendment permits different taxing schemes for different types of media).

99. Mill, *On Liberty*, 44.

100. *Masson*, 501 U.S. at 510, 517.

101. See Bartnicki v. Vopper, 532 U.S. 514, 527 (2001) (ruling that the First Amendment protects press disclosure of a recording of negotiations between a school board and a teachers' union that was illegally obtained by a third party because "state action to punish the publication of truthful information seldom can satisfy constitutional standards"); Tory v. Cochran, 544 U.S. 734 (2005) (holding that the First Amendment is violated by a permanent injunction in a defamation case where the plaintiff is a public figure).

102. Mill, *On Liberty*, 15.

103. Terence H. Qualter, "John Stuart Mill, Disciple of de Tocqueville," *Western Political Quarterly* 13, no. 4 (1960): 880–89, 882.

104. Rust v. Sullivan, 500 U.S. 173, 180 (1991) (upholding a federal rule that did not allow recipients of public funds to "encourage, promote or advocate abortion as a method of family planning").

105. R.A.V. v. St. Paul, 505 U.S. 377, 380 (1992).

106. *R.A.V.*, 505 U.S. at 391.

107. *R.A.V.*, 505 U.S. at 393 (emphasis in original).

108. *R.A.V.*, 505 U.S. at 392.

109. Gooding v. Wilson, 405 U.S. 518, 528 (1972); Edwin Chemerinsky and Howard Gillman, *Free Speech on Campus* (New Haven, CT: Yale University Press, 2017), 95.

110. Chemerinsky and Gillman, 95.

111. Wisconsin v. Mitchell, 508 U.S. 476 (1993).

112. Mill, *On Liberty*, 53.

113. See Forsyth County v. Nationalist Movement, 505 U.S. 123, 134–35 (1992) (striking down an ordinance charging higher security fees based on expression's content, reasoning that "speech cannot be financially burdened . . . simply because it might offend a hostile mob"); Lee v. International Society for Krishna Consciousness, 505 U.S. 830 (1992) (overturning a ban on the distribution of literature in an airport terminal). But also see International Society for Krishna Consciousness v. Lee, 505 U.S. 672 (1992) (upholding a ban on solicitation of funds in an airport terminal); Burson v. Freeman, 504 U.S. 191 (1992) (upholding a state law banning campaigning within one hundred feet of a polling place on Election Day).

114. Edenfield v. Fane, 507 U.S. 761 (1993) (ruling that certified public accountants may engage in direct face-to-face solicitation); Cincinnati v. Discovery Network, 507 U.S. 410 (1993) (striking down a prohibition on the distribution of commercial advertisements from news racks on city property).

115. United States v. Edge Broadcasting, 509 U.S. 418, 426 (1993).

116. *Edge Broadcasting*, 509 U.S. at 426.

117. *Edge Broadcasting*, 509 U.S. at 439 (Stevens, J., dissenting).

118. *Edge Broadcasting*, 509 U.S. at 439.

119. Mill, *On Liberty*, 94.

120. Mill, 94, 96.

121. Mill, 99.

122. Mill, 99.

123. See, e.g., Ibanez v. Florida Department of Business and Professional Regulation Board, 512 U.S. 136 (1994) (striking down a state reprimand of an attorney who advertised her designation as a certified financial planner and certified public accountant).

124. Ladue v. Gilleo, 512 U.S. 43, 45 (1994).

125. *Gilleo*, 512 U.S. at 58.

126. *Burson*, 504 U.S. at 199.

127. See Edward J. Eberle, "Hate Speech, Offensive Speech, and Public Discourse in America," *Wake Forest Law Review* 29, no. 4 (1994): 1135–213, 1147–92.

128. Eberle, 54–55.

129. Mill, *On Liberty*, 53.

130. *Gilleo*, 512 U.S. at 58 (internal citations omitted) (emphasis in original).

131. Turner Broadcasting System v. FCC I, 512 U.S. 622, 664 (1994).

132. *Turner I*, 512 U.S. at 637.

133. *Turner I*, 512 U.S. at 641. See also Denver Area Educational Telecommunications Consortium, Inc. v. FCC, 518 U.S. 727 (1996).

134. Bruce C. Hafen, "The Constitutional Status of Marriage, Kinship, and Sexual Privacy—Balancing the Individual and Social Interests," *Michigan Law Review* 81, no. 3 (1983): 463–574, 519.

135. Helen J. Knowles, *The Tie Goes to Freedom: Justice Anthony M. Kennedy on Liberty* (Lanham, MD: Rowman & Littlefield, 2019), 55.

136. See, e.g., Waters v. Churchill, 511 U.S. 661 (1994) (ruling a public employer can constitutionally fire an employee for speech the employer reasonably believed was not protected by the First Amendment).

137. Madsen v. Women's Health Center, 512 U.S. 753, 763–64 (1994) (internal citation omitted).

138. *Madsen*, 512 U.S. at 768.

139. Cohen v. California, 403 U.S. 15, 25 (1971); *Madsen*, 512 U.S. at 772–73.

140. *Madsen*, 512 U.S. at 795 (1994) (Scalia, J., concurring in part and dissenting in part).

141. *Madsen*, 512 U.S. at 792–93.

142. *Madsen*, 512 U.S. at 793.

143. *Madsen*, 512 U.S. at 776.

144. Florida Bar v. Went for It, 515 U.S. 618 (1995).

145. See Rubin v. Coors Brewing, 514 U.S. 476, 485 (1995) (overturning a federal prohibition on beer companies disclosing alcohol content on labels, holding that government power to regulate commercial speech was limited to situations where a true "social harm" would be prevented); Lorillard Tobacco v. Reilly, 533 U.S. 525 (2001) (striking down a ban on outdoor tobacco product advertising within one thousand feet of a school); Thompson v. Western States Medical Center, 535 U.S. 357 (2002) (finding that a federal ban on advertising compounded drugs violated the First Amendment).

146. 44 Liquormart v. Rhode Island, 517 U.S. 484, 503 (1996) (internal citation omitted).

147. *44 Liquormart*, 517 U.S. at 502–3 (internal citations and quotations omitted).

148. *44 Liquormart*, 517 U.S. at 518 (Thomas, J., dissenting).

149. *44 Liquormart*, 517 U.S. at 518.

150. *44 Liquormart*, 517 U.S. at 528 (emphasis in original).

151. Mill, *On Liberty*, 99.

152. Brudney, "First Amendment and Commercial Speech," 1209–10, nn.187–90.

153. Greater New Orleans Broadcasting Association v. United States, 527 U.S. 173, 195 (1999).

154. *Greater New Orleans*, 527 U.S. at 182.

155. *Greater New Orleans*, 527 U.S. at 195.

156. Kathleen E. Burke, "*Greater New Orleans Broadcasting Association v. United States*: Broadcasters Have Lady Luck, or at Least the First Amendment, on Their Side," *New England Law Review* 35, no. 2 (2001): 471–510, 496–97.

157. Mill, *On Liberty*, 95.

158. Reno v. ACLU, 521 U.S. 844, 875 (1997) (internal citations omitted).

159. *Reno*, 521 U.S. at 868, 885.

160. *Reno*, 521 U.S. at 885.

161. Maureen E. Browne, "Play It Again Uncle Sam: Another Attempt by Congress to Regulate Internet Content. How Will They Fare This Time?," *CommLaw Conspectus* 12, no. 1 (2004): 79–99, 84.

162. United States v. Playboy Entertainment Group, 529 U.S. 803 (2000) (ruling unconstitutional a requirement that cable companies had to block or scramble channels "primarily dedicated to sexually-oriented programming" from 10:00 p.m. to 6:00 a.m.).

163. Donald K. Brazeal, "Precursor to Modern Media Hype: The 1830s Penny Press," *Journal of American Culture* 28, no. 4 (2005): 405–14, 406.

164. City of Erie v. Pap's A. M., 529 U.S. 277, 294 (2000).

165. *Erie*, 529 U.S. at 297.

166. *Erie*, 529 U.S. at 317 (Souter, J., concurring in part and dissenting in part).

167. *Erie*, 529 U.S. at 317–18 (Stevens, J., dissenting).

168. *Erie*, 529 U.S. at 331.

169. *Erie*, 529 U.S. at 320.

170. Steven D. Smith, "Is the Harm Principle Illiberal?," *American Journal of Jurisprudence* 51 (2006): 1–42, 2.

171. Los Angeles v. Alameda Books, 535 U.S. 425 (2002) (upholding adult business zoning requirements).

172. Ashcroft v. Free Speech Coalition, 535 U.S. 234, 241 (2002). See also Kennedy's opinion of the Court, using a harm-based analysis, in Ashcroft v. ACLU, 542 U.S. 656 (2004) (ruling unconstitutional the Child Online Protection Act's provision that prohibited one from knowingly posting online "material that is harmful to minors").

173. *Free Speech Coalition*, 535 U.S. at 251.

174. *Free Speech Coalition*, 535 U.S. at 253.

175. Mill, *On Liberty*, 53.

176. *Free Speech Coalition*, 535 U.S. at 253.

177. Mill, *On Liberty*, 53.

178. Robert L. Tsai, "Speech and Strife," *Law and Contemporary Problems* 67, no. 3 (2004): 83, 94–95.

179. See Sarah Kagan, "Obscenity on the Internet: Nationalizing the Standard to Protect Individual Rights," *Hastings Constitutional Law Quarterly* 38 (2010): 233–57.

180. See Olivia B. Waxman, "This Is What Americans Used to Consider Obscene," Time, June 21, 2016, https://time.com/4373765/history-obscenity-united-states-films-miller-ulysses-roth/.

181. McIntyre v. Ohio Elections Commission, 514 U.S. 334, 342 (1995).

182. *McIntyre*, 514 U.S. at 357.

183. *McIntyre*, 514 U.S. at 357.

184. *McIntyre*, 514 U.S. at 342.

185. *McIntyre*, 514 U.S. at 371 (Scalia, J., dissenting) (internal citation omitted).

186. See Colorado Republican Federal Campaign Committee v. FEC, 518 U.S. 604 (1996) (finding First Amendment protection for political parties' independent expenditures that are uncoordinated with a candidate); Buckley v. American Constitutional Law Foundation, 525 U.S. 182 (1999) (finding unconstitutional a state law requiring name, badge, and financial disclosure requirements on initiative-petition proponents and circulators); Nixon v. Shrink Missouri Government, 528 U.S. 377 (2000) (upholding state campaign contribution limits on candidates for state office, following Mill's notion of preventing corruption); Republican Party of Minnesota v. White, 536 U.S. 765 (2002) (holding that judicial candidates have a First Amendment right to announce their views on legal and political issues).

187. McConnell v. FEC, 540 U.S. 93, 138 (2003) (internal quotation omitted).

188. *McConnell*, 540 U.S. at 206.

189. *McConnell*, 540 U.S. at 248 (Scalia, J., concurring in part and dissenting in part).

190. *McConnell*, 540 U.S. at 258.

191. See Mill, *On Liberty*, 3–4.

192. Mill, 12.

193. See Schenck v. Pro-Choice Network, 519 U.S. 357 (1997) (upholding a fifteen-foot fixed buffer zone around abortion clinics while striking down a floating buffer zone around persons or vehicles accessing or leaving clinics).

194. Hill v. Colorado, 530 U.S. 703, 715 (2000).

195. *Hill*, 530 U.S. at 716.

196. In chapter 4 of *On Liberty*, Mill insisted that interfering with a person's life choices was justified only if they violate the harm principle. Otherwise, "there is no room for entertaining any such question [of intervention] when a person's conduct affects the interests of no person besides himself" (73). For Mill, freedom of expression was a means to an end; it is valuable only insofar as it opens legal and social space for individuals to lead the lives they have chosen for themselves, rather than those that others have chosen for them. In the case of private citizens, Mill was adamant that there is no right to take action that aims at "the oppression of his individuality" (75). The offended have choices, but they are limited. Mill suggested simply not associating with those whom one finds offensive or who engage in unwanted invective; if one engages another about their behavior, one should adopt an attitude of "disinterested benevolence" and eschew "whips and scourges, either of the literal or metaphorical sort" (74).

197. *Hill*, 530 U.S. at 765 (Kennedy, J., dissenting).

198. *Hill*, 530 U.S. at 767.

199. Knowles, *Tie Goes to Freedom*, 72; Mill, *On Liberty*, 6–8.

200. *Hill*, 530 U.S. at 792 (Kennedy, J., dissenting).

201. See Good News Club v. Milford Central School, 533 U.S. 98 (2001) (ruling that religious groups have free speech rights to hold meetings after hours in public school district classrooms if nonreligious groups are permitted to reserve such meeting spaces); Watchtower Bible and Tract Society v. Stratton, 536 U.S. 150 (2002) (striking down an ordinance criminalizing door-to-door solicitation without a permit).

202. See Shaw v. Murphy, 532 U.S. 223 (2001) (upholding a ban on prisoners providing legal representation to other inmates); Overton v. Bazzetta, 539 U.S. 126 (2003) (upholding a ban on prison visitors against a freedom of association claim).

203. Virginia v. Black, 538 U.S. 343, 358 (2003).

204. Steven G. Gey, "A Few Questions about Cross Burning, Intimidation, and Free Speech," *Notre Dame Law Review* 80, no. 4 (2005): 1287–375, 1305; *Black*, 538 U.S. at 359.

205. Joseph Russomanno, "Facebook Threats: The Missed Opportunities of *Elonis v. United States*," *Communication Law and Policy* 21, no. 1 (2016): 1–37, 17; *Black*, 538 U.S. at 357.

206. *Black*, 538 U.S. at 363.

207. *Black*, 538 U.S. at 365–66.

208. Mill, *On Liberty*, 51.

209. *Black*, 538 U.S. at 366.

210. Mill, *On Liberty*, 53.

211. *Black*, 538 U.S. at 387.

9. Special Protection

1. See Helen J. Knowles and Steven B. Lichtman, "Conclusion: It's Complicated . . . ," in *Judging Free Speech: First Amendment Jurisprudence of US Supreme Court Justices*, ed.

Helen J. Knowles and Steven B. Lichtman (New York: Palgrave Macmillan, 2015), 239–54, 243–44.

2. Ryan J. Owens and David A. Simon, "Explaining the Supreme Court's Shrinking Docket," *William & Mary Law Review* 53, no. 4 (2012): 1219–85, 1228–29; "Supreme Court Caseloads, 1880–2015," Federal Judicial Center, accessed July 24, 2020, https://www.fjc.gov/history/exhibits/graphs-and-maps/supreme-court-caseloads-1880–2015; John G. Roberts Jr., *2022 Year-End Report on the Federal Judiciary* (Washington, DC: Supreme Court of the United States, 2022), https://www.supremecourt.gov/publicinfo/year-end/2022year-endreport.pdf, 5.

3. Owens and Simon, "Supreme Court's Shrinking Docket," 1230–33.

4. See Randall v. Sorrell, 548 U.S. 230 (2006) (overturning overly low state expenditure limits and contribution limits); Davenport v. Washington Education Association, 551 U.S. 177 (2007) (ruling that a state may constitutionally require labor unions to obtain permission from nonunion members before using the nonmembers' fees for election-related purposes).

5. FEC v. Wisconsin Right to Life, 551 U.S. 449, 457 (2007).

6. *Wisconsin Right to Life*, 551 U.S. at 470.

7. *Wisconsin Right to Life*, 551 U.S. at 474.

8. *Wisconsin Right to Life*, 551 U.S. at 488 (Scalia, J., concurring) (quoting First National Bank of Boston v. Bellotti, 435 U.S. 765, 777 (1978)), 494 (quoting Virginia v. Hicks, 539 U.S. 113, 119 (2003)).

9. *Wisconsin Right to Life*, 551 U.S. at 508 (Souter, J., dissenting) (internal quotations omitted).

10. *Wisconsin Right to Life*, 551 U.S. at 467–68.

11. Raymond J. La Raja, "Political Participation and Civic Courage: The Negative Effect of Transparency on Making Small Campaign Contributions," *Political Behavior* 36, no. 4 (2014): 753–76, 754.

12. See Davis v. FEC, 554 U.S. 724 (2008) (striking down BCRA's "millionaire's amendment").

13. John Stuart Mill, *On Liberty*, ed. Elizabeth Rapaport (Indianapolis, IN: Hackett, 1978), 79–80.

14. Garcetti v. Ceballos, 547 U.S. 410, 418 (2006) (internal citations and quotations omitted).

15. *Garcetti*, 547 U.S. at 419.

16. Mill, *On Liberty*, 80.

17. *Garcetti*, 547 U.S. at 438 (Souter, J., dissenting).

18. *Garcetti*, 547 U.S. at 429.

19. *Garcetti*, 547 U.S. at 447 (Breyer, J., dissenting).

20. Mill, *On Liberty*, 16.

21. Eric T. Kasper and Troy A. Kozma, "Absolute Freedom of Opinion and Sentiment on All Subjects: John Stuart Mill's Enduring (and Ever-Growing) Influence on the Supreme Court's First Amendment Free Speech Jurisprudence," *University of Massachusetts Law Review* 15, no. 1 (2020): 2–53, 46.

22. Morse v. Frederick, 551 U.S. 393, 397 (2007).

23. Mill, *On Liberty*, 9.

24. *Morse*, 551 U.S. at 403, 407.

25. *Morse*, 551 U.S. at 412.

26. *Morse*, 551 U.S. at 444 (Stevens, J., dissenting).

27. *Morse*, 551 U.S. at 445.

28. Jonathan David Shaub, "Children's Freedom of Speech and Expressive Maturity," *Law and Psychology Review* 36 (2012) 191–242, 198.

29. Shaub, 214, n.149.

30. *Morse*, 551 U.S. at 435.

31. *Morse*, 551 U.S. at 396–97, 403–6, 435–38.

32. United States v. Williams, 553 U.S. 285 (2008) (upholding, on a split vote, the PROTECT Act, which bans persons from advertising or distributing material believed or claimed to be illegal child pornography, even if that material is not actual child pornography).

33. Beard v. Banks, 548 U.S. 521, 528 (2006) (internal quotation omitted).

34. *Beard*, 548 U.S. at 543 (Stevens, J., dissenting) (internal quotations omitted).

35. *Beard*, 548 U.S. at 552.

36. Nicole B. Godfrey, "Suffragist Prisoners and the Importance of Protecting Prisoner Protests," *Akron Law Review* 53, no. 2 (2019): 279–312, 299.

37. United States v. Stevens, 559 U.S. 460, 464 (2010)

38. *Stevens*, 559 U.S. at 469 (emphasis in original).

39. *Stevens*, 559 U.S. at 476.

40. *Stevens*, 559 U.S. at 470.

41. *Stevens*, 559 U.S. at 479–80.

42. Frederick Schauer, "Harm(s) and the First Amendment," *Supreme Court Review* 2011, no. 1 (2011): 81–111, 86.

43. Even Justice Alito in his *Stevens* dissent emphasized a Millian concern: the harm caused to animals by depictions of animal cruelty fostering a market for animal cruelty. See *Stevens*, 559 U.S. at 494–98.

44. Christian Legal Society v. Martinez, 561 U.S. 661, 672 (2010).

45. *Christian Legal Society*, 561 U.S. at 690.

46. *Christian Legal Society*, 561 U.S. at 694 (emphasis in original).

47. *Christian Legal Society*, 561 U.S. at 689.

48. Mill, *On Liberty*, 8.

49. *Christian Legal Society*, 561 U.S. at 706 (Alito, J., dissenting) (quoting United States v. Schwimmer, 279 U.S. 644, 654–55 (1929) (Holmes, J., dissenting)).

50. Mill, *On Liberty*, 12.

51. *Christian Legal Society*, 561 U.S. at 731 (Alito, J., dissenting) (internal quotations omitted).

52. Holder v. Humanitarian Law Project, 561 U.S. 1, 29–30 (2010).

53. *Holder*, 561 U.S. at 38.

54. James Hart, "Revisiting Incitement Speech," *Quinnipiac Law Review* 38 (2019): 111–35, 128.

55. *Holder*, 561 U.S. at 44 (Breyer, J., dissenting) (emphasis in original).

56. Mill, *On Liberty*, 53, 12.

57. *Holder*, 561 U.S. at 53 (Breyer, J., dissenting).

58. See Rebecca L. Brown, "The Harm Principle and Free Speech," *Southern California Law Review* 89, no. 5 (2016): 953–1010, 958–59.

59. Citizens United v. FEC, 558 U.S. 310, 329 (2010).

60. Mill, *On Liberty*, 15.

61. *Citizens United*, 558 U.S. at 339 (internal citations and quotations omitted).

62. *Citizens United*, 558 U.S. at 340–41.

63. *Citizens United*, 558 U.S. at 342.

64. Helen J. Knowles, *The Tie Goes to Freedom: Justice Anthony M. Kennedy on Liberty* (Lanham, MD: Rowman & Littlefield, 2019), 213.

65. *Citizens United*, 558 U.S. at 354.

66. *Citizens United*, 558 U.S. at 355.

67. Santa Clara County v. Southern Pacific Railroad Company, 118 U.S. 394 (1886).

68. *Bellotti*, 435 U.S. at 776–77.

69. *Citizens United*, 558 U.S. at 394 (Stevens, J., dissenting).

70. *Citizens United*, 558 U.S. at 393; Austin v. Michigan Chamber of Commerce, 494 U.S. 652, 656 (1990).

71. Mill, *On Liberty*, 108.

72. See Melina Constantine Bell, "*Citizens United*, Liberty, and John Stuart Mill," *Notre Dame Journal of Law, Ethics & Public Policy* 30, no. 1 (2016): 1–23, 2.

73. *Citizens United*, 558 U.S. at 326–27, 339.

74. See also Reed v. Gilbert, 576 U.S. 155 (2015) (striking down an ordinance that placed size and time limits on temporary directional signs that were greater than the restrictions on political or ideological signs).

75. Snyder v. Phelps, 562 U.S. 443, 458 (2011).

76. *Snyder*, 562 U.S. at 458 (quoting Hustler Magazine v. Falwell, 485 U.S. 46, 55).

77. *Snyder*, 562 U.S. at 460–61.

78. Piers Norris Turner, "Mill and the Liberal Rejection of Legal Moralism," *History of Philosophy Quarterly* 32, no. 1 (2015): 79–99, 88–89.

79. Knowles and Lichtman, "Conclusion," 249–50.

80. Brown v. Entertainment Merchants Association, 564 U.S. 786, 792–93 (2011).

81. *Brown*, 546 U.S. at 790.

82. *Brown*, 546 U.S. at 790.

83. Mill, *On Liberty*, 84.

84. *Brown*, 546 U.S. at 798.

85. *Brown*, 546 U.S. at 799 (emphasis in original).

86. *Brown*, 546 U.S. at 799.

87. *Brown*, 546 U.S. at 790 (quoting United States v. Playboy Entertainment Group, 529 U.S. 803, 818 (2000)).

88. *Brown*, 546 U.S. at 794 (internal citations omitted).

89. Mill, *On Liberty*, 9.

90. Kasper and Kozma, "Absolute Freedom of Opinion," 38–39.

91. See Arizona Free Enterprise Club's Freedom Club PAC v. Bennett, 564 U.S. 721 (2011) (applying strict scrutiny to overturn a state law that provided both public financing to candidates and additional funds to match what was spent by privately financed opponents and independent groups).

92. McCutcheon v. FEC, 572 U.S. 185, 191 (2014).

93. *McCutcheon*, 572 U.S. at 191.

94. *McCutcheon*, 572 U.S. at 191.

95. *McCutcheon*, 572 U.S. at 203.

96. *McCutcheon*, 572 U.S. at 193.

97. *McCutcheon*, 572 U.S. at 236 (Breyer, J., dissenting).

98. *McCutcheon*, 572 U.S. at 237.

99. Rodney A. Smolla, "The Meaning of the 'Marketplace of Ideas' in First Amendment Law," *Communication Law and Policy* 24, no. 4 (2019): 437–75, 456.

100. Williams-Yulee v. Florida Bar, 575 U.S. 433, 452, 454 (2015).

101. Mill, *On Liberty*, 79–80. Other cases during this time raised that issue of an incumbent duty to the public in public employee speech, most notably Duryea v. Guarnieri, 564 U.S. 379 (2011) (upholding a public employer's use of retaliation against an employee for the employee speaking on a matter of private concern) and Lane v. Franks, 573 U.S. 228 (2014) (finding that the First Amendment protects a public employee who provided truthful sworn testimony that was outside the course of his ordinary job responsibilities).

102. *Williams-Yulee*, 575 U.S. 433, 444 (2015).

103. *Williams-Yulee*, 575 U.S. at 444–45.

104. *Williams-Yulee*, 575 U.S. at 449.

105. *Williams-Yulee*, 575 U.S. at 442–49.

106. Knowles, *Tie Goes to Freedom*, 206–7.

107. *Williams-Yulee*, 575 U.S. at 474 (Kennedy, J., dissenting).

108. *Williams-Yulee*, 575 U.S. at 476.

109. *Williams-Yulee*, 575 U.S. at 477.

110. United States v. Alvarez, 567 U.S. 709, 718 (2012).

111. *Alvarez*, 567 U.S. at 727.

112. Mill, *On Liberty*, 9.

113. *Alvarez*, 567 U.S. at 733 (Breyer, J., concurring) (quoting New York Times v. Sullivan, 376 U.S. 254, 279, n.19 (1964) (quoting Mill, *On Liberty*, 15 (Blackwell ed. 1947)).

114. *Alvarez*, 567 U.S. at 733.

115. *Alvarez*, 567 U.S. at 734.

116. Mill, *On Liberty*, 50.

117. Mark Tushnet, "Stephen Breyer and the First Amendment as Legal Doctrine," in Knowles and Lichtman, *Judging Free Speech*, 225.

118. *Alvarez*, 567 U.S. at 752 (Alito, J., dissenting).

119. James Weinstein, "What Lies Ahead? The Marketplace of Ideas, *Alvarez v. United States*, and First Amendment Protection of Knowing Falsehoods," *Seton Hall Law Review* 51, no. 1 (2020): 135–67, 142, 148.

120. *Alvarez*, 567 U.S. at 752.

121. *Alvarez*, 567 U.S. at 742, 744.

122. *Alvarez*, 567 U.S. at 723.

123. Mill, *On Liberty*, 79.

124. See K. C. O'Rourke, *Stuart Mill and Freedom of Expression: The Genesis of a Theory* (New York: Routledge, 2001), 19–20.

125. See FCC v. Fox Television Stations I, 556 U.S. 502 (2009).

126. *Fox Television Stations I*, 556 U.S. at 510.

127. *Fox Television Stations I*, 556 U.S. at 510.

128. FCC v. Fox Television Stations II, 567 U.S. 239, 247–48 (2012).

129. *Fox Television Stations II*, 567 U.S. at 253–54.

130. *Fox Television Stations II*, 567 U.S. at 254.

131. *Fox Television Stations II*, 567 U.S. at 259 (Ginsburg, J., concurring) (internal citation omitted).

132. Willmoore Kendall, "How to Read Milton's *Areopagitica*," *Journal of Politics* 22, no. 3 (1960): 439–73, 451.

133. USAID v. Alliance for Open Society International I, 570 U.S. 205, 213 (2013) (quoting Rumsfeld v. FAIR, 547 U.S. 47, 61 (2006)).

134. *USAID I*, 570 U.S. at 218.

135. *USAID I*, 570 U.S. at 220–21.

136. John Stuart Mill to Lord Amberley, February 2, 1870, in *The Letters of John Stuart Mill*, ed. Hugh Elliot (New York: Longmans and Green, 1910), 2:241; Mill, *On Liberty*, 98–99.

137. USAID v. Alliance for Open Society International II, 207 L. Ed. 2d 654, 658 (2020).

138. *USAID II*, 207 L. Ed. 2d at 678 (Breyer, J., dissenting).

139. McCullen v. Coakley, 573 U.S. 464, 472 (2014).

140. *McCullen*, 573 U.S. at 487, 488.

141. Mill, *On Liberty*, 17.

142. Mill, 16.

143. Mill, 51.

144. *McCullen*, 573 U.S. at 496.

145. It is debatable whether, in practice, all "sidewalk counselors" engage in "close, personal conversations" rather than protest. See National Abortion Federation, *2020 Violence and Disruption Statistics*, 2020, https://prochoice.org/wp-content/uploads/2020_NAF_VD_Stats.pdf.

146. Jacqueline Ahearn, "You Speak an 'Infinite Deal of Nothing': Prioritizing Free Speech over Other Fundamental Rights," *Journal of Civil Rights & Economic Development* 30, no. 1 (2017): 1–30, 20–24.

147. See also Heffernan v. Paterson, 136 S. Ct. 1412 (2016) (ruling that the First Amendment prohibits a public employee from being demoted because of perceived involvement in protected political activity).

148. See also Sorrell v. IMS Health, 564 U.S. 552 (2011) (striking down a state law banning the sale, transmission, or use of a doctor's prescription records without the doctor's consent).

149. Matal v. Tam, 137 S. Ct. 1744, 1751 (2017).

150. *Matal*, 137 S. Ct. at 1763.

151. *Matal*, 137 S. Ct. at 1751.

152. *Matal*, 137 S. Ct. at 1764 (quoting *Schwimmer*, 279 U.S. at 644 (Holmes, J., dissenting)).

153. *Matal*, 137 S. Ct. at 1763.

154. Mill, *On Liberty*, 4.

155. Mill 51.

156. Niki Kuckes, "Free Speech Meets 'Disparaging' Trademarks in the Supreme Court," *Roger Williams University Law Review* 23, no. 1 (2018): 122–68, 147–53.

157. Packingham v. North Carolina, 137 S. Ct. 1730, 1735 (2017).

158. *Packingham*, 137 S. Ct. at 1735 (internal citation and quotation omitted).

159. *Packingham*, 137 S. Ct. at 1735–36 (quoting Reno v. ACLU, 521 U.S. 844, 870 (1997)).

160. *Packingham*, 137 S. Ct. at 1737.

161. Michal Lavi, "Publish, Share, Re-tweet, and Repeat," *University of Michigan Journal of Law Reform* 54, no. 2 (2021): 441–523, 466.

162. *Packingham*, 137 S. Ct. at 1737.

163. *Packingham*, 137 S. Ct. at 1737.

164. See also Minnesota Voters Alliance v. Mansky, 138 S. Ct. 1876 (2018) (finding that a state ban on wearing political apparel at polling places on Election Day violated the First Amendment).

165. National Institute of Family and Life Advocates v. Becerra, 138 S. Ct. 2361, 2376 (internal quotations omitted).

166. *Becerra*, 138 S. Ct. at 2374 (quoting *McCullen*, 573 U.S. at 476).

167. *Becerra*, 138 S. Ct. at 2378.

168. *Becerra*, 138 S. Ct. at 2382 (Breyer, J., dissenting).

169. *Becerra*, 138 S. Ct. at 2388.

170. Janus v. AFSCME, 138 S. Ct. 2448, 2478 (2018) (quoting *Wisconsin Right to Life*, 551 U.S. at 500 (Scalia, J., concurring in part and concurring in judgment)).

171. *Janus*, 138 S. Ct. at 2464 (internal citations omitted).

172. *Janus*, 138 S. Ct. at 2476 (internal quotation omitted).

173. *Janus*, 138 S. Ct. at 2463–64, 2469–70, 2478.

174. Although Mill believed it just to require one to testify in court (*On Liberty*, 10), his example involves providing evidence, not being compelled to declare certain beliefs.

175. One exception has been *USAID II*, noted above. See also Manhattan Community Access Corp. v. Halleck, 139 S. Ct. 1921 (2019) (ruling that a private company overseeing public access channels is not bound by the First Amendment like a state actor is).

176. Iancu v. Brunetti, 139 S. Ct. 2294, 2297 (2019).

177. *Iancu*, 139 S. Ct. at 2297.

178. *Iancu*, 139 S. Ct. at 2299.

179. *Iancu*, 139 S. Ct. at 2300.

180. *Iancu*, 139 S. Ct. at 2300.

181. *Iancu*, 139 S. Ct. at 2300.

182. Mill, *On Liberty*, 11.

183. See Mill, 22–23.

184. Marc Jonathan Blitz, "The Pandora's Box of 21st Century Commercial Speech Doctrine: *Sorrell*, *R.A.V.*, and Purpose-Constrained Scrutiny," *Chapman's Journal of Law & Policy* 19, no. 1 (2014): 19–49, 24.

185. Mill, *On Liberty*, 99.

186. David M. Peterson, "Do the Swift Boat Vets Need to Move On? The Role of 527s in Contemporary American Democracy," *Texas Law Review* 84 (2006): 767–99, 788.

187. Barr v. American Association of Political Consultants, 140 S. Ct. 2335, 2346 (2020) (internal quotations omitted).

188. *Barr*, 140 S. Ct. at 2354 (quoting *Williams-Yulee*, 575 U.S. at 470 (Scalia, J., dissenting)).

189. *Barr*, 140 S. Ct. at 2347.

190. Mill, *On Liberty*, 94.

191. *Barr*, 140 S. Ct. at 2358 (Breyer, J., concurring in part and dissenting in part) (internal citation omitted).

192. *Barr*, 140 S. Ct. at 2359.

193. *Barr*, 140 S. Ct. at 2359.

194. *Barr*, 140 S. Ct. at 2360.

195. See also Americans for Prosperity Foundation v. Bonta, 141 S. Ct. 2373 (2021) (finding that a state requirement that nonprofit organizations disclose their donors' identities violates the First Amendment); Shurtleff v. Boston, 142 S. Ct. 1583 (2022) (finding unconstitutional a city's decision to refuse to temporarily fly a private organization's flag on a flagpole, based on viewpoint, when other organizations had been extended the same right); FEC v. Cruz, 142 S. Ct. 1638 (2022) (finding BCRA's cap on candidate campaign committees' ability to repay personal loans made by the candidate to the campaign to unconstitutionally burden core political speech). See also Austin v. Reagan National Advertising, 142 S. Ct. 1464 (2022) (upholding a city's distinction of allowing digitized signs on premises but not permitting digitized off-premises signs, with the Supreme Court applying intermediate scrutiny to an ordinance the majority found to be content neutral).

196. Mahanoy Area School District v. B.L., 141 S. Ct. 2038, 2043 (2021).

197. *Mahanoy*, 141 S. Ct. at 2046.

198. *Mahanoy*, 141 S. Ct. at 2046.

199. *Mahanoy*, 141 S. Ct. at 2046.

200. *Mahanoy*, 141 S. Ct. at 2044–47.

201. David L. Hudson Jr., *"Mahanoy Area School District v. B.L.*: The Court Protects Student Social Media but Leaves Unanswered Questions," *Cato Supreme Court Review* 2021 (2021): 93–108, 93–94.

202. See Kennedy v. Bremerton School District, 142 S. Ct. 2407, 2430 (2022) (finding a First Amendment violation when a public school district disciplined a football coach for offering prayers on the fifty-yard line after a game, with the Supreme Court reasoning that "learning how to tolerate speech . . . of all kinds is part of learning how to live in a pluralistic society, a trait of character essential to a tolerant citizenry" (internal quotations omitted). However, as explained by the dissent, the case also raised the specter of a public school employee leading students in prayer, which could cause religious coercion of students (2434) (Sotomayor, J., dissenting).

203. *Austin*, 142 S. Ct. at 1476–77 (Breyer, J., concurring).

204. Houston Community College System v. Wilson, 142 S. Ct. 1253, 1258 (2022).

205. *Wilson*, 142 S. Ct. at 1259 (internal citation omitted).

206. *Wilson*, 142 S. Ct. at 1261.

207. *Wilson*, 142 S. Ct. at 1261.

208. *Wilson*, 142 S. Ct. at 1262.

209. *Wilson*, 142 S. Ct. at 1263.

210. Counterman v. Colorado, No. 22–138, slip op., at 1 (June 27, 2023), available at https://www.supremecourt.gov/opinions/22pdf/22-138_43j7.pdf.

211. *Counterman*, No. 22–138, slip op., at 11–12.

212. *Counterman*, No. 22–138, slip op., at 5–6.

213. *Counterman*, No. 22–138, slip op., at 6–7 (internal citations and quotations omitted).

214. *Counterman*, No. 22–138, slip op., at 7–8, 10, 12.

215. *Counterman*, No. 22–138, slip op., at 5–8.

216. 303 Creative LLC v. Elenis, No. 21–476, slip op., at 4 (June 30, 2023), available at https://www.supremecourt.gov/opinions/22pdf/21-476_c185.pdf (internal quotations and citations omitted).

217. *303 Creative*, No. 21–476, slip op., at 8 (internal quotations and citations omitted).

218. *303 Creative*, No. 21–476, slip op., at 7 (internal quotation omitted). For another case emphasizing the harm principle and making use of the "marketplace of ideas" analogy, see United States v. Hansen, No. 22–179, slip op., at 4–5 (June 23, 2023), available at https://www.supremecourt.gov/opinions/22pdf/22-179_o75q.pdf. (In upholding a conviction for soliciting financial fraud (a clear Millian harm), Justice Barrett wrote the following for the majority: "Overbroad laws may deter or 'chill' constitutionally protected speech, and if would-be speakers remain silent, society will lose their contributions to the 'marketplace of ideas.' To guard against those harms, the overbreadth doctrine allows a litigant (even an undeserving one) to vindicate the rights of the silenced, as well as society's broader interest in hearing them speak.")

219. *303 Creative*, No. 21–476, slip op., at 25-26 (internal quotations and citations omitted).

220. Mill, *On Liberty*, 51.

221. *303 Creative*, No. 21–476, slip op., at 6-10.

222. Mill, *On Liberty*, 94.

223. *303 Creative*, No. 21–476, slip op., at 2 (Sotomayor, J., dissenting) (emphasis in original).

224. *303 Creative*, No. 21–476, slip op., at 6 (Sotomayor, J., dissenting).

Conclusion

1. United States v. Alvarez, 567 U.S. 709, 726–27 (2012) (internal citations omitted).

2. Mary E. Johnston, "Combating Thieves of Valor: The Stolen Valor Act of 2013 Is Constitutional Yet Unenforced," *William & Mary Bill of Rights Journal* 25, no. 4 (2017): 1355–92, 1358.

3. See Lee Epstein et al., "Do Justices Defend the Speech They Hate? An Analysis of In-Group Bias on the US Supreme Court," *Journal of Law and Courts* 6, no. 2 (Fall 2018): 237–62.

4. See, e.g., McKee v. Cosby, 139 S. Ct. 675, 676 (2019) (Thomas, J., concurring in denial of certiorari); Berisha v. Lawson, 141 S. Ct. 2424, 2429 (2021) (Gorsuch, J., dissenting from the denial of certiorari); Coral Ridge Ministries Media, Inc. v. Southern Poverty Law Center, 142 S. Ct. 2453, 2455 (2022) (Thomas, J., dissenting from the denial of certiorari); Counterman v. Colorado, No. 22–138, slip op., at 1–2 (June 27, 2023) (Thomas, J., dissenting), available at https://www.supremecourt.gov/opinions/22pdf/22-138_43j7.pdf.

5. See, e.g., Near v. Minnesota, 283 U.S. 697, 714, 717, 722 (1931); Roth v. United States, 354 U.S. 476, 488 (1957); New York Times Co. v. United States, 403 U.S. 713, 716–17, 719 (1971) (Black, J., concurring); McIntyre v. Ohio Elections Commission, 514 U.S. 334, 369 (1995) (Thomas, J., concurring); Houston Community College System v. Wilson, 142 S. Ct. 1253, 1261 (2022); see also Eric T. Kasper, *To Secure the Liberty of the People: James Madison's Bill of Rights and the Supreme Court's Interpretation* (DeKalb: Northern Illinois University Press, 2010), 227–36.

6. See Whitney v. California, 274 U.S. 357, 375 n.2 (1927) (Brandeis, J., concurring); Gertz v. Robert Welch, Inc., 418 U.S. 323, 356–58 (1974) (Douglas, J., dissenting); *McIntyre*, 514 U.S. at 372 (Scalia, J., dissenting); Citizens United v. FEC, 558 U.S. 310, 427 (2010) (Stevens, J., dissenting); Brown v. Entertainment Merchants Association, 564 U.S. 786, 829 (2011) (Thomas, J., dissenting).

7. See *Near*, 283 U.S. at 713–14; Dennis v. United States, 341 U.S. 494, 522 n.4 (1951) (Frankfurter, J., concurring); Joseph Burstyn v. Wilson, 343 U.S. 495, 524 (1952) (Frankfurter, J., concurring); Times Film Corp. v. Chicago, 365 U.S. 43, 53–54 (1961) (Warren, C. J., dissenting).

8. See *Dennis*, 341 U.S. 590 n.5 (Douglas, J., dissenting); Scales v. United States, 367 U.S. 203, 278 (1961) (Douglas, J., dissenting); *Brown*, 564 U.S. at 824–26 (Thomas, J., dissenting).

9. See American Communications Association v. Douds, 339 U.S. 382, 415–16 (1950) (Frankfurter, J., concurring); Time v. Firestone, 424 U.S. 448, 477 n.7 (1976) (Brennan, J., dissenting); NAACP v. Claiborne Hardware, 458 U.S. 886, 933 n.80 (1982); Austin v. Michigan Chamber of Commerce, 494 U.S. 652, 693–94 (1990) (Scalia, J., dissenting).

10. For Zechariah Chafee, see Chaplinsky v. New Hampshire, 315 U.S. 568, 572 nn.4–5 (1942); *Dennis*, 341 U.S. at 567 n.9 (Jackson, J., concurring). For Alexander Meiklejohn, see *Dennis*, 341 U.S. at 524 n.5 (Frankfurter, J., concurring); Konigsberg v. State Bar of California, 366 U.S. 36, 65 n.19 (1961) (Black, J., dissenting); Red Lion Broadcasting Co. v. FCC, 395 U.S. 367, 390 (1969); *Gertz*, 418 U.S. at 382 (White, J., dissenting); Police Department of Chicago v. Mosley, 408 U.S. 92, 96 n.4 (1972). For Thomas Emerson, see Rosenbloom v. Metromedia, 403 U.S. 29, 44 (1971); CBS v. Democratic National Committee, 412 U.S. 94, 151 (1973) (Douglas, J., concurring); First National Bank of Boston v. Bellotti, 435 U.S. 765, 777 n.1 (1978); Connick v. Myers, 461 U.S. 138, 164 n.4 (1983) (Brennan, J., dissenting). For Burt Neuborne, see Barr v. American Association of Political Consultants, 140 S. Ct. 2335, 2358 (2020) (Breyer, J., dissenting).

11. For a list of comparable cases making use of Madison as an authority or appealing to Madisonian rhetoric, see Kasper, *To Secure the Liberty*, 227–36.

12. John Stuart Mill, *Autobiography*, ed. Jack Stillinger (Boston: Houghton Mifflin, 1969), 150.

13. Mill, 150.

14. Mill, 152.

15. Mill, 152.

16. Jacob Mchangama, *Free Speech: A History from Socrates to Social Media* (New York: Basic Books, 2022), 214.

17. Mill, *On Liberty*, ed. Elizabeth Rapaport (Indianapolis, IN: Hackett, 1978), 27.

18. See *McKee*, 139 S. Ct. at 676 (2019) (Thomas, J., concurring in denial of certiorari); *Berisha*, 141 S. Ct. at 2425 (2021) (Thomas, J., dissenting from the denial of cer-

tiorari); *Berisha*, 141 S. Ct. at 2430 (Gorsuch, J., dissenting from the denial of certiorari); *Coral Ridge Ministries Media*, 142 S. Ct. at 2454–55 (2022) (Thomas, J., dissenting from the denial of certiorari); *Counterman*, No. 22–138, slip op., at 1–2 (June 27, 2023) (Thomas, J., dissenting).

19. Dobbs v. Jackson Women's Health Organization, 142 S. Ct. 2228, 2301–2 (2022) (Thomas, J., concurring).

20. Mill, *On Liberty*, 34.

21. Oliver Wendell Holmes Jr., "The Path of the Law," *Harvard Law Review* 10, no. 8 (1897): 457–78, 469.

INDEX

Printed in the USA
CPSIA information can be obtained
at www.ICGtesting.com
CBHW031324010424
6200CB00009B/16/J